SOLDIER FIELD

CHICAGO VISIONS AND REVISIONS

Edited by Carlo Rotella, Bill Savage, Carl Smith, and Robert B. Stepto

ALSO IN THE SERIES:

Barrio: Photographs from Chicago's Pilsen and Little Village
by Paul D'Amato

The Plan of Chicago: Daniel Burnham and the Remaking of the American City
by Carl Smith

· LIAM T. A. FORD

SOLDIER FIELD

A STADIUM AND ITS CITY

THE UNIVERSITY OF CHICAGO PRESS · CHICAGO AND LONDON

The University of Chicago Press, Chicago 60637
The University of Chicago Press, Ltd., London
© 2009 by Liam T. A. Ford
All rights reserved. Published 2009
Printed in the United States of America

18 17 16 15 14 13 12 11 10 09   1 2 3 4 5

ISBN-13: 978-0-226-25706-8   (cloth)
ISBN-10: 0-226-25706-1   (cloth)

Portions of chapter 15 appeared in different form in the *Chicago Tribune*. Used by permission.

Library of Congress Cataloging-in-Publication Data

Ford, Liam T. A.
    Soldier Field : a stadium and its city / Liam T. A. Ford.
        p. cm.
    Includes bibliographical references and index.
    ISBN-13: 978-0-226-25706-8 (cloth : alk. paper)
    ISBN-10: 0-226-25706-1 (cloth : alk. paper)
    1. Soldier Field (Chicago, Ill.)—History. 2. Stadiums—Illinois—
    Chicago—History. 3. Sports—Illinois—Chicago—History. I. Title.
    GV584.5.C4F674 2009
    725'.8270977311—dc22
                                            2009016521

♾ The paper used in this publication meets the minimum
requirements of the American National Standard for Information
Sciences—Permanence of Paper for Printed Library Materials,
ANSI Z39.48-1992.

Liam T. A. Ford, a fifth-generation Chicagoan, returned home after a stint at the *Advertiser* in Montgomery, Alabama, and joined the City News Bureau, eventually becoming its lead City Hall reporter. Since 1998 he has covered housing, politics, regional development, and the Chicago Park District for the *Chicago Tribune*.

Dedicated to the memory of my grandparents,
especially Paul H. Ziemer, who served in World War II

CONTENTS

Part 1   Getting It Built

Part 2   A Stadium for All Chicago

Part 3   The Fall and Rise of Soldier Field

FIGURES

The Chicago Bears had lost to the Philadelphia Eagles, 33 to 19, and fans streamed out of Soldier Field, a few lingering to take snapshots of the old stadium. Hopes for a trip to the Super Bowl were gone, and most people wanted to put a good season with a disappointing finish behind them.

As soon as the stands were clear, crews wielding crowbars began yanking up seats from the north stands. These seats had been added in the early 1980s, part of a $32 million renovation that the Chicago Park District had declared would make the building usable for another fifty years.

It was January 19, 2002, and the game was the last event at a lakefront arena designed early in the twentieth century to lure the Olympics to Chicago. Twenty months and $675 million later Soldier Field would reopen, transformed into an entirely modern structure, still framed by the neoclassical columns many Chicagoans consider the city's greatest war memorial. My assignment that evening as a reporter for the *Chicago Tribune* was to talk to Bears fans about the old stadium: what they remembered about it, what they hated, what they would miss. But minutes after the game clock ran out, almost no one remained, except those two hundred workers pulling out seats, a spokesman for the renovation project, myself, and Tom and Trevor Kay.

Tom Kay had brought his son to the game that night because he wanted Trevor, then twelve, to remember the stadium Tom had grown up with. As crews began lowering the goalposts, Tom and Trevor climbed down onto the field carrying a football. I went down and talked to them for a few minutes. Tom threw the football to me, I shot a few photos of him and his son with a disposable camera, and they left. Two weeks later, Tom Kay e-mailed me:

"It was, even in a Bears' loss, a great day for my son and me." The photos, he wrote, "helped us to remember it and memorialize a great stadium and tradition that the Bears are."

At the time, I knew little about Soldier Field's history beyond its thirty years as the Bears' home turf. But a sense of tradition permeated the place, and I wanted to learn why this monumental building mattered so much to so many people. Along the way, I learned about Chicago's struggle to attract the Olympics at the dawn of the twentieth century, and how the city had won the 1904 games, only to give them up so that St. Louis could have both an Olympics and a world's fair in the same year. After the Great War—what we now call World War I—the city's Olympic hopes were rekindled and city leaders of all political persuasions backed building a stadium they promised would be the greatest ever constructed. A tribute to the city's war dead, it would also bolster Chicago's quest for recognition as one of the world's great cities. Its central location would make it the perfect place to encourage and show off the athletic achievements of Chicago's youth—young men who, as a result, would be better prepared if the United States ever again entered an international war.

Grant Park Municipal Stadium rose on land reclaimed from Lake Michigan, rooted in the ashes and debris of the teeming Loop and the sands of northern Indiana. From the beginning, Chicagoans and out-of-towners hailed it as one of the most remarkable achievements in modern architecture—a melding of classical structure and modern convenience. A celebration honoring the athletic prowess of Chicago's police officers opened the stadium; a re-creation of the Great Chicago Fire marked its first dedication. A West Side high school played a Kentucky high school in the first football game on its gridiron. In 1925 the South Park Commission, the government body that built the stadium, renamed it Soldier Field. The *Tribune*, insisting that the singular "soldier" implied a memorial for only one serviceman, christened it "Soldiers' Field," confusing generations of Chicagoans.

In 1926 the largest gathering of Roman Catholic faithful ever assembled anywhere in the world flocked to the still-unfinished stadium to venerate the Holy Eucharist. The following year, the biggest crowd ever to attend a college football game packed the stadium. A decade later that record was topped when the largest crowd ever to attend any football game hung from the stadium colonnades and squeezed onto its wooden benches to see a young Catholic boy from the Austin neighborhood lead his public school to victory over a Catholic school.

Chicagoans came together at Soldier Field, celebrating their history through German folk dance, the singing of spirituals, and reenactments of military battles. Stadiumgoers marked the beginning of the age of transatlantic flight and the end of America's years of isolation. They bore witness as new religious movements swept America and the globe. Soldier Field welcomed

Franklin Roosevelt, Harry Truman, Dwight Eisenhower, Liberace, Bozo the Clown, and Humphrey Bogart. It stood sentinel as Navy midshipmen paraded before Bears games, as warplanes flew overhead, and as Chicago celebrated American independence over and over. Its giant scoreboard tallied points as stars of college and professional football faced off each year in one of the country's most anticipated games. As Soldier Field became a symbol of the city's progress, it also fostered the Democratic Party's political power in Chicago, particularly that of the faction controlled by South Sider Edward J. Kelly and West Sider Pat Nash. Kelly's rise began with his presidency of the South Park Commission; millions of dollars in park contracts went to his and Nash's allies, even before he became mayor in 1933, and for years thereafter the money flowed.

Kelly and the South Park commissioners struck a deal with 1920s reformers and businessmen to bring about a grand transformation of the lakefront. Soldier Field was part of that change from an ash-choked, desolate waterfront to the verdant front yard we know today. For decades, the stadium stood as a monument not just to fallen soldiers but to the way Chicago worked, with politicians adapting the message and plans of the good-government types to advance their own ends. Reformers got new parkland, lakefront beaches, and cultural institutions like the Shedd Aquarium. Businessmen got tourist attractions. And politicians like Kelly could boast of a revitalized, modern city while using their control over an ever-growing list of public works projects— each with a budget that included jobs and maintenance contracts—to reward their loyalists and amplify their power.

But the alliance that built Soldier Field and kept it vibrant for half a century had frayed long before the Kays and I tossed around their football on the Bears' 30-yard line that chilly January night. Soldier Field fell victim to changes in American culture and Chicago history that were beyond the control of its owners, the people of Chicago and the Chicago Park District. Many traditions that fell dormant during World War II never revived when the conflict ended, as veterans began moving their new families to the suburbs. Television devastated the movie business and places like Soldier Field as it altered the way Americans amused themselves and connected with their fellow citizens. By the time the Rev. Billy Graham and the Rev. Martin Luther King Jr. used the stadium as a stage to inspire Chicago to religious and political reform in the mid-1960s, Soldier Field was dying. Annual attendance, which had reached almost two million some years in the 1950s, dipped as low as a quarter of a million by the late 1960s. The only real draws some years were Mayor Richard J. Daley's Prep Bowl, the *Tribune*'s College All-Star Game, and the Bears' Armed Forces Benefit Game.

In 1971, in a desperate attempt to keep the stadium alive, the Chicago Park District turned to an unlikely savior: George Halas, one of the founders of the National Football League and owner of the Chicago Bears. For years Halas had wanted a new stadium for his team, and the NFL had goaded him to relocate the Bears from Wrigley Field to a larger venue. Halas never got his new stadium, but with the Bears as Soldier Field's chief tenant, the Park District was able to pour money into the structure and keep it operating until the end of the century. The Bears' new home at first did little to change the team's fortunes, but fans in Chicago and across America who saw the stadium's colonnades in the background of every televised game grew to think of Soldier Field as a monument to Chicago history and Bears football. Then running back Walter Payton, coach Mike Ditka, and the rest of the 1985 Bears captured a whole new generation of fans, many with little memory of the years at Wrigley. As Chicagoans came to think of Soldier Field as primarily a football stadium, much of its history and original purpose was forgotten.

Two visions of the stadium competed: park advocates and architectural buffs thought of it as a grand gathering place usurped by the Bears, while many Bears fans thought of it as a beautiful but crumbling relic, lacking even adequate restrooms. The 1985 Super Bowl title resurrected demands for a new stadium, but renovations to accommodate World Cup soccer matches in 1994 and a Bears lease that lasted through the 1990s helped postpone Soldier Field's day of reckoning. Meanwhile, the Bears continued to look for a way to acquire a home field that would put the team on a par with other NFL franchises.

Finally, the whim of an architect who had drawn up plans for one of the team's many proposals and the development of new laser measuring technology convinced the team that Soldier Field could be retrofitted. In 2000 the political stars aligned, and Mayor Richard M. Daley—with the help of Illinois governor George Ryan—did what his father had not been able to do when a new stadium was first mentioned in the 1950s: strike a deal to rebuild Soldier Field as a modern stadium, designed for football.

During the debate over the Bears' plans for Soldier Field, I began learning about the stadium's real history and got to know fans like Tom Kay, who loved the stadium as it was. While researching this book—reading yellowed, brittle newspaper clippings about Mayor Kelly and the South Park Commission—I came to see that Soldier Field's story is the story of Chicago in the twentieth century: its achievements and disappointments, its continual striving to meet its potential and live up to its hyperbolic self-image. As the old Soldier Field fell and the new stadium rose between its historic rows of columns, I realized that if we can no longer sit precisely where crowds roared their approval of President Roosevelt or strained to hear Charles Lindbergh exhorting Chicago to take to the air, we should at least recall what this place has done for its city and recognize that even the most historic and beautiful buildings must sometimes be remade when they no longer serve their original purpose.

Chicago Challenges the World

We have Soldier Field because Chicagoans of the early twentieth century wanted to outdo Paris. To top the French capital—modernized in the mid-1800s by a sweeping new urban plan and host, in the century's closing decades, to two world's fairs—they set out to build the largest, most beautiful public arena in the world, so that anyone planning a national track meet, a convention, or an American Olympics would think first of Chicago. They wanted to draw tourists, throngs of visitors to sleep in the Lexington Hotel, eat at the Stevens Building Restaurant, and shop for clothing at the Boston Store.

They also wanted to tame decades of unbridled growth and to banish the city's reputation as a monstrously dirty, notoriously corrupt metropolis. Its "air is dirt," wrote Rudyard Kipling in 1891, and its streets teem with "barbarians." Though it was, he conceded, a "real city," he "urgently" desired never to see it again. Many visitors shared the British author's reaction.[1]

For a brief time, Chicagoans thought the 1893 Columbian Exposition had shown the world what a great American city could do. By the end of that year, the world press had proclaimed that no city could outshine Chicago. In the fair, America saw a new vision of itself, as the land of the City Beautiful, where the great minds of the New World would take the best of the Old and refashion the backstreet rabble as upright citizens of an enlightened democracy. "The Chicago of today is a magnificent city; it is a city of the twentieth century, brought in upon us before its time," wrote journalist and historian Charles Dwight Willard in the *Los Angeles Times* near the close of the fair. "The Western Giant is pushing ahead with vast strides," closing in on New York.[2]

But the glories of the fair swiftly faded, and outsiders' opinions of Chicago seemed, if anything, to get worse. Few could ignore all else in favor of the city's unparalleled industrial achievements. Upton Sinclair's *The Jungle*, published in 1906, focused the nation's attention on the brutality of that industry and the corruption that allowed it to thrive. The city's open tolerance of prostitution and vice made it a reliable source of scandal and a regular target of reformers. Even those who sang Chicago's praises decried its dank streets, moldering waterways, and soot-covered buildings. "Her filthy and rotting streets, her dilapidated and decaying bridges, and her dirty and dingy City Hall, in whose chambers and corridors lurk all the diseases incident to uncleanliness and foul atmosphere, tend to impress the stranger with the conviction that he is in a city already well advanced on the road of decadence," wrote Judge Lambert Tree, an early Chicago patron of the arts, survivor of the Great Chicago Fire, and prominent city booster, in 1900.[3]

Chicago, and America's other great cities, suffered growing pains. The air was tainted with more than just industrial soot; it was politically charged as well. In the decades preceding publication of *The Jungle*, Chicago was a center of radical politics. Anarchism and the dangers of leftist radicals using the discontent of Chicago's poor to their advantage obsessed the city. In 1893 a crazed job seeker had killed Mayor Carter Harrison I; eleven years later, police captured Abraham Gobinski, a man they identified as a Saint Louis anarchist, after a gunfight at Huron and Clark streets. A notebook found on Gobinski identified his planned targets, including Mayor Carter Harrison II. The younger Harrison had closed down a lecture by radical Emma Goldman three years before. (It was to have been a repeat of the lecture that supposedly inspired Leon Czolgosz to assassinate President William McKinley a month before.)[4]

Prominent families like the railcar-building Pullmans and the hotel-mogul Palmers felt their grip on the city—always somewhat tenuous—slipping. Vice reformers of the early twentieth century decried the bordellos in the Levee, just west of then-fashionable Prairie Avenue. The growth of prostitution and gambling, the constant push of immigrant workers into middle-class areas, and the seemingly ceaseless expansion of industry into residential areas helped convince middle- and upper-class Chicago that something had to be done to guide—and control—the changing city.[5]

Into the fray stepped men like Daniel H. Burnham, master planner of the Columbian Exposition, proclaiming that if only America's civic leaders would give them the money and the time, they could build a City Beautiful, where all would be content and business would thrive. Several late-nineteenth-century reform movements had come together to make the fair a success. Its architects, including Burnham, adapted neoclassical ideas to American uses. The Chicago businessmen who backed the fair saw it not only as a way to boost their economic fortunes but to show visitors and Chicagoans alike how much the city had progressed since the Great Fire of 1871. Prominent women took active roles in planning. And day-to-day operations benefited from advances in urban sanitation and transportation technologies. Long after the Midway closed, this coalition continued working to change the nature and reputation of Chicago. With the fair receding into history, Burnham began crusading to transform Chicago as a whole on the model of the fair's "White City." Soldier Field would grow out of this impetus.[6]

The political genius of the City Beautiful movement was to connect aesthetic reactions like Kipling's to the actions of radical agitators like Goldman. To calm the roiling waters of radicalism, its leaders claimed, America's cities must be transformed so that workingmen could join with their fellow citizens in admiration of their civilization's achievements. The real Chicago, the one beyond the grounds of the fair's fantastic White City, was called by some the "Black City."[7] As the impact of the Columbian Exposition spread, disciples of Burnham argued that to make the city a healthful place, and to instill civic pride, cities must establish and follow rational plans. "Life in our cities would be vastly easier if only they had been planned with some reasonable foresight," wrote one planner, John Coleman Adams, a few years after the fair. Uncoordinated and unguided growth bred the subversive elements endemic to American's cities, those men claimed. Without a change in how cities developed, America would never reach its potential, would never best Europe, would never become what God had meant it to be.[8]

Chicago, in particular, was in need of saving.

Secular prophets like Jane Addams crusaded for changes both sweeping and small. Even before the 1871 fire, the city had prided itself on its parks: in the late nineteenth century and continuing into the early twentieth, reformers and businessmen helped carve out playgrounds and built fieldhouses citywide as centers of neighborhood play for the children of the immigrant slums. A United States captivated by Horatio Alger's rags-to-riches stories felt a moral imperative to improve young slum dwellers through organized sports. College football stars—real and fictional—were bursting onto the American scene as an ideal for the sons of the new middle class, and sports stadiums were built across the city.

The City Beautiful movement had at its core the idea that making a city a better place to live would cause its residents to become better citizens. Structuring the urban landscape was seen as a means of taming chaos and holding off the onslaught of radicals. Paving roads and installing sewers might promote public health, and thus were worthy goals. But aesthetically pleasing parks, public squares, and public buildings—beyond being places for citizens to come together, take leisurely strolls, and engage in government business—would instill a sense of civic pride and democratic engagement. For architectural inspiration, these reformers looked to Greece and Rome, which they considered exemplars of civic patriotism. Grand structures and scenic promenades would inspire Chicagoans to greater appreciation for their city and the democratic capitalism that made it possible. Those selling the idea of a lakefront stadium adopted these high-minded sentiments.

In 1906, the year of *The Jungle*, the Merchants Club of Chicago turned to Burnham, the great mind behind the fair, who for years had been putting forward plans to save the entire city. Burnham wanted to remake Chicago—to do right what three decades of unplanned economic growth had, he believed, done wrong. Now the Merchants Club commissioned him to create a comprehensive plan for the city.

Though it's called the 1909 Plan of Chicago, Burnham's vision grew out of his work on the Columbian Exposition, and he first proposed a large-scale lakefront redevelopment in 1896. Burnham and other Chicago adherents of the City Beautiful movement admired what they viewed as the exemplary planning of Paris but bragged that, with similar restructuring, their city could outshine the City of Light. "Putting his statements together it seems that D. H. Burnham's ambitious plan for Lake-Front improvements has in view making Chicago so beautiful it will outrival Paris," the *Tribune* wrote in 1897.[9]

Beauty was a selling point for the Burnham Plan, especially among the high-minded, but the underlying motivations were much more practical. The middle class was already fleeing the teeming immigrant city. A new order of urban living and a reinvigorated democracy, Burnham reasoned, would also bring economic progress. Beauty would bring people to Chicago, to visit, to live, and to work. The Merchants Club, and later the Commercial Club, agreed with him.

Others, however, disagreed. Burnham and his Progressive allies wanted to regulate industry and wield the visible hand of government to improve the soul of the city. But they saw arrayed against them corrupt forces that put the ambitions of industry ahead of other goods, allowing business magnates to determine the shape of Chicago. These factions saw the lakefront as ripe for development. Even before the fair, in 1890, the mayor and the city council had proposed putting city buildings in what was then known as "Lake Park."[10] In his 1896 plan, which covered the area from Grant Park, downtown, south to Jackson Park, the site of the world's fair, Burnham proposed extending the lakefront through further landfill. And he too proposed buildings: a museum near where Buckingham Fountain now stands and an armory roughly at Monroe Drive.[11] Both the city's and Burnham's plans conflicted with the wishes of a number of prominent citizens—the most prominent being Aaron Montgomery Ward—to keep the lakefront free of construction.

At the time, the downtown lakefront was strewn with debris and choked with smoke from the Illinois Central Railroad. The railroad had persuaded Chicago's budget-conscious city council to give it rights to the lakefront in the 1850s in exchange for building a retaining wall to hold back the waters of Lake Michigan. A railroad switching yard and repair shops sat where the Field Museum and the north end of Soldier Field would later be.

Ward knew about the original land maps that laid out downtown Chicago. The 1836 Canal Commissioners Map states plainly that what is now Grant Park should "remain forever open, clear, and free of any buildings, or other obstructions whatever." The 1838 Fort Dearborn Addition Map reaffirms that the land is "forever to remain vacant of buildings." As a lakefront property owner, Ward believed those early plans guaranteed his right to an unobstructed view of Lake Michigan, and he fought for that right in court. Other prominent Chicagoans decried his legal obstructionism, asserting that public buildings in the lakefront park could only help the city's economy and pride, but Ward persisted and eventually triumphed in court. In the early 1900s the success of military, sporting, and other events in Grant Park—even stopovers by cross-country aviators—helped convince Ward's opponents that a stadium was needed. And Chicagoans who remembered the city's preparations for the 1904 Olympics knew that a temporary lakefront stadium had been part of the plans, despite Ward's objections.[12]

Another important force, which had shaped the lakefront since before the 1871 fire, was the South Park Commission. One of almost three dozen government bodies that developed and ran parks in Chicago, the South Park Commission had jurisdiction over some of the most prized yet neglected land in the country: the lakefront from the Chicago River south to Jackson Park. Although it had been able to develop Washington Park early and Jackson Park following the fair, the commission had been unable to move forward with ambitious plans for the south lakefront due to legal and political obstructions. Commission members were appointed by judges chosen, in party-line elections, from the geographic area covered by the parks. Throughout much of the early twentieth century, Republicans had a controlling vote on the board, but that was to change in the early 1920s, with profound consequences for Chicago.[13]

In 1909, with the patronage of the Commercial Club of Chicago, Burnham and his partner in the undertaking, Edward H. Bennett, finished their Plan of Chicago. Chicagoans greeted their vision enthusiastically. The plan is, in many ways, a paean to the burgeoning twentieth-century American city but also contains a tirade against it. Burnham and Bennett open with a quick historical survey of city planning, saving their highest praise for the planners of Paris.[14]

We in twenty-first-century America might think it odd, given the authors' expressed admiration for democratic values, that they would cite as a model for the modern industrial city the work of autocratic planners chosen by Louis XIV, Napoleon, and Napoleon III—France's longest-serving monarch, its most belligerent dictator, and the leader of a coup d'état. But even as they embraced industrial capitalism, Burnham, the City Beautiful movement, and the Progressives who were their political allies rejected laissez-faire economics, the idea that business left unregulated by government could best provide what its customers demand. The Progressives admired Teddy Roosevelt, the great imperial president who finally got the Panama Canal built after failed attempts by the French. While some historians claim the City Beautiful movement's influence diminished in the era following the Burnham Plan, replaced by more practical planning ideas, many modern-day urbanists still hearken back to Burnham and look on Napoleon III's Paris as the apogee of nineteenth-century planning. In Chicago, debates over city planning still often center on the Burnham Plan, and all debates over changes to the city before World War II took the plan—and its City Beautiful underpinnings—as their starting point.[15]

Burnham looked to the reorganization of the city's physical structure both to calm the disturbed souls of the populace and to keep Chicago on its path of unrivaled expansion. Since its founding in 1833, the city had grown more rapidly than any other in human history. Burnham observes in his plan that as wealth increases, cities come to play a larger part of nations' lives. And successful cities, he argues, are those that have coherent plans for growth: "Men are becoming convinced that the formless growth of the city is neither economical nor satisfactory." Many of Chicago's business leaders eagerly agreed with Burnham's ideas. Even industrialists, despite their enthusiasm for laissez-faire economics, often favored social regulation, expressing a decidedly paternalistic notion of how their employees' lives should be organized. Company towns like Pullman, however, were unsuccessful in keeping radicals at bay. Urban planning that engaged the imagination of the populace and gave them a reason to support the grand plans developed by experts like Burnham was seen as the solution. The idea that a well-planned city would inspire loyalty and breed patriots instead of bomb throwers was a key part of Burnham's appeal. "Chicago, in common with other great cities," Burnham wrote, "realizes that the time has come to bring order out of the chaos incident to rapid growth, and especially to the influx of people of many nationalities without common traditions or habits of life."[16]

To make real Burnham's plan, Republican mayor Fred Busse and the city council appointed a 328-member Chicago Plan Commission, headed by Charles H. Wacker. Busse, the first Chicago mayor of German ancestry, served only one four-year term. The creation of the Plan Commission, which had much broader powers and greater autonomy than today's version of the same body, was one of Busse's few reformist accomplishments in office.

Following a term most notable for his alliance with early organized crime figures, Busse lost to Carter Harrison II in 1911. Meanwhile, Wacker and his publicity agent, Walter D. Moody, popularized the plan so well that almost a century later, many Chicagoans still look on Burnham as the city's most important citizen ever. And Chicago politicians still invoke Burnham's vision when they are dreaming big dreams, especially those that will cost taxpayers hundreds of millions of dollars.

Among Burnham's proposals for the lakefront, one became important for the eventual building of Soldier Field. The Field Museum, then housed in the old Palace of Fine Arts from the Columbian Exposition (today the site of the Museum of Science and Industry), was looking for a new home. Burnham, in line with the thinking of the South Park Commission, proposed putting the new building in Grant Park. "Grant Park readily lends itself to the function of a spacious and attractive public garden. The location of the Field Museum in the center of this space is a special instance of good fortune," Burnham wrote. His proposal, however, triggered Montgomery Ward's last great legal fight. Invoking state law, the park commission sought to take the waterfront rights that gave Ward and other Michigan Avenue landowners veto power over structures in Grant Park. But Ward would have none of it. He sued again and on February 8, 1911, won his last lawsuit defending the open lakefront. It looked like the Field Museum would have to build its new home in Hyde Park.[17]

But by the end of the year, the Illinois Central Railroad and the South Park Commission came to an agreement that resulted in the extension of the lakefront parks from Roosevelt Road south to Jackson Park. In 1910 the Illinois Supreme Court had forced the railroad, commonly known as the IC, to pay what amounted to back rent to the state for the lakefront land. Hit hard for being a blight on the lakefront and smarting from its impending tax liabilities, the railroad decided to give up much of its land, including a large railyard built on landfill. Backers of the Burnham Plan and a downtown Field Museum were ecstatic. The south lakefront part of the plan could now move forward, with its museum built just south of Grant Park, out of reach of Ward and his lawyers.[18]

A few years after the Chicago Plan Commission started its work, the *Tribune* published an essay by Wacker in support of a bond issue for the widening of Michigan Avenue that summed up the argument in favor of the City Beautiful proposals: "A new era is dawning which cannot be dimmed by doubt or pessimism," Wacker wrote in 1914, going on to cite new parks, harbors, street improvements, and the Field Museum (then under construction) as examples of Chicago's progress. "These improvements, when completed, will make Chicago a real cosmopolitan city . . . and at the same time prove to be a good business investment."[19]

Even as Wacker and his cohorts drummed up public support, the South Park Commission and the other park districts in Chicago moved ahead with what work it could without final federal approval to fill in vast swaths of Lake Michigan. A Special Park Commission mapped out the whole city's boulevard system, connecting existing parks with broad parklike streets. Some began talking about how the city needed a new stadium in Grant Park. Bennett, Burnham's partner in drafting the Plan of Chicago, became the commission's chief architect. And the city's new mayor, William Hale "Big Bill" Thompson, a Republican, saw that the popularity of the Burnham Plan gave him a new mantle with which to cloak government spending.

Thompson's corruption in comparison to other politicians of his era likely has been exaggerated—partly because *Tribune* publisher Robert R. McCormick—known as "the Colonel"—was hostile to him as a member of a rival GOP faction. All Chicago mayors since Thompson have emulated his adoption of City Beautiful rhetoric to further his own ends. City Beautiful planners wanted to involve the public at large in their projects—they could not lift up the populace if the populace didn't care. But their attempts to tame the growth of the city ultimately provided a justification for City Hall to involve itself in every major business development in the city, a perverse effect completely counter to the movement's reformist aims. Thompson and subsequent mayors have consistently used the planning and zoning powers acquired by municipal government in the City Beautiful era to their political advantage, taking credit for positive changes and blocking plans they disapproved of. The rhetorical and spending power that flowed from Burnham Plan public works projects, Thompson realized, would allow him to appeal to working-class Chicagoans, who would get jobs and new places to spend their free time; to businesspeople, who would get the contracts for and the profits from such developments; and to reformers and elites, who believed Burnham's City Beautiful would help convert the city's unruly lower classes to a manageable and productive citizenry. By taking the Burnham Plan and the South Park Commission as his instruments, he could satisfy both the grasping political class and the reformers at the same time. Soldier Field embodies this combination of reform and business as usual.

Wacker himself at first thought Thompson's election would bring about the realization of the Burnham Plan. At a mass rally Thompson organized at the Auditorium Theatre soon after his inauguration, Wacker gushed about the prospects of the plan—and inveighed against its opponents. "Give civic patriotism a chance where patronage may not defeat efficiency, economy and dispatch in the accomplishment of the people's will!" Wacker declared. Thompson took his cue from the enthusiastic endorsement of Wacker and businessmen like chewing gum magnate William Wrigley Jr. and department store moguls William A. Wieboldt and James Simpson, of Marshall Field & Co., declaring it his mission to build a new Chicago. "We ought to have all the good things we have pictured, but we must do more than just talk. We must get together and act," Thompson told the assembly, billed as a "revival meeting" for Chicago's "I will" spirit.[20]

But World War I soon intervened, making financing for improvements harder to come by and taking Thompson's political career in a new direction. Thompson publicly opposed American involvement in the war, decrying the draft, blaming the conflict on "the commercial rivalry between Great Britain and Germany," and denouncing the prowar *Tribune*.[21] In 1917, when the United States joined the war effort on the side of England and France, Thompson voiced his reservations loudly, figuring the war would become unpopular—and hoping he might ride the nation's doubts to the White House. Thompson believed the war would end up as a Democratic quagmire, and he knew what many Chicago politicians and historians have almost ignored: despite its reputation as an Irish city, Chicago has always had more German citizens than Irish ones. He continued to rail against Woodrow Wilson's "hunt for trouble" but softened his opposition a bit by setting up a relief fund for children and orphans of soldiers.

Thompson's political instincts had often served him well. In his first campaign, the New England native had endorsed the Chicago Plan, and throughout the war, despite constraints on funding, Thompson and his cronies took advantage of the public's enchantment with the Burnham Plan. He worked with Wacker as the head of the Chicago Plan Commission fought for approval of some of the more mundane elements of the plan: building a Roosevelt Road bridge, widening Michigan Avenue, creating Wacker Drive. Funding for each project had to be approved by voters, but even in the face of political delays, bond issues began to be passed. These projects, Thompson realized early on, would give any politician controlling them an advantage over his competitors. What the City Beautiful reformers demanded, Thompson knew politicians could take credit for delivering.[22]

Almost as soon as he took office, Thompson had changed the way the city paid the private consultants who appraised property that the city might need to acquire to complete the changes called for by the Burnham Plan. Eventually, the property assessment fees became the cornerstone of what was known as the Expert Fees Scandal, in which a Cook County judge found Thompson, his allies, and his political operation had bilked taxpayers of more than $2.2 million (more than $28 million in 2008 dollars), all made possible by the Burnham public works activities. (The suit, mounted by the *Tribune*, ultimately was defeated on appeal to the Illinois Supreme Court.)[23] Big Bill manipulated taxpayers' money more blatantly than his successors, but every

Chicago mayor since has emulated his use of City Beautiful garb to dress up the enrichment of his friends.

WORK FOR VETERANS

In tune with the public mood, civic leaders who supported the war came up with their own public works proposals, plans that would benefit industry—and, they said, returning veterans. While the Burnham Plan envisioned many monumental works, it did not, of course, include plans for a memorial to those who lost their lives in the Great War. But by early July 1918, five months before the end of the war, a committee had formed to advocate for a temporary memorial, with a permanent one to follow at war's end.[24] The project soon became another opportunity for neoclassical-obsessed architects to showcase their knowledge of the Chicago Plan's style; indeed, Edward Bennett, Burnham's collaborator and now the South Park Commission's lead architect, led the charge.

Some of the proposals put forward by architects, artists, and the public (solicited by the ad hoc committee through a call published in the *Tribune*) almost dwarfed Burnham's plans for a City Hall as large as the U.S. Capitol. Chicago artist Oscar D. Soellner suggested an obelisk like the Washington Monument, standing on the lakefront and visible "for miles up and down."[25] The proposal of the official memorial committee was no less grandiose: a building with colonnades surmounted by a five-hundred-foot tower topped by a statue. One report noted: "It will have a rotunda as large as the largest monument in the world. . . .The plans include moving picture halls, a museum for war relics, safe deposit vaults for records of all the heroes from Chicago, and a place for the public to view all of the flags and guidons of the regiments."[26] The memorials and other public works projects were advertised as a way to help soldiers returning from the war reenter the civilian workforce, and to rejuvenate the civilian economy. The Plan Commission went so far as to put forward a postwar "reconstruction platform," which declared, "Valuable time has been lost, but it is not yet too late to replace procrastination with our vigorous and enthusiastic support of the reconstruction program of the Chicago plan commission." The city's first duty, the document asserted, was toward returning soldiers.

In its postwar platform (revealed less than a month after the war's end), the Plan Commission also states flatly that along with traffic relief and better railway terminals, places like Soldier Field were vital: "The public health, ample means for healthful recreation . . . which were of fundamental importance before the war, now become matters of absolute necessity." In the years before the war amateur athletics had become a rallying point for urban reformers, many of whom were also advocates for the construction of playgrounds and parks—parks designed for sports and health rather than the Sunday strolls of the rich.

Mayor Thompson was among those pushing for ever more playgrounds and parks, to make Chicago a city of "broad shouldered, red cheeked boys and girls—regular people." Parks gave joy to the reformers who wanted to see the city's children healthy and happy. And they gave joy to Thompson, who used his favored contractors to build them and filled them with equipment from his favorite suppliers.[27] As part of this movement, athletic groups such as the Chicago Athletic Association had, in the first decade of the century, urged the South Park Commission to build a monumental stadium. Everett Brown, chairman of the CAA's Athletic Committee, wrote to the commission in 1907, notifying it that the group's board of directors had passed a resolution to "petition the South Park commissioners to erect a Stadium for athletic games and sport on the new made land of Grant Park. This would be in line with your park play ground policy and be a grand consummation of it. It will not only make Chicago the center of athletics in America, but international events would be held which would make Grant Park the best known of any in not only the United States but throughout the world." As with so many Chicago plans, visionaries had one eye on local benefit and the other on world reputation.

The South Park Commission did construct a temporary stadium in Grant Park, just north of the Field Museum construction site. Olympic-style athletic events were held there in 1913, along with several military shows. But calls for a permanent stadium continued, with advocates pointing to the growing popularity of spectator sports like the Olympics as evidence that such an arena would attract visitors to Chicago.

Then, in the early months of 1919, the plans for a memorial and the hopes for a stadium converged. In February, Charles Fox, of the architecture firm Marshall and Fox, proposed a stupendously elaborate memorial building that, in the end, was a stadium. The *Tribune* gushed: "Not a big mute monument—but a live memorial, busy every day in the year, a structure of utility and beauty, surpassing in size anything on earth . . . that is the sort of memorial plan presented yesterday."[28] Fox's concept—a bowl rather than an arena with one rounded end—bears little resemblance to Soldier Field, looking more like a French duke's palace than a Greek temple. But it shares one crucial feature with the stadium we know today: a grand sweep of columns, stretching along both sides of the structure.[29]

Marshall and Fox were best known for their hotels, such as the Blackstone, and their apartment buildings, including the Edgewater Beach Apartments. Because he happened to be on retainer to the South Park Commission, Fox was enlisted to draw up a rough sketch for the proposal. At the time, a faction of the state Republican Party opposed to Mayor Thompson—the so-called

Deneen wing—controlled the commission, and the city was gearing up for the 1919 mayoral election. Still, Thompson's allies hoped the memorial stadium could be approved under the guise of Chicago boosterism and would help negate the disastrous stand Thompson had taken against the war.[30] Despite his tarnished reputation as a patriot, Thompson was able to use his clout as a backer of Burnham Plan improvements to join the movement to build a stadium as the city's primary World War I memorial. By March 1919, the stadium-as-memorial idea had already been endorsed by several groups, including one spearheaded by W. E. Skinner, chairman of the National Dairy Council. Yet other organizations, including the Chicago chapter of the American Association of Engineers, had asked that the stadium not be built in Grant Park.

Thompson brought his own proposal to the South Park Commission. The hold the Burnham Plan had on Chicagoans was so powerful that the commissioners reacted favorably to the plan and—for a time—let Thompson take credit for it. Although it was divided among Republicans and Democrats, the commission voted unanimously to go forward with the creation of a new stadium. Either Thompson's idea was mightily compelling or all sides saw in it a scheme from which they could benefit. Burnham's allies saw it as a way to bring the city together, and to bring in more business, by showing off the best of Chicago's cultural, sport, and civic life. Political Chicago saw the opportunity to create a grand new public works project; for as long as the building would stand, the money would flow to them.[31]

Primed by Wacker, the *Tribune*, and other Burnham Plan zealots, the city prepared to build Grant Park Municipal Stadium, soon to be renamed Soldier Field. This monumental public space, so central to Chicago's political, cultural, and sporting life throughout much of the twentieth century, had its birth in a marriage between high-minded reformers and venal politicians. In concrete and steel, Soldier Field embodied Chicago's myriad contradictions.

SOLDIER FIELD

PART 1

GETTING IT BUILT

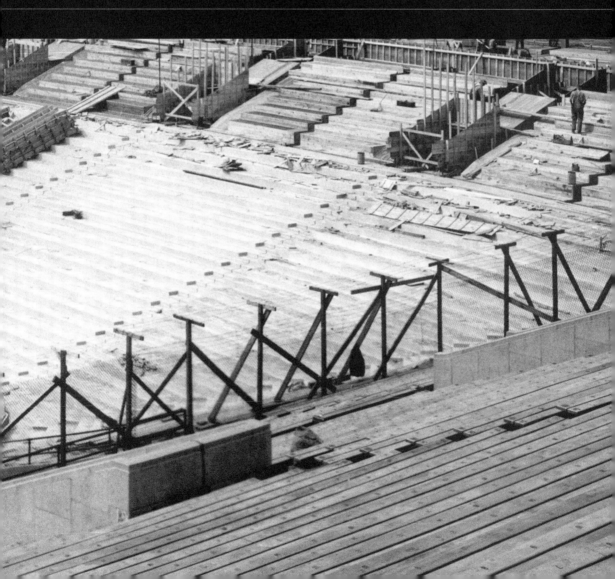

1 *Born Republican, Adopted by Democrats*

Buildings like Soldier Field can become so much a part of a city that's it hard to imagine their absence. Before the stadium rose south of the Field Museum, few would have suggested that Chicago government should own and run a place that would compete with the city's private ballparks and convention arenas.

The Progressive ideas Burnham represented meshed in many cities with a blossoming interest in organized sports and great gatherings that brought city folks—many of them recent immigrants or former farm dwellers—together in the way small-town celebrations had in the previous century. Measures of a city's success at the beginning of the twentieth century included how well it provided for the health and well-being of its youth and how captivating it made its parades, civic celebrations, and public pageants. Football, rugby, and even polo teams were organized in Chicago neighborhoods not just for physical exercise but as ways of creating community. City leaders eagerly encouraged mass gatherings sponsored by civic groups with close but sometimes hidden ties to their own political groups, like Mayor William Hale Thompson's "Chicago Boosters." The aim, for "Big Bill" and others, was to "Americanize" the waves of new immigrants, while justifying to city natives the increased spending—and increased taxes—that inevitably accompanied the City Beautiful improvements.

In Chicago, as in other cities, enthusiasm for more and better parks, sports facilities, and pageants led to the building of an immense stadium only because all of the city's most powerful political factions saw that they could gain something from supporting—and claiming credit for—the arena. What Progressive backers of the Burnham Plan failed to anticipate or willfully ignored was that the push to build a new Chicago would inevitably increase the power of the type of politicians they had been crusading against for decades. As the city was transformed in the first four decades of the century, spending on projects like Soldier Field fueled the political machines Progressives had set out to destroy.

At the end of the Great War, the Republican Party was split into three factions, one of which endorsed Thompson's Democratic rival in the 1919 mayoral election.[1] The Democratic Party was similarly split, with good-government types following former mayors Carter Harrison II and Edward Dunne, and supporters of the ascendant machine following Irish boss Roger Sullivan.[2] Yet despite the enmity between Republicans like Thompson and Democrats like Edward Kelly, the South Park Commission decided to override the letter of the Burnham Plan and the principle of a lakefront "forever open, clear, and free" and to endorse Thompson's proposal and hold a competition to design a new stadium. Chicago's unreformed politicians, Republican and Democrat, were tired of spending restrained by wartime austerity. Chicago needed new streets. It needed new parks. It needed new lakefront beaches. Its people needed jobs—especially, though this wasn't usually said in public, its political people.

The politicians' lust for new fountains of patronage could hardly be contained. Almost as strong, though, was the public impulse to commemorate, in a lasting way, the Chicago men who had lost their lives in the Great War. Thompson, cribbing from proposals by several civic groups, realized he could bring the two forces together in the concrete form of a stadium.

Thompson originally put forward a plan for a stadium that, if built, would have rivaled the much-ridiculed Il Vittoriano monument in Rome, better known as "the wedding cake." Thompson's proposal was ambitious, "twice the size of the Yale Bowl," with the cost, about $10 million, to be paid for by "public subscription" and construction to be completed within two years. The *Herald and Examiner*, which reported the mayor's proposal in glowing terms, took partial credit for the proposal itself. Chicago parks already had many prominent war memorials, including the statue of Civil War Union general John A. Logan, the originator of Memorial Day, at the south end of Grant Park. Nor was the idea of memorial buildings entirely new, though it had become more popular since the Great War. A few stadiums, such as Harvard Stadium at Soldiers Field in Boston, had been built before the war as memorials to war dead. But after the Great War, a rise in popular sports, combined with a movement to create useful buildings as memorials, resulted in scores of stadiums being built across the country. Federal officials, notably chief Labor Department spokesman George W. Coleman, urged the creation of "living memorials" both to help remember the dead and to provide employment for returning soldiers.[3]

Even as they claimed credit for the scheme, Thompson and the *Herald and Examiner* were drawing on a proposal that had grown out of months of back-and-forth among civic leaders. It's hard to determine who came up with the idea first, but all through the late winter and spring of 1919, Chicago's most prestigious architects had been drawing up schemes for war memorials. In late February, Edward H. Bennett, Burnham's collaborator on the 1909 Plan of Chicago, had hatched an idea for a giant triumphal arch in Grant Park, leading to an open-air stadium.[4] (He had first proposed a stadium in Grant Park, north of 11th Street, before the war.) A few weeks later, Marshall and Fox, architects under contract to the South Park Commission, put forward their own proposal, which the *Tribune* and other newspapers praised highly.

The Marshall and Fox idea appears to have been a brainchild of the memorial committee put forward by former Judge John Barton Payne, the Democratic president of the South Park Commission (the board was, however, controlled by Republicans unfriendly to Thompson). In the first two decades of the twentieth century, Grant Park often had been used as a staging area for immense military shows. Payne alluded to that when he speculated about what the proposed arena could be used for: "The stadium, of course, can be used for military maneuvers, out of door theatricals, intercollegiate meets, football games, and I don't see any reason why we could not have the world series of baseball played there," raved Payne, who later would join Woodrow Wilson's cabinet while still serving on the park board. "The place would be an ideal one for an Olympic meet and for any huge out of door theatrical performance."[5]

Though Payne may not have been the first to think of putting a grand, permanent stadium on the lakefront—possibly on the site used for the temporary stadium since 1913, just northwest of the Field Museum—his vision of its uses came closest to the expansive vision the South Park Commission proclaimed when decided to build the stadium, and what actually came to pass at Soldier Field—except, of course, for the World Series.

Thompson leapt on the bandwagon, talking up the stadium wherever and whenever he could.

Tribune publisher Colonel Robert R. McCormick, Thompson's onetime ally, had begun to turn against his fellow Republican, and the *Tribune* had lent its support to Thompson's opponent in that year's mayoral primary. Given the animosity between the two, the paper might have been expected to oppose the stadium. But the sports palace had begun to catch the public's—and the *Tribune*'s—imagination. As with other lakefront improvements, editors held their noses at the stink of Thompson's corruption and endorsed the stadium plan. In an editorial, the *Tribune* urged the South Park Commission:

If we are going to make Chicago a pleasant place to live in, a home fit for heroes to live in and not merely to fight for, we should be about the business of registering our intention in a substantial way.

There is proposed a stadium for athletic games and out of door festivals in Grant Park. Most citizens will be in favor of a project that is to serve the purpose of the greatest number. Grant Park should be a vast forum of the people. It has its Art Institute, its museum, and its recreation grounds. It should have a great Amphitheatre where many thousands may gather for whatever purpose seems desirable.[6]

When the city council approved ordinances clearing the way for lakefront development, aldermen supporting the plan touted the new stadium as one of four big selling points. Hundreds of acres of new lakefront parks, an aquarium, a new passenger terminal (which was never built), and the stadium were to be "Chicago's quartet of world beaters." This grand hoped-for status reflected a tendency in Chicago after the Great Fire to want always to be or to have the best, the first, the biggest, the fastest growing, whatever the category.[7]

Thompson, accompanied by members of his Chicago Boosters club, brought his garish stadium proposal to the South Park Commission. In a letter to the board, Thompson hinted at some of the more compelling reasons why city fathers wanted stadium built—reasons that reappear to this day whenever a new stadium is proposed:

Not only would the stadium give the people of Chicago a great deal of enjoyment, but it would attract thousands of visitors. It would be centrally located and could be used by other cities as well as Chicago for post-season games and for holding world championship contests.[8]

In referring to "world championship contests," Thompson alluded to the city's hopes to host the Olympic Games, a goal Chicago promoters claimed the stadium would help to fulfill. Though today we might think of football, baseball, and basketball as America's great sports, in the early twentieth century, track and field competitions captivated the U.S. public and were popular in most European countries as well.[9]

"Here, south of the new Field Museum and within ten minutes of the Loop, will be held athletic contests, great military and civic parades and spectacles, which 100,000 persons can witness," the *Chicago Herald and Examiner* declared.[10] The *Chicago American* was even more effusive:

More than two thousand years ago a great stadium was erected on the hills of Olympia. . . .

One Milo, bodyguard of an emperor, held his little finger so rigid that none could bend or even move it; another, Melamcomas, stood two days with arms outstretched. They were heroes. . . .

Chicago is now to have a great revival of the games which promises to out-Olympia the Athenians.

The *American*'s boosterish ardor echoed the hopes of many Chicagoans, declaring that the Grant Park stadium could help lead the way toward a revival of athleticism among Chicago's—and the nation's—youth.[11]

In the spring and summer of 1919, it seemed as though all Chicago was backing the stadium, and the rest of the South Park proposals. At the end of May, the South Park Commission unanimously voted to have its general superintendent draw up detailed plans for the construction of a stadium.[12] Initially, everyone assumed it would go up just north of the Field Museum, as laid out in the 1919 city council legislation approving Burnham-inspired lakefront development. But Thompson and the South Park commissioners were mindful of recent court battles. To sidestep controversies over what could be put up in Grant Park, Thompson sought legal advice. One newspaper reported that "under the law no buildings can be erected in Grant Park, but the Mayor has been advised by attorneys a stadium is not a building."[13] The commissioners decided not to risk litigation but to build the new stadium south of the Field Museum instead.

With the site selected, attention turned to choosing a design. Six architectural firms were invited to draw up plans for the stadium: Marshall and Fox, Holabird and Roche, Edward H. Bennett, Coolidge and Hodgson, Zachary T. Davis, and Jarvis Hunt.[14] For several months before the competition kicked off, the park commissioners, city leaders, and the architects had haggled over requirements and restrictions. Thompson, among others, had hoped for the largest stadium ever built, seating 150,000 and "outdoing anything . . . that the Romans had ever built."[15] Dwight Perkins, the South Park Commission's advisor on the competition, took a close look at the area of landfill—at the time still mostly underwater—and quietly raised some doubts about that ambition: "There is not room enough in the plat selected for so large a number," he wrote in a letter to the commissioners.[16] Perkins recommended a maximum capacity of about 100,000 people—the figure that was cited throughout Soldier Field's history until the field was reconfigured in the 1970s. (Standing-room crowds could greatly exceed this number.) The size of the playing field—"unusually large, larger than any Stadium ever built, so far as I am able to discover," Perkins noted—itself limited the seating. So even if the stadium failed to outrank the Yale Bowl in seating capacity, its gargantuan arena would impress spectators.

When it came time for the six architects to submit their designs, the South Park commissioners treated the competition as seriously as a medieval coronation ceremony. The request for proposals went through several revisions, with a final letter going out from the commission in August 1919. All of the architects invited to compete were renowned builders and artists, many of whom—including Fox and Bennett—had gained their reputation from their association with Burnham. The commissioners wanted to make sure no one could accuse the advisory panel of any bias. If the stadium were to be taken seriously as a new mecca for American sport and society, the design must be chosen fairly and the construction must satisfy the highest standards.

Because a trained eye might be able to differentiate a Marshall and Fox schematic from one by Edward H. Bennett, the letter to competitors warned, "No design will be considered the drawings or wrappers of which bear any note or mark revealing their authorship."[17] Perkins arranged tight security for the submitted proposals, securing them in a vault at the Art Institute. The letter to competitors appears detailed for the times: "The proposed stadium shall consist of an open amphitheatre for spectators surrounding (wholly or partially) an arena. It shall be so arranged that large numbers of people may view processions, pageants, military maneuvers, concerts, out door dramatics, athletic contests, track meets, horse shows, fairs, winter sports, ice carnivals, etc., etc." (Today, by contrast, its eight pages would hardly be enough space for Chicago Park District attorneys to clear their throats.) The *Tribune* wrote on August 22, 1919, "Beauty is the most necessary attribute for the Grant park stadium to be submitted by six architects to a jury appointed by the south park board, according to an announcement yesterday. . . . It is hoped to bring the next Olympics to Chicago."[18]

The rules of the competition specified a massive playing field: "An arena, the longest dimension not less than 1,000 feet," with a one-third-mile running track thirty feet wide, suitable for modification for bicycle races. (There was no acknowledgment of the possibility that such distances might make it had for some in the stands to see what was going on.) In addition to its use for various sports and festivals, the stadium was to be a showplace for America's military might. Entrances onto the field were to be designed "for incoming and outgoing processions so that armies may approach at one end, maneuver within the stadium and leave at the opposite end." An ancient purpose for outdoor arenas was drama; Chicagoans of the early twentieth century felt themselves in competition not just with the modern-day Europe but with the Greek and Roman founders of Western civilization, and so concluded that the stadium needed a theater space. One end of the stadium was thus to be convertible into an outdoor stage—the origin of the rounded south end of Soldier Field.[19]

The north end of the stadium was to be south of the Field Museum, its south end at 16th Street. A detailed statement of the physical requirements sent to the architects in June 1919 shows the maximum size of the stadium as about 1,200 feet long by 450 feet wide. The last of several such letters sent by the commission points out a topographical detail that would prove essential to the character of the stadium as it was eventually built: the site, created as landfill in the shallows of Lake Michigan, slopes down, from thirty-one feet above lake level at what was originally the north end of Soldier Field to only fifteen feet above the lake at its south end.

Four of the six competitors submitted plans very similar to each other and to the 1919 Marshall and Fox drawings. They envisioned the stadium as an oval, with colonnades framing the field, a popular design for stadiums of the time. Marshall and Fox, Bennett, and Holabird and Roche set aside the south end of the stadium for the outdoor theater, by grouping close-in stands around a stage area. Jarvis Hunt proposed having the grand entrance to an elongated oval stadium face the lake.

Most of the architects voiced the enthusiasm of the times, boasting of the achievements of American civilization—and how their version of the stadium would advance Chicago's place in it. Zachary T. Davis, the designer of both Comiskey Park (1910) and Wrigley Field (1914), and William F. Kramer, known mostly for his churches and west suburban homes, boasted of the good their stadium would do for the city. They claimed the South Park stadium would instill civic pride in Chicagoans, in the same way great stadiums and monuments in ancient Greece and Rome instilled nationalism in those civilizations' residents. The dream of hosting the Olympics captivated many Chicagoans, and like the *Tribune*, Davis and Kramer evoked the Yale Bowl. In the same way East Coast

> colleges look to the Yale Bowl as the most perfect place so far provided for athletics and exhibitions, so will the entire country look upon Chicago as the most probable setting of any great athletic meet. It will necessarily be the center of national and state athletics, and thus a feature toward promoting a national rivalry in athletics, and, by virtue of its magnitude, recognition of the benefits derived from athletic contests and the interests centered therein.[20]

Though some of the entries extolled the symbolic uses of the stadium, the firm of William Holabird and Martin Roche, the eventual winners of the competition, concentrated more on its practical aspects. Holabird, whose son would take over his duties at the firm after he died in 1923, had studied at West Point before becoming an architect. His firm had made its name on famous skyscrapers such as the Gage Building and the Marquette Building. (They would go on to design the University of Illinois Memorial Stadium.) By spending most of their energy answering what they considered the two main requirements the park board had set, Holabird and Roche appear to have won over the jury in the contest. But they may also have set up their arena for its own eventual demise.

First, Holabird and Roche decided that the primary requirement was not that the stadium be usable for popular sports, or even for the pageants, military parades, and political demonstrations popular at the time. The most important consideration, they believed, was aesthetic: "The Field Museum is considered the head of the composition, the axis of [the] stadium being the same as that of the museum," the architects wrote. This attempt to conform with the Field Museum explains in part why the stadium was only three hundred feet wide,[21] but the justification the architects gave for keeping the stadium so narrow was what they saw as the second key requirement: by concentrating seats around the central portion of the field, they sought "to afford to the greatest number the best view of those athletic games and similar events as could not be expected to fill the stadium to capacity." Holabird and Roche had good reason to make the stadium conform with the Field Museum's dimensions. Letters between the competing architects as a group and Perkins, the park commission's point man, made it clear that whatever they did, the architects were not to overwhelm the Field Museum.[22] Holabird and Roche followed the restrictions carefully—with two exceptions. Mindful of the idea that the stadium was to be a tribute to fallen soldiers, they included a massive memorial that would constitute a towering addition to the skyline. And they violated the height requirements slightly, increasing the height of the center stands to sixty feet, thus allowing for more seating around the playing field than the competing plans.

The memorial as proposed looked like a cross between the Washington and Lincoln monuments. It would have risen over the central stands of the stadium, with columns at the same level as the current stadium's colonnade. Most likely modeled after the ancient Mausoleum of Mausollos, one of the seven wonders of the ancient world, it would have matched or even outdone the Field Museum's entrance facade. And that was only its base. Topping the soldiers' temple would have been an obelisk four times as tall as the top of the colonnade. In designing the colonnades, Holabird and Roche collaborated with a designer who recently had worked on the Lincoln Memorial, another structure that uses Doric columns.

When the jury met in late 1919, its decision was swift and businesslike. It considered the six submissions, in four meetings over a week, and on December 1 decided unanimously in favor of Holabird and Roche. The jurors' three-paragraph report on their findings gives scant indication as to why they chose this design. The only real comments in the minutes dismiss Holabird and Roche's proposal that the stadium be given "a memorial significance," through the inclusion of a tower at its south end, because the memorial plans were outside "the scope of the competition." Amos Alonzo Stagg, the famous University of Chicago football coach, offered no objections regarding the stadium's suitability for football or its bad sightlines—an oversight that was to plague Soldier Field for the rest of its life and eventually result in its 2001–2003 renovation.[23]

Despite the jury's unanimity, the South Park Commission quickly decided that it could not build the whole stadium as Holabird and Roche had envisioned it. At the time, the United States was struggling to emerge from a postwar recession. Having accepted the winners at its meeting of December 3, the board met again, five days later, and voted to seek contractors for the colonnade sections of the stadium immediately but to hold off on the rest of the project. The stands in this first part of the stadium would hold about fifty thousand people—a respectable number. Still, the delay in finishing had two major effects, one political and one aesthetic. First, it meant that the nominally Republican-controlled park board in power in the early 1920s had control over contracts for only part of the stadium. A few years later, Democrats, including Edward J. Kelly, would take over, using the South Park Commission as a foundation for the Democratic machine that would eventually bring Richard J. Daley to power. Second, it meant that Holabird and Roche's monumental tower would never be built.

By the end of the twentieth century, Chicagoans had grown accustomed to thinking of Soldier Field's colonnades as its main memorial feature. That was not the architects' original vision. Until the Park District building rose to block it, the north end of the stadium was open, with the Field Museum a constant backdrop for spectators. Holabird and Roche wanted their monument to be as much of a visual exclamation as the museum. In their submission, they describe "the commanding nature" of the expanse between the museum and the proposed monument at the south end of the stadium. They imagined spectators entering the stadium and sitting awestruck at the giant arena, the towering monument, the gleaming museum, all framed by the neoclassical colonnade. "Here should be placed a monument worthy of Chicago's effort in the Great War," they urged.[24]

When the newspapers originally reported the choice of the Holabird and Roche plan, they left out any mention of the memorial, but renderings that included the tower ran in the newspapers and in the *American Architect*.

Backers of the stadium ignored the objections raised by a few architectural purists, lakefront advocates, and others. One of the most enduring criticisms—mentioned even by Lois Wille, an avowed partisan of the old Soldier Field, in her book *Forever Open, Clear, and Free*—is that it was not envisioned in Burnham's plan. Indeed, it can be argued that no stadium belongs on the lakefront. In the end, the South Park Commission headed off legal challenges to constuction by separating the newly built parkland from Grant Park and renaming the area south of Roosevelt Road "Burnham Park."

Interior of the Soldier Field colonnades, ca. 1924. Photograph by Raymond W. Trowbridge. Courtesy Chicago Park District Special Collections.

Despite this sleight of hand, Soldier Field's placement violates the principle of maintaining an open lakefront.

Though Burnham's vision is the one politicians always cite, it was not his plan that popularized the idea of a stadium. Few remember that before

World War I, Montgomery Ward had tentatively endorsed the idea of a stadium in Grant Park, telling a Chicago newspaper that it was "an excellent idea, and the best possible use to which the lake front could be put. There will be no objection from me as long as the view is not interfered with by any buildings."[25] Ward, it would seem, envisioned a simple structure that fit in a sunken field at the south end of Grant Park rather than a towering cross between a Greek temple and Roman coliseum; he likely would have disapproved of Soldier Field. However, by the time preliminary plans for the stadium were announced, few purists like Ward objected. Instead, the most vociferous arguments against the stadium came from parents of the war dead the stadium was intended to memorialize.

Fred W. Bentley became a leader of the Gold Star Fathers after his son, Paul Cody Bentley, died when a German shell hit the ambulance he was driving at the French front. Paul Bentley was the first Chicagoan killed in the war, and his death made banner headlines in the city's newspapers. A Harvard student and friend of President Theodore Roosevelt's youngest son, Quentin, Paul Bentley had left school and volunteered for the American Field Services ambulance corps. (The corps was founded by a Harvard professor to help the American Hospital in Paris two years before the United States entered the war.) In an odd twist of fate, the French Line steamer that carried Bentley, twenty-nine other Harvard students, and students from other colleges to France on May 19, 1917, was named *The Chicago*. The following month, Harvard awarded Bentley his bachelor's degree while he was in the field. Bentley served with fellow Chicagoans in a unit largely made up of young men from Illinois. Less than two weeks after the United States entered the war, Paul Bentley and another ambulance attendant were "riding through a part of the western theater of war, which was under bombardment."[26]

"During a gas attack . . . we were at the front and were ordered to transport five French soldiers to the rear who had been badly gassed," a friend, Carson Ricks, later told reporters. "Paul was driving. He stopped and tried to back, when they laid down another tier barrage behind us. Then big shells commenced to fall in between. I put on my gas mask and put on Paul's while he was running the car. We had passed through the fire and gas in safety when a shell struck the rear of the ambulance. The five wound French soldiers died instantly.

"I helped Paul to a shell hole and then made my way to a poste de secours, but I don't remember how. A stretcher bearer went out after Paul."[27]

"He never complained," said his friend and fellow driver, Robert Redfield Jr. "He took the dangers as they came without flinching. . . . Anyhow, Bentley was every inch a man—a true man. He died as he worked—bravely."[28]

The press lionized Paul Bentley and his family, calling him the "first Chicago martyr" and covering his funeral like that of a prominent public figure. Reports noted that his ambulance unit had been the first American unit in action—and that the French commander in the area where Bentley was killed had praised its bravery.

Families with members in the service would display a white flag with a blue star in their windows; if the serviceman died in the war they would cover the blue star with a gold star. The parents of the dead thus came to be known as Gold Star Mothers and Fathers. Through the prominence of their son's death, Fred Bentley and his wife became de facto representatives of all Chicago parents who had lost sons in the war. Fred Bentley became head of the Chicago Gold Star Fathers, and his wife, Josephine Bentley, became head of the Gold Star Mothers.

After Big Bill Thompson helped popularize the idea that the stadium should be a monument to the war dead, the American Legion took up the cause, urging the South Park Commission to name the stadium in their honor. But the Bentleys vociferously objected. The Gold Star Mothers had somehow obtained the rights to land in Grant Park and wanted to build a $3 million memorial there. The "noisy athletic strife" of a stadium would not be "a fitting background for a memorial," Josephine Bentley told the park board.[29]

Calling the idea of a memorial stadium "a travesty," Fred Bentley said, "We resent the efforts that some persons are making to create sentiment for the stadium and bond issue by representing it to be a memorial to the dead soldiers." The protests against the stadium, however, went nowhere. The idea of a "living memorial" appealed to most patriotic organizations. At the same time, it appealed to politicians of every persuasion because of its public works possibilities. The South Park commissioners moved forward. In the late twentieth century, if the mayor of Chicago wanted something built, there was little question but that it would be built; voters today have no real say in what the Chicago Park District builds, or how it builds it. Only the district board—and perhaps the Plan Commission and the city council—has to approve it. In 1920, however, park districts in the city had to go directly to the voters to raise taxes to build anything. The board's first order to the architects had been to estimate how much it would cost to build the stadium. Before workmen could turn the first spade of dirt, officials had to drum up public support for funding.

The enthusiasm surrounding the Burnham Plan helped the South Park Commission convince voters that funding the stadium was their civic duty. And even as they campaigned against the tax-wasting city scandals surrounding Big Bill Thompson's Burnham Plan improvements, the *Tribune* and other newspapers urged the approval of bonds to pay for the stadium and other park projects.[30] Voters, the paper declared, could bring to life the dream of what Chicago could be. "When will it be a reality?" the *Tribune* asked under a half-page image of Holabird and Roche's design for the stadium.

If the stadium were built, it would "provide one of the most impressive civic centers in the world."[31]

Newspapers and other reform advocates seemed to forget their concerns about corruption and overspending when the "dream" of the Burnham Plan seemed in sight. Civic groups such as the Chicago Church Federation, the Illinois Manufacturers Association, and the Chicago Political Equality League—a group that had fought to gain women the right to vote—banded together to urge South Siders to vote for the bonds. "Never before has all Chicago been united for a great public improvement as it now is for the lake front plans," the civic groups declared.[32]

When voters went to the polls on Tuesday, February 24, 1920, they voted almost three-to-one in favor of all six of the South Park bond issues. City leaders were ecstatic, with Wacker saying that the victory opened the way for "the biggest, finest and most far-reaching undertaking for the public good Chicago has launched in its entire history."[33]

The park commission gave Holabird and Roche permission to exhibit the plans for the stadium, and they were displayed at the Art Institute, along with a model.[34] Because the commission had decided not to include the war monument at the south end of the field, however, the architects had to rejigger their plans before work could begin. The commissioners had at first raised Chicagoans' hopes that the stadium would be open within a year or two after the first bond issue in spring 1920, but it took until August 1920 even to advertise for test piles for the stadium's foundation. The commission then also voted to pay the architects 3½ percent of the full cost of the stadium.[35]

Several other factors also delayed construction. First off, once the South Park commissioners decided to build south of the Field Museum rather than north of it, they had to wait until crews finished landfilling south of 14th Street, where they were dumping ashes and other debris from the Loop.

"Setting the stage for this great structure in an area as yet inundated with an average of fifteen feet of water gave occasion for a brilliant engineering performance," wrote Linn White, the South Park Commission's chief engineer during Soldier Field's construction, in a short book on the stadium's history written in the late 1930s but apparently never published. "The first act consisted of plunging right out into navigable waters, where gulls and white-caps still had their own way, and reclaiming the land upon which Soldier Field now stands."[36]

The South Park commissioners, meanwhile, were having trouble deciding who should build the stadium. Most bids for the construction came in far above the $2 to $2.5 million that voters had approved spending; the lowest initial bid was for $2.4 million. In the years following the United States' entry into World War I, wholesale prices skyrocketed, more than doubling by the end of 1919. In the early 1920s these price increases still affected the

Crowds arrive for the Chicagoland Music Festival, August 18, 1934. This photo shows the northwest corner of the stadium as it appeared before the Chicago Park District administration building was erected. Courtesy Chicago Park District Special Collections.

economy, and inflation hampered construction throughout the country. On December 21, 1921, the board voted to extend the time to receive bids. Then, in a meeting on February 21, 1922, the board made public that all fourteen bids for stadium construction had come in at $4 million or above, and it rejected them all. "The plans will be modified to permit cheaper construction, but I do not think the size will be altered," John F. Foster, the South Park general superintendent, said. The next call for bids omitted from the plans an impressive set of terraces, thirty-two feet long, that were to have led from the north end of the field to a promenade connecting the stadium to the Field Museum (they were built later). Another change was the final removal of the memorial structure Holabird and Roche had envisioned for the south end of the stadium. Within a few years, South Park president Edward J. Kelly, in attempt to obscure the board's scratching of the memorial plans, described the colonnades as rising "like guards of honor" around the stadium. The obfuscation appears to have succeeded. Almost eighty years later, the Chicago Bears would propose and execute a renovation plan that demolished the original Soldier Field arena but kept the colonnades, in part because many Chicagoans considered the columns an almost sacred monument to veterans and the war dead.

Finally, Blome-Sinek & Co., which had built Wrigley Field and constructed a number of South Park District fieldhouses in the early part of the century, was awarded a $2.3 million contract to build the colonnades and stands on the east and west sides of the stadium. Rudolph Blome was a longtime supporter of Republican candidates, including former governor Frank O. Lowden, a onetime GOP presidential contender. Aside from its political qualifications, Blome-Sinek also was a pioneer in the construction of concrete buildings. And instead of building the stadium of concrete faced with stone, the South Park Commission had decided to face it with panels of composite concrete made to look like stone, again to save money.[37]

Even with the design changes, the cost of the stadium far surpassed the initial $2.3 million Blome-Sinek estimate, and while park officials later said the stadium cost about $8.5 million to build, that does not appear to include the cost of extending the lakefront south of the Field Museum. The extension of the lakefront from Roosevelt Road south to Jackson Park cost a total of $8 million. Several hundred thousand dollars of that money went toward raising land for the stadium out of the lake. And Blome-Sinek was only the largest contractor on the first phase of the stadium construction; there were numerous smaller contracts for matters such as filling in areas of the arena with clay and sand and areas outside the stadium with sand and cinders, as well as electrical and plumbing work. After the delays caused by revising the plans and rebidding the contracts, work finally got under way with a groundbreaking on July 19, 1922.

Even as work commenced, the South Park commissioners, and Holabird and Roche, continued to make changes to the stadium design, reworking the plans for the driveways leading into the stadium a few weeks after construction started and approving changes in the colonnades twice around the time ground was broken. By the end of August, although two construction shacks and two cranes were set up on the site, there was still little evidence of work between the south steps of the Field Museum and the water that filled the area where the Soldier Field south parking lot and McCormick Place East now stand. Photographs documenting the progress of construction show a number of dams out in the lake, as well as construction boats.

The first year of work was mostly preparatory. Crews sank test pilings to determine how far down supports for the stadium would have to go. Great Lakes Dredge & Dock Co. filled in the rest of the land. Other companies scraped the existing ground to level it off, and laid railroad spurs around the stadium site to bring massive steel girders and faux-stone blocks as close to the site as possible. "Construction problems were many and varied,"

GRANT PARK STADIUM CHICAGO, ILL.
NO. 21 FOR THE DATE JUNE 20-23
SOUTH PARK COMMISSIONERS OF CHICAGO
HOLABIRD & ROCHE · ARCHITECTS
BLOME SINEK CO. · CONTRACTORS

Façade of the west stands under construction, June 20, 1923. Courtesy Chicago Park District Special Collections.

White wrote. "Newly made water-front land, some of it about as unsettled as a marsh, challenged the ingenuity of the engineers at the very start." The engineers decided to drive pilings down "in a network sufficient to provide the required support." To build the floor of the arena just seven feet above the lake level, the land had to be filled in to a depth of at least twenty-two feet. Crews drove the sixty- to sixty-six-foot pilings in the months following the groundbreaking so that by mid-September 1922, the areas where the colonnades would later stand looked like a clear-cut forest of stumps.

Photographs from October show that the west side of the stadium progressed more rapidly than the east. The stands and colonnades began to rise in the spring of 1923, and by May the first outlines of the west stands were visible, towering over the nearby Illinois Central railroad lines.

The first year of stadium construction ended with yet another delay. On June 1, 1923, laborers at the stadium site received a raise from 72½ cents an hour to 82½ cents an hour. Still, the Industrial Workers of the World, a radical union better known as the Wobblies, convinced caisson diggers throughout the city to go on strike three weeks later. By July 2, however, most of the

Stadium interior under construction, August 29, 1923. Courtesy Chicago Park District Special Collections.

workers were back on the job.[38] After the strike, construction moved ahead swiftly, although Blome-Sinek suffered a minor setback when its payroll was robbed of $5,000 in early August. By then, the composite stone for the stadium facade sat on a spur in New York Central boxcars, and huge crane platforms towered over the site. In October, visitors to the Field Museum—itself only two years old—saw the colonnades taking shape at the south end of each side of the stands. The composite stone covered the concrete skeleton of the stadium to about a third of the height of the stands; farther north, toward the Field Museum, workers still toiled to erect the skeleton, half of which was still enclosed in wooden scaffolding. Three crane platforms, two about the height of the columns, another about twice the height of the completed stadium, towered over the east stands. The ground east and north of the stadium remained largely bare earth.

Early the following month, work progressed to the point that the entire east colonnade was complete or under construction, with workers capping off the southern part, and the columns at the north end were about two-thirds done. By November 22, 1923, Blome-Sinek had reached the topmost part of the west colonnade and was about to start on the column caps and roof. In mid-December, crews largely left the site, clearing most of the wood, concrete, and earthen debris from what would become the arena. The exterior of each colonnade appears in photos to be almost complete, except for the top of the east colonnade's north end. As Soldier Field rose on the shore of the lake, the national press took notice. "The outstanding example of concrete stone construction during the year was the Chicago Stadium, still unfinished," wrote the *New York Times* at the end of 1923. "This structure is being faced entirely with concrete stone, requiring 130,000 cubic feet of dressed material. This represents the largest concrete stone construction project ever undertaken."[39]

Even as work progressed, the commissioners continued to tinker with the design. White optimistically told newspapers on January 1, 1924, that freezing temperatures were not slowing down the work. "The exterior is about 90 percent complete and the interior about 60 percent," he said. "We hope to have it entirely finished by the latter part of July." By April 14, 1924, the first caps on the colonnades, at the south end of each row of columns, were going up. The arena area once again filled up with wood and other construction debris. Sometime during the spring, however, it became clear that part of the west stands closest to the arena had sustained damage during the winter, and the South Park Commission and the contractor began sniping at each other about who would pay to redo it. Soon enough, though, the commissioners agreed to pay Blome-Sinek the cost of the work, plus $2,000 in office expenses.[40]

Meanwhile, the commissioners debated whom the stadium concessions contractor would be and put out to bid contracts for seats—really benches—temporary seats, and clay and sand for the stadium arena. J. F. Fisher and Co. received $205,000 to supply and install the electric wiring system. In April 1924, Luminous Fixtures Supply Co. received a $9,000 contract to install the stadium's original light fixtures. At the construction site, all the caps on top of the colonnades were in place or under construction by the beginning of May. By the end of June, the lower sections of the east stands were completed to the north end of the stadium—an area known as the Court of Honor until the park district headquarters was built—with workers building steps up to stands from what would later be McFetridge Drive. Railroad cars pulled up next to the rising hulk of the stadium, and horse carts hauled material from one part of the site to another. The west colonnades were largely complete and the scaffolding removed, although scaffolding still sheathed the east colonnades. By mid-August, the east and west colonnades were complete, with doors and other fixtures—minus lighting and gate number signs—largely in place on the ground level. In construction photos, doors are also visible inside the stadium, and grass is

Horsecarts move material at the construction site, June 25, 1924. The west colonnade is largely complete. Courtesy Chicago Park District Special Collections.

growing at the north end, though the south end appears barren. Kenwood Trucking Co. of Chicago received almost $11,000 to fill in the stadium arena with clay and sand and another contract to create the stadium's cinder running track in July 1924. Kenwood used more than twenty-five thousand cubic yards of gravel and cinders to raise the arena to the level of seven feet above the lake level of the time, with the center of the arena floor higher than the sides to allow for drainage.[41]

By late August, the stadium was ready for the first of its many dedicatory events—at least six in its opening two years, with four in the first five weeks. The first, an athletic meet with policemen as competitors, was a fund-raiser for the Chicago Police Benevolent Association, which provided support for police widows and officers disabled in the line of duty. On Friday, September 5, 1924, Sergeant John Walsh of the Chicago Police Department's Traffic Division became the very first winner of an athletic contest at what would become Soldier Field, throwing a sixteen-pound hammer 132 feet, 10 inches. The next day, at the meet's official opening, twelve hundred police officers paraded in formal blue dress through the arena, led by police chief Morgan

Exterior of the west colonnade at night, soon after its completion in 1924. Courtesy Chicago Park District Special Collections.

A. Collins. The South Park commissioners had enough seats set up to accommodate sixty thousand people—in addition to seating on the arena—and about forty-five thousand showed up. The event included fireworks, music by two police bands, and the antics of forty clowns, as well as an actor playing Barney Google, a popular comic strip character of the time, riding his horse Spark Plug. One of the contests, a chariot race, resulted in the injury of several policemen when something spooked the horses and they took off toward their temporary stables at the south end of the arena. A horse trampled Buck Weaver of the 34th District and injured him seriously enough to send him to the hospital.[42]

One of the purposes the commissioners had envisioned for their new building was as a showplace for pageants celebrating Chicago culture and bringing together the city's people. The first of many such programs took place September 10, 1924, when schoolchildren who received singing instruction at South Park fieldhouses joined professional musicians in the Pageant of Music and Light, which one newspaper called a "preliminary dedication" of Grant

Park Stadium. "It is a lesson to foreigners and those socialistically inclined showing that Americans still have the old pleasures and love of beauty, that they haven't lost all these qualities in the modern rush of life," Edward Kelly told the *Daily News*. At the beginning and end of the program, red lights bathed the colonnades, publicly illuminating them for the first time at night. About three thousand children marched into the stadium from the north carrying lanterns as much as four feet tall that they had made in crafts classes at South Park playgrounds. They paraded around until they formed a giant wheel, then set down the multicolored lights. The children then joined a fifteen-hundred-voice adult chorus in the stadium's east stands. Floodlights atop each colonnade illuminated the arena, and beams of colored light bathed conductor Harry Barnhart as he led the crowd in singing. In a performance that ten years later would be echoed in the first of many Chicagoland Music Festivals at Soldier Field, William Boeppler also led the Chicago Saengerfest Chorus in the "Hallelujah Chorus" from Handel's *Messiah*, as well as "Beautiful Savior" and—as it was raining slightly—"The Heavens Declare." Bears made their first appearance on the field, as about a thousand of the youngsters sang tunes including "The Big Brown Bear," a popular children's song of the time. The evening ended with the singing of "America the Beautiful."

Less than two weeks later, the South Park Commission brought hundreds more schoolchildren to Soldier Field for another dedication ceremony. No other Soldier Field event ever was so dominated by children's handiwork. Many youngsters wore costumes reflecting their ethnic heritage—at least, those not dressed as elephants, giraffes, and other animals. Photos of the event show the children frolicking through the arena, apparently having the time of their lives.[43]

With these early ceremonies, the South Park commissioners showed that they supported the city's police and offered ways for the city's children to celebrate their various heritage while joining its mainstream culture. The stadium's promise lay in its ability to bring together private citizens for some larger purpose, even if simply for the hope of enjoying themselves in the company of a great crowd. As Chicagoans discovered how they could use the facility, however, the City Beautiful ideals that helped create it mixed with a force made more potent by its control of the South Parks: Chicago's rising Democratic Party. In his booklet on Soldier Field, Linn White, the South Park engineer, laid out clearly what the commissioners hoped the stadium would be for Chicago: the stadium was to represent

> an impulse to glorify their city with noble effort . . . an enshrined temple . . . to Chicago's fallen heroes. . . . More than that, Soldier Field represents those ideals for all sorts of recreational and physical diversions. It is a lofty example of changing sand wastes into the grandeur of a dream of the City Beautiful."

Chicagoans quickly accepted the new stadium as a central place for gatherings celebrating the city's achievements and honoring its heroes. Meanwhile, Soldier Field, born as a monument to Republican mayor Big Bill Thompson's attempts to remake himself, was adopted as the child of the South Park Commission and its Democratic leaders. The stadium had become an essential part of Chicago—and essential fuel for the rising Democratic political machine.

2 *Soldier Field and the Democratic Ascendancy*

By the fall of 1924, Big Bill Thompson had lost his post as mayor to a reforming Democrat, William Dever, and languished on the sidelines of Chicago politics, flirting with the Progressive Party. With the mayor who first proposed the stadium out of the picture, the Democrats who controlled the South Park Commission could freely claim credit for it, and the ways they used the grand creation defined Soldier Field's place in Chicago's cultural and political life for the next half century. Edward J. Kelly embraced the City Beautiful ideas Thompson had championed, making his own the rhetoric about the higher purposes of landfill, road construction, and concrete pillars.[1]

Soldier Field hosted only a few overtly political rallies over the years, but they were massive in both size and importance. More important was the extent to which the Democratic Party used other events at the stadium to promote itself, and the way it used Soldier Field's day-to-day operations and frequent need for repairs to reward political workers and favored contractors.

Thompson's attempts to use the Burnham Plan had earned him praise even from newspapers such as the *Tribune*, and had blunted some of the incessant political criticism from Democrats and rival factions within his own party. That reformers and good-government types opposed politicians like Thompson and Kelly on principle did not stop them from praising their achievements on behalf of the city.

When Kelly joined the South Park Board in June 1922, Irish Democrats, long the power brokers in the party, stood on the margins of Chicago politics. Republicans sat in City Hall and the governor's mansion in Springfield, and though a Democrat held the Cook County presidency, it was Anton Cermak, a Bohemian, who controlled the county purse strings.

For several years, Kelly had used the Metropolitan Sanitary District as his power base. Kelly owed his position as chief engineer for the Sanitary District to *Tribune* publisher Robert McCormick, who befriended the Democrat when McCormick headed the district. Sometime in Kelly's early years at the Sanitary District, the story goes, McCormick came across the young foreman fighting with a Republican coworker. Instead of firing Kelly, as the Democrat had feared, McCormick raised his salary, telling him, "I'm glad someone around here has guts."[2] Despite their political differences, McCormick continued to look favorably on Kelly throughout his public life. Over the years, the *Tribune* subjected Kelly's use of the park board and the stadium as sources of patronage to much less scrutiny than it might otherwise have faced. When Kelly joined the South Park Board, Republicans still nominally controlled it, though its longtime president, Judge John Barton Payne, was a Democrat. A year later, Kelly replaced Payne as president and from then on used the parks as an important source of patronage, contracts, and prestige for his party and himself. Despite his clear partisanship, Kelly rarely was called out on his Democratic Party ties or his use of the South Park Commission, and later the Chicago Park District, for his own ends.

In his tenure as president first of the South Park Commission and then of the Chicago Park District, and later as mayor, Kelly used beautification of Chicago as a way to reward everyone from ward heelers to construction contractors. Even as they reported on his political activities—and his ambitions—Chicago's newspapers largely portrayed Kelly as a civic-minded public servant striving to complete Chicago's lakefront transformation. Chicagoans considered the stadium a civic jewel, the culmination of the Burnham Plan's City Beautiful vision and a symbol of the city's final ascent to world-class status. Newspapers, radio and later television covered almost any charitable or public event held there, even events sponsored by their competitors.

Kelly's use of Soldier Field to increase the prestige of the Democratic Party began almost as soon as it opened. The formal dedication ceremonies for the stadium took place on October 9, 1924, the anniversary of the Great Chicago Fire, which Chicagoans of the time regarded as the central event in the city's history. For decades the city marked the anniversary of the fire as Chicago Day, including during the World's Columbian Exposition. The ceremonies sometimes featured parades and often included a reenactment of the fire's beginning. For the fifty-third anniversary and the official opening of the stadium, the descendants of the fire's two most famous characters reenacted their ancestors' legendary—although apocryphal—roles. Marie O'Leary Cannon, the great-great-granddaughter of Catherine O'Leary, owner of the barn where the fire is thought to have started, dressed up as a milkmaid for the Soldier Field opening, despite her family's customary reticence about their role in the fire. The day before the opening ceremonies, she and a

Rubbish in Soldier Field concourse following a College All-Star football game, September 1, 1938. The game was one of many events at the stadium promoted by one newspaper (in this case, the *Chicago Tribune*) but covered by others. Courtesy Chicago Park District Special Collections.

cow advertised as Bessie, granddaughter several times over of the O'Leary's cow, paraded through the downtown streets urging Chicagoans to come to the Chicago Day event at Soldier Field. Cannon made light of her family's persecution for a fire that historians have concluded one of their neighbors almost certainly started. When a photographer asked Cannon to milk the cow, she replied that "It may be poor policy to admit it in view of Mrs. O'Leary's well-known ability along that line, but I, her great-great-granddaughter, never milked a cow in my life."

The opening ceremonies gathered a bizarre jumble of entertainments and memorials. The fire department started things off, parading through the Loop to the stadium. Mayor William Dever, Kelly, and William J. Sinek stood by as a flag was raised, and then each addressed the crowd. In typically bombastic style, Kelly welcomed the crowd of sixty thousand and told them the stadium stood as a symbol of Chicago's rebirth and future ascendancy. (At that point, Soldier Field could accommodate only about thirty-eight thousand in its permanent seats.) "There is no doubt, there is no doubt in the world that Chicago will someday not so long hence be the largest and leading city in the world," Kelly opined.

Several military troops, from the 14th Cavalry, 2nd Infantry, and 14th Artillery, drilled and attacked each other in a mock battle. Riders from the 14th Cavalry's Troop A urged their horses to a gallop and jumped through giant rings of fire. Then came the star attractions: The crowd sat rapt as Cannon took her place on a milking stool at the center of the newly sodded arena, next to Bessie in a mock-up of her great-great-grandmother's barn. Accounts don't record whether Bessie kicked over the lantern, but the barn began to burn. Firemen, including ten who had fought the Great Fire, came onto the field with Fire King No. 1, the first Chicago pump engine. Letting the mock barn burn to the ground (as it had in the historical fire, while the O'Leary home was spared), they set to work fighting another fire in a mock three-story building using modern equipment.

Once the fire spectacular ended, policemen drilled on the field. Two police quartets sang. Then *Tribune* publisher and owner Robert R. McCormick and the manager of the Hotel Sherman, Frank Bering, led teams in a polo match. (McCormick's team won, 5–4.) Aside from the odd pageantry, the event also included the first instance of children getting lost at a Soldier Field event. Sinek announced over the newly installed loudspeakers that a girl, age four, and her brother, age six, were lost, and that anyone who found them should take them to the reviewing stand. A police officer soon did just that.[3]

Questions about the stadium's cost plagued it from the beginning. In 1919 Holabird and Roche estimated it would cost $2.6 million to realize the entire plan, including $350,000 for the memorial structure.[4] But by the time the South Park commissioners signed contracts with Blome-Sinek, it was clear that building Soldier Field would cost much more than that. (Mayor Thompson's $10 million estimate came closer to the mark than the architects' calculations.) As they opened the stadium, Kelly and the other commissioners were looking for a way to cut costs. Blome-Sinek alone had cost them $2.3 million, close to the original allocation for the entire structure.[5]

Two weeks before Chicago Day, White had written a memo to the acting general superintendent of the South Park Commission, estimating that the completion of the stadium would require $3 million—doubling the project's cost. If the memorial structure in the original plans was completed, the cost could go as high as $4 million. The commissioners quietly abandoned the memorial temple. Two days after the October 9 dedication, the commissioners voted to put a measure on the ballot asking voters to approve $3 million in bonds to complete the stadium. "Although the stadium as it now stands is a monument to Chicago, its real beauty cannot be appreciated until the south end is closed to form the horseshoe," Kelly told the *Tribune*. From that time on, South Park officials and their successors at the Chicago Park

District refered to the colonnades themselves as the memorial element of the stadium, contrary to the designers' intent. (Although the colonnades' design does resemble that of Lincoln Memorial and the Mausoleum of Mausollos, both obviously memorial structures.) One news account mentioned that the stadium would be dedicated "as a memorial to the heroes and veterans of the world war."[6]

Politicians and the newspapers once again went to bat for the commissioners, with the *Tribune* declaring, "A vote for the $3,000,000 bond issue to complete the stadium is only good business." Soldier Field could be popular enough that "it may make the south park system well nigh self-supporting," a *Tribune* editorial concluded. But the Gold Star Fathers and Mothers opposed the bond issue, saying that Kelly and other backers were playing on voters' sentiments to gain approval of a financial boondoggle. "We resent the efforts that some persons are making to create sentiment for the stadium and bond issue by representing it to be a memorial to the dead soldiers," Fred W. Bentley said. Civic groups contended that the commissioners had known from the outset that the earlier bond issue would be insufficient but had misrepresented the cost in order to lure voters into allowing more spending. A perfectly fine stadium could have been built for only $2.5 million—as was being done in Los Angeles at the time.

Meanwhile, Kelly and others pushed hard to get the new bonds approved. The board president explained that postwar building costs were much higher than anticipated. Leaving only the colonnade section of the stadium would mean that "the original investment will be practically lost," Kelly claimed. Already skilled at playing on voters' pride in their city, Kelly conjured the dream of Chicago hosting the annual Army-Navy football game, which until then had always been played on the East Coast. "However, it all depends on passage of the . . . bond issue to complete the stadium." South Side business associations and the Chicago Association of Commerce backed the bonds. Voters looked at the successes of the stadium in its first few months of operation and agreed with Kelly. The referendum passed with more than 70 percent of the vote.[7]

With the bonds approved and their City Beautiful legacy assured, the commissioners moved to award contracts to finish the stadium. At the same time, those who supported renaming Grant Park Stadium to honor America's war dead began to press their case. Bidding on the new contracts began in the spring, and in July the bids were opened. On August 19, the South Park commissioners bypassed a lower bid and awarded John Griffiths & Sons a $2.28 million contract for most of the remaining construction, except for the north end of the stadium. Three years later, the same firm received a $1.3 million contract for the north end work—an amount $320,000 greater than the low bid by Avery Brundage & Co.

The 1925 and 1928 Griffiths & Sons contracts stand as a landmark in Chicago political history. Up to that point, contracts related to Chicago's wastewater treatment and drainage canals had been Edward Kelly's most visible claim to power. Now, however, Kelly had a new means of rewarding a frequent contributor to his Democratic campaigns. Chicago got a celebrated new stadium, while Kelly built the foundation of the political machine that helped bring the Democratic Party to permanent ascendancy in the city. Newspapers paid little attention to the questions raised about the contracts until years later, when Kelly had moved up to the mayor's chair at City Hall.[8]

While the South Park Commission worked to ensure the fortunes of its friends, it also decided that the naming of the field in honor of U.S. war dead could not wait for the completion of the stadium. At the commissioners' April 14, 1925, meeting representatives of the Grand Army of the Republic, the Civil War veterans' group, asked that the Grant Park Stadium be renamed United States War Veteran's Field. The commissioners referred the matter to the parks' general superintendent, and on August 19 the commissioners voted, 3–2, to name the stadium Soldier Field. The very naming demonstrated the control and influence of Chicago's rising Democratic Party. The commissioner who proposed the name Soldier Field was Louis J. Behan, an attorney with Kelly's sanitary district who was also the Fifth Ward Democratic committeeman. (Now part of the 11th Ward, Bridgeport, Kelly's center of power and the center of Democratic politics for the rest of the twentieth century, was then in the Fifth Ward.) A dedication was set for November 11.[9]

In late October the *Tribune* latched onto an issue that illustrates—almost as well as Colonel McCormick's efforts to reform English spelling single-handedly—how its editorial policies bent to the whims of its sometimes cantankerous and eccentric owner. More importantly, it explains why generations of Chicagoans, including both mayors Daley, have referred to the stadium as "Soldiers Field" (or "Soldiers' Field") and why several high-ranking park district officials—including Erwin "Red" Weiner, who was in charge of the stadium throughout the 1950s—went into conniptions whenever the paper was mentioned, despite the numerous events the paper sponsored at the stadium over the years. On October 21, 1925, a *Tribune* editorial criticized a *Tribune* news article about Armistice Day events for calling the arena "Grant Park Stadium." The South Park commissioners, in part at the urging of the paper, had renamed it "Soldier field," the writer asserted, even if it hadn't yet been ceremonially christened. "Then for the purpose of an American Legion celebration of Armistice Day it reverts on the *Tribune* local copy desk to the Grant park stadium."

A second editorial, likely written by McCormick, followed the next day, under the headline "This Is Going to Be Soldiers' Field If It Takes the 1st Division":

> It is, whatever the south park commissioners may have put in the record, Soldiers' Field, and not Soldier Field. . . . [The commissioners] changed Soldiers' Field to Soldier Field. Try to say Soldier Field. Then ask what soldier. Maybe Mike, or it might have been Jan or possibly Sven. Maybe because Harvard has the old Soldiers' Field the south park commissioners thought they ought not to be copycats entirely. Harvard will not object. . . .
>
> It is Soldiers' Field, plural in the hope that America will have more than one when more are needed and will regard more than one when more have been used.
>
> It is Soldiers' Field, now and forever in this space on this newspaper.[10]

Ignoring the *Tribune*'s jeremiad, the American Legion and the South Park commissioners helped coordinate a massive commemoration of Armistice Day, November 11, to mark the name change—to Soldier Field. Despite renewed isolationism after the Great War, even relatively antiwar cities like Chicago marked Armistice Day, the anniversary of the declaration of peace. Celebrations sometimes resembled a second Independence Day but also emphasized the loss of life in the Great War—and the need to avoid such losses in the future. While we still observe the date, as Veterans Day, Armistice Day was in the decades immediately following the Great War a much more solemn holiday. Commissioners had hoped the stadium would become the site of grand civic celebrations and commemorations, and events like the Armistice Day memorial helped make this a reality.

The day began with the firing of guns at dawn. Then at 11 a.m., a twenty-one-gun salute was fired in Grant Park and the crowds in the Loop stopped to bare their heads (men almost always wore hats at the time) and pause for a moment of silent prayer and reflection. In the afternoon, former governor Frank Lowden and naval commander John A. Rodgers were the guests of honor. Just two months before the Soldier Field dedication, on August 31, Rodgers, a World War I veteran and the second naval officer ever licensed as a pilot, had piloted one of two Navy planes making the first attempt to fly from the West Coast to Hawaii. Rodgers's plane went down the next day, about four hundred miles short of the islands. The crew survived the downing and subsisted on scanty emergency rations until a submarine found the plane floating fifteen miles from Kauai on September 10. Rodgers was immediately hailed as a hero and his name splashed on front pages across the country. So it was a coup that Chicago brought him to the city for the official renaming ceremony.

The ceremony began with decorated combat veterans escorting the Gold

Star Mothers and Fathers to their seats and field artillery firing a salute. The U.S. flag was raised, followed by a large banner reading "Soldier Field," which the Gold Star Mothers had carried into the stadium with them. A parade led by an Army general included sailors from the Great Lakes Naval Station, ROTC units, and numerous veterans groups, including the Grand Army of the Republic. Rodgers described his flight, relating how his crew could receive but not send radio messages and so was able to follow the fading hope of the Navy ships searching for them. "The eulogies you voice for us apply also to you," Rodgers told the twenty thousand people at the ceremony. "Let us remind you that in living it becomes your duty to be prepared to see that the country is ready, so that in the event this nation is drawn again into war the young men who fall will be as few as possible." Lowden, the Republican governor of Illinois during the war, gave the main dedication speech, praising the veterans of the wars of the last fifty years, and telling them that they had preserved American democracy and defended freedom. Himself a veteran of the Spanish-American War, Lowden declared that Soldier Field stood as a "memorial of our soldier dead, not only in the Great War, but in all the wars in which we have been engaged."

But none that day waxed more grandiloquent than Kelly. The future mayor and political powerhouse gave speeches at each opening of the stadium. From the start, Soldier Field stood as one of the most impressive signs of the city's civic advancement—and Kelly made sure people knew who to credit for it. The stadium was a place for people to come together and feel pride in their city. Kelly did his best to embed that idea in the mind of the public, and his speeches at the stadium used the most high-flown rhetoric possible to describe its place in Chicago's culture. In his speech on Armistice Day 1925, he linked the soldiers' sacrifice to the lakefront improvements the South Park commissioners had embarked on a few years before. The stadium fulfilled the city's grand vision of itself, and served to lift Chicagoans up from mundane pursuits to flights of glory.

"The soldiers who died did their work well," Kelly told the crowd:

They gave us security. We who survive have much of our work still to do. Who would have thought, twenty-five years ago, that Chicago would be . . . the city it is today? Who could foresee this great Stadium, the new Lake Front, our great new boulevards, our other public improvements? Only a few. I like to think of this stadium not as an achievement, so much as a pledge and a symbol. It helps us all to visualize the city Chicago must become. . . . This is the Armory of the Soldiers of Citizenship.[11]

As Kelly mentioned, work had started just before Armistice Day on the south end of the stadium. Griffiths & Sons had taken over the construction

The east stands in winter, December 26, 1925. Note the wooden pilings being driven to support the stadium's foundation. Courtesy Chicago Park District Special Collections.

that fall, and a new series of photographs documents the swift completion of the project. By November 13 the south bowl of the stadium was starting to take shape, with sewers capped at the southeast end of the colonnades and a railroad spur at the south end of the property once again in use. Crews worked through December, driving piles to support the south end's foundation. Work stopped around Christmas but resumed in January 1926, with workers battling the cold to keep water for concrete flowing. In a photo dated March 5, 1926, horses drawing a cart are visible right where Gate 0 later stood.

Even before its opening, Soldier Field became a sought-after venue. As the stadium neared completion, Kelly and other South Park officials negoti-

Roman Catholic Eucharistic Congress, June 1926. Courtesy Chicago Park District Special Collections.

ated plans for the first high-profile events to be held there. Cardinal George Mundelein, Chicago's archbishop, wanted to show the world the power and presence of Catholics in the United States. He and other leaders of the U. S. church decided that there would be no better place to display that power than Soldier Field, and reserved the still-incomplete stadium for the June 1926 International Eucharistic Congress (see chapter 6).

At the same time, Kelly and other city leaders wanted to make as big a splash as possible in their final dedication ceremony. And they succeeded, bringing the Army-Navy Game to Chicago for the first and—so far—only time. During the first half of the twentieth century, the two military academies were college football powerhouses. Their status as winning teams was enhanced by the patriotic sentiment Americans who had championed the war effort felt toward two teams made up entirely of military officers in training. Kelly's old friend, Colonel McCormick, worked his Washington connections to get the game, and Republican congressman Fred Britten, a senior member of the Illinois delegation, carried the proposal to the Naval Academy at Annapolis, Maryland, in late December 1925.

As city leaders negotiated for the Army-Navy Game, the main work still to be finished was the horseshoe-shaped south end of the stands, which were to add thirty-two thousand seats. The South Park commissioners planned also to install ninety-six hundred temporary seats within the horseshoe and ninety-five hundred seats in bleachers at the north end of the football field. More distant seats at the north end would not be used in the game, because they stood too far from the gridiron. Already, Soldier Field's builders had discovered that it required retrofitting for football games, a fact that would become even clearer fifty years later when the Bears considered adopting it as their home field.[12]

On January 22, 1925, Kelly and the rest of Chicago learned that the military academies had chosen the new stadium for their game, scheduled for the last weekend in November. But of course, no major event in Chicago would be complete without charges of political influence. East Coast congressmen who had sought the game accused Britten of abusing his influence as a member of the House Naval Affairs Committee to force the military academies' hand. But other factors probably had at least as much influence. The South Park commissioners had promised to pay for the cadets' and midshipmen's travel to the city, and Chicago businesspeople had sweetened the pot with $300,000 toward the academies' expenses.[13]

In early April, a spring snowstorm covered the construction site, freezing water piped in to mix concrete. More serious than weather-related setbacks, however, were legal challenges to funding for the stadium. William E. Furlong, a Chicago attorney, pursued a lawsuit alleging that bonds approved by voters for the renovation of the Columbian Exposition's Fine Arts Building—now the Museum of Science and Industry—added too much to the debt carried by the South Park Commission. Furlong contended that other projects, including the stadium, should wait until the city finished the rest of the south lakefront plans, such as for building new parklands and beaches.

The suit, filed as a taxpayer action, had failed in Cook County Superior Court, but the Illinois Supreme Court at first sided with Furlong, ruling that renovating the Fine Arts Building violated state law authorizing the improvement of land owned by the South Park Commission. A few months later, however, the court reheard the case and in April, even as stadium construction crews fought the elements, ruled that the commissioners were acting within their rights: "Park purposes are not confined to a tract of land with trees, grass and seats. . . . Museums, art galleries, botanical and zoological gardens . . . for the public benefit, are recognized as legitimate purposes."[14]

Just as their successors at the Chicago Park District would do almost eighty years later when park advocates challenged the new Soldier Field, the South Park commissioners had pressed ahead, regardless of ongoing lawsuits. By the time the court made its final ruling, a railroad spur removed temporarily after the completion of the colonnades was back in place, ringing the area where the horseshoe would rise. The southeast corner of the stands was under construction, with framing up at the south end of the east colonnades. Construction photographs show work on the south end of the stadium proceeding quickly, while at the north end of the stadium the altar for the Roman Catholic Eucharistic Congress, scheduled for June, goes up. Workers started building supports for the second tier of seating in the bowl in May, and by July the concrete steps for the seating benches were almost half done.

While construction moved ahead and the court fight raged, Kelly and other parks and city officials continued negotiations with the military academies. By May the South Park commissioners had acceded to demands from West Point and the Naval Academy that they pay to bring several thousand cadets and midshipmen to Chicago. The estimated cost of bringing eighteen hundred midshipmen, the football team, the band, and school officials on duty with the football squad was $97,516, including $1.50 per person per meal for eating in Chicago. The academies signed a separate contract for the costs of the game itself, which the park commission was to cover with gate receipts.[15]

Workers were close to finishing the stadium by August, and newly planted trees were visible along the lakefront. The south end of the bowl was finished by mid-October, and the outer walls were being faced with composite stone. By the end of the month, wooden benches were in place in the seating area. In one of the last photographs from this first phase of construction, taken three days before the Army-Navy Game, the stadium scoreboard, with a clock, is in place and the stands extend above the enclosing walls. Painted gate signs are in evidence; permanent, lit signs would come later. Flagpoles line the rooftop promenade, and streetlamps line the sidewalks outside. Flags were, from the start, an essential element of Soldier Field's decor. Along with small cast-iron eagle decorations that at one time stood atop the railings along the colonnades, they called attention to the stadium's memorial function.

In the wake of the Great War, with its heavy loss of life, the country was ambivalent about international organizations like the League of Nations, but a generation of politicians and civic leaders was unified in putting a patriotic and memorial cast on as many public events as possible. With Soldier Field arguably the country's largest war memorial, outside such places as Arlington National Cemetery, the South Park commissioners hoped that the Army-Navy Game—the occasion of Soldier Field's final, most important dedication—would cement the stadium's place as a premier venue for national events. When the week of the game arrived, journalists from across the country flocked to Chicago.

In the days leading up to the game, Navy and Army officials inspected the stadium arena and found the playing field satisfactory. Two days before the game, the two teams' trains pulled into Chicago, within about half an hour of each other, to the cheering of enthusiastic crowds. Banners with Army's black, gold, and gray and Navy's blue and gold decorated Loop streetlights. The two contingents marched to the Marshall Field department store for a lunch where Kelly and others, including U.S. vice president Charles G. Dawes, regaled them with speeches about how important the game was to Chicago.

Southeast stands under construction, with both black and white workers, August 21, 1926. Courtesy Chicago Park District Special Collections.

After lunch, the Army cadets led a parade to Soldier Field, although Navy had been granted home team advantage that year.

Many later assumed that the stadium officially became Soldier Field on the day of the Army-Navy Game. That's doubly wrong. The South Park Commission had renamed the stadium the year before, on Armistice Day. The renaming ceremony, however, was deferred until 1926, and took place as a free event, open to the public, after the parade on November 26—the day before the game. Although they apparently conceded in the end that it was all right for a stadium to double as a memorial, Fred and Josephine Bentley and the other Gold Star parents would likely not have accepted a football game, even a game between the nation's two most prestigious military academies, as an appropriate dedication. A separate, more solemn ritual dedicating the field was called for, and of the many ceremonies Kelly engineered to focus local and national attention on the unique dual function of the stadium, this one best deserves to be remembered..

South façade of stadium under construction, October 29, 1926. Courtesy Chicago Park District Special Collections.

Yet despite free admission and intense interest in the game, the ceremony failed to draw many people. Only the hardiest of souls braved the freezing sleet to see rows of chilled cadets and midshipmen assembled in the stadium. Joining the young men were marchers wearing the historic dress of U.S. soldiers and sailors and carrying flags from conflicts from the Revolutionary War on. Still, people lined the parade route six deep along Michigan Avenue. Much as fans fifty years later would boast of their ability to withstand below-freezing temperatures to see a game, the newspapers of the time touted the ability of the young men to perform military maneuvers despite the harsh weather. While Vice President Dawes wore a silk top hat, he also donned the Army coat he had worn as a brigadier general in the Great War. The snow blew through Grant Park, around the stadium and the Field Museum, and into Soldier Field's bowl. The cadets marched onto the field and past the reviewing stand to the strains of, incongruously, both "John Brown's Body" and "Dixie." Cannon salutes and drumrolls competed with the lakefront gale for the crowd's attention. To the north of the reviewing stand, the West Point cadets stood at attention in gray uniforms, white belts crossed on their chests, the only color breaking up the mass of gray the red sashes worn by their officers. To the south, the midshipmen massed in blue uniforms and white pants, as their officers' dark, yellow-lined cloaks blew in the wind.

Dawes's speech was "mercifully brief," given the inclement weather, but not short on patriotic rhetoric. Soldier Field was dedicated, he said, to all "who made the supreme sacrifice. . . . They gave us freedom and this government of liberty under law." Kelly used his address to remind the crowd of the place the South Park Commission hoped Soldier Field would assume in Chicago's cultural and political life from that time on: "This noble coliseum will stand for generations as a temple of patriotism, of manhood, of fine sportsmanship, as a gathering place for all loyal-hearted citizens." Fittingly, the ceremony closed with the playing of taps.[16]

After the ceremony, the young military men received a respite from their official duties and the brutal Chicago weather. That evening, the city held a massive dinner dance at the Drake Hotel, a new grand hotel designed by Marshall and Fox, the architectural firm that had drafted the original Grant Park stadium plans. The night included a buffet dinner and six jazz orchestras, but the main attraction for the cadets and midshipmen was the girls—just shy of thirty-five hundred young women recruited for the evening to dine and dance with the three thousand or so young military men.

Kelly and other civic leaders went far beyond providing the cadets and midshipmen with dates for a dance, paying for almost every expense imaginable. The South Park commissioners arranged everything, down to how the baggage was handled when the two contingents got off their chartered trains. Transporting the cadets from West Point to Chicago on the Baltimore & Ohio Railroad cost just over $72,000. The midshipmen's lodging at the Palmer House cost about $9,000. (The Army cadets stayed at the LaSalle Hotel, and the teams stayed in separate accommodations from their classmates.) Some of the Naval Academy brass who attended the game racked up large bills during their stay, no doubt entertaining national political luminaries who had flocked to the city to see the game. In all, the transportation of about thirty-one hundred people to the game, hotel bills and miscellaneous expenses set back the South Park Commission at least $100 per person to bring Army and Navy students, faculty, and staff to Chicago—a total of about $310,000, or $2.3 million in 2008 dollars.[17]

The game was not in itself political, but as with scores of events at Soldier Field in later years, Kelly and the Democratic Party took full political advantage of their control of the stadium. The patriotic spectacle reminded Chicagoans of the Democratic South Park Commission's loyalty to country. And the tickets party leaders distributed or sold reminded their recipients of the party's generosity, while at the same time helping to stuff its campaign chest.[18]

Game day dawned with clearer weather, although the temperature in Chicago peaked two degrees below freezing. The members of the Army team, who stayed at the South Shore Country Club, took a short run before breakfast. The Navy team, staying at the Windmere Hotel, did the same, then packed up extra provisions to take to the stadium. About a thousand spectators from Washington, D.C.—Army and Navy officials and just plain football fans—took a late train for Chicago the day before the game, although the wire services reported that fewer officials than usual planned to attend, Chicago being much farther afield than the usual East Coast host cities. The secretary of the Navy made the trek, but General John J. Pershing, the recently retired Army chief of staff, said he would miss the game because of a cold. The students formed ranks downtown at about 1 p.m. and marched to Soldier Field in another parade, arriving about 1:30.

There they joined the football teams, which had arrived at the field about three hours before the 2 p.m. game time. Thousands of fans poured through the Loop and south to the stadium starting around noon. Scalpers hustled to sell tickets before they became worthless, with many losing money on high-priced seats they failed to resell. Because so many of the tickets were bought by Chicago politicians well in advance of the game, a few experienced ticket agencies had passed up the opportunity to buy any tickets at all. And despite the throngs that did make it to Soldier Field, many opted to listen to the game on the radio rather than brave the cold on the chance tickets might still be available at the stadium.

The cold and the disappointed scalpers were about the only low notes, however. Newspapers described the crowds as bigger than for any event in Chicago since Armistice Day in 1918. Souvenir vendors worked the street corners, selling miniature footballs, toy goats and mules (representing the Navy and Army mascots), and pins with a reproduction of the Holabird and Roche drawings of Soldier Field—complete with the unbuilt obelisk. The Annapolis band and students came onto the field first for drills, then filed into seats in the east stands. The Army cadets followed, ending their drills by singing the Army fight song before decamping for the west stands. As the students drilled on the field, a crowd of 110,000—purportedly the largest for a football game up to that point—filled the stadium. Spectators included Notre Dame coach Knute Rockne, who considered the Army-Navy Game at Soldier Field important enough that he missed a game his own Fighting Irish played against Carnegie Tech that day.

Fans were anticipating a great game, and they got one. Sixty years later, some still called it the best Army-Navy Game ever. (More than a decade later, readers of *Esquire* magazine chose the game as the best football game ever.) Navy had a sensational year in 1926, losing only their first game, against the University of Hawaii at Manoa, and then winning nine in a row before

A man and two boys watch auto racing from the colonnades, 1947. Note the eagle decorations on the railings. Courtesy Chicago Park District Special Collections.

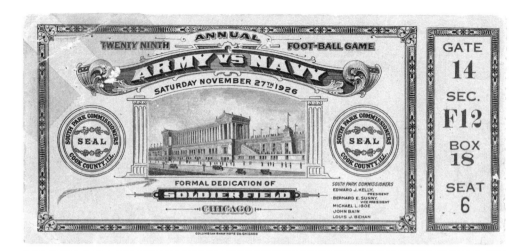

Ticket from 1926 Army-Navy Game. Courtesy Chicago Park District Special Collections.

coming to Chicago. Both teams had a lot to lose and played hard. The game also featured a few technological innovations that sports fans now take for granted. Because of the great size of the stadium—and the bad sightlines, something football fans would complain about for the next seventy-five years—the two coaches had assistants stationed in the stands, telephoning details of the teams' movements to them during the game. Meanwhile, in an early example of the power of radio, President Calvin Coolidge and many bureaucrats in the War Department stopped what they were doing to listen to a broadcast of the game. The stadium's fortunes rose with the new medium, and the national broadcast of the Army-Navy Game helped cement Soldier Field's reputation as a grand national stadium.

Play started with the Army coach, Lawrence "Biff" Jones, putting his second-string players on the field. After a few changes of possession, Navy got to the 50-yard line, and James B. Schuber passed thirty-five yards over the heads of an Army defensive box to Harry "Hank" Hardwick (who would coach Navy in the 1930s). Henry Caldwell then scored a one-yard touchdown. In the second quarter, Caldwell made a first down on Army 18-yard line, then Schuber rushed through Army's center line for a touchdown, making the score 14–0. But Army tied it up before halftime with a seventeen-yard touchdown run by Harry Wilson, the team's right halfback, and a fumble recovery that left end Morris Harbold ran in for a score.

In the second half, Army scored again, taking the lead, 21–14. On the seventh play of the fourth quarter, as darkness started to fall, Alan Shapley, who had come in late in the third quarter at right halfback, ran three yards

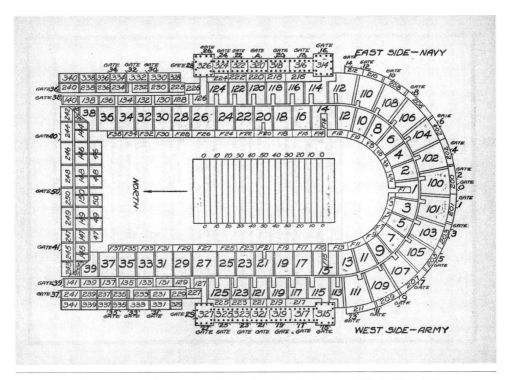

Detail of pamphlet given out with Army-Navy Game tickets, showing layout of Soldier Field, including temporary north stands. Courtesy Chicago Park District Special Collections.

for a Navy touchdown. Tom Hamilton, another future Navy coach who won a Bronze Star in World War II, then tied the game at 21 with a drop kick. By this time, the players were so mud-caked, and the light so dim, that spectators had trouble distinguishing one team from the other. Twice more, Army nearly scored but came up short. Shapley was the hero of the game, for the tie ensured Navy of the national college football championship. "Just about the best game I ever saw," Navy's coach Bill Ingram said after the game. "I was glad to see the boys perform with such style before that great crowd."[19]

The game was a resounding success for Chicago, and for Kelly's South Park Commission. Parker Brothers even commemorated the contest with a board game, called "Tom Hamilton's Pigskin Football Game." Coming on the heels of the Eucharistic Congress in June (see chapter 6), the game secured Soldier Field's reputation as *the* place to hold an event in Chicago—if not the entire country. The Army-Navy Game also brought in about $850,000 in ticket sales. Some $300,000 of that went toward South Park expenses, including a $70,000 bonus paid to Kelly's favored contractor for quick completion of work so that the stadium would be ready for the game. Construction workers still had a few details to finish up after the game, and minor work on the interior of the stadium continued until December 15, when the commissioners accepted the stadium as finished.[20]

Soldier Field's preeminence as an object of civic pride and place for pageantry meant that events held there attracted greater attention than they would have at other venues, and any successful event at the stadium reflected well on the Democratic Party that controlled it. The 1920s were an era of political spectacle, a heyday of torchlight parades and hours-long floor demonstrations at political conventions. But nonpolitical events and control over contracts for stadium maintenance and operations were more significant sources of political capital. A decade after Kelly joined the South Park Commission, Thompson was exiled from City Hall, and Anton Cermak became the first in an as-yet-unended string of Democratic mayors. Cermak died after an assassin's bullet hit him as he rode in a car with president elect Franklin Roosevelt in Florida in 1933. So Kelly ascended to the post of mayor soon after Roosevelt entered the White House.

In building the power base that helped him step into the vacuum when Cermak died, Kelly had followed Thompson's pattern, using the Burnham Plan to justify spending and win over reformers, newspapers, and masses of voters. Joyful events at Soldier Field justified constant Democratic spending on upkeep and renovation at the stadium, even when the press began calling it a white elephant in the 1950s. An idealized picture of the stadium, first crafted by Kelly and South Park leaders like Linn White, took root in the popular mind and helped to ensure that for years the public was more interested in saving Soldier Field than the city was in making money from it.

When the political importance of the South Park Commission became too obvious to ignore, the papers did report on it—but then seemed to forget its ties to politics almost immediately. Due to a peculiarity of Illinois law, Cook County Circuit Court judges appointed the commission's members, and the judges gained their seats through partisan elections. Thompson and his allies, who controlled the Cook County Republican Party in 1920, understood this. They also knew that the South Park Commission was finally embarking on the long-anticipated lakefront project sketched out by Burnham, and they itched to keep control of the tens of millions in contracts for the work.

When Kelly became president of the South Park Commission in March 1924, the *Tribune* proclaimed it the end of an era: the "Deneen Republicans," a South Side GOP faction allied with Colonel McCormick, had lost control to Democrats.[21] Kelly soon began to shape the commission to his purposes. The high-flown rhetoric Burnham, Wacker, and Thompson had adopted now became the everyday vocabulary of a man who started life as a window washer and beer carrier. While he spoke of the beauty of the city's parks, he also emphasized the utility of the lakefront transformation.

On returning from one six-week trip to Europe in 1927, Kelly gushed to the *Chicago American*, "In America, we built parks for service—that the people might enjoy them. But there is no reason why we cannot build for both beauty and service."[22]

Soldier Field's growing national prominence and ability to attract large crowds—and good press—made it an ideal example of the progress Kelly and his Democratic allies could bring the city. Soldier Field was only one part of a much larger plan to transform the industrial wasteland of the lakefront. What beaches there were on the stretch between downtown and Jackson Park were almost inaccessible and marred by the soot and grime of the Illinois Central Railroad. South Siders rejoiced at the prospect of the electrification of the IC's coal-powered trains—another proposed improvement. Though Thompson received credit for the change in a plaque at the Randolph Street Station in downtown Chicago, Kelly claimed some of the credit. In an essay for the *Herald and Examiner*, Kelly said South Siders were now "free to enjoy the beauties, recreations and utility features of the entire South Shore district without the present attendant business district congestion, and without the grime and soot . . . prevalent throughout this entire stretch."[23] The ceremony marking the beginning of the changeover—the switch to electric trains took place over a month or more—was a classic early-twentieth-century pageant, lasting for four days in August 1926.[24]

On the day of the main celebration, spectators at Soldier Field took in a parade re-creating the various modes of transit used along Chicago's lakefront over the years: "First there came, down the green northern slopes of the field, the red man with his . . . rude wagon, and his pony," the *Tribune* noted. Players dressed as trappers and hunters, white covered wagons, stagecoaches, and pony express couriers followed in turn. Behind them came primitive cars, then "the high powered motor car," fire engines and finally the electric railroad locomotive.[25]

The electrification pageant, like many events Kelly orchestrated, was nominally apolitical, but others explicitly promoted either charities and causes he championed or the Democratic Party itself. And these were not the only benefits that accrued to Kelly and his successors. In the early 1930s, Chicago's newspapers started looking into some of Kelly's Soldier Field construction contracts. Records showed that he heavily favored businesses with ties to his branch of the Democratic Party, the *Herald and Examiner* reported:

> Just as the mayor took care of boss Patrick A. Nash in 1928, in connection with the Nash Brothers contract for the Sanitary District's West Side sewer, so he took care of his friends, John Griffiths & Sons, construction contractors, who also had done work for the Sanitary District, from 1925 to 1928. This he did in his capacity of park board president, a post incidentally, which he still holds.[26]

29TH ANNUAL FOOT-BALL GAME
ARMY VS **NAVY**
NOVEMBER 27TH, 1926
FORMAL DEDICATION OF
SOLDIER FIELD
CHICAGO

Packed house at the 1926 Army-Navy Game. The Field Museum is framed by the east and west colonnades. Courtesy Chicago Park District Special Collections.

Around the time of the Century of Progress Exposition in 1933–1934, newspapers carried the first accounts questioning the quality of Soldier Field's construction. Concrete was flaking and falling. The exhibition halls, finished with indoor plaster but open to the elements, were a mess. A few years after these criticisms began, Kelly prevailed upon the Democratic administration in Washington to provide millions of dollars in aid through the Works Progress Administration to renovate and alter Soldier Field, as well as to build a permanent home for the newly formed Chicago Park District, which combined all the city's old districts into one.

In 1946, when Kelly was near the end of his tenure as mayor, two Republican aldermen, Theron Merryman and William M. Devine, the latter

COPYRIGHT 1926
KAUFMANN & FABRY CO.
CHICAGO

SCORE
Y 21 NAVY 21

a candidate for the county tax appeals board, put forward a study of all of Kelly's contracts. Kelly had been on the public payroll for fifty years, they noted, with an average salary of $50,000 per year, and they calculated that over the years he had controlled $6 billion in contracts. "What did Chicago taxpayers get for 6 billion dollars?" the two asked. "The Kelly political machine is what the taxpayers got for their 6 billion dollars. It operates to perpetuate Mayor Kelly and his New Deal spenders in office."[27]

Though it's hard to agree with Merryman and Devine that Chicagoans got nothing for their money, it's also hard to argue with their conclusion that the spending of taxpayer money helped entrench the Chicago Democratic Party. The half-billion dollars in Burnham Plan improvements created the south lakefront of today. The new lakefront parks unquestionably enriched Chicagoans' daily lives, but just as clearly they helped enrich businesses favored by Kelly and other Democrats.

Over the years, Kelly also was accused of having Democratic operatives strong-arm government employees to attend events that benefited charity—specifically, charities controlled by the Democratic Party. The Prep Bowl, the championship game between Catholic and public league high school football teams, brought together young people and parents of all walks of life. But for years, it also was a fund-raiser for "Chicago's Own Christmas Benefit Fund," which bought clothes for needy children during the holidays. Kelly's Democratic Party tightly controlled the fund.

In 1938 Democratic precinct captains pledged to buy $130,000 in tickets for the Prep Bowl and a Christmas event at the Chicago Stadium, both of which benefited the Chicago's Own fund. In 1941 teachers in schools run by the Chicago Board of Education complained about pressure from schools superintendent William H. Johnson to buy tickets to the Prep Bowl. They objected because Democratic precinct committeemen distributed the goods bought with game proceeds, and at a meeting of union delegates, five hundred members vowed not to buy or sell the tickets.[28] But the Prep Bowl continued as a Democratic Party concern for many years.

In addition to milking contracts for the arena for his friends, Kelly used Soldier Field to show off Chicago's achievements—and to prove to the national Democratic Party his importance in the city's politics. His successors as mayor continued the tradition of sponsoring ostensibly nonpolitical events that enlisted the help of party regulars, but the highest-profile explicitly political functions at the stadium took place during Kelly's years of prominence. The largest Democratic event ever held at the stadium was an appearance by Franklin D. Roosevelt, the only Midwestern speech of his final reelection campaign, in October 1944. Kelly used a tried-and-true method of packing the stands that was repeated countless times over the life of the stadium. For the Chicago machine, a successful event entailed more than just booking the best entertainers or the most famous public figures. A good political show also required that people who stayed home and heard about it later think, "Hey, I should have been there." Part of the recipe for such a success was word of mouth, and having an impressively large crowd increased the chances that attendees would talk about it afterward to neighbors and fellow patrons at the corner tavern. And the best way to ensure a huge crowd was to make tickets easily available—by having political workers hand them out indiscriminately, like candy at Halloween.

J. Leonard Reinsch, who set up the sound system and radio broadcast for Roosevelt's speech and in later years was a high-ranking Democratic Party official, described how Kelly made certain that Soldier Field was

North stands and Chicago Park District headquarters under construction, September 6, 1938. Park officials used Mayor Edward J. Kelly's clout with the Roosevelt administration to get funding for the projects, as well as other renovations. Courtesy Chicago Park District Special Collections.

packed for the event: "We had a hundred and twenty-five thousand for President Roosevelt's speech. This was when I first learned how to 'paper the house.' Mayor Kelly had issued tickets for about four hundred and fifty thousand people. They couldn't handle the crowd that showed up at Soldier Field."[29] In reality, Kelly handed out at least seven hundred thousand tickets, including ten thousand to each Democratic ward organization and another hundred thousand to CIO union members.[30] Union leaders went so far as to make certain that shifts at war production plants ended early, so their members could get to the rally on time. CIO members were expected to gather north of the stadium, near the Field Museum, where union political bosses marked them present or absent. The night of the event, there was "a solid mass of humanity extending for blocks trying to get into the huge stadium."

Roosevelt had traveled by rail, stopping in Fort Wayne, Indiana. His

President Franklin D. Roosevelt arrives at Soldier Field for his only major speech in Chicago during the 1944 campaign. With him in the car was Mayor Edward Kelly. Courtesy Chicago Tribune.

train arrived in Chicago several hours before his speech and parked on an Illinois Central siding near Cermak Road.[31] At the stadium, Roosevelt spoke for forty-five minutes. Dressed only in his suit, hatless—a rarity for an outdoor fall event in those days—the president went on the offensive against his critics, from Republican politicians to the *Tribune*.[32] Roosevelt laid out a postwar program that addressed some military issues but largely dealt with economic conditions. His campaign and the "greatest war in history" were being fought "for the same essential reason: Because we have faith in democracy," Roosevelt said. But the campaign was "the strangest . . . I have ever seen," with Republicans calling Democrats "incompetent bunglers," then promising not to change any of the programs instituted by the Roosevelt administration.[33] Roosevelt continued, using the acerbic wit that so galled his GOP opponents,

> They also say in effect, "Those inefficient and worn-out crackpots have really begun to lay the foundations of a lasting world peace. If you elect us, we will not change any of that, either."
>
> "But," they whisper, "we'll do it in such a way that we won't lose the support even of Gerald Nye or Gerald Smith—and this is very important—we won't lose the support of any isolationist campaign contributor. Why, we will be able to satisfy even the *Chicago Tribune*."

Though some reports noted that the sound system faded in and out or that the wind made the speech hard to hear—even for reporters on the field—the comment about the *Tribune* drew a roar of approval from the crowd.[34]

Largely because of his attempts to combat the Great Depression, Roosevelt had promoted greater federal involvement in the economy than had previous presidents. Citing an "economic bill of rights" he had first advocated in his State of the Union speech the previous January, Roosevelt signaled that this emphasis would not end with the war. Roosevelt said he hoped to create conditions that would generate sixty million postwar jobs, what one newspaper called a "Second New Deal." Naysayers might scoff at "the dreams of starry-eyed New Dealers," but Roosevelt said he knew that "the American people have a habit of going right ahead and accomplishing the impossible."[35]

Chicago has long been known as one of the most segregated U.S. cities outside of the South, but political and cultural events at Soldier Field often drew racially mixed crowds. At the Roosevelt speech, the crowd included a large number of black spectators, who had particular reason to cheer the president's postwar plans for the U.S. economy. In 1941 Roosevelt had created the fair Employment Practices Committee to enforce an executive order against racial discrimination in hiring by munitions contractors for the war effort.[36] A large part of the crowd—not just the black spectators—cheered Roosevelt's references to the committee. Roosevelt emphasized in his Soldier Field speech that his new bill of rights "must be applied to all our citizens, irrespective of race, creed or color." Though this aspect of his talk went largely unnoted by the mainstream press, the plan was later enthusiastically endorsed by the *Defender*, Chicago's leading black newspaper, with distribution and influence far beyond Illinois. It would be almost twenty years before another major rally at Soldier Field focused so directly on discrimination against blacks.[37]

After Roosevelt, many other prominent Democratic politicians spoke at Soldier Field, both at rallies and at ostensibly nonpolitical events. Harry Truman was the last Democratic president to make a speech at the stadium until Bill Clinton spoke at the 1994 World Cup opening ceremonies—but he spoke there twice as president and at least once after leaving the White House.

Truman's first speech, in 1946, took place on Army Day—April 6, the anniversary of the entry of the United States into World War I (later known as Armed Forces Day). At the time, he and Soviet dictator Josef Stalin were negotiating long-distance on ways to bring their countries together. He was joined by Mayor Kelly and by General Dwight Eisenhower, then the U.S. Army Chief of Staff. At a lunch at the Blackstone Hotel, Kelly feted the president and the general, praising Truman as "a sturdy oak who is bringing the United States out of chaos." Later, at Soldier Field, cold spring weather kept the crowd relatively small until just before Truman's speech. Newspaper vendors did a brisk business, as people used layers of newsprint as padding under their spring jackets, and the stadium's coffee stands saw long lines. But Chicago's Democratic ward heelers were out in force.

Truman's motorcade entered the stadium to a twenty-one-gun salute just before 3 p.m. and drove around the cinder running track. The crowd applauded loudly when Eisenhower's car entered the arena. The Cold War had not yet begun, but in his speech Truman outlined many of the themes that would dominate the next forty years of U.S.–Soviet relations—and almost eradicated the traditional assumption that the United States should remain aloof from foreign conflicts. The United States was, Truman said, the strongest country in the world militarily, and it was resolute in its decision to stay strong. Most importantly, he hinted at the creation of the North Atlantic Treaty Organization, which throughout the Cold War was to bind together the Western democracies in their opposition to the Soviet bloc—and which has kept U.S. military forces in Europe to this day.

Truman also took a moment to praise his predecessor: "The army itself, as well as the American people, will always remember the inspiration, leadership, courage, and determination which came from that gallant warrior in the White House—Franklin D. Roosevelt."[38]

Truman's next speech at Soldier Field was a June 19, 1949, address to the convention of the Ancient Arabic Order of Nobles of the Mystic Shrine—the Shriners—as the group marked its seventy-fifth anniversary. In addition to Truman's talk, one of the first Soldier Field events to be televised, the convention featured one of the largest parades in Chicago history. Some five hundred thousand spectators looked on as fifteen thousand Shriners from a thousand chapters of the group in Canada and the United States walked a three-mile route through downtown to Soldier Field, with 130 bands accompanying the five-hour procession. Among the Shriners was Hollywood comic actor Harold Lloyd, who became "Imperial Potentate," the national leader of the group, at the end of the convention.

Democrats made the most of the president's appearance and did their best to pack the stadium. Jacob "Jake" Arvey, the head of the Cook County Democratic Party, required Democratic officeholders to buy premium $150 tickets to the Shriner's event. In addition, he ordered each of the fifty ward organizations to buy a block of 150 $1 tickets, thus raising $10,000 that ostensibly went to the Shriners. But that alone would not fill the stadium, and the White House dispatched Truman aide Donald S. Dawson to help draw people in. "That was a little sleight of hand," Dawson said thirty years later. "I found that 4 o'clock Thursday afternoon was not really a popular time for people to take off from work and spend five or ten or fifteen dollars [$46 to $138 in 2008 dollars] for a seat to hear the President of the United States, so that sales were going slow." Democratic workers went around the city with sound trucks, announcing the speech. Finally, to make Soldier Field seem smaller than it was, Dawson borrowed an immense American flag from the *Tribune*, one so large that it stretched from one grandstand to the other.

When he finally came to the podium, Truman decried communist tyranny and said it would ultimately be compelled to "abandon its attempt to force other nations into its pattern" or else it would destroy itself. "Some leaders"—meaning Stalin and the leaders of his client states—had "cut off communications and built barriers of suspicion between their people and the outside world," but Truman said war could be avoided. America's "faith" in democracy was "more appealing, more dynamic and stronger than any totalitarian force," he said.[39]

Truman last appeared at Soldier Field on July 13, 1955, during another Shriners convention. It was a full day, but between events he stopped by City Hall and held a press conference with the newly elected mayor, Richard J. Daley, tackling such hard-hitting questions as whether he missed being president ("Heck no"). In several speeches throughout the day, the former president warned of the need to use the United Nations to prevent the use of nuclear weapons in war. "If you make up your minds to turn your back on peace, you may have complete destruction," he told a group gathered for a dinner preceding the evening's festivities. After reviewing the Shriners' parade, he spoke at Soldier Field as part of "Shrinearama," one of the most diversely entertaining post–World War II events the stadium hosted: More than fifty-eight thousand People saw Jack Dempsey and Gene Tunney, who had boxed for the heavyweight title at Soldier Field in 1927, stage a brief mock rematch in a miniature ring; a band of fifteen hundred Shriner musicians

Former president Harry S. Truman and other dignitaries review a Shriners parade at Soldier Field, 1955. Courtesy Chicago Park District Special Collections.

and a thousand-voice choir sang; and after circus acts and military drills, fireworks closed out the evening.[40]

Though Truman's staff helped bring in the crowds even on a weekday afternoon, and many Democratic politicians made Soldier Field a stop over the years, others found its mammoth size—and its exposure to often raw lakefront weather—a reason to avoid the stadium. The stadium's selling point as the largest public venue in the city also could be a drawback, as it required immense organization and coordination to fill it. Sometimes, an event just did not work out.

In the summer of 1928 local Democrats had tried to persuade New York governor Al Smith, the first Catholic to run for president, to give a speech at the stadium during his fall campaign. Smith, however, fearing the cold night air might harm his health, asked organizers to find him an indoor hall instead. When this proved difficult, Cook County Democratic chairman Martin J. O'Brien proposed moving the rally back to Soldier Field. To calm Smith's fears of the chill, he told the *Tribune*, "We're going to inquire at once into the possibility of putting up a platform enclosed in clear glass, which would save the governor from exposure and let the thousands see him while he speaks. His speech would have to be carried by amplifiers even in a large hall and we hope the glass can be handled in such a way that it won't mar the effect."[41]

But a few days before he was to arrive in Chicago, Smith told a *Tribune* correspondent that he had no interest in such an experiment. He had been to Soldier Field, he said, and the "glass cage" would never work: "You might as well sit in your undershirt in a hotel room and try to talk to a city full as stand in a glass house in the middle of Soldiers' field and try to put yourself and your thoughts into the thoughts of 150,000 people."[42] In the end, Smith led a rally at the 131st Regiment Armory at Michigan Avenue and 16th Street, not far from Soldier Field.[43] While seven thousand people packed the armory, another fifteen thousand crowded the surrounding streets.

Smith lost the option of using Park District property a few years later, when Kelly took charge of the Democratic machine. Under Kelly, Chicago Democrats did everything they could to ingratiate themselves with the Roosevelt administration, and it paid off handsomely. Along the way, political opponents of Roosevelt's felt the sometimes petty but always effective hand of the Chicago machine. Park administrators made certain that events they allowed either were apolitical or worked for some Democratic constituency or a political leader's friends.

Among the slighted were Republicans, radicals, and racists, as well as some Democrats. In October 1936 Smith spoke in Chicago on behalf of Alf Landon, the Republican nominee against Roosevelt. The sponsors of Smith's speech, conservative Democrats who were backing Landon, asked the Chicago Park District for permission to use Jackson Boulevard, which the district controlled, for a parade welcoming Smith after he arrived at the LaSalle Street railroad station. Permission was denied. George Donoghue, the park district's general superintendent, said he thought it "unwise" to allow a 10 a.m. parade that would "interfere with traffic" on the downtown street.[44]

Kelly's corrupt ways finally became so galling that after the war, Chicago Democrats slated a reform candidate, Martin Kennelly. In 1947 Kennelly took office and swept many old machine retainers out of City Hall, much to the chagrin of loyal Democratic ward heelers. He was less successful, though, with the park district. Though the mayor appoints them, park district commissioners serve terms that don't coincide exactly with those of the mayor, giving them a degree of independence, especially in times of political conflict. (A more serious conflict between Chicago Park District leadership and a sitting mayor occurred forty years later, when Harold Washington clashed with general superintendent Edmund Kelly.) For a while, because of difficulties in reforming the parks, there was talk of consolidating the city and the park district. One alderman estimated that the merger, which would have required the approval of the state legislature, would save the city as much as $4 million in payroll costs ($36.5 million in 2008 dollars). Even without the merger, Kennelly moved a few Democratic politicians off the public payroll by handing over to the district some administrative duties previously handled by the city.[45]

Chicago patronage has a way of persisting even after the patrons are gone. Edward Kelly left the South Park Commission soon after he ascended to City Hall's fifth floor in 1933, and left that office in 1947. But in 1950, a few months before the former mayor's death, his brother, Evan I. Kelly, came into the spotlight, in one of the most titillating public controversies ever involving Soldier Field. Evan Kelly, younger than the former mayor by a quarter century, went to work for the South Park Commission just before the Chicago Park District was formed. He first came to public attention in 1935, when some questioned his appointment as director of the new division of special services, in charge of Soldier Field. Kelly also supervised the Lincoln Park Zoo, Indian Boundary Park Zoo, the Adler Planetarium, and the city's harbors, all of which are now run by either private foundations or private contractors.

Some fifteen years later, he had a more colorful run-in with fame. A small item in the *Tribune* in May 1950 reported that Grace D. Kelly, forty-three, "was awarded $300 a month temporary support from Evan I. Kelly."[46] Before Mrs. Kelly left her husband, he had appeared a few times in the press, but usually in a favorable light. He had defended the operations of Soldier Field occasionally, once writing to the *Tribune* to say that the field had thirty-two working water fountains after a fan wrote in to say there were none.[47] Usually, he made the news only when fishing lagoons opened or other minor public events required his presence.

A few weeks after Grace Kelly was awarded support, it became apparent that the family was feuding. Evan Kelly accused his family of harassing him and petitioned the court to bar his wife and children from seeking him out at home or at his Soldier Field office. Grace Kelly countered that "Evan Kelly is a drunkard and maintains a 'love nest' under the stands," which he used for trysts with his secretary, and thus wanted no one in the office near Gate 0, "to obviate the possible discovery . . . of the fully-equipped 'love nest' that he maintains in connection therewith."[48]

Evan Kelly and his boss, James H. Gately—Edward Kelly's handpicked replacement as president of the Chicago Park District—promptly denied that such a hideaway existed. The secretary likewise denied Mrs. Kelly's charges, stating, "My office is on the third floor of the park district administration building. . . . I never got to the office under the stands except when on duty at special events." Gately said no one should be suspicious. "There's a deep freeze, a refrigerator and a stove in the office under the stands at gate 0," said Gately, "but they are there with full knowledge of the park board for preparation of sandwiches and coffee at special events in the field. No one stays in the place over night or anything like that. You couldn't call it a love nest."

"Mrs. Kelly was jealous of my previous secretaries, too," Evan Kelly sneered.[49] But in the end, the battle with his family became too much for him. Kelly "resigned his $8,000 a year park district job as director of special services . . . citing poor health caused by his family difficulties as impairing his efficiency," the *Tribune* announced.

Gately, who appears to have been genuinely disappointed that Kelly left, said, "Under Evan Kelly's direction Soldiers' field was developed from a white elephant and financial liability into a park board asset." Kelly had brought new events to Soldier Field, and Democratic leaders such as Donoghue knew that he brought shows to the stadium that would be a hit with their precinct workers. The bookings during his time there show that he regarded Soldier Field as more than a venue for sports and carried on his brother's vision of the stadium as a gathering place for all of Democrat-approved Chicago.[50]

A native West Sider soon took over and began shaping Soldier Field according to his own philosophy, which included always hiring political workers, as long as they were qualified for their jobs. Red Weiner had started out at Columbus Park as a recreation supervisor. He worked his way up to general superintendent of the Chicago Park District, largely on the strength of his work at Soldier Field and his loyalty to the Democratic Party. Weiner's time at Soldier Field and in charge of the park district show once again the mundane but important advantages the party derived from its control of the stadium. Tickets or free passes to nonpolitical events at the stadium served as ways to reward members of the party. And the numerous renovation projects that began only a decade after the stadium's opening provided ample opportunity for successive Democratic administrations to reward political donors with rich contracts.

As the age of mass political rallies faded with the advent of the television era, the importance of Soldier Field for overt political organizing diminished. No longer content to listen to someone hundreds of feet away, at a podium in the middle of a vast crowd, people expected to see their politicians up close, even if it was only in close-up on a television screen. Both John F. Kennedy and Lyndon Johnson were supposed to speak at Soldier Field during their years as president, but in each case Vietnam kept them away.

Kennedy, gearing up for his reelection campaign, had worked with Mayor

Richard J. Daley to bring the 1963 Army–Air Force Game to Soldier Field, the first game between two military colleges there since the Army-Navy Game in 1926. He planned to attend the game, scheduled for early November, and to avoid seeming to take sides, was to cross the field at halftime from one cheering section to the other. One of Chicago's few Republican aldermen, John Hoellen, protested. Hoellen, just returned from a vacation in Colorado where he had visited the Air Force Academy, claimed that "a minor rebellion" was brewing among the cadets there. Kennedy's maneuver would disrupt the halftime show, preventing the teams' bands from playing. Air Force cadets, Hoellen claimed, were incensed. "They feel like I do," he said. "This is using a sports event for political purposes."

Hoellen was onto something. And Colonel Jack Reilly, Daley's director of special events, offered a typical Democratic response to such challenges. No one in the Daley administration had told Air Force—playing as the home team—that its band could not play at halftime, he told reporters. "The only thing I'd like to see parade across the field is John Hoellen—and at the point of a bayonet."[51]

The day before the teams were to arrive in the city—about three weeks after the alderman's initial protest—officials announced the details of Kennedy's trip. A "large turnout" of Democratic political workers and political leaders was to meet Kennedy at O'Hare Airport and accompany him to the Loop. The next day, newspapers even published the exact time of his anticipated arrival in Soldier Field: thirteen minutes before the scheduled kickoff.[52]

Kennedy's visit was to have taken place only twenty days before his fateful trip to Dallas. The president failed to make the Chicago trip because of developments in "the South Vietnam crisis," which later developed into the Vietnam War.[53]

Lyndon Johnson's appearance at Soldier Field was to have coincided with the 1968 Democratic National Convention. That convention is so well remembered for the riots in Lincoln Park and Grant Park, that Mayor Daley's pride at landing the event and his wish to show off the city in the media spotlight is usually overlooked. Aside from helmeted police officers using billy clubs to subdue excrement-throwing protesters, one of the most enduring images from the convention is of Daley, his face distorted in rage as he yells what many thought were obscenities at Connecticut senator Abraham Ribikoff, who had criticized from the convention podium the "Gestapo tactics" of the mayor's loyal police department.

But the violence in the streets, aside from embarrassing Daley in front of the national press, also quashed an event of personal significance to the mayor. The Democratic Party had reserved Soldier Field for an entire week during the convention, with a giant rally planned for August 27. Though the perceived defeat of the Tet Offensive in Vietnam had led Johnson not to seek reelection, the president had planned to attend the rally, which was to double as a party for his birthday. Instead, the riots led to the cancellation of all regular Democratic rallies, and Johnson stayed at the White House to watch the convention unfold on television.[54]

The Democratic Party's use of Soldier Field went well beyond holding rallies there. Ultimately, its control over who could get a permit for the stadium had much more impact. The reformers who envisioned the stadium as the staging ground for athletic competitions had many sports in mind. They especially wanted to reward the youth of Chicago and the Midwest who bested their competition, by giving them a grand arena to play out their rivalries. But from its earliest days, Soldier Field was enmeshed with politics. And when the focus was on athletics, the stadium came to be associated with one sport in particular: football. Until the Bears moved there in 1971, one of the most anticipated events at Soldier Field each year made young football players famous—and packed the coffers of Democratic mayors' favorite charities.

PART 2

A STADIUM FOR ALL CHICAGO

3 *A Game for Our Youth: Amateur Football at Soldier Field*

Football fans today know Soldier Field primarily as the home of the Chicago Bears. But football always has been a part of the stadium's history. For a half century it welcomed amateur games, especially high school championships and high-profile college games, and rarely played host to professional teams. Football was one of the uses envisioned for Soldier Field even as it was under construction, though the South Park Commission's Division of Playgrounds and Sports actually ranked baseball as its most important use. Although the parks staff noted that the field was probably too small for cricket matches, they apparently failed to recognize that it was also too narrow for regulation baseball games, and only a few softball tournaments were ever played there.[1] From the first, Chicagoans associated Soldier Field with football. The South Park commissioners had made sure that Amos Alonzo Stagg, one of the most innovative, influential, and long-serving coaches in football history, helped choose the design. And the biggest, most memorable dedication at the stadium coincided with the Army-Navy Game of 1926.

The people who built Soldier Field thought of football as more than just an amusement. Its boosters promoted the relatively new sport as a pastime that could improve both body and spirit. Professional football, then in its infancy, was scarcely considered; rather football was associated with the country's great universities.

In pitching the stadium to voters, the South Park commissioners and the newspapers had emphasized how athletic competition would help to invigorate Chicago's youth. So it was fitting that the first several football games played there were high school contests. The first football game ever at the new Grant Park Stadium—even before it was officially opened—was an exhibition game between Austin High School and Louisville Male High School, the oldest U.S. high school west of the Allegheny Mountains, on October 4, 1924. It was the second year the Austin team had met Louisville; in 1923 the Austin squad had traveled to Kentucky to meet the Colonels and lost 72–0. The Austin Kiwanis Club decided to sponsor a rematch at the new stadium, the first big high school game of the season in the Chicago area. Austin had improved its team since the previous year, and coach Arthur Miller expected to win the 1924 game, newspapers reported.

The score was not as lopsided as the previous year, but Louisville still won 26–0. The more experienced southern squad showed its superior skills, cutting through the Austin defense repeatedly. The Colonels' captain, fullback Jack C. "Tuffy" Norman, scored two touchdowns himself, though it is unclear from press reports whether he or fellow starter Tom Ford, who played left halfback, scored the first touchdown ever at Soldier Field. The game was so one-sided that Louisville sent in its second string early in the game. It was a historic year for Austin losses: the week before, Oak Park High School had beaten Austin, 13–0, in the first game in the near west suburb's new stadium.[2]

High school football remained an important part of the Soldier Field schedule each year until the early 1970s. There were at least six high school games just in the stadium's first season. Attendance at some games was so low that it is hard to believe the stadium even rented to individual high schools. Phillips High School, for example, played several games at Soldier Field in 1943, including one against Tilden Technical High School that drew only twenty-five hundred people. Such low numbers were not typical, but it was rare for high school teams to draw more than twenty thousand people, even for Catholic or public league championships. In the last years before the Bears became permanent residents of the stadium, games sometimes drew only a few hundred people. As early as 1925, however, the *Southtown Economist* observed that the stadium was an exception to the rule at the time against charging admission for games at public parks, and that apparently helped attract high schools. While the *Southtown* stated that Soldier Field was "so far out of the district that the support of the students would be greatly diminished," high school football brought fans from Chicago and elsewhere together in the stadium for many years.[3]

The biggest exception to the rule that high school games drew underwhelming crowds was the Prep Bowl, the game that for decades decided whether a public school or a Catholic school had bragging rights as city football champion. During its heyday, the Prep Bowl brought together Catholic and Protestant Chicagoans in a way that few other events did. And Chicago's mayors, particularly Edward Kelly and Richard J. Daley, took advantage of its popularity to fund their favorite charities, garner free publicity, and inspire their own supporters.

Although Catholic and public schools had met in interleague play for years, the first real Prep Bowl took place in 1927 as a charity game sponsored by the *Herald and Examiner* and other newspapers. The rivalry between Catholic and public school football teams in the city had been developing since 1912, when Catholic high schools, snubbed by the Cook County High School Athletic Association, had formed their own athletics league. Teams with local rivalries, such as Loyola Academy and Senn High School, had clashed regularly, but the Catholic and public leagues had separate championships. The establishment of a separate league was consistent with the general insularity of American Catholic culture at the time, which not only kept Catholics apart from public schoolers but fed the rivalries among various Catholic ethnic groups. Although ethnic rivalries were more pronounced in Chicago's parochial grammar schools, many Catholic high schools were also associated with religious orders favored by particular ethnic groups. The Catholic League thus reinforced ethnic rivalries, but it also emphasized how all of the groups were part of one Catholic whole. Thereafter, teams from Catholic and public schools did not compete until the *Herald and Examiner* and other papers established the game as a unique charitable opportunity. Catholic League leaders also saw the game as an opportunity to prove their schools' equality with secular institutions, and so agreed to the game.[4]

Schurz High School, the public league champion in 1927, used the run-oriented playbook of Stanford football coach Glenn Scobey "Pop" Warner, which had evolved as the sport became standardized and grew, between 1906 and 1912, from something like rugby into a game today's American football fans would recognize. The guiding light for Catholic football in Chicago, by contrast, was Knute Rockne's Notre Dame team; indeed, Catholic football fans had come to regard Warner-style play as Protestant and therefore suspect. That year's top Catholic League team, Mount Carmel High School—the Caravan—had adopted many of the techniques of Rockne's Fighting Irish. It excelled at passing, as evidenced in its 19–0 win over Saint Rita High School for the Catholic League championship a few weeks earlier. Newspaper accounts at the time detailed the religious backgrounds of the two coaches, noting that Mount Carmel's Tom Reardon was Catholic and Schurz's coach Protestant.

Led by Reardon, the Mount Carmel team had gone undefeated in 1927, giving up only two points all season. Team captain Mel Brosseau led a backfield line that could launch "offensive plays with dazzling speed and real deception and on defense back[ed] up the line in fine fashion." Schurz had lost only in two exhibition games. With college football in the 1920s mostly over for the season by the beginning of December, many fans were "turning to the [Prep Bowl] for one last sight of the battle along the scrimmage line," as one writer put it.[5]

In a precedent-setting game December 3, 1927, fifty thousand people watched Mount Carmel defeat Schurz by a score of 6–0. Fans stood throughout much of the second half, with the east side of the stadium on its feet for Mount Carmel and the west side cheering on Schurz. The game remained scoreless until the fourth quarter, when Brosseau, who later became a halfback for Marquette University, finally pushed through the Schurz line for a touchdown, the only score of the game. The game raised $35,000 for charity and gave the Catholic League school bragging rights as city champion.[6]

"There are football games and football games. And then there is the annual game between the Catholic and Public High school league champions for the city title," wrote the *American* in 1928. That year Tilden Tech took on DePaul, and won 12–0. Still, persistent arguments arose about whether the public league champion should agree to play against Catholic teams, which competed under different eligibility standards, and the game took a hiatus in 1929 and 1930, with the 1930 public league championship substituting for the Prep Bowl as a Soldier Field charity fund-raiser. But in 1931, with the Depression increasing the need for charitable events and Catholic League rules having moved closer to public league rules, the series resumed, with twenty-five thousand people watching Harrison pummel Mount Carmel, 44–6. That year's event raised about $15,000 (over $200,000 in 2008 dollars) for the Joint Emergency Relief Fund of Cook County, a charity headed by area businesspeople that, in the days before government-mandated unemployment insurance, provided aid to the unemployed and indigent.[7]

In 1932, however, the fathers of six players on the winning public league team, Morgan Park, refused to let them play, claiming that the weather would likely be bad, that their sons were behind in their studies, and that they needed their rest. The fathers refused to consider an indoor game, and that year's Prep Bowl, scheduled for December 3, was called off. Catholic fans insisted, even to recent years, that Morgan Park was simply afraid to face Mount Carmel, following the public school's defeat by Catholic Fenwick High School of Oak Park in a preseason game. Sports historian Gerald Gems argues that the inability of Catholics to force Morgan Park to come to the field emphasized Catholics' lack of real power in Chicago, despite the advances made in the preceding decades, as Catholic immigrants became an important force in city politics and events such as the Eucharistic Congress brought them greater positive recognition.[8]

In 1933 the uninterrupted tradition of the Prep Bowls began, though only after a complicated dispute as to the winner of the Catholic League title. After games—and disputes—involving Saint Rita and Loyola Academy, as well as Oak Park's Fenwick, Mount Carmel finally emerged victorious. Because of the delay in deciding the Catholic champion, officials announced the Prep Bowl's date just a few days before the contest, and only about five thousand people attended. Mount Carmel won, 7–0, against Harrison, and the resulting profits went to the Junior Association of Commerce's Christmas Basket fund.[9]

The following year, Mayor Kelly took over the Prep Bowl to raise funds for his own charitable organization, putting the Catholic League formally on par with the public league in the city's most prominent sports arena. (Catholic League fans still got the short end of the deal, however, and had to sit in the east stands, with the sun in their eyes for at least part of the Saturday afternoon game.) With the mayor's sponsorship, the 1934 game became officially the first Prep Bowl, though in reality it was the fifth. The game saw Leo High School lose to Lindblom, in a result that Catholic fans—and even the *Daily News*—attributed to the referees' bias in favor of the public league.[10]

Most of the patterns for the Prep Bowl, at least until the death of the first Mayor Daley, were set in the 1934 and 1935 games. Kelly and the other organizers—particularly Barnet Hodes, the law partner of Cook County Democratic leader Jake Arvey and the secretary of Chicago's Own Christmas Benefit Fund, a de facto arm of the mayor's political organization—made sure that the games were on a par with high-profile college games at Soldier Field. At the 1934 game, about a thousand band members from eleven Chicago high school bands—five public and six Catholic—played, led by the Chicago Police post band of the American Legion and a high school ROTC group. With the addition of Democratic precinct workers who wanted to make sure their political bosses saw them at the event, plus the families of the many band members, fifty thousand people attended in 1934 and seventy-five thousand in 1935.[11]

Even though Kelly was Catholic, he sat on the public school side of the stands. Subsequent Catholic mayors similarly balanced their own Catholic loyalties against their status as the city's highest elected official. A diagram of the field setup for the 1957 Prep Bowl shows that Mayor Daley and his family and guests sat in Section 21 of the lower seats, just off the 50-yard line—about the same place Kelly had sat. As the years went on, the Prep Bowl became a symbol of the mainstreaming of Catholic culture, a longtime goal of Chicago's Cardinal Mundelein. The game could be read as an indicator of how that project was progressing, and how divisions between mainstream Protestant culture and Catholicism both faded and lingered.

The high point of the Prep Bowl's history was undoubtedly the 1937 game between Leo and Austin high schools, which included Bill DeCorrevont, perhaps the most famed high school athlete in American history before the advent of television. Although a public school student, DeCorrevont was Catholic, and his fame and football prowess helped both to solidify the rivalries between Catholic and public schools and to bring together the two leagues' fans, with members of each group regarding him as a product of their own

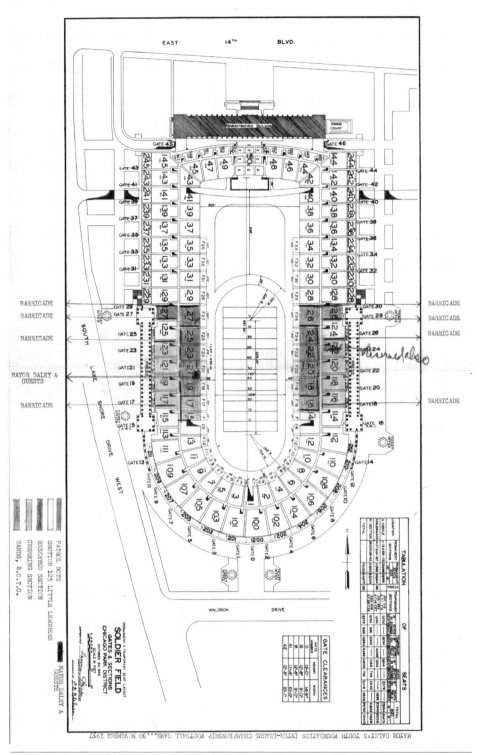

Plan of Soldier Field showing seating arrangements for the Mayor's Inter-League Championship Game (the Prep Bowl), 1957. Note the block of seats reserved for "Mayor Daley & Guests," in section 21 of the west stands. Courtesy Chicago Park District Special Collections.

culture. He had played in the 1936 game, in which Austin tied Fenwick, 19–19, and his individual achievement contrasted with the communal spirit of the Catholic team. Newspapers, magazines, and newsreels touted DeCorrevont's athleticism weeks in advance of the bowl game, hailing him as "making 'em forget the exploits of Harold 'Red' Grange, famed as the galloping ghost of Illinois a decade ago." One Associated Press report described DeCorrevont as drawing scores of adult fans: "The spectators leave the field with looks of amazement in their eyes, convinced that what they have read is true that he is as great a high school player as his record indicates." Newspapers across the country followed his progress through the season, as he scored thirty touchdowns and six extra points in eight games—a total of 186 points by the time of the Prep Bowl.[12]

Local papers, too, gushed over DeCorrevont and, to a lesser extent, his rival team captain, Johnny Galvin of Leo High School. Though the *Garfieldian*, a West Side paper, said Austin was "all set to bring foot ball title here," it also noted that the Austin coach, Bill Heiland, conceded that both players were "uncanny open field runners, great passers, and long, safe kickers."[13]

By mid-November, fans had already purchased $80,000 in tickets, many of them at a dollar each, which were easy to find, because charity game tickets were oversold at the time. "If everyone who bought a ticket from the police and firemen showed up for the game, they would have needed three stadiums the size of Soldier's Field," *Tribune* reporter Edward Harold Burns said in 1966. "But the day of the Leo-Austin game was a wonderfully warm day. Kids who ordinarily would have stayed at home because of the late season snow and sleet decided they wanted to see DeCorrevont. They remembered that they could pick up tickets, for the asking, at the neighborhood saloon or horse parlor. They grabbed those tickets and filled Soldiers' Field." Much of the crowd consisted of "skinny kids."[14] "Two of those kids could crowd in the space that would be taken up by an adult fan." One youngster who attended, Edmund Kelly, would later serve as general superintendent of the Chicago Park District. Sitting the stands with as many as 125,000 other people, he recalled,

> [I] thought I was back in Rome. That's the image I had. It was the Super Bowl to us. It was like going to the Super Bowl. Not just the thrill of being able to go to Soldier Field and see the game, but the excitement of the Catholic school going against the public school, all the Catholic school kids and all the public school kids being there.[15]

The size of the crowd, often cited as the largest ever for an American football game, has been disputed ever since, because there was no accurate tally of the number of people who bought tickets or were admitted to the stadium.

Crowds arrive for the record-setting 1937 Prep Bowl game, in which Austin High School star Bill DeCorrevont scored three touchdowns. Courtesy Chicago Park District Special Collections.

The seating capacity was thought to be about seventy-six thousand at the time—the north stands had been removed while the park district administration building was under construction—but the young people who attended were crowded in close, as well as filling the aisles, crowding the colonnades and even spilling onto the arena floor itself. Police who had handled crowd control at other Soldier Field events and Andy Frain, the legendary usher in charge at the stadium, both estimated the crowd at as high as 125,000.

Reinforcing the Super Bowl comparison, the 1937 Prep Bowl—at the time called the Mayor's Bowl, or even the Kelly Bowl—had plenty of pregame entertainment. Organizers again harnessed the musical talents of a thousand high schoolers, as well as Paul Whiteman, known in his own publicity and in *Downbeat* magazine as the King of Jazz. DeCorrevont and Galvin were overwhelmed. "I couldn't imagine there would be this many people coming to see a high school football game," DeCorrevont said fifty years later. "All I could say to myself was, 'Don't louse things up now.'" Galvin's shoulder had been injured in the Catholic championship against Saint George High

School, and he recalled much less of the atmosphere of the event: "The game was over so fast I never had a chance to look up to see how many people were there. Besides I was hurting so much. They gave me a shot of Novocaine before the (Austin) game, and I wore some oversized shoulder pads, but it didn't help."[16]

College officials refereed the game, and it ended in a blowout for Austin. DeCorrevont suffered a charley horse and a case of jitters brought on by the size of the crowd, but still managed to score three touchdowns and pass to a teammate for a fourth. The first touchdown came in the second quarter, on a forty-seven-yard run that ended with teammates making key downfield blocks to get him clear of Leo's defensive line. "That first touchdown was a strange play," DeCorrevont said in a *Tribune* interview fifty years after the event. "I was supposed to hand off to the right halfback, Ozzie Lange, but he was too far away. Everyone was going left, so I went right. Today, you call it a misdirection play. Then, it was just a mistake play." That was followed the same quarter by a high diving catch that ended in a touchdown. DeCorrevont scored again in the third, then in the fourth passed the ball to teammate Sonny Skor, who caught it in the end zone. "There was no kid stuff about the process of the victors," Burns wrote. "And the losers, too, performed like they knew their stuff." After being injured again in the first quarter, Galvin left the game in the second half, to applause from both sides.[17]

The weeks following the game showed how events at Soldier Field could bring Chicagoans together, even off the field. Both DeCorrevont and Galvin were inducted into the Catholic Youth Organization Club of Champions. The CYO, run by Bishop Bernard J. Sheil, played a large role in popularizing organized sports in the Catholic community and constantly stoked the rivalry between the Catholic and public schools. The move to honor both boys—recognizing that both were Catholic—was one of many signals that despite the rivalry, Catholic culture was becoming more integrated into Chicago society. The *Chicago American* picked all-stars from both Catholic and public school football teams to play against an all-star Arizona team in Phoenix on New Year's Day, but DeCorrevont did not attend. Instead, he and his mother traveled to Los Angeles, where a movie studio hosted him and he attended the Rose Bowl—as a spectator.[18] After months of national hype, DeCorrevont chose to stay in the Chicago area and attend Northwestern University rather than taking one of the numerous offers from colleges in other cities; he later played professional football with teams including the Chicago Cardinals and, for two seasons, the Bears. He was Soldier Field's first superstar.

The Prep Bowl's significance lasted into the 1970s, though its popularity waned as pro football became more popular. The 1938 contest saw about eighty thousand people attend, as Kelly emphasized to his political underlings that the game proceeds went to a good cause, a point also stressed by the Chicago

Fans at the 1939 Prep Bowl. Courtesy Chicago Tribune.

newspapers—particularly the *Tribune*, controlled by Kelly's friend, Colonel McCormick. As the newspapers promised, Mount Carmel and Fenger put on a good show, and though Fenger won, 13–0, Mount Carmel kept the public school's star player, Don Griffin, from scoring.[19] Fenger's dominance in the Prep Bowl lasted into 1940, when its team beat Leo, 13–0. Overall, though, the Catholic League has dominated the Prep Bowl, winning fifty-one contests to the public league's twenty-three, if the pre-Kelly city championships are included (two games, in 1936 and 1939, ended in ties). The 1930s and 1940s, along with a few years in the early 1960s, were the heyday of the game, with those decades' Prep Bowls accounting for eleven of the Illinois High School Association's top fifteen football games in terms of attendance.[20]

Over the years, a few games came close to matching the 1937 Prep Bowl, and several high-powered Catholic and public league teams developed rivalries. After Leo lost to Fenger in 1940, Leo defeating Tilden Tech in 1941 and 1942, kicking off the long-standing Catholic school dominance of the match. The 1941 game, just days before the Japanese attack on Pearl Harbor, drew the second-highest number of spectators ever to an Illinois high school game, about ninety-five thousand. Through the end of the war, the game continued to sell well; only in 1944 did the attendance dip below seventy-five thousand.[21]

After 1946, however, attendance dipped and did not regain those levels until the mid- to late 1950s. Some years the drop was merely a function of bad weather, common in the weeks following Thanksgiving in Chicago. In 1947, a decade after their first contest, Austin and Leo had a rematch, but with temperatures well below freezing at kickoff time, fewer than thirty thousand people came out to see Austin win by a point.

Over the years, fog has also disrupted a number of events at the stadium, including several football games. Of these, however, only the 1950 Prep Bowl, between Lane Tech and Mount Carmel, and the 1988 Fog Bowl, in which the Bears bested the Eagles, were playoff or championship games. As in 1988, "television cameras were practically useless" at the 1950 Prep Bowl, and Jack Brickhouse, who was broadcasting the game, used an extension microphone to announce from just behind the Lane Tech bench. Mount Carmel, appearing for the sixth time in the interleague championship, had what many thought to be the best Illinois high school football team up to that point, and its Caravan squashed Lane's Indians, 45–20, with three players scoring two touchdowns each. "I know we could have beaten many a team that has won this game in other years," said Lane's coach, George Ring. "I think the difference is we were a high school team, and a great one, but they played like no high school team I've seen." The Mount Carmel coach, Terry Brennan, a recent Notre Dame graduate, led Mount Carmel to two more city championships, in 1951 and 1952, and then returned to Notre Dame, serving first as assistant coach and then as head coach. The Caravan's record of three straight titles has yet to be bested and was only tied twenty years later by Burbank's Saint Laurence.[22]

Until at least 1976, the year Richard J. Daley died, the Prep Bowl often carried with it a strong whiff of politics. Kelly had long used the proceeds of the game as a way to reward his ward leaders. During Mayor Martin Kennelly's years, the proceeds went to prominent Chicago charities, but Chicago's Own Christmas Benefit Fund, still headed by Kelly's former corporation counsel, continued to get some funds. Daley then further centralized control over the money, making the game a fund-raiser for his own scholarship foundation.

The zeal with which political workers have sold tickets to the Prep Bowl over the years provides a prime example of how the Democratic political machine helped to keep a hold on city politics, even as it brought Chicagoans together for a popular yearly event. On at least one Sunday a few weeks before the 1936 game, the *Tribune* reported, police officers actually made traffic stops just to solicit people to buy tickets. One officer who stopped a *Tribune* reporter defended his actions, saying, "I know it has earmarks of a shakedown because drivers are frightened when we stop them, but don't get me in bad with my captain. . . . I was given a dozen tickets and told to sell them or eat them."[23]

Newspapers generally agreed that the Chicago's Own fund, and later the Mayor Daley Youth Foundation, which took over sponsorship of the game in 1955 and provided college scholarships for Chicago students, were genuinely worthy causes. But at times the more venal political nature of the groups shone through. In 1935 the Christmas fund raised $300,000 to help eighty-five thousand poor children. Like similar funds in other cities, the fund had what the *Tribune* called "the backing of a powerful local political organization," but its director, Barnet Hodes, claimed that 86 percent of what was raised went to buy clothing for children, while only about $24,000 went to running the Prep Bowl and another fund-raising event. The mechanics of the ticket sales and financial distribution were, however, more complex. In addition to the police, other public employees, including firemen and school principals, were coerced to sell tickets for the game. About the a third of the money came to ward committeemen, who would use any money in excess of what they had pledged to the fund for the Christmas baskets their own political organizations handed out to needy but loyal voters each year. It's little wonder that Prep Bowl attendance records were set in the years when the Kelly and Daley machines were at their peaks of power.[24] Still, saying that the Prep Bowl was defined by its political taint would ignore the benefit high school players gained from having college-size crowds at their games, and the pleasure other Chicagoans derived from an event that focused on the achievements of young people.

THE BENEFITS OF SOLDIER FIELD

Other benefit games also were a popular ticket at Soldier Field in the days before televised football. One annual game that ran from the 1920s into the 1950s benefited the Sisters of Mercy, the order's Catholic high schools, or Mercy Hospital. Most often, it involved a matchup of two Catholic League schools, for years Saint Rita and Leo, and drew between twenty and thirty thousand spectators. (It also featured professional and college teams some years, although not playing each other.) The game got started in 1926 when her superior asked Sister Mary Ricardo, the former Helen M. Ganey, to found a regular fund-raiser for the sisters. Sister Ricardo, a native of Chicago, knew little about football, but set up a meeting with Chris O'Brien, the owner of the Chicago Cardinals. O'Brien decided that a scheduled game with the Kansas City Cowboys could be played at Soldier Field. In 1946, after twenty of the annual games had been played (some of them at Comiskey Park), Sister Ricardo told a group of people—including then–state senator Richard J. Daley—at a dinner preceding that year's match that she had "never seen a game." The 1946 contest, on the centennial of the Sisters of Mercy's work in Chicago, was one of several that helped raise $6 million to build Mercy Hospital. The games continued until 1951, after which the sisters moved toward other types of benefits that entailed less overhead.[25]

COLLEGE FOOTBALL TAKES THE TURF

Many of the college games played at the stadium were also fund-raisers—in fact, the first college football game ever held at Soldier Field was an Armistice Day match—the Midwest Catholic League championship for 1924—between Saint Viator College of Bourbonnais and Columbia College of Dubuque, Iowa (now Loras College), to benefit an American Legion fund for disabled veterans. After the teams plunged through "a deluge of rain and a sea of mud," the game ended in a scoreless tie. Bad weather kept the crowd down to two thousand people, an inauspicious beginning for the stadium's history of hosting college games. Perhaps because of the game was unremarkable, or perhaps because Saint Viator went out of business in 1938 and Columbia is now know by another name, the game is little remembered. Instead it's often claimed that the Notre Dame–Northwestern game, played ten days later, was the first college football match at Grant Park Stadium.[26]

It might not have been the first ever, but the Notre Dame–Northwestern game certainly was the first important game at the stadium, pitting the rising Catholic university against a well-established Methodist school. Another milestone that year also helped popularize Notre Dame football: the first radio broadcast of a Fighting Irish game, a home game against the University of Nebraska, which aired on WGN-AM a week before the team's first appearance at Soldier Field. Although the team had played in Chicago before, at smaller venues, the prosperity of the decade had enriched Chicago's Irish American and Catholic communities. Anticipating high demand, Rockne urged relocating the game to the Grant Park stadium, and his instincts proved correct. Ticket sales were hot, with Notre Dame and its Chicago alumni club selling out a week before the game. Officials expected a capacity crowd, as many as forty-five thousand people, which would yield Northwestern and Notre Dame each $27,000 from ticket sales, after the usual 10 percent of the gate went to the South Park Commission. Notre Dame struggled more than usual to overcome the Wildcats, as Northwestern's Ralph "Moon" Baker scored on two drop-kick plays. Northwestern lost 13–6, however, after Elmer Layden, one Notre Dame's famed Four Horsemen (so dubbed the month before by Grantland Rice), made a fourth-quarter touchdown.[27]

Notre Dame was one of the most avidly followed football teams of the era and was particularly popular in Chicago. Before its next game at Soldier Field, against the University of Southern California in 1927, the team's ticket manager said he could have sold a hundred thousand more seats. More than four thousand Californians, including Los Angeles mayor George E. Cryer, traveled to the game, scheduled for November 26. As with the Prep Bowls, Notre Dame games helped show off the best of Catholic education, and the games were a focus of pride for Chicago-area Catholics. For the USC game, the South Park Board added a thousand seats to the stadium, and Chicago mayor Big Bill Thompson issued a proclamation urging Chicagoans to decorate their homes with the American flag and the colors of the two opposing teams.

Adding to Notre Dame's popularity was a peculiar relationship between Rockne and one of the game officials. *Tribune* reporter Walter Eckersall not only wrote about college football but officiated at some of the games he covered for the paper. In what looks from the distance of eighty years like a complex payoff scheme, Rockne took out advertisements in a magazine run by the commissioners of the Big Ten, who decided which referees worked which games. Rockne preferred to have Eckersall for Notre Dame games, and Eckersall he often got. For the 1927 game at Soldier Field, letters to Eckersall from Rockne indicate not only that Eckersall acted as the head lineman but also that Rockne sent him $250 to promote the game. Eckersall also received what Rockne called "good" tickets for his family and friends for Notre Dame games. And, despite officiating, Eckersall wrote at least four advance stories for the *Tribune* about the game, as well as a page-one story the day after; changes in media culture make such an arrangement unimaginable today.[28]

The game itself was a cliffhanger, though all the scoring happened in the first quarter. USC halfback Russell Saunders scored on a pass in the first few minutes of the game, but quarterback Morley Drury slipped in the wet grass while trying to make the extra point, putting the score at 6–0 "before the spectators had settled into their seats," one reporter wrote. Then, about ten minutes into the game, Notre Dame right halfback Ray Dahman caught a seventeen-yard pass in the end zone and successfully kicked the extra point. A number of passes by the Trojans were intercepted, but the Irish were unable to score again. The *Tribune* reported a record crowd of 117,000, generating profit of about $150,000 for each team and $125,000 for the South Park Commission. Park district tallies put the crowd at 123,000. Notre Dame and the NCAA record it as an even 120,000. Whatever the exact number, the NCAA deems it the largest pre-1948 regular-season crowd for college football.[29]

The only game Notre Dame played at Soldier Field in 1928, against Navy, also set an attendance record, with about 120,000 spectators, despite Notre Dame's coming off a 22–6 loss to the University of Wisconsin. (It was to be Rockne's worst season as a coach, with the Irish winning five and losing four.) Radio broadcasts were helping to make the team more popular, even as they began to turn big-city sports fans' attention away from local high school and amateur teams. Among the dignitaries at the game was New York mayor James L. Walker, who was in town for a Democratic political rally. Once the game got going, Walker made his way to the sidelines, lighting cigarettes and shouting advice to Notre Dame throughout the game. Notre Dame gained momentum when Navy punted poorly in the third quarter, giving the Irish possession of the ball at the Navy 28-yard line. Still, the game remained a scoreless tie until the fourth quarter, when Notre Dame's John Niemiec passed to John Colerick, a substitute left end, in the end zone. Frank Carideo, the team's quarterback, kicked the extra point. Walker, still kibitzing, had told the Democratic candidate for governor, Floyd E. Thompson, just before the winning touchdown, "I'd never make a pass on this play." When the pass was thrown and caught, Walker still jumped to his feet, "flourishing his derby and prancing a victory prance."[30]

In 1929 a new stadium was under construction at Notre Dame, and the team played its entire home season at Soldier Field. The head coach, however, was ailing and missed the first home game, against Wisconsin. Notre Dame won, 19–0, with two of the touchdowns scored by Joe Savoldi, who the next year played a season with the Bears before becoming a professional wrestler. Rockne went on the road to Pittsburgh for a game against Carnegie Tech, then stayed home from the next game at Soldier Field, against Drake, which the Irish won, 19–7, coming from behind after Drake led for the first three quarters.[31] The following week was to be a rematch with the USC Trojans, and Rockne made it known that he was still in charge of his team, being photographed in a special wheelchair he used to direct drills in a Notre Dame gym.[32] On game day, the formidable USC team played Notre Dame to a 6–6 halftime tie. In the Irish locker room at halftime, Tom Lieb, the assistant coach who had been running the team during Rockne's illness, talked about what the team could do better. Rockne, in his wheelchair, sat silent, until former Notre Dame punter Paul Canter told the team: "Here he is, fellows: here's Rock. He's the fellow you turn to no matter what the trouble. Rock's sick, fellows . . . He came because he wanted to be here when you won." Then Rockne himself spoke briefly, telling the team, "Go on out there, go on out there, and play 'em off their feet in the first five minutes." After Rockne's pep talk, Savoldi, the team's fullback, scored a touchdown, breaking through USC's center, and Carideo got the extra point. USC scored again, but missed the point after, leaving the score 13–12, Notre Dame. Fighting Irish fans celebrated in the Loop.[33]

The next year, Rockne's last, demand for tickets to the game against Northwestern was so high that the president of Northwestern tried to get it moved to Soldier Field, proposing that the teams donate the proceeds to charity. Although Notre Dame usually shied away from charity contests, the leadership at the university agreed, only to have the Big Ten veto the move because of a rule against moving a game from one Big Ten school to a stadium within a hundred miles of another conference member (the University of Chicago was then in the Big Ten). Instead, Notre Dame agreed to move its 1931 home game against Northwestern to Soldier Field for the same purpose, and Northwestern preemptively donated $100,000 to the Illinois unemployment commission. Alumni complained that despite Soldier Field's size, they had difficulty getting tickets. In fact, Kelly's South Park Commission was secretly forcing Notre Dame to sell it fifteen thousand tickets at face value. For the time being, Notre Dame did nothing about it.

The 1930 Army–Notre Dame game was previewed by newspapers as yet another epic contest. The day turned out cold and gray, and though almost all the seats filled eventually, the rain and mist made it hard to distinguish one teams' players from the other. The game remained scoreless for almost fifty minutes as the two teams dirtied each other up. "A cold winter rain beat down upon the great crowd which sat and watched the two teams skid and slip, slide and tumble over the treacherous turf that gave no spikes a gripping chance upon any fast start," wrote Grantland Rice.

It was not until the fifty-five-minute mark that Notre Dame succeeded in scoring. When Marchmont Schwartz returned an interception to the end zone, many in the crowd didn't realize what had happened until the referee threw up his arms to signal a touchdown. Carideo followed up with the extra point. Soon after, a Notre Dame punt was blocked and the ball landed in the end zone. Army's Dick King pounced on it to score, but Army missed the extra point and lost the game by one. Despite the weather and the gloomy press accounts that followed it, Rockne was all smiles after the game.[34] It was to be his last game at Soldier Field, and one of the last for Notre Dame. After the Northwestern game in 1931, the Irish did not return until 1942, for a game against Army. That game was followed by a fifty-year absence; they returned in 1992 to beat Northwestern, 42–7.

Northwestern too played several games at Soldier Field over the years, including, besides the Notre Dame matches, two games in 1925 and two in 1933. Having Notre Dame and other high-profile teams at the stadium fulfilled one of the main objectives of building Soldier Field, that of attracting prestigious sports events to Chicago that might otherwise have been played elsewhere, even if, as in the case of Northwestern, elsewhere was no more distant than Evanston, an adjacent Chicago suburb. Although college games were popular events at Soldier Field in the 1920s and early 1930s, they became rarer as the Depression wore on and many colleges, including Notre Dame, concentrated on holding games at their own stadiums. Soldier Field also appears to have been a victim of its own success—or at least of the way park officials treated that success. Take, for example, the fifteen thousand tickets the South Park commissioners bought for the Notre Dame games, then resold or gave away as favors. Over the years, many sponsors of events at the stadium complained to park officials about having to provide free tickets to events. Such political maneuvering eventually helped kill the golden goose.

BLACK COLLEGES AT THE STADIUM

From the mid-1930s to the 1990s almost the only prominent college games played at the stadium were fund-raisers of one type or another or special bowl games. Outside of matches involving professional players, such as the annual College All-Star and Bears Armed Forces games (see chapter 7), the longest running football face-off at the stadium involved two historically black colleges, the Tuskegee Institute (now Tuskegee University) of Alabama and Wilberforce University of Ohio. Tuskegee hosted the first game between the two schools in 1928. The following year the contest moved to Soldier Field, in part because the 1928 game had cost the two schools money, and promoters guaranteed each university $6,000 if they played at the new stadium.

The Tuskegee team arrived a couple days before the contest and toured the city. Most of the team members had never been outside the South. "I've seen a couple of big buildings in Atlanta, but I never laid my optics on any as high as Chicago's and, boy, I never saw 'em so copious," one remarked. Fans of the two teams were eager to see the match, but it wasn't only the game that attracted people to Chicago. As the *Defender* noted, many parties were planned with visiting alumni in mind, and the clubs of the two schools worked overtime to outdo each other in planned festivities.[35]

In addition to being a meeting of rivals, the October 26, 1929, game also was for the football championship among historically black colleges. Wilberforce was within sight of the end zone three times in the first half but was blocked by Tuskegee's center line. Tuskegee had lost only one game in five years, and the second half showed off the team's abilities. Tuskegee's star was Benjamin Stevenson, a running back who in 1926 had ensured numerous wins for the team, including a game against Lincoln University of Pennsylvania in which he scored all the Tuskegee points, including a ninety-yard run for a touchdown. At Soldier Field, Tuskegee came within half a yard of a touchdown early in the second half, but the game remained scoreless until the fourth quarter. Stevenson finally scored the only touchdown when a Tuskegee halfback passed him the ball and he ran twenty yards. Tuskegee won its first Soldier Field contest, 6–0. The College Football Hall of Fame inducted Stevenson in 2003.[36]

Though it's remembered as a classic rivalry in the annals of black college sports, the Tuskegee-Wilberforce game never garnered the media attention or public support its organizers hoped for. The first match at Soldier Field drew only about twelve thousand people, and that turned out to be an average crowd for the contest in subsequent years. In the days of segregation and parallel sports organizations and colleges, games involving black college teams rarely drew crowds as large as those for all-white or largely white institutions, even for title bouts. The 1930 contest brought out one of the larger crowds in the history of the contest, about fifteen thousand, but the teams battled to a scoreless draw. In 1931, with Soldier Field unavailable, the teams faced off at Mills stadium on the West Side, with Wilberforce winning, 15–6.[37] In 1932 Wilberforce played another team elsewhere in Chicago.

The series resumed at Soldier Field in 1933 and ran there through 1936, only to be canceled at the last minute in 1937. It returned in 1938, and the two schools' alumni associations in Chicago worked hard to get a decent crowd to the stadium that year. Their efforts, the presence of five Chicagoans on the Wilberforce team, and a warm fall evening helped bring in a crowd of fifteen thousand to see Wilberforce win, 25–6. The largest attendance at the game appears to have come during World War II, at the 1942 game. The proceeds of the game were donated to Army and Navy relief funds, and Wilberforce won again, 13–7.[38] After 1942 the games moved to Comiskey Park, a smaller venue that organizers could come closer to filling. The series ended in 1949, with Wilberforce defeating Tuskegee, 22–7. Overall, Wilberforce won nine games to Tuskegee's eight, and three games ended in ties.

Many who grew up in Chicago's African American community at the time remember the Tuskegee-Wilberforce games fondly. Beyond adding to the colleges' bottom lines, games at Soldier Field raised the profiles of the universities involved, whether Tuskegee and Wilberforce or Notre Dame. And they added to Chicago culture in the way the stadium builders intended. When singer Lou Rawls received an honorary degree from Wilberforce, more than fifty years after the last game, he remarked, "Growing up in Chicago, I was aware of Wilberforce University because every year they would have the Tuskegee-Wilberforce football game. That was something we looked forward to."[39]

For years, before interest in high school football at the stadium declined, Soldier Field's owners used the stadium, at least in part, for what they had originally contended was its main purpose: to foster amateur sports and athletics of all kinds and, if possible, to bring the Olympics to Chicago.

4 *Chicago's Olympic Legacy*

When the stadium that would become Soldier Field first rose south of the Field Museum, machine politicians, reformers, and businessmen all hoped it would herald a new era in Chicago's history. Two decades before, the city had landed the Olympic Games for 1904. But Chicago allowed St. Louis to take the games, so as not to compete with that city's Louisiana Purchase Exposition, a world's fair scheduled for the same summer. "We did not oppose the transfer . . . in view of the fact that [the fair] is a national enterprise, and because we realized that the holding of the games in Chicago at the same time would seriously jeopardize the success of the exposition," said H. J. Furber, who had headed Chicago's Olympic bid.[1]

As part of Chicago's preparations for the games, organizers had planned a temporary stadium on the lakefront. Over the next two decades, leading up to the construction of Soldier Field, the popularity of Olympic-style athletic competitions had increased in Chicago, as the city developed a system of small parks to provide recreation for every citizen, particularly the city's youth. Grant Park Stadium was to be the culmination of that development, bringing the city together in the mutual goodwill that reformers thought sport fostered. In its early years especially, park officials encouraged amateur competitions at Soldier Field and used the stadium to show off the accomplishments of children participating in programs at the smaller parks, as well as students in the city's public schools—among the first in the country to have a physical education requirement (in part because of the German American Turners, discussed in chapter 8). City leaders understood that one of their best hopes for bringing the Olympics to Chicago lay in demonstrating to the U.S. and international Olympic committees that a town that had given up so much to become one of the leading industrial centers of the world—sunlight, clean streets, clean air—also could go all out in encouraging its youth in sports.

ATHLETICS IN A MODERN SPORTS PALACE

And Soldier Field certainly encouraged *every* kind of sport, especially in its early years. Most remain familiar, though a few now appear quaint. In the 1920s horses still were a common sight in the city. Many tradesmen used them; the lakefront paths we now use for bicycling and running were largely designed for equine traffic; and horses even played a part in building Soldier Field. So it may not have seemed unusual when the Ogden Park Horseshoe Pitching Club and the Chicago Playground Council cosponsored the state amateur horseshoe pitching tournament at the stadium in December 1924. Ogden Park's pitchers swept the competition, coming away with eight of the fourteen trophies.[2]

From the opening of the stadium in 1924 until the early 1930s, track and field meets were common, especially in the spring and early summer months; competitions included those sponsored by the *Chicago Daily News*, the *Herald and Examiner*, and the *American*, as well as public and Catholic school meets. The University of Chicago and Loyola University also regularly used the stadium for intercollegiate events, as did the Amateur Athletic Union.

With the city's hopes for an Olympics so tied to the Grant Park Stadium, the South Park Commission worked hard to make it a center for area athletic meets, starting even before the stadium's first dedication on the fifty-third anniversary of the Chicago Fire. On September 27, 1924, the *Chicago Daily News* helped sponsor a women's track meet that brought together more than five hundred competitors from across the Chicago area, especially from local parks. Competitions took place in the usual events, such as the high jump, as well as now-forgotten contests like the basketball distance throw. The 1920s was the last decade in which other athletic events competed with sports like baseball and football for popular acclaim, and the newspapers paid considerable attention to the event, which the *Daily News*, as was common at the time, termed an Olympic field meet. The Amateur Athletic Union, which up until 1976 ran U.S. Olympic qualifying events, had started holding women's athletic events in the Chicago area in 1923. The city produced a crop of talented, highly visible athletic stars like Norma Zilk, one of four women working with University of Chicago track coach Tom Eck, and Helen Filkey. (Zilk would later set a world's record in the women's 80-yard dash.)[3]

Typical of early competitions at the stadium were two held in the spring of 1925: an intercollegiate track meet sponsored by Loyola University held on April 19 and the "first annual Chicago Olympics," sponsored by the Finnish

American Athletic Association. The Loyola event featured one of the most famous athletes of the 1920s, Paavo Nurmi, who the year before had won five Olympic gold medals for Finland. The fastest middle- and long-distance runner of the era, Nurmi was in the last few weeks of a five-month tour of the United States, during which he competed in fifty-five races. The meet was hampered by rain the morning of the competition, but in the 3,000-meter race Nurmi beat Willie Ritola, another Finnish Olympian who was an American resident and who had been traveling with him. In the Finnish American meet, the following month, women competitors included Filkey and female Eck protégés Zilk and Nellie Todd. Filkey established what event organizers claimed was a record in hurdles, while Illinoisan Harold Osborn won as best overall athlete of the event. And Ritola, who was back in Chicago, won a two-mile race. But even with the fierce Olympic-style competition, temperatures hovering around 90 degrees appear to have kept many people away, as only about twenty-five hundred spectators turned out.[4]

Even in good weather, low attendance plagued track and field events at Soldier Field from the beginning. The 1924 women's track meet appears to have been an exception to the rule that even high-profile Olympic athletes could do little to raise attendance above ten thousand. For the first decade of the stadium's operations, this doesn't seem to have concerned the South Park commissioners. They perhaps were content to provide a venue for a sport that added to the prestige of the stadium, if not to its bottom line.

Chicago newspapers continued to sponsor many of the highest-profile track meets at the stadium over the next two decades, even after athletic events declined in popularity in the 1930s. One of the most important turned out to be the 1928 women's meet sponsored by the *Chicago Evening American*. Filkey and other familiar female competitors participated, and the *American* noted, on the front page, the records that were broken. A newcomer from south suburban Riverdale named Elizabeth Robinson—also known as Betty or Babe—won the 100-meter race, equaling a world record for the event the first time she ran it in an outdoor meet. She set the mark—12 seconds, beating a previous record of 12.6 seconds—in a semifinal qualifying heat, despite a whistling north wind that whipped through the stadium (at the time open at the north end), then finished with the same time in the final, beating Filkey by a yard. The *American*'s reporter matter-of-factly noted that the newspaper would pay to send Robinson, at the time only sixteen years old, to New York City for the Olympic trials.

It was the beginning of an incredible career for Robinson, who had started running competitively only weeks before when one of her teachers at Thornton Township High School in Harvey noticed her abilities. The story varied depending on when Robinson told it. About two months after the Soldier Field meet, she told reporters:

> About a year ago at a church picnic, I attracted the attention of one of my teachers when I ran in a race. He complimented me, but apparently forgot about it until he saw me running to catch a train this spring. Later he gave me my first instructions in sprinting.

"I was just lucky that this teacher was up at the station," Robinson said in 1988. "It was lucky he saw me running. If he hadn't, I wouldn't have known I was a fast runner."

Her first competition came when her sister entered an early spring track meet sponsored by area bankers and got Robinson an amateur card, allowing her to run in the indoor meet. When Robinson finished second, close behind Filkey, the Illinois Women's Athletic Club invited her to join, and she started training with the club regularly. After her record-setting run at Soldier Field, "there was no end of talk until I tried out for the American Olympic team in the meet at Newark, N.J.," Robinson told reporters in 1928.

Her coach had set Robinson on the course to becoming a legend. The 1928 summer games in Amsterdam were the first Olympics that included women's track events. Fanny Rosenfeld, a Canadian, was the odds-on favorite to win the 100-meter race, but halfway down the track Robinson pulled even with Rosenfeld and then passed her, taking the race by a foot. With her win, she became the first woman to win an Olympic gold medal in a track event. "Everything has been so far beyond my fondest dreams," Robinson told the *Tribune* afterward. Over the next several years, while attending Northwestern University, she appeared in many local races, including several at Soldier Field.

Robinson continued to set records into 1931, and many expected her to repeat her star performance at the 1932 Olympics in Los Angeles. But her career as an athlete almost ended on a hot summer day in 1931. She had been trying to cool off without violating training rules against going for a swim, and so took a airplane ride with her cousin. The plane crashed and burrowed into marshy ground near 156th Street and Cicero Avenue. At first, the two were presumed dead. "A man came up and threw her in the trunk of the car and took her to the mortician," Robinson's nephew, Jim Rochfort, said after Robinson's death in 1999. When the mortician realized that Robinson was still alive, she was taken to the Oak Forest county infirmary, where doctors treated her left leg and left arm for fractures. Despite being told by doctors that she would have a lifelong limp, Robinson told the *Tribune* late in 1931, "Of course I am going to try to run again." Although she was unable to compete at the 1932 Olympics and could never again crouch in a sprinter's starting position, Robinson made the 1936 Olympic team as part of its women's relay crew—and won another gold medal in Berlin.[5]

Another Chicagoan who competed at Soldier Field in the late 1920s and

1930s and went on to Olympic fame was Ralph Metcalfe, a graduate of Tilden Technical High School. Metcalfe first came to the attention of many Chicagoans in the spring of 1928, as he led Tilden Tech to victory in a downstate meet and set records in national competitions at Marquette University. He continued to set records over the next two years, and his star rose even further in a 1930 meet at Soldier Field that on its last night attracted one of the largest crowds for any athletic meet ever held there, about forty thousand people. That meet was an international competition between athletes from the British Empire and a team from the United States. Similar events had been held in England following the previous three Olympics, and the Soldier Field meet was the first one held in the United States. Metcalfe appeared on the front page of the *Tribune*, just about to break through the tape to win the 100-yard dash against some of the best sprinters in the world. In 1932 Metcalfe won a silver medal and a bronze medal at the Los Angeles Olympics. That same year, he was one of the stars at a post-Olympic meet that brought teams from fifteen countries to Soldier Field.

The many high school athletic meets held at Soldier Field each spring always had suffered from low attendance, but adult events enjoyed a strong following for a few years. The 1932 meet, however, appears to have been one of the last to draw a big crowd—and even that was small by Soldier Field standards. A June 1933 NCAA meet that included Metcalfe and Jesse Owens and saw five world records set, including one by Metcalfe, still drew coverage from the newspapers but was sparsely attended. A national black athletic meet held in conjunction with the poorly attended Negro Day at the Century of Progress world's fair featured such athletes as Olympic gold medalists Edward Gordon and William DeHart Hubbard, the first African American to win a gold medal, but attracted even fewer people. Later that summer, attendance at the forty-sixth annual National Amateur Athletic Union meet in August barely hit the eight thousand mark. "Judged solely by the caliber of the athletes, [it] was one of the best in the history of the modern games," wrote one commentator. "By the standards of attendance . . . the games flopped. . . . Chicago isn't a track town." After 1933, fewer and fewer track and field events graced the stadium. [6]

ETHNIC SPORTS SHOWCASED

Some of the better-attended athletic competitions in Soldier Field's first two decades were presented by northern and eastern European ethnic groups, especially Germans and Czechs. German Turnerbund groups put on a number of athletic demonstrations as part of German Day events (see chapter 6), and Czech-Slovak Sokol societies began holding some of their larger Midwest athletic competitions at Soldier Field early in the stadium's history. The latter movement (*sokol* means "falcon" in Czech) began in 1862 and spread to the United States with Czech and Slovak immigrants in the late nineteenth century. Its founder, Dr. Miroslav Tyrs, harkened back to Greek and Roman ideals of the well-rounded person whose harmony of body and mind were enhanced by vigorous physical activity. Sokol remains a vibrant organization today, promoting gymnastics, athletics, and cultural heritage through numerous local affiliates; it is especially strong in the Chicago area, which hosted the first American Sokol *slet*—or gathering—in 1893. In the United States, national slets generally have been held every four years, often in Chicago. The first at Soldier Field was in 1929 and brought out twenty-five thousand people, among them U.S. representative Ruth Hanna McCormick, Illinois' at-large congresswoman and the first woman to win statewide office in Illinois. Athletes participated in Olympic-style individual gymnastics events against representatives of as many as twelve hundred other Sokol organizations from around the country. The Soldier Field slets also showed off Sokol members' skills at mass gymnastic drills. In the first Soldier Field slet, two thousand children from the Chicago Sokol organization participated in a mass drill in time to orchestral music. Always an expression of Czech and Slovak national pride, early slets were attended by representatives of the Czechoslovak government; the country's ambassador, for instance, participated in the 1947 slet, the first held since the start of World War II. (This changed, however, in the 1950s, when representatives of the Communist Czechoslovak government were pointedly excluded.) Slets in the 1930s and 1940s attracted the largest crowds of any such events in the United States, bringing fifty thousand to Soldier Field several times.[7]

The 1954 slet was the last one held at Soldier Field. American taste in sport had changed significantly in the quarter century since the stadium was first proposed, and while slets retained a following, track and field events were no longer in vogue. Long after such competitions fell out of favor with sports enthusiasts, however, many Chicagoans remembered that the stadium designers had in mind the world's greatest athletic gathering when they drew up plans for Soldier Field.

From even before the stadium's opening until the late 1950s, Chicago made frequent efforts to lure the Olympic Games to the city, and many—especially those who believed that the lack of a lakefront stadium had been a decisive reason why the International Olympic Committee had agreed to transfer the 1904 games to Saint Louis—regarded Soldier Field as one of the amenities that would help their bid succeed. In 1920 Everett C. Brown, a longtime member of the U.S. Olympic Committee and former head of the Chicago Athletic Association, proposed to a meeting of the committee in Belgium that Chicago get the 1924 games, citing the proposed new stadium as a selling point. When that bid failed, city officials tried to drum up support for Amateur Athletic Union events, in part because they realized that Olympic officials in the first half of the twentieth century often looked at the popularity of athletic events in a city as a portent of how well the Olympic Games might do there. In 1924 Chicago fire commissioner John F. Cullerton, who was involved in several athletic leagues, including indoor baseball, traveled to France with the mayor of Minneapolis to support Chicago's bid for the 1928 Olympics. They pitched Chicago as the summer venue and Minneapolis as the winter venue for the quadrennial games, but again failed to convince the Olympic committee.

Almost every four years over the next three decades, Chicago civic leaders would put in a bid for the Olympics. And every four years the attempt would be shot down, though occasionally the city would host Olympic tryouts, as in the run-up to the 1932 Los Angeles Olympics. In 1928 Chicago boosters planning the 1933 Century of Progress Exposition invoked the decision to move the 1904 games in an effort to persuade the Olympic committee to postpone the 1932 games to 1933 and to hold them in conjunction with Chicago's world's fair, but the idea went nowhere. In 1946 and 1947, Mayor Edward Kelly set up a Chicago committee to present a bid to the International Olympic Committee in Stockholm. The city got as far as scoping out sites for the Olympic village, suggesting a lakefront site between 23rd and 31st streets—basically the same site as that in Chicago's 2016 proposal. Organizers were discouraged when they learned Los Angeles was again lobbying for the Olympics, only fourteen years after hosting the 1932 games, but they went ahead anyway, and the head of the *Tribune*'s London bureau, William Fulton, presented the city's case to the committee. Ultimately, Helsinki, Finland, was awarded the games, and Paavo Nurmi had one last moment in the sun when he carried the Olympic flame on the last leg of its journey and lit the Olympic torch.[8]

The disappearance of smaller athletic competitions at Soldier Field was influenced by an ever-increasing demand by park officials that most events—except those sponsored by a favored few organizations—cover their own expenses. An "event in the structure should pay its own costs, where people are charged admission to the structure," V. K. Brown, the Chicago Park District's director of recreation, wrote in a 1945 letter to the Los Angeles recreation superintendent, replying to a query about the stadium. The park commissioners "do not think the taxpayer should contribute to the cost of an event and then be denied admission unless he pays a fee for entrance." Although exceptions appear to have been made for high schools, college events and track meets generally charged admission, and so would have been required to pay their own way. With the sparse turnout for most track events, Soldier Field became a less popular destination for meets—probably contributing further to athletic events' decline. Sponsoring organizations just couldn't pay the fees necessary.[9]

EVERY SPORT—ALMOST

Of course, Soldier Field's builders envisioned the stadium as a center for other amateur sports as well. Some sports had only limited success, and others were more successful than their present lack of popularity might suggest. Robert McCormick, owner of the *Tribune* and friend of Kelly, was a longtime fan of polo, and the 1924 official opening of the stadium included a polo match in which McCormick took part. Polo made a few more appearances at the stadium over the years, once or twice in conjunction with rodeos (see chapter 9), and as a regular feature of the American Legion Fourth of July shows in the late 1930s and early 1940s. In 1938, for example, the 124th Field Artillery team and a Cuban army team played to a 3–3 draw as part of the Legion's celebration.

Another short-lived, albeit well-publicized, sport at Soldier Field was rugby. In 1939 the Chicago Rugby Club (not related to the club of the same name founded in the 1970s) played two games at Soldier Field, one against a Hollywood club and another against a New York–East Coast all-star squad. A number of the players were good enough to have played football professionally, but as the *Tribune* put it, the teams were "playing for nothing but the genuine lust of combat, as rugby is an amateur sport." Chicago won, 24–9, in front of a crowd of about ten thousand, advancing to a Los Angeles game against the Hollywood Lighthorse Lancers for the national amateur rugby championship.[10]

One consequence of the park district's effort to make Soldier Field pay for itself was the introduction of sports and events that might otherwise never have found a widespread Chicago audience. Conversely, in its early years, the stadium had hosted many events in which the South Park Commission sought to showcase the vast array of recreation available in its parks. On May 9, 1925, the stadium hosted an event that not only was unlikely to draw crowds but was almost impossible to view from the stands: the South Parks Marble Championship. Although it sounds odd, the tournament, which included both juvenile and adult competitions, was in keeping with the idea that the stadium was the perfect place to bring new pursuits to a wider audience. It wasn't the only time the marble-playing championship took place at Soldier Field, either. In a tournament held in 1929, Judd Spear, a "youngster of 50" and master mechanic employed by the South Parks, triumphed in the thirty-to-one hundred age category. Yet another championship was held in conjunction with the 1933 world's fair.[11]

After the marble tournaments and a game of motorcycle polo played as part of the 1924 police meet, one of the least likely sports ever at Soldier Field was ski jumping. In late 1924 the South Park commissioners had a skating rink set up at the stadium, but that does not appear to have been repeated until 1936. That year, the Park District set up both a skating rink and a giant ski slide that descended from a mammoth scaffold that extended high above the colonnades. From then until 1938, the U.S. Central Ski Association held its annual ski meet there. (The skating rink appears to have been set up most years the ski jump was.) In 1936 a Chicago-area ski group also sponsored an invitational tournament. At the February 1937 Central Ski Association meet, entertainment included a dogsled race, a ski-equipped car, and a demonstration by the Chicago Figure Skating Club. The jerry-built ski jump was not without its problems, however. At the 1937 *Chicago Daily Times* ski meet, the bottom section of the slide broke, injuring two brothers who were coming down the slope. The ski meets ended after 1938, although there was brief talk of renewing them for 1939. They would be revived only for a brief time, years later.

One sport Soldier Field always has been considered good for, by contrast, is soccer. From 1926 until the early 1950s, local teams regularly played matches—especially amateur league championship games—at the stadium. Professional teams also played there from early on. The National Soccer League of Chicago—then known as the International Soccer Football League of Chicago—was only a few years old when the stadium was built but was already an important part of Chicago sports life. Teams such as Sparta, named after the AC Sparta Club of Prague, were technically amateur but included professional players on their rosters, often blurring the line between full-time athletes and weekend warriors. The first highly publicized amateur matches at Soldier Field were 1927 exhibition games involving Uruguay's national team, which had won the gold medal in soccer at the 1924 Olympics. Uruguay's first opponent was Sparta Chicago, and the South Americans prevailed, with Héctor Pedro Scarone, still Uruguay's all-time leading scorer, scoring the lone goal. That same spring, Vienna's Hakoah soccer club, part of an all-Jewish sports organization, played against the Peel Cup All-Stars, drawn from teams that had participated in the Chicago league's yearly championship. Hakoah had played against a similar all-star team in 1926 at Comiskey Park, and in 1927 lined up matches against the Peel all-stars, Sparta, and an all-star team of the Illinois State Football Association. Hakoah won the first two matches before losing, 2–1, to the Illinois all-stars.[12]

Soccer was a popular sport at the stadium into the early 1930s, though it never drew the crowds that American football did. The Peel Cup final was played at Soldier Field several years, including in 1928 and 1933. Soccer then faded out for a dozen years or more, rarely making an appearance until after World War II, except as part of a few celebrations of cultural heritage, such

One of many teams that competed in softball tournaments at Soldier Field in the 1930s. Courtesy Chicago Park District Special Collections.

as Swedish Day or German Day. The game reappeared after the war, though fewer games were played in any given year than had been in the late 1920s, when soccer matches often dominated the May schedule. In 1947 twenty thousand or more spectators watched a Chicago all-star team play to a tie against Hapoel, a team billed as the champion of Palestine (made up largely of Jewish refugees from Nazism). After fading again in the mid-1950s, soccer reappeared at Soldier Field in the early 1960s, with Peel Cup playoff games for a few years and several exhibition games by international professional teams each year until a Chicago-based professional team took the spotlight in the late 1960s (see chapter 13).[13]

There is no record of baseball games being played at Soldier Field—much less the playoff series the South Park commissioners had anticipated. The stadium is simply too narrow for regulation games. Softball, however, made a few appearances over the years, with national championships for both men and women played there from 1936 through 1939. The arena of those years was large enough to allow five softball diamonds for the 1936 championship, with their home plates along the west stands, on the running track that circled the field. All five were used at once for day games, but only three were used simultaneously for night games. Teams came from forty states and Canada, but rain delayed the beginning of the tournament, which finally started two days late. Most of the teams were supported and sponsored by companies such as the National Screw Manufacturing Co. or Montgomery Ward. About fifteen thousand people watched as Harold "Shifty" Gears, a sheet metal worker for Eastman Kodak in Rochester, New York, held the Cleveland Weaver-Walls to four hits in the final, leading Kodak to a 2–0 win. Gears was a legend in softball; by 1940, after playing for eighteen years, the glasses-wearing amateur had pitched fifty-four no-hit games.[14]

BOXING BRINGS THEM IN

Even as track and field athletics faded from Soldier Field, another traditional amateur sport remained popular, at least for a few years. Boxing became popular among both park district and Catholic school athletes in the late 1920s and 1930s—once it became legal again in 1927 following a three-year period in which Illinois had outlawed it. Long after the stadium hosted its only high-profile professional boxing match, the Jack Dempsey–Gene Tunney bout of 1927 (see chapter 9), youth boxing tournaments were a highly anticipated part of each year's sports calendar.

Amateur boxing at Soldier Field started in 1931 when a Golden Gloves tournament sponsored by the *Tribune* outgrew the Chicago Stadium. *Tribune* sports editor Arch Ward, who had advanced the idea for the Golden Gloves tournament, was an old-fashioned sportswriter who often crossed the line between covering sports and promoting them. (A few years later, Ward would start both the College All-Star Game, which pitted top collegians against the year's professional football champions [see chapter 10], and the baseball All Star Game.) The Chicago-based Golden Gloves tournament, which was held in 1923, before the state ban, and then again starting in 1928, began as a local contest and quickly became a Midwestern and finally a national amateur championship. The Chicago bouts and a New York equivalent, started by the *New York Daily News*, as well as an intercity tournament involving boxers from both cities, had become so popular by 1930 that Ward decided a bigger, better tournament could be held—one involving international competitors.[15]

The first international competitors to take up the Golden Gloves challenge were ten young French boxers, selected from among the winners of their country's annual amateur championships. The group arrived in Chicago on May 7, 1931, for the May 12 matches. Their American opponents, as well as *Tribune* representatives and the French consul to Chicago, met the team at Union Station, with the U.S. boxers shouting "Vive la France!" in welcome. Once again, Soldier Field served to unite cultures through sport. "No matter the outcome, the cause of friendship between two great nations will have prospered," Mayor Anton Cermak told the competitors at a City Hall ceremony. "Victor or vanquished, that rivalry must add to the mutual regard, long standing."[16]

In four short years since becoming legal again, boxing had reestablished itself as a popular sport in Illinois. To make sure that the event could be held in the Chicago Stadium in case of rain, only twenty-one thousand tickets were sold in advance, but on the day of the fights, forty thousand people showed up. Ward compared the seating for the bouts to those for the 1927 Dempsey-Tunney fight, noting that seats that cost $30 for the professional fight would cost 50 cents for the Golden Gloves. The ring was set in the center of the arena, surrounded by twenty-two thousand so-called ringside seats, set on a giant, slightly sloped floor. After a band concert and fireworks, the fights got under way with exhibition matches between Golden Gloves team members and other boxers who had competed in the preliminary rounds of Golden Glove competitions. The international matches started with three American wins; in the first, Leo Rodak of South Chicago beat André Perrier for the flyweight title (112 pounds and under). The Americans went on to win five of the eight fights, although two French alternates also won matches that did not count toward the title.[17]

After the 1931 contest, the *Tribune* sponsored international Golden Gloves competitions for many years, although they appeared at Soldier Field only a few more times. On March 6, 1932, the paper announced that the amateur boxing champions of Germany would travel to Chicago that summer to take on the winners of the city's late-winter Golden Gloves tournament. The German boxers were, in effect, their country's 1932 Olympic boxing team. On the day of the fights, July 27, more than forty-five thousand people showed up—a crowd hailed by organizers as the largest group ever to see an amateur boxing tournament anywhere. The Germans' tactics showed that they had absorbed many of the techniques of American amateur boxing. Chicago's champions looked outclassed at first, as the first three German boxers triumphed. But the Americans' footwork, modeled on that of Dempsey, helped them to win the next three matches and, after another loss, the final one, producing a 4–4 tie. Three members of the German team—bantamweight Ziglarski, featherweight Josef Schleinkofer, and welterweight Erich Campe—went on to win silver medals at the Los Angeles Olympics a few weeks later.[18]

The final Golden Gloves international tournament at Soldier Field came in conjunction with the Century of Progress world's fair in 1933. That year the *Tribune* announced that Chicago's team, the winners of that year's intercity

Golden Gloves tournament, would face a team of Irish boxers. The Irish team had won no medals at the 1932 Olympics but had done better than expected, and that had helped revive interest in the sport in Ireland. Amateur clubs had sprung up throughout the country, and "we are confident we shall show the world at Chicago next summer that we still have plenty of fighting men," the head of Irish amateur boxing wrote the *Tribune*. After the success of the 1932 fights, the *Tribune* had wisely chosen to bring in boxers with ties to another large Chicago ethnic group, and the city's Irish Americans responded enthusiastically. Ethnic rivalries, though damped down by events such as the Prep Bowl, still ran strong, and Soldier Field helped them to play out in a friendly manner. When the Irish team arrived at Union Station on July 20, crowds packed the station and brought traffic outside to a standstill. In the two weeks before the August 2 tournament, the Irish boxers lived at the Midwest Athletic Club at Hamlin Avenue and Madison Street, in the heart of the Irish West Side. (The club building still stands, and is listed on the National Register of Historic Places.) Chicago treated the boxers to several receptions, including one at Garfield Park, across the street from the athletic club, that police said drew two hundred thousand people or more.

Rain on August 2 forced a one-day postponement. But despite the delay, about forty-eight thousand people showed up to see the fights. The Irish boxers entered the arena to the strains of "The Wearing of the Green," and the first two bouts went to the foreign team. "Thereafter, however, the Irish adherents had little to cheer for save the determination and fighting spirit of the visiting team," wrote Warren Brown in the *Herald and Examiner*. Irish heavyweight champion Patrick Mulligan was knocked out and his ankle broken, and his team lost to Chicago, six matches to two.[19]

As successful as they were, the Golden Gloves events at Soldier Field were something of a disappointment; even the largest crowds did not come close to filling the vast stadium. After 1933 organizers usually held the contests at the Chicago Stadium. But boxing did not disappear from Soldier Field immediately. Beginning in 1936 the Chicago Catholic Youth Organization held intercity and then international boxing tournaments at the stadium for several years. The first bouts were against New York's Catholic Youth Association, the second annual intercity boxing meet between the two groups. Sports wags considered Chicago's team weaker than usual, because several of its best boxers had traveled to the 1936 Berlin Olympics. But the Chicago CYO triumphed in eleven of sixteen matches, held July 22 before a crowd of about thirty-eight thousand. The proceeds of the tournament went to the CYO Milk Fund to help feed thirty-five thousand students in nonsectarian summer schools run at Chicago Catholic schools.[20]

The matches took on an international flavor the following year, when the CYO team faced off against sixteen South American boxers, including eight members of the Argentine Olympic boxing team, which had won four medals at the 1936 Olympics. The South Americans received much the same treatment as their Irish counterparts had four years before, although only thirty thousand people showed up for a rally in their honor at Garfield Park. The Olympic medal winners were not among the boxers who came to Chicago, however, and the CYO again won eleven of its sixteen matches. The CYO tied against an Irish amateur team in 1939 and won tournaments against groups of Hawaiian boxers in 1940 and 1941. Although the bouts consistently drew thirty thousand fans or more, after World War II they did not reappear at Soldier Field.[21] While they lasted, though, the bouts were a lucrative fund-raiser for the CYO, and they helped to bring to Chicagoans' attention the prowess of their homegrown pugilists. At the same time, the matches highlighted one of the most democratic of sports—and one that possessed simultaneously a great deal of prestige and an association with organized crime. Like the Prep Bowl, the CYO matches helped to bring Catholics further into mainstream Chicago society, and politics. Boxing was a harder sell, however, and it did a lot less than the Prep Bowl to mainstream the youth involved. Just as important over the years was the stadium's role as a forum for Chicagoans hoping to change their city, just as the adherents of the City Beautiful movement had wished before them.

5   *A Stage for Acceptable Dissent*

For most of the twentieth century, political groups opposed to Chicago's Democratic machine had difficulty getting access to Soldier Field, except when granting them a place on the stadium's civic stage would pacify a group with Democratic ties or please an individual connected to one of the party's leaders.

Over the years, a hierarchy of public gathering places developed. Chicago Stadium, the Coliseum, and the Amphitheatre all provided important venues for political rallies and conventions, but organizers seeking public recognition for their events were more likely to request the use of Soldier Field. If you could get Soldier Field, you could claim to be holding your event in the city's greatest venue. The denial of a permit, by contrast, might signal social disapproval—or at least, the disapproval of Chicago's Democratic Party. Several national political leaders, including Harry Truman, spoke at the stadium more than once, often at the beginning of their movements, or at a high point. By exercising their ability to keep out its rivals, or at least groups that lacked a large Democratic constituency, Chicago Democrats made it more difficult for competitors to gain wide public recognition while allowing the favored to take the limelight.

SOME SAY ARMISTICE MEANS PEACE

After the Great War and the surge of militaristic nationalism it provoked, the United States went through a period of resurgent isolationism, especially among old-style Democrats and conservative Republicans. Many populist political leaders preached a doctrine of "America First," and many Americans thought Armistice Day should mark a return to focusing on domestic troubles. Soldier Field played a role in one episode of us-versus-them politics that focused many Americans on the conflict U.S. leaders were experiencing with the country's Great War allies.

In 1928 William Randolph Hearst's newspapers, including the *Herald and Examiner*, published the details of a secret naval pact between Britain and France. In 1930 Hearst visited Europe, traveling to Germany and Italy before arriving in Paris. When he tried to check into a hotel there, Hearst received an expulsion order from the French government, requiring him to leave the country within thirty-six hours "because his newspapers were considered 'hostile' to France," according to a *New York Times* report. At first, Hearst kept his ejection secret, only making it public when a reporter phoned him to ask why he had left France. In a sharply sarcastic statement he then released, Hearst said the French commissioners who delivered the order had informed him he was "an enemy of France and a danger in their midst."[1]

With the mass media Hearst had helped to create working on his behalf, the banishment provoked an immediate and fierce reaction in the United States. When he returned to the country, Hearst found eager allies in Chicago mayor Big Bill Thompson and Boston mayor James M. Curley. Though a longtime Democrat, Hearst had at times made common cause with the Republican Thompson because of the mayor's America First political views. Thompson invited him to be part of that year's Chicago Day celebration, which commemorated the October 9 date of the Chicago Fire. The event was to include a parade and culminate in ceremonies and speeches, including one by Hearst, at Soldier Field. The stadium was controlled by South Park Commission president Edward Kelly, a Democrat, but Thompson had helped Kelly secure one of the biggest events ever staged at the venue, the Jack Dempsey–Gene Tunney boxing match. So Kelly allowed Thompson's Chicago Day celebration to take over the stadium for a day.[2]

Chicago Day 1930 was one of a number of attempts by city leaders—especially Republicans like Thompson—to counteract the dismal mood that had descended on the United States with the onset of the Great Depression the previous year. Some of these events served to show off the city's culture in the hope of attracting tourism, while others were fund-raisers for the many who were out of work. For the most part, partisan politics were not overtly on the program, though Thompson and other boosters did have an interest in getting voters to see the positive aspects of city life. The twenty-five-mile Chicago Day parade followed the circuit of Chicago's boulevard system before arriving at Soldier Field, where about fifty thousand people waited to see Hearst and the city leaders accompanying him. Thompson waved his signature cowboy hat as Hearst sat sedately next to him in the mayor's open car.

By the time Hearst got up to speak following a rendition of Thompson's campaign song—"America First," of course—much of the crowd had melted away. But Thompson seemed unperturbed. "Thanks to this great organization of Republicans and Democrats, we will go forward to another Chicago day and make jobs and prosperity for the people," Thompson said. He thanked Kelly for hosting the event at Soldier Field before introducing Hearst as "the greatest living American."[3] Hearst himself provided a little verbal stretching. It was a practical application of Chicago's "I Will" spirit that had allowed his correspondent to obtain the secret French-English documents, he said, and not any sort of dishonesty.[4]

Over the next decade, Hearst's and Thompson's isolationism found a ready audience. In Chicago and elsewhere, as the country struggled to regain its economic footing, many disaffected Americans turned to leaders who attributed the country's travails to its domination by purportedly foreign-influenced elements and what early American leaders had called "entanglements" with Europe. Most Americans, the memory of a horrific Great War still in their minds, hoped simply to sit out Europe's next conflict. Even after Germany invaded Poland in 1939, the Gallup Poll found that 84 percent of Americans opposed sending U.S. troops or naval forces to aid England and France.[5]

FATHER COUGHLIN LOSES OUT

In the years leading up to World War II, one of the most popular but controversial personalities in the United States was the Reverend Charles E. Coughlin, a Detroit diocesan priest who rode the tide of America First to fame as one of the nation's first radio preachers. Though his superiors would later silence him when his rhetoric devolved into anti-Semitic rantings, in the early to mid-1930s he drew crowds wherever he went. Coughlin had started as a radio preacher a half decade before, wholeheartedly endorsing Franklin Roosevelt when the New York governor first ran for president. He even spoke at the 1932 Democratic convention in Chicago, coining the phrase "Roosevelt or Ruin" to describe what he saw as the stark choice facing American voters. By 1934, however, a disillusioned Coughlin had founded the National Union for Social Justice, in part to advocate policies opposed to Roosevelt's. By May 1935, when he requested a permit for a rally at Soldier Field, Coughlin had turned against Roosevelt entirely. Because Coughlin's group had members throughout the Midwest, Chicago was a natural place to hold a rally, and Coughlin sent an advance man, E. J. Steiner, to appear before the park district board on his behalf. The board president, Robert J. Dunham, spoke against giving Coughlin a permit, on the grounds that he and his group would preach "controversial political propaganda." The unanimous vote against the permit was no surprise to Steiner, given the board's deference to Kelly, who was by then mayor. "We had expected it but we wanted to give them a chance to refuse us," Steiner told reporters.[6]

The board's decision set up the Chicago Park District for a long battle with Coughlin—and a long period of public ridicule. Coughlin defiantly said the mass meeting would go ahead on June 12 in Chicago. The Chicago Civil Liberties Committee sent a telegram to Dunham, protesting the refusal to issue a permit to Coughlin and urging the board to reconsider.[7] On June 1 Coughlin renewed his request, firing off a sharply worded telegram to Dunham that all but accused the board of burning the Constitution: "Even the sovereign power of the federal government cannot interfere with the right of the people peaceably to assemble."[8]

Dunham replied in a two-page letter that the board's decision would stand. The stadium and other park facilities were created for recreation and health purposes, not for promoting political viewpoints that many Chicagoans might find objectionable. The parks existed for nonpartisan recreation, Dunham wrote, and there were plenty of private places in Chicago where Coughlin could hold his rally.[9] Practical considerations figured in too. In most cases since its opening in 1924, agreements for the use of the field had been negotiated months ahead of time and signed at least five or six weeks in advance.[10] Still, it was possible to set up the field relatively quickly, if need be. So it's unlikely anything other than the political enmity between Coughlin and the New Dealers motivated the board's decision.

On learning of Dunham's decision, Coughlin almost immediately retained a lawyer. His group claimed seven million members by 1935, so he could afford the best. Showing that he knew how things worked in the city, Coughlin hired a former Chicago corporation counsel, Samuel Ettelson, who echoed his client's assertion of his constitutional rights to peaceable assembly and free speech.[11]

Reaction to the park board's decision was mixed, but the first volley of ridicule was discharged within a few days of Dunham's letter. The *Chicago Heights Star* said in an editorial, signed "Starling," that the board was afraid Coughlin might "start a fight about matters of principle." But hadn't a real fight, the Dempsey-Tunney boxing match, been fought in the stadium a few years before, "with the benediction of the board"? Obviously, yes—so Father Coughlin's "snubbing" meant that, in the board's view, boxing was all right, "but it is dangerous and reprehensible . . . to argue about such questions as the money system and the future of the country."[12]

Coughlin's fight for the stadium went on for another year, during which successive levels of the Illinois courts issued conflicting decisions as to whether he should get a permit. Coughlin vowed to fight to the finish, but the Illinois Supreme Court finally found that the Chicago Park District had the discretion to decide who could use the stadium, and thus no constitutional questions were involved. As he fought on, Coughlin held a couple of large rallies in Chicago, but never one at Soldier Field.[13]

Coughlin's was not the only more or less controversial group denied use of the the stadium. A few weeks after he first asked for a permit, other opponents of the New Deal proposed having a "Constitution Day" at the stadium. The board nixed their permit as well, forcing them to use Chicago Stadium, where they received some publicity, but much less than they would have at Soldier Field.[14] The district also denied several permits for the Ku Klux Klan over the years.

LINDBERGH BECKONS TO CHICAGO

One of the few public figures allowed to hold an anti-Roosevelt event at the stadium had close connections to *Tribune* owner Robert McCormick, who arguably had enough influence with Edward Kelly to use the field whenever he wanted. Charles Lindbergh, who held a high place in the American pantheon following his transatlantic flight in 1927, gave speeches at Soldier Field that year and, more contentiously, in 1940, both of them organized by McCormick.

Aviators such as Lindbergh were among the rock stars of their era. Following World War I, which Lindbergh had been too young to participate in (he was sixteen when it ended), he dropped out of the University of Wisconsin and soon was attempting new feats of flying. Lindbergh spent a little over a year as an aviator for hire in Saint Louis and inaugurated airmail service between Saint Louis and Chicago in April 1926.

In May 1927 Lindbergh had completed the first nonstop transatlantic flight, from New York to Paris. His first Soldier Field appearance came less than three months later, in the middle of a national tour. (His previous stop was in Detroit, where he gave Henry Ford his first two airplane rides.)[15] McCormick, a friend of Lindbergh's, had recruited the Chicago Association of Commerce to host the famed pilot, and the city went all out for his visit, with groups such as the Boy Scouts preparing weeks in advance to welcome him. Lindbergh was to guide his plane, the *Spirit of St. Louis*, nicknamed "We," over downtown; land at the municipal airport (now Midway); and then drive to Comiskey Park and on to Soldier Field.[16]

The day before Lindbergh's visit, bunting and flags hung from many homes and businesses, and Soldier Field's sound system had been checked and rechecked. Each of the city's hundred Boy Scout troops had chosen a scout to represent it in a delegation that was to greet Lindbergh and escort him to the stadium.[17] Mayor Thompson, always ready to bask in the glory of another, declared August 13 "Lindbergh Day." Lindbergh was coming to Chicago not to seek glory, but to advance the cause of aviation, Thompson said.[18]

Lindbergh flew into the city about 1:45 p.m. that Saturday afternoon, and flew over downtown as far north as Chicago Avenue, to the cheers of hundreds of thousands people gathered on the lakefront. The *Spirit of St. Louis* roared over the Michigan Avenue Bridge, a link between the north and south sides of the city envisioned by Daniel Burnham and Edward Bennett in the 1909 plan. He flew over Soldier Field, then on to the airport, where forty thousand waited fifteen people deep to see him. There, police had the hardest time of the day keeping the crowd in check as they rushed toward his plane the moment it hit the runway.[19]

The visit by Lindbergh coincided with the sixth annual Chicago police meet, which for many years was held at Soldier Field but that year was at Comiskey Park. The host committee brought the flier there first before taking him to Soldier Field. Thousands more people lined his route through the city. Arriving at Soldier Field, the convertible in which Lindbergh was riding wheeled around the park with the "hero of the hour" seated on the trunk, his legs dangling onto the rear seat. The crowd broke into deafening cheers. Lindbergh, dressed in a rakish quarter-length leather overcoat with one button fastened, waved to the crowd as the car made its way around the field. When the car stopped at the reviewing stand, Thompson, dressed in a light-colored suit, took up a megaphone. "This is America's hero!" he announced to the crowd. Lindbergh opened his mouth to speak but was drowned out. After the noise died down, Chicago police chief Michael Hughes pinned a gold star on him, making him an honorary member of the department.[20]

Lindbergh's speech advocated developing aviation as a means of tying Chicago more closely to other cities and spurring economic development—especially with the addition of a planned lakefront airport. "Chicago has been in a position to observe the development of aviation as probably no other city in the world," Lindbergh told the crowd, detailing how airmail had developed, between Saint Louis and Chicago and New York and Chicago. "You have a good airport in Chicago. I understand that you intend to construct a landing field on the lake front. If so it will probably be one of the best, if not the best, in the country. . . . By constructing such an air field, you will do more to put your city out front of other large cities." Given Lindbergh's acclaim at the time, even the presentations of gifts to the aviator at an evening banquet had to be limited, and many groups failed to get in.[21]

But the hero of 1927 would not be so highly esteemed on his next visit to Soldier Field. In 1940 Lindbergh—who had by then spent several years in Europe, including much time in Germany—returned to Chicago to lead a rally against U.S. involvement in the new European war. The rally was organized by a number of city leaders, including Avery Brundage—the vice president of the International Olympic Committee, who later was kicked out of the America

Aviator Charles A. Lindbergh addresses a crowd at Soldier Field in 1927. Courtesy Chicago History Museum. Chicago Daily News archive, glass negative DN-0083855.

First movement for being too pro-Nazi (and whose company had lost out in bidding to build Soldier Field)—but also the heads of many veterans groups and several business associations.[22] That this antiwar rally was able to attract as much support as it did speaks to the number of Chicagoans who still held anti-interventionist sentiments before the bombing of Pearl Harbor. Both the *Tribune* and Hearst's papers were isolationist, and isolationist groups such as We the Mothers Mobilize for America were based in Chicago.

About forty thousand people—half the number who had heard his speech in 1927—greeted Lindbergh at the stadium. There he decried the growing drumbeat for America's entry into the war and predicted that the people would not stand for intervention: "When the danger of foreign war was fully realized by our people, the underlying tradition of American independence arose, and in recent weeks its voice thundered through the weaker cries for war." Lindbergh counseled against thinking that the defeat of England and France would have tragic consequences: "In the past we have dealt with a Europe dominated by England and France. In the future we may have to deal with a Europe dominated by Germany. But whether England or Germany wins this war, western civilization will still depend on two great centers, one in each hemisphere."

Today it is hard to imagine how a respected public figure could be as opposed to intervention in World War II as Lindbergh was. But we must imagine the mood of the country in the 1930s, when the United States was struggling to feed its own people and memories of the Great War were still fresh.

The *Tribune* hailed Lindbergh's Soldier Field speech, but many others, throughout the country, saw it as more evidence that he was a puppet of Hitler. The lack of a large crowd shows that even in heavily German cities like Chicago, sentiment was turning toward Roosevelt's internationalist views. The Chicago speech, like others he gave that summer and fall, led to denunciations both by ordinary citizens and by more liberal journalists and politicians. The liberal New York newspaper *PM* editorialized against Lindbergh as "Spokesman No. 1 of the Fifth Column," a reference to subversives who had supposedly undermined the Spanish Republican government in Madrid during the Spanish Civil War. Lindbergh's FBI file, started in the late 1930s when he returned from living in Europe, runs to more than thirteen hundred pages. When the war came, Lindbergh tried to enlist but was denied because of his suspect connections to Germany, and ended up working as an aviation consultant for Henry Ford.[23]

Charles Lindbergh at Soldier Field in 1940. Courtesy Chicago Tribune.

GENERAL MACARTHUR COUNSELS WAR

War opponents weren't the only dissidents to speak at Soldier Field. General Douglas MacArthur, one of the rare Republican to be given the platform, spoke at a rally backed by then-mayor Martin Kennelly at the height of a conflict with a Democratic president. MacArthur's warm reception in 1951 also can be read as an endorsement of the anticommunist fervor that was gripping America. As commander of U.S. troops in Korea, MacArthur had defied President Truman, threatening to expand the Korean War and attack North Korea's ally, China, more directly. Truman, in response, had relieved him of his command. On his return to the United States, MacArthur headed to the Midwest for a series of events intended to highlight support for his position in the heart of the country.

Chicago hailed MacArthur when he arrived on April 26. (Something that might not have happened had Kelly still been mayor.) Though a ticker-tape parade was usual for visiting heroes at the time, it was almost unheard of to turn on Buckingham Fountain several weeks early, as was done for MacArthur. In all, between 3 million and 4.5 million people greeted the general in the streets of the city, and many appeared to agree with a hand-painted sign held by South Sider Dennis O'Keefe or one of his friends, who were among a group that gathered near the Tribune Tower, waiting to see MacArthur. It read, referring to Truman's World War I rank, "Since When Does a Captain Fire a General?"[24]

In his speech that night before about fifty-five thousand people at Soldier Field, MacArthur argued that what was being ignored in Korea was what should have been the objective of the war: "victory over the nation and men who without provocation or justification have warred against us"—in other words, defeating China. The lack of a clear political policy regarding China—a "political vacuum"—and interference by other United Nations allies in war planning, were preventing victory, he said. At the same time, MacArthur called for a "realistic" policy aimed at minimizing the loss of American lives. The crowd, according to the *Tribune*, had expected nothing more than a "routine greeting." Instead, MacArthur's sharp rhetoric resulted in his speech being interrupted nineteen times by applause and cheering. Though he said his public life was over, MacArthur said he would "continue to fight against that greatest scourge of mankind, communism, as long as God gives me the power to fight." Although MacArthur's was far from the first speech televised from Soldier Field, it was an early example of how a speech may be perceived differently by those in attendance and those at home. Television, it appears, failed to convey the emotional impact of MacArthur's speech, and the audience at home reportedly felt little of the passion experienced by those in the stadium.[25]

After his Chicago speech, MacArthur went to Washington, giving his famous "old soldiers never die, they just fade away" speech to Congress. He was talked about as a vice presidential running mate for Senator Howard Taft in 1952, but Taft lost the nomination to General Dwight Eisenhower. MacArthur faded into relative obscurity, to be sought for counsel by President John Kennedy briefly in the early 1960s, following the Bay of Pigs debacle.

Later in the 1950s, under the leadership of Erwin "Red" Weiner, the Chicago Park District became more tolerant of some dissenters—as long as they appeared to have a good deal of local backing. As divisive as some political events at Soldier Field have been, they have also often served as great unifiers for movements striving for recognition by the larger Chicago society. The stadium's role as a place to bring together large groups as they entered the mainstream of American culture began early in its history. But it was not a political event that marked the stadium as the focus for Chicago's public display of American culture and politics. A Catholic religious festival, unprecedented in American life, made Soldier Field the place to be noticed by Chicago—and the whole country.

The City's Altar

Soldier Field might not have been the perfect place for a football game, as many people remarked over the years, but it was ideal for mass rallies. Some of these, of course, were political, but to an even greater extent the major religious gatherings held there demonstrate how Soldier Field in fact fulfilled the dream of City Beautiful advocates.

A 1954 Catholic Holy Hour event holds the official record for the largest single event at Soldier Field, but accounts from the time indicate that the mass at the center of the 1926 Eucharistic Congress may have been larger. Cardinal George Mundelein began angling for the event at least two years earlier, when he asked Pope Pius XI to name Chicago as the host city for the next Eucharistic Congress. Such assemblies are gatherings focused on veneration of the Eucharist, also known as communion, and on discussions of the theology of the sacrament in Catholic life. The congresses had originated in France in 1881, and by 1926 twenty-seven had been held, mostly in Europe and Asia, with only one in the Americas, in Montreal in 1910. Bringing a Eucharistic Congress to Chicago would show the entire Catholic world, and Mundelein hoped, non-Catholic Americans, the importance of the church in U.S. culture. Mundelein promised the pope "a million communicants as a spiritual banquet to your august presence."[1] Though the pope did not come, railroad executives estimated that the Congress did indeed draw about a million people to Chicago.[2]

The first official word came in February 1925, when Mundelein announced that Pius had approved holding the next congress in Chicago. It was to be the largest Roman Catholic gathering in the church's nineteen-hundred-year history, he bragged. All the Catholic bishops from the

United States would attend, as would bishops and cardinals from every continent.[3]

Chicago was, at the time, still run largely by a Protestant elite, some of whom harbored deep prejudices against the Church of Rome. The loyalty of Catholics to the United States was often called into question, due to their putative allegiance to the pope, who until a few decades before had ruled much of Italy. Mundelein knew that holding the congress in Chicago could help to solidify the Catholic Church in Chicago as a force to be reckoned with. He would flaunt his flock's patriotism before Catholics from around the world to the city.

Detailed planning for the event began almost immediately. The president of the Eucharistic Congress, Bishop Thomas Louis Heylen of Namur, Belgium, and its secretary, Count Henri D'Yanville, of Paris, journeyed to Chicago in March 1925 to start scouting locations and conferring with railroad and steamship companies about transportation.[4] Preparations went into full swing in January 1926, as the South Park Commission approved a contract to allow several masses at Soldier Field as part of the congress.[5] The 1910 congress in Montreal had been the last such event, and the Catholic Church in the United States expected a massive turnout, with clergy and lay people coming from across the globe. Indeed, response was so overwhelming that by February organizers announced that the Eucharistic Congress would start three days earlier than originally planned, making it a weeklong event. "Nothing that has ever happened in the history of Chicago will put Chicago on the map like this congress," Monseigneur C. J. Quille, the general secretary of the congress, told the press.[6]

Catholics from around the world soon began to select delegates to the congress. In March all the bishops of Poland met in Warsaw and voted to send a bishop, a priest, and a professor from the University of Lublin as the country's primary representatives.[7] In Mexico, where the Catholic Church was in the midst of a long power struggle with the secular authorities, planning began for the largest pilgrimage ever to a foreign country, larger even than pilgrimages to Rome.[8]

Meetings planned to coincide with the congress were to be conducted in at least sixteen languages, not counting Latin. By the end of April representatives from the German delegation were already in Chicago planning their meeting, to be held in the Broadway Armory; the French delegation was to use the 16th Street Armory on Michigan Avenue, and the Italian group was to use Navy Pier (then known as Municipal Pier).[9]

Throughout the spring, the *Tribune*, which had a history of anti-Catholicism, broke with that tradition and ran a number of articles, several of them by Catholic priests, explaining in detail the meaning of the Eucharistic Congress.[10] A month before the congress, a regular contributor to the *Tribune*,

Kathleen McLaughlin, worried that while most in the area probably knew something of the logistics of the congress—how transportation and traffic would be handled and thousands of people housed—fewer understood why all these Catholics were about to converge on Chicago. She went on to explain that Christ, according to Catholic doctrine, had instituted the Eucharist at the Last Supper, and that the bread and wine consumed in the sacrament were truly his body and blood.[11]

Even as discussions of the Real Presence graced the pages of an uncharacteristically tolerant Chicago newspaper, local businesspeople focused on the more mundane aspects of what amounted to a giant convention—a juxtaposition not unlike the blending of high-flown City Beautiful rhetoric and pragmatic political and commercial interests that had led to the stadium's construction. From the start the dual purpose of Soldier Field had been to bring citizens together and to enrich the city by drawing visitors. Each successful event held there brought new revenues into government coffers, and padded the bottom line of Chicago restaurants, hotels, and department stores.

Twenty-five committees drawn from various civic groups collaborated to ensure that the congress ran smoothly. The Chicago Association of Commerce and the Hotel Owners' Association worked on housing, while railroad and steamship companies offered special rates for those attending. The Rock Island Line announced that each of its trains bound for the congress would carry a special missionary mass kit, containing everything needed to say mass, including vestments, a chalice, and other essential containers.[12] Transportation companies also sketched out plans to handle visitors who were unable to find accommodations; sleeping and dining cars would be parked on spur tracks and boats docked in Lake Michigan and along the Chicago River. All in all, one correspondent wrote, "Visitors can be assured of a courteous and gallant welcome."[13]

Laypeople who were part of the effort to host the pilgrims planned to entertain and guide them so that they would "be able to carry home with them a comprehensive story of the greatness of Chicago."[14] Others focused specifically on the financial benefits the event would bring to the city. The Chicago Association of Commerce estimated pilgrims would spend about $15 million during the congress ($186 million in 2008 dollars). The group's president, George Hull Porter, said that the event "represents to Chicago more cash per day spent than any other meeting ever held here. . . . There will be a great reward for the city if the congress is handled properly."[15]

Cardinal Mundelein, preparing for his archdiocese's moment of glory, preferred not to encourage souvenir sellers, but he did want to make sure that Catholics who attended the congress received a memento of their participation. His solution was to commission a special bronze medal by Silvio

Procession from the Field Museum into Soldier Field at the start of the Eucharistic Congress, June 1926. Much of the stadium had yet to be completed; there are, for instance, no permanent stands between the north end of the west colonnade and the museum. In the background (upper left), machines pump water from behind dams in order to extend the lakefront east of the stadium. Courtesy Chicago History Museum. Chicago Daily News archive, glass negative DN-0081914.

Silva, the official medal artist for the Vatican. A million were ordered, and they started arriving almost two months before the congress, in a shipment of one ton of the medals.[16]

On May 21, Count D'Yanville, the secretary of the Congress, arrived in Chicago. Described by one observer as having "the vigor of a LaSalle Street bond salesman," the sixty-year-old count moved through the city with whirlwind speed to check on various preparations.[17]

Meanwhile, workers rushed to erect giant altars at Soldier Field and, thirty-five miles to the north, at a seminary in the village of Mundelein, the latter surrounded by fifteen thrones for fifteen cardinals. At Soldier Field the altar arose under a latticework of scaffolding alongside intense construction on the stadium itself. At the time of the congress, the south stands were still under construction, as were the north end of the east and west stands—but the stadium's final official opening, the Army-Navy football game, was slated for that November. Pilgrims would find the impressive new stadium a work in progress, with cranes, concrete forms, and piles of lumber littering the landscape.[18] A peristyle draped with laurel marked the north end of the altar, with the columns surmounted alternately by crosses and bronze eagles. As a note of welcome, a similar peristyle surrounded City Hall and the County Building, with a shield of welcome attached to each column.

On June 6 the papal delegation to the congress set sail from France aboard the *Aquitania*, which flew the papal flag. Headed by Cardinal Giovanni Vincenzo Bonzano, the group included five other cardinals and sixty bishops.[19] Over the next two weeks, numerous princes of the Catholic Church arrived in New York, and from there on June 16, after a rousing reception by New York dignitaries, they embarked for Chicago on a train with cardinal-red cars.[20] It was all city and railroad police could do to keep in line the thousands of people who jammed Grand Central Station's massive main room and train platforms to see off Bonzano and the other cardinals. The crowd gave a final cheer as the train pulled out of the station, and the clergy gave a final blessing.[21]

Along the way to Chicago, tens of thousands of people turned out in "what appeared as a continuous line 960 miles long" to glimpse the train, many kneeling and taking off their hats out of respect. Reaching Chicago on June 17, the cardinals were welcomed by Mayor William Dever, thirty-five aldermen, and large, enthusiastic crowds—by then almost a hundred thousand pilgrims had already flooded into the city, bolstering the ranks of resident spectators (and making hotel rooms hard to come by).[22] The crowds could scarcely be contained. As with Lindbergh's visit the following year, police locked arms to keep people outside the station from overwhelming the car in which Mundelein and Bonzano rode. Even so, a number of spectators broke through and kissed Bonzano's ring.[23]

Bonzano had last visited Chicago in 1921, but in the five years since, many of the buildings that still define the Chicago skyline had risen along Michigan Avenue: the Wrigley Building, the London Guaranty Building, the Allerton Club Building (now the Crain's Building and Allerton Hotel). Mundelein pointed these out as they drove to Holy Name Cathedral, where in a short prayer service Bonzano delivered a blessing in the name of the pope. Bonzano told the *Tribune* that he was impressed by the city's achievements but added that the Eucharistic Congress could signal the beginning of the city's greatest era:

> I join with the rest of the world in offering to Chicago my heartiest congratulations on the proud pinnacle of success to which it has attained. . . . From an outpost

Eucharistic Congress at Soldier Field, June 1926. Note the prevalence of American flags, reflecting Cardinal Mundelein's wish to emphasize the loyalty of U.S. Catholics to their country. Courtesy Chicago Park District Special Collections.

on the shore of Lake Michigan to her present size, she shows a development for which history has no parallel. . . . Her unprecedented growth offers a field for the utmost rational conjecture. Be that conjecture as each one wishes it, may not the selection of your city by the vicar of Christ for the first Eucharistic Congress in the United States indicate the beginning of its realization; for I consider no greater blessing has ever come to your city than the one the Holy Father conferred upon her when he selected Chicago for this congress.[24]

At Soldier Field, the altar for the congress was almost complete. The sanctu-

ary, 30 feet above the field, stretched 224 feet long and 214 wide, and rising over the altar was a baldacchino, a golden canopy held up by four columns, surmounted by a cross. All the histories and guidebooks of the congress mention that this setting was modeled on the altar and sanctuary at Saint Paul-outside-the-Walls in Rome (a statement that may perplex recent visitors to that church, as the baldacchino now in place looks nothing like the one that figures prominently in almost all the photographs of the masses at Soldier Field).[25]

The unfinished stands held too few people for the ceremonies of the

Eucharistic Congress and so were supplemented with bleachers. There were also seventy thousand seats on the playing field itself, used primarily for the choirs that sang at the masses on three successive days. At each of the sessions, the stadium seated about 175,000 people; another 50,000 stood in every available space inside the stadium, while as many as 200,000 people, depending on the session, stood outside.[26]

The first day of events at Soldier Field opened at 10 a.m. on Monday, June 21—designated as Children's Day. Vehicles were barred from much of downtown, so the crowds making their way to the stadium, beginning before dawn, had little to block their path.[27] It was estimated that some six hundred thousand people had arrived for the congress by that first day. And just in case more devotees were needed, Mayor Dever allowed all Catholics who asked ahead of time to take the day off from their city jobs.[28]

Children chosen for the day's choir had been rehearsing for weeks, and early that morning they were quickly fed, dressed, and taken to their Catholic schools, where they boarded buses or cars bound for Soldier Field. They arrived in large groups, by parish, and filed into the center of the arena. The morning started out sunny but windy, and for a time rain threatened. A blare of trumpets sounded, and the cardinals and other priests started marching from the Field Museum toward the altar. All did not go as planned. The tens of thousands of eager pilgrims had so crowded the area north of the stadium and the stadium bowl itself that police had a difficult time clearing a path for the clergy. It took the procession almost an hour to get from the Field Museum to the altar—about one-tenth of a mile.[29]

One of the largest organs built up to that time in the United States had been installed by George Kilgen & Sons of St. Louis below the east stands. The almost outdoor conditions of the stadium required the builders to conduct a number of experiments to make sure it would be able to function given Chicago's volatile lakefront weather. But it was when the bishops ascended the stairs that the extensive sound system got its first real tryout. At first the wind off the lake made it difficult to hear anything coming out of the loudspeakers—except the organ. In era in which amplification was a novelty, the crowd was awed. "The music seemed to come out of the air itself," the official chronicler of the congress wrote.[30]

As Cardinal Mundelein came into view of the choir, the children, who had been applauding throughout the procession, clapped even more furiously, until Mundelein signaled them to quiet down. Cardinals and bishops ascended the dozens of green-painted, red-carpeted steps, with a single long carpet of red flowing down onto the field. When Bonzano reached the altar, the crowd rose to receive the first blessing of the mass.[31] The sixty-two-thousand-voice children's choir, dressed in papal colors, gold and white, sung the Latin mass—the *Missa de Angelis*, or "Mass of the Angels." Glenn Dillard

Gunn of the *Chicago Herald-Examiner* described the mass, composed by Irish monk Saint John Dunstable, as "lovely, simple music, pure Gregorian in mode, and the children, whose ranks completely filled the field between crowded tiers of the stadium, sang it simply, without effort at other expression than that which belongs to the song of childhood."[32]

Police estimated that only 160,000 of the 400,000 people who showed up for the mass were able to get into the stadium itself. And not all who did got a good look at the action; some women—perhaps mothers hoping to catch a glimpse of their children in their starring moment—reportedly used their vanity mirrors as periscopes to get a better view.[33] The crowd was a cross-section of the burgeoning Catholic community, which was usually divided by national origin or by parish (and often by both). As one report put it, "Men in frock coats accompanied by women attired to fashion's latest dictate, might be seen wedged side by side in this great crowd with Italian immigrant women surrounded by their little ones. Pilgrims from the Antipodes gazed over the shoulders of Catholic Negroes from Tennessee. Questions put in French were answered by neighbors who spoke German."[34]

Nearly seventy-five years later, one of the participants recalled how, before the Eucharistic Congress, his main contact with life outside his neighborhood of Bridgeport was counting the number of Buicks and Chryslers that passed by on Archer Avenue. At the congress, though, he was crowded in with Catholics from all over the city, and from places as far away as Philadelphia, Alaska, and Africa. "It was like a coming-of-age party for the church in Chicago. Catholics were flexing their muscles," the Reverend Edward Skupien told a reporter in 2000, when he was eighty-six. "They wanted to show they were somebody. To me, it was just like getting a side door into heaven." "Never in history," the *Tribune* noted, "have so many persons lifted their voices in the solemn devotional of the Catholic Church—the celebration of the mass."[35]

Archbishop Michael J. Curley of Baltimore delivered the homily, comparing the power of prayer to the power of governments. Prayer, he said, is a universal human need, so much so that "man might be defined as a praying animal." Jesus could have "set up an Empire into which all the nations of the earth should be brought, but He preferred to establish His kingdom in the hearts of men."[36] After a pontifical blessing ended the mass, "thousands of devout poured into the field from the stands and pressed inward through the policed ground to the space before the great outdoor altar." The worshippers continued to press forward until organizers used the public address system to ask people to move from the arena, and to warn those who had moved toward the altar that the wooden structure could not hold them all. Many did leave the stadium, but as many as thirty thousand others waited for hours for their turn to approach the altar.[37]

Much of the congress took place in other venues, and some of those disparate programs were impressive on their own, such as the Latin American meeting on Navy Pier, which included more than a thousand priests.[38] But only the events at Soldier Field brought all the pilgrims together as one crowd, and thus demonstrated to the world the reach and the power of the Roman Church, as Mundelein had hoped.

Though the first day, with its children's choir, was probably the most impressive, two more days of masses at the stadium followed, including three full general meetings. On Tuesday, June 22, officials estimated that more people came together at Soldier Field than had ever gathered in one arena in a single day, as two meetings were held in the stadium—a women's mass in the morning, and a men's meeting with a benediction in the evening. More than 170,000 women, including tens of thousands of nuns, gathered at Soldier Field, and tens of thousands gathered outside.[39]

In his sermon that morning, San Francisco archbishop Joseph Hanna called the women's day event the greatest honor ever to women—and said:

> Never since the pages of history have recorded the deeds of mankind has woman had the place of power she holds today. Never has this power reached such commanding sway as it does at this moment in our loved land—she is the mother of the race; she makes the first, the most indelible impression on the budding mind of the child.
>
> Her love makes her the ideal of the child's life. As life runs on, she is the guide, she is the upholder of life's high traditions of noble effort. When men fail in life's stressing conflict she speaks words of comfort, of courage and sends her men back to fight anew.[40]

In the afternoon, as many as two hundred thousand men—all members of the Holy Name Society—came together for a benediction. In a procession to begin the event, thousands of men marched toward the stadium in columns of four, carrying banners or candles, some eating sandwiches as they went, filing into the arena and flooded the seating. When, about an hour before the services started, it was announced over the loudspeaker that the Eucharist was on the altar, straw hats were doffed and smoking ceased. As the services began, everyone lighted candles. "The effect was magical, the steep sides of the stadium and the floor, where fifty thousand sat, were showered by golden spangles," and "as the sun sank, a cool wind rushed in from Lake Michigan to send the banners of the stadium into a series of ripples." The bishops, archbishops, and cardinals were seated, and the men stood to sing the national anthem. During the benediction, as the Eucharist in the giant monstrance was lifted, the gathered crowds made the sign of the cross with their lighted candles.[41]

The reaction to the weeklong event affirmed Mundelein's belief that bringing the Eucharistic Congress to Chicago would showcase the central role his archdiocese played in American religious life. "Nothing like this religious demonstration has ever been seen, and it will be years before it will be equaled, if it ever is," said Quebec Premier L.A. Taschereau after attending the congress.[42] The Reverend Dr. James Stone, former pastor of Saint James Episcopal Cathedral in Chicago, said in an address coinciding with the congress that he considered the gathering a sign of the "dawn of a new day" for Christianity. "It is significant there is gathered in this city the greatest body of Christians ever assembled here. The only power that could have brought these thousands to Chicago is the power of Christ," he said.[43]

The scale of the Eucharistic Congress made it difficult to ignore. And the positive press inevitably prompted anti-Catholic reactions from some Protestants. Among the most strident was an editorial in the *Herald of Christ's Kingdom*, a millennialist Christian paper with ties to a sect related to the Jehovah's Witnesses. The writer could not be sure what the result of the congress would be, but was certain that it was a sign of "the great conflict," in which "the complete overthrow of Satan's empire"—including the Catholic Church—"is assured."[44]

Such responses, predominantly positive, helped establish Soldier Field as a venue that could lend prestige and import to any large public event—a place to make headlines—solidifying its own place in Chicago culture for much of the twentieth century. For almost thirty years, the Eucharistic Congress was the event to which any other large gathering held in Chicago—whether religious or secular—would be compared, remaining unequaled until the celebrations of the Marian Year in 1954.[45]

PROTESTANTS TAKE THE ALTAR

Less than a week after the congress, the first Protestant gathering to be compared to the Eucharistic Congress was held when Lutherans of the Missouri Synod from across the Chicago area held a program in honor of the United States' sesquicentennial. Held June 27, the event was one of the first to commemorate the nation's 150th birthday, part of a series of celebrations that went on for more than a week surrounding July 4, 1926. As many as fifty thousand people, including a twenty-five-hundred-child choir, took part in the festivities, which included a pantomime accompanying a performance of "The Star Spangled Banner" and songs by a chorus made up of singers from 150 churches.

As was sometimes the case with Protestant gatherings, the Lutherans sought to distinguish themselves from Catholics by asserting their loyalty to the United States. The pilgrims at the Eucharistic Congress had knelt before a Roman bishop—a gesture often taken by American Protestants as a sign of disloyalty. In the mid-1920s, German Americans might also be considered suspect, because of the recently concluded Great War. At the Lutheran gathering, Dr. Martin Graebner, the president of Concordia College in Saint Paul, Minnesota, declared, "We Lutherans of Chicago and vicinity will pledge our lives to the flag and to the country."[46]

EASTER SUNRISE AT THE STADIUM

The next series of notable religious events at the stadium began with the Century of Progress Exposition, held in 1933 and 1934 along the lakefront.

Soldier Field would in later years host a nondenominational Protestant sunrise service each Easter. In 1933, though, what was billed as the first such service was held southeast of the stadium, at the Court of Honor of the fair's Hall of Science. The Illinois Central Railroad ran a special train from the South Side for the event, and at least a hundred buses brought people from other parts of town. About twenty thousand people attended the service, which was geared largely to young adults and open to people of all races.[47]

At the following year's service, at Soldier Field, the lead preacher was the Reverend Amos Hershey Leaman, a member of the Century of Progress religious council, a Mennonite missionary, and one of the Protestant ministers who in 1931 founded the Christian Business Men's Committee of Chicago (which later became a national group called CBMC). Leaman, whose dedication to proselytizing and missionary work was part of a general American upsurge in fundamentalism, made use of all the same instruments of popular culture that were making organized sports a part of most American men's daily lives: newspapers, radio, and large public venues, which, in rapidly urbanizing America, were replacing the more intimate gathering places of the small towns city folk had left behind. After the success of the Eucharistic Congress, it was men like Leaman who made Soldier Field a regular part of the city's religious culture. The Easter sunrise services he helped organize were sponsored by a variety of Protestant religious youth groups, though the list always included leaders from the Moody Bible Institute and the Salvation Army.

In 1935 about twenty-three thousand people attended the service, held at Soldier Field, where a giant white cross had been emblazoned on the playing field, with the motto "Christ Is Risen" running above it.[48] It was one of the first sunny Easters in years, and newspapers accounts of the annual Easter Parade expressed amazement at the good weather—hinting at a problem the organizers of the sunrise service had from the start. Given Chicago's frequently raw spring weather and lake breezes, they had to work each year to overcome congregants' hesitation about attending a service that would last hours and often require them to dress for winter weather.

Easter sunrise service at Soldier Field, 1938. Courtesy Chicago Park District Special Collections.

As with a number of religious events at Soldier Field in the 1930s, the park district let the Christian Business Men's Committee use the field for free. In the stadium's first several decades, the South Park Commission, and later the Chicago Park District, seemed to care more about making the space available to as many groups as possible than about making money. Even as they tried to profit off sports games, those who controlled the stadium viewed it as a venue that should bring people together, even if its maintenance and use involved a taxpayer subsidy.[49]

Though the city had celebrated its hundredth anniversary in 1933—and extended its celebratory Century of Progress Exposition into 1934—it decided also to celebrate the centennial of its incorporation in 1837 as a city.[50] So in 1937 Chicago planned a Charter Jubilee, in hopes of drawing tourists and stimulating spending among civic patriots. Special boxing matches, an event showcasing a hundred years of fashion, and a West Side businessmen's lunch featuring food from 1837 were among the varied and quirky events in the celebration spearheaded, of course, by Mayor Edward Kelly. The events stretched from March 4, the anniversary of Chicago's incorporation as a city, to October 9, the anniversary of the Great Fire. The Easter sunrise service that year was, of course, a Charter Jubilee event, but again it was marred by cold weather.[51]

The sunrise service grew in popularity over the next decade, though some years, like 1937, when only about twelve thousand people attended, the cold weather kept many at home. The next year, Easter fell several weeks later, and the temperature hovered around sixty, with a threat of rain.[52] In addition to Presbyterian, Baptist, and nondenominational churches, that year's sponsors included the American Legion. Most years, the service was broadcast on the radio, and in 1938, the organizers had as chief minister the Reverend Charles E. Fuller, a Los Angles radio preacher. That year, the group sent "flying squadrons" to all Protestant churches in the Chicago area to promote the service. The effort was successful, and about fifty thousand people turned out.[53]

Attendance the next year was about the same, though organizers had hoped for further growth. A new feature for the 1939 service was a giant electric organ and a choir of about ten thousand people under the direction of Homer Ammonite of the Moody Bible Institute.[54] Easter 1940 was one of the coldest on record, with temperatures barely cracking the double digits by the time the service started.[55] In 1941 the weather was more springlike, and attendance again topped fifty thousand.[56]

The annual service continued through World War II, with as many as forty-five thousand people attending. Then, in 1949, Easter fell in mid-April, often a good sign for attendance. However, the day, April 17, turned out to be not just cold but snowy; only about thirty-five hundred people showed up. The following year organizers announced that the bad weather had done in the service.[57]

The weather, however, was probably not the only factor. Also at work was a larger cultural trend that over the years would erode the popularity of the stadium and other downtown cultural icons. The 1930s and 1940s saw an exodus of the middle class from Chicago that had been arrested in the late nineteenth and early twentieth centuries by the annexation of formerly suburban towns and the expansion of middle-class residential areas in the city. For several years, other groups had been organizing sunrise services both in the growing suburbs and in more distant residential areas of the city. In 1950, for example, the Lutheran Church–Missouri Synod sponsored its ninth annual sunrise service in Norwood Park and a sixth annual sunrise service for suburbs along the Burlington Railroad line in the Riverside-Brookfield stadium.[58]

After the early juxtaposition between the Eucharistic Congress and the Lutheran Independence Day rally, the Easter sunrise services had helped set in motion what would be a longstanding rivalry between evangelical Protestants and Catholics in bringing souls to the Lord at Soldier Field. Beginning in 1940 the Catholic Holy Name Society took up the patriotic cause, sponsoring an annual "Holy Hour" service that rallied Chicago's Catholics to "combine love of country with adoration of 'Christ the King' in solemn benediction of the most Blessed Sacrament."[59] The 1941 gathering, held September 14, drew an estimated 150,000. The event was advertised as a great patriotic rally but also made a point of joining Pope Pius XII in praying for "the early coming of a just peace among men." Archbishop Samuel A. Stritch, in appealing to the faithful to attend, said that the event was intended to make "a true and honest petition addressed to God for a just peace." The crowd, from more than four hundred parishes in the six counties that were part of the archdiocese at the time, sang hymns and "The Star Spangled Banner." The climax of the night came when the crowd knelt in adoration of the Eucharist as trumpets blared, an airplane dropped rose petals, and cannons fired.[60]

With their mix of patriotism and Catholic ritual, the Holy Hour services drew crowds each year during the war. In 1942 a massive procession of altar boys and priests marched flanked by an honor guard of military troops nine hundred strong, and Stritch memorialized eighty-eight members of Chicago Holy Name Society chapters who had died in the war. "We reared them for peace. . . . We stressed in their hearts no hatreds for their fellow men," Stritch said. But when the war came, "Those sons of our homes gathered around the flag."[61] The services continued into the early 1950s, attracting as many as eighty thousand people in 1945. Subsequently Catholic events at the stadium became less frequent, though one landmark event was yet to come.

In the new millennium, religion might still be a large part of many people's lives, but large-scale outdoor religious gatherings are less common than they were in the pre-television era. The midcentury change had a profound effect on how Soldier Field was used, especially when it came to events that had nothing to do with sports, and everything to do with the city's cultural life off the playing field.

7 Military Marches, Music, and an Arsonist Cow

When the South Park commissioners first voted to build Soldier Field, on land that at the time was still submerged in the shallows of Lake Michigan, they envisioned the stadium as a stage upon which all the actors in Chicago culture could play a part. Within a few years Soldier Field became the most prominent venue in a city that regularly held events, from war shows to music festivals, that were open to all races—though at first some had segregated seating.

At one of the many official openings of the stadium, Edward Kelly, then the president of the South Park Commission, observed that the stadium's status as a memorial meant it should act as a silent inspiration to those still living to build a better Chicago. Survivors should show off the best of Chicago culture, whether in athletics or music or theater. "I like to think of this stadium not as an achievement, so much as a pledge and a symbol," Kelly said in his speech at the November 11, 1925, renaming dedication:

> This is the Armory of the Soldiers of Citizenship. . . . The uses which the people have made of it thus far have proved it a place where Life mounts to flood tide. What has been done here in Sport, or Game or Exhibition has been done to the limit of men's capacities. This is the Arena where men attempt to do their best. It is Chicago's place of Inspiration.[1]

The park board always envisioned the stadium as much more than a sports venue, and its first two years of use, between its opening and the official dedication, had seen a panoply of events. Many were sporting events that a twenty-first-century Chicagoan would recognize. But over the years, the stadium's popularity as an arena for other activities reflected the direction of Chicago, and American, culture in ways few other venues could.

FROM MEMORIAL FOR THE DEAD TO WAR SHOWS

Though in some ways it seems perverse that an arena dedicated to honoring war dead would host reenactments of the circumstances of their deaths, it makes a certain sense; in an age of spectacle, what better way to bring their sacrifice home, albeit in sanitized form? Military shows had become popular in Chicago following the Spanish-American War, and what amounted to war games remained a popular attraction throughout the first half of the twentieth century, until the military became less popular with many of Chicago's elite Democrats and the advent of the jet airplane made aerial dogfights over Soldier Field impractical. War shows then gave way to the milder Air and Water Show. In 1918, however, at the height of the Great War, Chicago's twenty-one hundred postmen and five hundred postal clerks sold more than a hundred thousand tickets to a military exposition in which eleven acres of Grant Park were remade as a battlefield, complete with trenches, barbed wire, and a no-man's land. More than 130,000 people came to gawk at the machinery of war, including one of the first British tanks ever, the Britannia, and see it in action.[2]

Despite widespread isolationism after the war, Americans still flocked to demonstrations of the country's military might (even as actual military strength declined markedly). The mock battles and exhibitions presented an idealized picture of war, one that sold itself as a way to see what our boys had been doing at the front—free, of course, of the stench of death and the lung-searing fumes of chemical warfare.

The first month the stadium was open, September 1924, included what the War Department called a national "Defense Day," intended to promote a general military preparedness that many military leaders felt had been lacking before World War I. Following the war, Congress had passed the Defense Act of 1920 to make U.S. military forces a true standing army and provide for continued upkeep of the National Guard and Reserve.[3] But while the South Park Commission had given Colonel Philip Fox of the 341st Reserve Infantry permission to use the stadium as a mobilization point in case of an emergency, Grant Park itself, and not the stadium, was used for Defense Day. The mustering, which happened throughout the country—though Wisconsin mostly abstained—drew about fifteen thousand people to Grant Park and an estimated million people to parks and other assembly areas throughout the Chicago area. Mainly, the assembled throngs heard speeches by military commanders about the need for readiness.[4]

Though Defense Day appears to have been a success, the War Department blundered the next year and tried to hold the event on November 11, Armistice Day (now known as Veterans Day). Churches and other groups objected, arguing that the date of the peace that ended World War I should not be marked with preparations for war. The War Department ended up canceling Defense Day that year and in 1926 announced that it would hold such mobilization exercises only every few years. After that, the event appears to have been largely forgotten.[5]

The spectacle that had drawn so many people to Grant Park in 1918, however, was not forgotten. Chicago-area commanders saw military exercises as a way to bring in new recruits and keep up the morale of their men. So the 65th Reserves and its superior outfit, the Army's Sixth Corps, sponsored the first of many military pageants at Soldier Field in May 1925. The 1925 War Show established the blueprint for shows that followed over the next twenty years, and because the troops were more likely to be battle-tested and the equipment to be relatively new, it was probably also one of the more spectacular shows prior to World War II.

Cavalrymen at Fort Sheridan practiced weeks in advance for the event. Organizers brought in examples of "all the fighting equipment of Uncle Sam's war machine and the men behind the guns," one report noted: more than one thousand soldiers, five hundred horses, five tanks, and twelve airplanes, along with several dirigibles and other equipment. The show included marching, of course, but that wasn't what the public flocked to see: they wanted a clash of armies in which they could imagine the gore of battle. "The ordinary sham battle has ceased to be entertaining because the bursting of shells and other effects of warfare are lacking when blanks are used," Colonel John G. Winter, one of those in charge of the spectacle, told the *Tribune*. Instead, the troops at the 1925 show were to use fireworks that would mimic "every detail of actual warfare."[6]

The show was held over three days at the end of May 1925, an extraordinarily unpredictable month for weather in Chicago. The opening day of the show, Friday, May 22, it was 94 degrees; on Sunday, the final day, temperatures only got up to 40. There were two performances a day, with airplane flights in the afternoon, and searchlights and antiaircraft-mimicking fireworks in the evening. Vice President Charles G. Dawes was among the twenty-three thousand spectators at the first show, Friday afternoon. The battle of the Argonne, in which almost twenty-seven thousand Americans were killed, was reenacted using a smoke screen and four tanks that "waddled and barked their way across the field," according to one account. This fake warfare did have its real dangers. In Friday night's reenactment, horses trampled one infantryman, and one policeman in a Roman-style horse race before the main show was thrown from his steed and injured.[7]

A highlight of the daytime entertainment was the radio-dispatched movement of warplanes over the stadium. Spectators listened in on the radio communication between air and ground over Soldier Field's state-of-the-art loudspeakers, and watched as the airplanes responded instantaneously to the orders of a commander on the ground, diving, soaring, and moving into and out of V and line formations. On Sunday winds kept the airplanes grounded and cold kept the crowds small; nonetheless, organizers still called the event a success and soon began planning the next year's show.[8]

Among the more spectacular war shows over the years was that held in 1932, the bicentennial of George Washington's birth. The show had grown in popularity since 1925, as the realities of war faded in the popular mind, and planners decided it should span eleven days instead of only three. Mayor Anton Cermak made sure that his followers knew he was behind the show and bought a ticket at a booth set up at an annual outdoors show at the Chicago Coliseum (a precursor of the outdoors shows of today, it was devoted to popular hobbies such as hunting and fishing).[9]

In mid-June fifteen hundred soldiers from Fort Sheridan moved to Chicago temporarily, camping next to Soldier Field for the duration of the show, which also featured about a hundred Army Air Corps planes. Show organizers also invited Amelia Earhart, the first woman pilot to cross the Atlantic, to take part in the military plane formation opening the show. Earhart, a graduate of Chicago's Hyde Park High School, professed herself "overwhelmed" when she was greeted by thousands of Chicago admirers after her transatlantic flight in 1928.[10] By the time of the 1932 war show, however, Earhart seemed to have gotten used to her fame, no longer shying away from the cameras when she landed in Chicago.[11]

To open the show, four squadrons of fighter planes escorted Earhart's plane—painted to resemble a red and white eagle—over the stadium at about 8 p.m. She landed a short time later and made her way to the stadium, where she received a gold medal and addressed the crowd (and radio audience), telling them about her solo flight across the Atlantic earlier that year. Numerous military units, including artillery, machine gunners and tanks, paraded around the arena, followed by floats depicting the influence of other countries' cultures on American history.

The 1932 war show was also notable for an accident, which appears not to have done anyone any physical harm—and pleased some who either couldn't or wouldn't pay the price of admission. As during many events before the construction, in 1938, of the Chicago Park District administration building, people had gathered on the steps of the Field Museum to get a glimpse into Soldier Field's open north end, but their efforts were frustrated by a temporary fence. During that year's aerial maneuvers, however, what was described as a "looping comet plane," apparently with a fiery tail, caused the canvas fence to catch fire and parts of it to burn to the ground, giving those on the steps a much better view.[12]

Attendance was high during the Century of Progress Exposition, in 1933 and 1934. In the latter year, troops were stationed in the fairgrounds at what they called Camp John Whistler, named for the builder of Fort Dearborn (and grandfather of painter James MacNeill Whistler), and each evening ended with a mock-up of the World War I battle of Cantigny, in which *Tribune* publisher Robert McCormick, a promoter of the war shows, had fought and won his title of colonel. Another popular year was 1937, when Chicago celebrated the hundredth anniversary of its incorporation as a city.[13]

As the war in Europe continued, the Illinois National Guard performed a 1940 show, including two-hundred-mile-an-hour observation planes and a demonstration of what a blitzkrieg might look like. In 1941 they were too busy preparing for the possibility of an actual war to hold a war show.[14] But in 1942 the shows resumed, with the aim of promoting the sale of war bonds; proceeds that year benefited Army Emergency Relief—a charitable group formed to help reserve and regular soldiers and their families with emergency financial needs. Early in the war, Kelly, having moved up to the mayorship, had made the sale of war bonds a priority for the city, and the Democratic political machine worked overtime to ensure his wishes were carried out. As a result, Chicago's sales of war bonds outstripped those of all other cities, as did its number of enlistees.[15]

The approximately two thousand soldiers and officers in the 1942 show once again camped around the stadium, equipped as if about to be shipped off to war. At an equipment exhibit installed just outside the southeast wall of the stadium, Chicagoans were able to take a look at the Army's big guns, as well as the remains of Japanese and German airplanes and the latest portable chaplain's kit.[16] Rainstorms dampened the first night of the show September 2, but by the next day there was nothing to stop the crowds from enjoying the spectacle of flamethrowers, machine guns, and tank cannons. The Army also showed off a new technology, what the *Tribune* called a "handy-talky." The large radio communications device was used by spectators in several spots around Soldier Field, with their conversations broadcast on the stadium loudspeakers.[17]

No war show was held in 1943, but as part of the national push to sell war bonds, a number of Hollywood celebrities, from James Cagney and Fred Astaire to Judy Garland and Lucille Ball, performed at Soldier Field on September 16. The show began with music from the Great Lakes Naval Training Station's band and choir, but quickly became more light-hearted, with comedian Harpo Marx running across the stage between acts, pursuing a shapely actress. War bond shows, a staple of the war effort, were also held in 1944 and 1945, but the 1943 show was the most successful, bringing in

The 1942 Army War Show at Soldier Field, a show of support for the war effort. Courtesy Chicago Park District Special Collections.

about $200 million. The 1945 bond show was staged on May 20, in connection with the fifth annual "I Am an American" day at Soldier Field. It included the presentation by General Alexander A. Vandegrift of the Congressional Medal of Honor to Nora Witek, the mother of Marine private Frank Witek, who had been killed in action on Guam, as well as a reenactment of the raising of the U.S. flag on Iwo Jima. (The Soldier Field reenactment was itself reenacted in Clint Eastwood's Oscar-winning movie *Flags of Our Fathers*, though because of the 2001–2003 renovation scenes could be shot only outside the stadium.) Stars at the show included Humphrey Bogart and Lauren Bacall. Also in 1945, the Chicago Bears held their first Armed Forces Game, an exhibition game played for charity.

One overlooked aspect of the war shows was that from the first they brought together black and white Chicagoans and acknowledged the contributions of black Americans in the military. Like the military, however, the shows were sometimes segregated, although some photographs of other events at the stadium do show blacks intermingled with white spectators.[18]

The military show returned in 1946, with the Army Day celebration at which President Harry Truman was the main speaker. A sign of the changing times—and changing warfare—was the magnificent sight of two jet-powered P-80A fighters passing over the stadium at six hundred miles per hour, stealing the show for the brief instants they were visible.[19] Though the popularity of military drills and battle reenactments waned in the late 1940s, the taste for displays of U.S. military might didn't go away. Soldier Field remained the focus of military preparedness campaigns—the stadium and its parking lots became the staging grounds for drills and inspections by the Illinois reserve militia each April and September—and other military displays, such as the annual Memorial Day parade, were held on Michigan Avenue and elsewhere in the city.[20]

In the 1950s the Chicago Park District's lakefront parks began sponsoring a water show that was initially a showcase for district swimmers but soon came to include Navy divers. By the early 1960s the shows also included the Air Force's Thunderbirds stunt flying team.[21] Though the 1946 Army Day celebration was the last strictly military show at the stadium, the Bears-sponsored Armed Forces Game took over a number of the shows' functions. The benefit usually included some sort of military parade, a salute to veterans and the military, and exhibits of military machinery such as Nike missiles.[22]

Though Soldier Field was dedicated to U.S. war dead, for years after the Armed Forces Games ended in 1971, when the Bears moved full-time to the venue, it hosted few, if any, official ceremonies or events honoring war dead or veterans until 2003, after its renovation. (The lone exception many years was Independence Day.)

COPS AND FIREMEN ENTERTAIN

The stadium's long tradition of celebrating Chicago police officers and firefighters also ended in 1971. As noted in chapter 1, the first event ever held at Soldier Field, while it was still under construction, had been the third annual Chicago Police Field Meet, a two-day contest at which more than thirty thousand people filled the west stands to watch some twelve hundred police officers competing in motorcycle polo, chariot racing, and tugs-of-war, as well as more conventional athletics.[23] And the Chicago Fire Department had taken part in the stadium's official 1924 opening, on the anniversary of the Great Chicago Fire of 1871, with veteran firefighters providing a demonstration of how fires were extinguished—or not, as the case might be—in 1871.[24]

After its success in 1924, the police meet became an annual event at Soldier Field, drawing high attendance throughout the rest of the 1920s. Enthusiasm was such that, in 1928, the *Tribune* declared that the shows were "now looked upon as one of Chicago's athletic institutions." Thirty thousand

Fireman clown Smoky Rogers with a group of boys in uniform at a 1929 Chicago Fire Department event. Clowns like Rogers were a regular part of the firefighting shows at the stadium. Courtesy Chicago History Museum. Chicago Daily News archive, glass negative DN-0089645B.

people turned up for that year's opening event, which consisted almost entirely of three hundred police officers doing calisthenics. The warm-ups were followed by a series of races and other competitions, and entertainment by a troupe of clowns.[25]

Firefighting shows had been conducted in the city since at least 1877, when the entertainment included the demonstration of Chicago's first horseless steam fire engine, then newly acquired.[26] The 1924 demonstration was, however, the only such event at Soldier Field until 1929. Then in 1930, the *Daily News* sponsored a firemen's demonstration, which became an annual event, as a fund-raiser for the firefighters' benevolent association. The opening for that first event was typical of fire department shows over the years: a parade of firefighters and bands intermingled with examples of the city's firefighting apparatus, with sirens blaring and bells ringing. In another of the periodic signs that Soldier Field was more tolerant than many city venues in matters of race, the 1930 event showcased the talents of at least one mixed-race junior

Firefighters compete, using high-pressure hoses to push a ball along a wire, at the 1973 American Legion Fourth of July celebration. Courtesy Chicago Park District Special Collections.

fire company from the South Side. Under the leadership of Junior Fire Chief Odulphus King, age fourteen, Junior Fire Patrol 3, stationed at a firehouse at 35th Street and Wabash Avenue, won a trophy for their drilling techniques. According to the *Defender*, "The color line is not drawn among the junior firemen. The dark skinned boys play, eat, and 'fight' fires along with white youths." Unfortunately, the harmonious race relations among the junior firemen of 35th Street were not typical of the city at the time.[27]

In 1938 about a thousand police officers and firefighters joined up for one show, a meet that benefited both departments' benevolent associations. Though still billed as something of an athletic event, the "thrill show" was more a chance for police to perform stunts; in one, a perennial favorite at the police shows, four or even six traffic officers rode on one motorcycle, contorting their bodies in poses more familiar in circus acts. Meanwhile, firefighting squads squared off in a contest that involved using their hoses to drive red and gold balls across the field and over the opposing squad's goal line. Deputy Chief Fire Marshal Anthony J. Mullaney explained that the game showed off a real firefighting skill: "At a fire it is of supreme importance to place the stream where it will do the most good. Misdirected streams can lose a fight against a fire." There were also displays of hand-drawn water pumping machines from 1837 and 1845, and the last survivor of the fire company that had lost seventeen men fighting a warehouse fire at the 1893 world's fair was given a place of honor.[28]

The combined police and fire shows were popular, with seventy thousand people attending in 1938 and eighty thousand in 1940, but the spectacle was canceled in 1942 because of the war.[29] In 1943 the shows' organizers sent a letter to the *Tribune*, thanking Chicagoans—and the newspaper—for four years of support and noting that a surplus of more than $10,000 was being turned over to "Mrs. Edward J. Kelly"—Margaret Kirk Kelly—to help in running Mayor Kelly's pet war project, a servicemen's center just west of City Hall.[30]

HIGH CULTURE, MATCH LIGHTING, AND FIREWORKS

Two other long-running events at Soldier Field fell victim to changes in local and national entertainment culture in the 1960s and 1970s. One, the Chicagoland Music Festival, ran from 1930 through 1964 and fed off the rise of celebrity musicians but lost popularity as televised musical variety shows and popular music supplanted more old-fashioned musical gatherings. The other, the Amerian Legion's Independence Day fireworks shows, made use of Soldier Field's status as a focal point of American patriotism but was overwhelmed by the Democratic Party's insatiable drive to control and take credit for popular events.

The Chicagoland Music Festival was probably the single most popular annual nonsporting event at Soldier Field, consistently drawing more spectators and participants than almost any other one-day event.[31] Though it was billed as a Tribune Charities event, from the start it involved the cooperation of newspapers covering at least fifty cities throughout the Midwest, from the *Evansville Courier-Journal* in southern Indiana to the *State Journal* of Madison, Wisconsin, to the *Hawk Eye* of Burlington, Iowa. In each newspaper's circulation area, hundreds, sometimes thousands, of people vied for spots at the festival, with the winners coming to Chicago to compete in the finals for a spot at the festival.

Its boosters billed the event as a successor to one of the city's legendary music festivals, the 1873 Chicago Jubilee, which was held to celebrate Chicago's rising from the ashes of the Great Fire. The *Tribune* bragged that its first festival would best the 1873 show in any number of ways, drawing triple the earlier event's attendance of forty thousand; where the Chicago Jubilee had a thousand singers, the Chicagoland Music Festival would have four thousand; where it had a band of three hundred, the new festival would have twelve hundred.[32]

Chicagoland programs were eclectic. The first, held August 23, 1930, included, as a tribute to the Chicago Jubilee, the "Anvil Chorus" from Verdi's opera *Il trovatore*, which had been performed at the 1873 event; the "Hallelujah Chorus" from Handel's *Messiah*, sung by the entire audience; a number of John Philip Sousa marches; and spirituals such as "Swing Low, Sweet Chariot."

The *Tribune*—which had a habit of exaggerating its accomplishments—estimated that about 150,000 people attended the event. As the sun set, the festival announcer boasted to the crowd that the stadium's 392,000 watts of illumination was "the greatest artificial illumination of a single arena in the world's history." As with almost any *Tribune*-sponsored event of the time, there was an emphasis on patriotism and on honoring veterans, especially veterans of the Civil War. Among the musicians in the crowd was veteran W. T. Kimsey, of Douglas, Michigan, who at the time was ninety-one years old. Kimsey, a drummer in Ulysses S. Grant's army at the battle of Shiloh, brought with him that night the drum he beat during the war.[33]

Even if the *Tribune*'s attendance estimate was an exaggeration, the festival was wildly successful and set the stage for more than three decades of well-attended, varied, and sometimes peculiar musical gatherings. Within a few years, the annual event had become a place for musicians from a cross-section of Chicago to become famous, sometimes for a night, sometimes for years. It also attracted numerous high-profile musicians from around the country.

Organizers made a point of trying to draw competitors from as many of Chicago's ethnic groups as possible. Though *Defender* readers noted that the seating for the event was segregated (at least into the 1940s), black musicians, conductors, and bandleaders were an essential part of the festival from the outset. At the first festival, the *Tribune* bragged, "probably the largest Negro chorus ever assembled, 1,000 voices," performed, under the direction of James A. Mundy and J. Wesley Jones, and George Garner, a celebrated black tenor who was originally from Chicago, sang a solo. Black Chicagoans could be proud of their contribution to the city's musical culture, and at the Chicagoland Music Festival, at least, they were considered equal participants in shaping that culture.

James Mundy had a long and storied musical career. Though best known in Chicago, his musical group, the Mundy Choristers and Singers, was nationally famous. Born in 1886, Mundy was inspired to enter the musical field by a mother who herself sang professionally until she was seventy-five and came to public attention in Chicago when he directed the first black chorus to sing at Orchestra Hall in 1914. By 1916 the Mundy Choristers were prominent enough to be part of the opening of what's now known as Navy

Pier. When the first Chicagoland Music Festival was being planned, "It was a new baby," Mundy told an interviewer in 1970. "Nobody knew whether it was going to crawl or walk. But it had an amazing birth—like a little yellow chick at Eastertime."[34]

Black groups became a mainstay of the festival, providing some white Chicagoans with their first exposure to black music. In the mid-1930s, Mundy and Jones explained the origins of spirituals as they were understood at the time by many in both the white and black communities: "The Negro had no music when he roamed the African Jungle, and it was not until he was sold into slavery that he found this outlet for his emotions," Mundy told the *Tribune*. "Then, oppressed by burdens, he communed with nature and learned to chant his appeals to God."[35]

The *Defender* also urged its readers to attend the music festival. [36] But despite their prominence at the festival, black singers weren't treated as equals with white singers in its early years. The *Tribune* often hit a condescending note even when praising black singers. In the run-up to the first festival, for example, the paper wrote an article praising a black baritone, but called the thirty-two-year-old, John Burdette, an "elevator boy" in a headline, and referred to him by his first name in its second reference.[37] Mundy himself criticized some of the arrangements in a 1940 letter to the editor of the *Defender*, noting that at a 1939 music festival at Northwestern "the races mixed freely . . . [while] in the Chicagoland Soldiers Field festival, the one thousand Negro singers are segregated far in the rear in Georgia style."[38] Nonetheless, the festival remained popular with black performers and black music lovers up to the end, and Jones was involved until his death in 1961.

The music festival started out dominated by classical music but soon began a turn toward more popular songs. From the start, though, it included homespun elements, notably the tradition of massed accordion bands. For the 1959 festival, for example, an ensemble of two thousand accordionists was assembled. And that didn't include the solos by accordion players who won competitions sponsored by local newspapers and music groups and made their way to the festival finals.[39]

The Chicagoland Music Festival always tried to be both an uplifting event, bringing classical music to the masses, and an overwhelming spectacle. At the 1932 festival, three thousand girls ages eight to sixteen waltzed under colored searchlights to the strains of Richard Strauss's "Blue Danube." At the 1939 festival, modern popular music first made its appearance, with the inclusion of Fats Waller's band on the program.[40]

In its peak years, the music festival attracted ninety thousand to a hundred thousand people, drawing participants and spectators from as far away as Hawaii.[41] From its early years, an hour or more of the Soldier Field event was broadcast on radio, and later on television. As with *American Idol*, and

The *Chicago Tribune* claimed that the tradition of lighting matches and lighters at concerts started at a qualifying event for the Chicagoland Music Festival. This match-lighting took place in 1953. Courtesy Chicago Park District Special Collections.

other talent competitions of its own era, the festival had the potential to rocket formerly unknown musical talents into stardom.

Before reaching the Soldier Field stage, musicians competed in local talent contests and then in the finals, held in Chicago, usually at a hotel like the Drake or the Palmer House. Starting in 1938, the two top singers in each of several categories would often sing at the festival, with the winners announced during the broadcast portion, the last two hours of the event.[42] Not every singer became famous, but many who won top honors were able to boost their careers. One success story was the 1957 male winner, Richard Best, an operatic bass who would go on to sing seven seasons with Chicago's Lyric Opera, twelve with the Metropolitan Opera in New York, and ten with the Santa Fe Symphony.[43]

In addition to individual singers, men's and women's choruses, concert bands, individual and team baton twirlers, and accordionists, both individually and in bands, competed at the festival. And, as with Garner's appearance at the 1930 festival, it was common for famous musicians to be part on the program. One of the high points of the festival's thirty-five-year history came in only its second year, when John Philip Sousa, arguably the most famous band director and conductor in American history, served as guest conductor. In later years, popular musicians as diverse as Waller, W. C. Handy, Al Jolson (twice, in 1934 and 1949), Liberace, Duke Ellington, Lawrence Welk, and Johnny Cash and June Carter headlined at the festival.[44]

The vastness of Soldier Field, always a problem for performers trying to connect with audiences, often was overcome by the enthusiasm of the vast crowd, and professionals and amateurs alike considered the festival a memorable night in their careers. "At first, I felt the spectators were too far away from me," June Carter told the *Tribune* in 1964. "But before long I found they were swinging along with me and it almost seemed like they got closer all the time." Jazz clarinetist Pete Fountain, a regular on Welk's show at the time, closed out the three-and-a-half-hour show that year and said playing the festival was "unbelievable . . . by far the greatest kick I've ever gotten from a performance."[45]

One tradition said to have originated at the Chicagoland Music Festival is now a cliché of large pop music concerts. H. Philip Maxwell—the *Tribune*'s editorial promotions director, and the director and emcee of the festival through its history—claimed that the tradition of audience members' lighting matches en masse during a show was inspired by a concert held in Garfield Park in 1938, one of the run-ups to the main music festival at Soldier Field. Maxwell, who was running the concert, noticed, as the evening sky darkened, a "constant flicker" as spectators sitting on benches beneath the park's trees lit pipes and cigarettes. The twinkling complemented that if fireflies in the grass, and "from that came the match lighting idea," Maxwell wrote fifteen years later.

A few weeks later, as part of its drumbeat of publicity for the festival, the *Tribune* published an article exhorting anyone planning to attend to bring matches or a lighter to light at a specified time during the evening. (In an early example of corporate sponsorship at the stadium, the Diamond Match Company supplied matches for the ceremony throughout much of the festival's history.) At the festival, at the selected moment, the lights went down and the announcer gave the crowd its cue: "One, two, three, strike!" Maxwell boasted that many other events, including concerts by Danny Thomas and Bob Hope, had copied the match-lighting, "and the little trick that started in Garfield Park has lit up countless stadiums."[46] Years before the crowd at Woodstock held candles aloft to keep away the rain during a set by folk singer Melanie Sofka (often cited as the beginning of the tradition), spectators at the Soldier Field festival held up their lights, to the accompaniment of the song "The Glow Worm."[47]

The longest-running annual nonsports event at Soldier Field, however, is still the American Legion's Fourth of July fireworks show, which lasted until the early 1980s. The Legion's involvement with Soldier Field began early, as it lobbied the South Park Commission to rename Grant Park Stadium in honor of America's war dead, though its influence is sometimes exaggerated—Kelly's park commission had used the idea of the stadium as a memorial as a selling point for the project from the beginning.

The first Independence Day event at the stadium was a for-profit fireworks show with a 50-cent admission, put on by a South Park concessionaire on July 4 and 5, 1925. (Another ticketed fireworks show was held the same year at Wrigley Field.)[48] The following year, as part of the nation's sesquicentennial celebrations, the Loyal Order of Moose put on a show depicting the founding of Chicago, and Native Americans from what is now Haskell Indian Nations University acted in a pageant said to depict the history of Native Americans in the Chicago area up until the Fort Dearborn Massacre of 1812. As part of the festivities, South Park Commission president Edward Kelly and four other park commissioners were initiated into the Chippewa tribe and given Native American names.[49]

For several years after the 1926 show, no Independence Day events were held at the stadium, though the American Legion was involved in several other events. It was not until 1935 that the annual show was inaugurated, as a fund-raiser for the Cook County American Legion.

The fireworks show evolved over the years, though it did retain popular elements from older-style shows. Beginning in the mid-nineteenth century, when large fireworks displays became a mainstay of Independence Day celebrations, set pieces—pictures drawn by setting off small fireworks mounted on elaborate frames—drew in audiences and were part of almost every fireworks show. Over the years, as audiences came to expect larger shows with more rockets, set pieces fell out of favor at the Soldier Field show, which usually lasted about half an hour. Changes in the stadium's configuration also forced the Legion to shift the emphasis to aerial fireworks. The stadium was open-ended, with a 1,014-foot-long arena, until 1938, when the addition of north stands shortened the arena to 887½ feet—still enough room for set pieces. In the early 1970s, though, when the Bears moved in and new north stands were built to form a seating bowl, the arena was effectively shortened to about six hundred feet, making it harder for the smoke from set pieces to blow away. "We've had to get away from using many set pieces because of the facilities," said Albert Swiderski, the chairman of the Fourth of July celebration. "We used to have them at the north end of the field, but that's where George Halas put up those stands.

Now we have them just below the level of the stadium peak. . . . The smoke sometimes obliterates the piece."[50]

In its early years, the American Legion event resembled some of the military shows at the stadium. In 1935, spectators had to put up with only two minutes of speeches; the rest of the event was spectacle. A dozen young women gathered on the field, where judges crowned seventeen-year-old Bernice Slaby, of the Far West Side, Queen of the Great Lakes. A military band marched onto the field, with an accompanying regiment, followed—in the air—by six stunt-flying airplanes from Great Lakes Naval Training Station. Then the stadium lights were turned off and a half-hour fireworks show commenced, as searchlights swept the night sky.

The show seems to have been a success, and the following year members of about two hundred American Legion posts participated. about eighty thousand people attended the 1936 show. Police estimated that southbound traffic on the Michigan Avenue Bridge, going to the stadium, peaked at fifteen thousand cars an hour.[51]

The beginning of the Legion shows coincided with Mayor Kelly's push to enforce a Chicago ban on the private sale and use of fireworks. A fight by the *Tribune* and others to end fireworks sales began around 1903, when, according to American Medical Association statistics, fireworks in the United States killed 60 people outright and another 406 who contracted tetanus from fireworks-related injuries. When the ban finally went into effect the *Tribune* trumpeted it, saying that for the first time, the state would have a "legally sane" Independence Day.[52] Encouraging large, "safe and sane" fireworks shows like the Legion's became a big part of the effort to convince people that the prohibition need not diminish people's enjoyment of the celebration of American freedom.[53] American Legion posts had for years sponsored fireworks shows in smaller towns throughout the area, so it was natural that the Cook County Legion would sponsor a big one in Chicago.

Within a few years, the Legion's fireworks show became as established a summer ritual as the Air and Water Show is today. Marching bands, patriotic music, and massed troops were regular features. Typical was the 1940 show, at which mechanized units and airplanes demonstrated military maneuvers. Military men also turned up in less expected roles. In 1938, for example, along with color guards and drum and bugle corps, the program included a match between the 124th Field Artillery polo team and that of the Cuban Army.[54] And some entertainments had no obvious relation to the military or the holiday: most years there were circus acts—trained animals or at least acrobats and clowns—and from the late 1950s on, the show often included car racing, the stadium's most popular sport before the Bears moved in, or an "auto thrill show."

Fewer people than usual attended the 1956 show, but its program was typical of the event's later years. It began with a flag-raising ceremony at 7:30 p.m. that included the Stock Yards Post's Kiltie Band and several other posts' bands. A chaplain gave an invocation, and the crowd said the pledge of allegiance and sang the national anthem, after which the bands left the field. Cook County Legion commander Milton Applebaum then welcomed the crowd. After another number by the Kiltie Band were several acrobatic and circus acts: Alarno's Trained Pork Chops, a group of pigs that jumped through hoops and rode teeter-totters, plus two separate chimpanzee troupes, dancing bears, and clowns. Then came some ramp-to-ramp car jumping, and finally the half-hour fireworks show.[55]

While many of the stadium's signature events recurred each year for decades, others were one-time affairs that nonetheless had a tremendous impact on how Chicago and the nation saw the groups that staged them.

8   *Americans All: Culture in an Epic Space*

During its years of popularity, the Chicagoland Music Festival inspired a number of other celebrations. Meanwhile, Soldier Field played host to numerous other cultural and musical events, including several operas, as well as other ethnic and cultural celebrations, such as a tribute to a thousand years of Christianity in Poland. The diversity of the events and their importance in familiarizing Chicagoans with the cultures and ways of life of their neighbors vindicated those who had advocated building a great civic stadium as a way to bring the city together. With every such event, those who had backed Soldier Field's creation could point to its usefulness as a showcase for the best of American culture. And the South Park Commission, and later the Chicago Park District, could point to another example of how its governance—and by extension, that of the Democratic Party—helped bring together the city.

Many cultural events at Soldier Field celebrated the heritage of one ethnic group or another, and one of the first groups to take advantage of the visibility that the stadium afforded to anyone holding an event there was Chicago's large German community. Chicago had a long history of ethnic conflict, dating back at least to 1855, when anti-immigrant Know-Nothings, running on the "Law and Order" ticket, won city elections and began a crackdown on drinking establishments frequented by Irish and German immigrants. The conflict came to a head in what was known as the Lager Beer Riot, in which German Americans from the North Side and others banded together to storm City Hall on the day the first case against a tavern was scheduled. Several people were gravely wounded and a large number arrested. From that time on, Germans became more involved in city politics, though less prominently than their fellow immigrants, the largely English-speaking Irish.

The early twentieth century was not kind to the reputation of German Americans, especially after the United States entered World War I and all things German were actively suppressed. But by the 1920s the city's German population was eager both to celebrate its European heritage and to prove its Americanism; one way it did so was through a yearly festival some German American groups had been holding even before the war. In addition to singing and dancing to traditional music from German-speaking countries, the first German Day event at Soldier Field, held September 20, 1925, included athletic contests and a soccer game. As part of the effort to emphasize the community's loyalty to the United States, the event also included a twenty-one-shot salute to the U.S. flag by Battery F of the 124th Field Artillery, using a 75-centimeter gun that had been used on the Western Front during the Great War. Profits benefited a fund to provide free ice to poor Chicagoans and the *Tribune*'s Camp Algonquin, which allowed city children to visit what was then the rural setting of northwest suburban Algonquin.

The German Day festivals, mounted with the help of as many as 250 German American organizations, continued to be held into the late 1930s, usually in June or September, and consistently drew forty thousand people or more. Delegations from German-speaking countries were regular participants, as were groups from Milwaukee, Gary, Peoria, and other Midwestern cities. Politicians such as U.S. senator Charles Deneen and Mayor Anton Cermak often made appearances, though that became less common in the late 1930s. And most years' festivals included demonstrations of American patriotism. In 1928, while the program was dominated by feats of athletic skill, the crowd reserved its greatest applause for American songs—and the crowd stood to attention when "The Star-Spangled Banner" was played, "with a respect more profound than is usually noticed in strictly English speaking assemblies." The festival celebrated both the German and Austro-Hungarian empires of the past and those countries' democracies of the 1920s and early 1930s, as well as German Americans' love of the United States. (Despite criticism at several German Days of the Eighteenth Amendment, which had outlawed the sale of alcohol in the United States.)[1]

As the Depression wore on the nature of the festival changed, and as the Nazi Party rose to power in Germany the event became controversial. German Americans were fighting among themselves over the direction of their community, with many aghast at the growing influence of Nazism. At the 1933 festival George Seibel of Pittsburgh, an attorney, writer, and friend of novelist Willa Cather, spoke about the contributions of German immigrants to American democracy. Seibel was also national president of the American Turnerbund, an organization created by German immigrants fleeing Europe in the late 1840s and 1850s to promote physical education and socialist political causes. Heavily represented on the Union side in the

Civil War, Turners also were influential in the nineteenth-century push for compulsory public education and in establishing physical education as part of public school curricula throughout the country, including in Chicago. Turner groups dwindled starting in World War I, though many members served in the U.S. military in both world wars and leaders like Seibel worked to counteract anti-German sentiment.[2]

In his 1933 speech at Soldier Field, Seibel emphasized that German immigrants had actively supported American democracy from the very beginning. "Our liberal and progressive institutions in America we owe chiefly to the German immigrant," he said. "The first rebel against British tyranny was Jacob Leisler," who led a rebellion against the English in New York in 1689—almost a hundred years before the American Revolution. "The first who proposed the name of Abraham Lincoln for the presidency was the German Gustav Koerner," an 1836 immigrant to Illinois who was a founder of the Republican Party.[3]

But recovery from the harm done to German American identity by the Great War came to nothing as Nazi control over Germany strengthened. In 1936, for example, a number of Jewish groups protested the Chicago Park District's decision to issue a permit for German Day because of the possibility that swastika flags might be displayed. Park board president Robert J. Dunham acknowledged that "the swastika is to be flown as a courtesy to representatives of the German government who plan to come . . . for the festival." More than previous German Day programs, the 1936 event focused on pageantry and German dancing rather than athletics. The next year, the hundredth anniversary of Chicago's incorporation as a city, saw the last German Day at Soldier Field, though it does not appear to have caused the same controversy. Organizers in 1937 took pains to publicize Germans' long history in the city, noting that the first German citizen of Chicago was Matthias Meyer, a baker and grocer who settled in the area in 1831. Unlike other cultural events at Soldier Field, German Day saw no postwar revival. In fact, on July 19, 1942, the American Slav Congress held a rally at the stadium to mark the 532nd anniversary of the battle of Grunewald—in which Slavs defeated the Germans and their allies—and to tout German defeat in the ongoing war. Later that same year, the Park District and several other groups sponsored a pageant of American patriotism.[4]

CENTURIES OF PROGRESS DEPICTED AT THE FAIR

Other ethnic celebrations at Soldier Field over the years included the three-hundredth anniversary of the first Swedish immigrating to the United States in 1638.[5] But few cultural events were as groundbreaking as *The Romance of a People*, depicting the five-thousand-year history of Judaism, and *O, Sing a*

New Song, a pageant of African American culture and music, both mounted in connection with the 1933–1934 Century of Progress Exposition. *The Romance of a People* helped coalesce the U.S. movement in favor of creating Israel. And while it is less remarked on today, *O, Sing a New Song*, produced by noted jazz composer Noble Sissle, marked a new high point in public recognition of black Americans' contribution to American culture.

Much as the Columbian Exposition and 1909 Burnham Plan had been intended to erase Chicago's image as a dirty, teeming industrial town, the Century of Progress Exposition was geared toward undoing the damage to the city from a decade as a center of national attention during the gangster era of Prohibition. Civic leaders like Major Lenox Lohr, the general manager of the fair, attributed the city's bad reputation to envy of Chicago's status as a great city. It was a defense echoed by mayors in later years, who often derided their critics as do-nothings who only knew how to criticize. Lohr said in a 1929 radio broadcast:

> There are many people in the outside world who give us the atmosphere of a wicked city. Chicago, I believe, is forty-ninth in the list of American cities in the matter of homicide on the basis of population.
>
> Then why this reputation? It is one of the invariable penalties of greatness. . . . If the big man, let us say, wears even a gay necktie, it is a matter of comment just because he is outstanding.[6]

One way to help dispel this reputation was to hold a world's fair showing off the best of the city and of American civilization. The monumental spaces of the Century of Progress Exposition served to highlight for the national and international press how far Chicago had come since its founding—and how it continued to move forward with the transformation first promised in 1893.

The fair's opening day, May 27, 1933, included ceremonies at Soldier Field that displayed the great diversity of Chicago and American culture. Opened by postmaster general James Farley—who also was head of the Democratic National Committee, the ultimate manifestation of the political spoils system—the fair was hailed as a triumph for Chicago, and particularly for Mayor Edward Kelly, who saw it enhance his popularity, especially after he extended its run to 1934. What one reporter called "a congress of nations" included men dressed in Scottish kilts, Native Americans in traditional garb, and black-shirted Italians giving the Fascist salute as they went past the reviewing stand. Cadets from Midwest military academies and a few remaining Civil War veterans from the Grand Army of the Republic joined in a military parade that also included African American veterans, who were "heartily cheered" by the crowd.[7]

The opening ceremonies gave a glimpse into the way that Soldier Field, already one of the most sought-after venues in the nation, served as a showplace for diverse ethnic, cultural, and religious groups. From its earliest years, the stadium helped to bring less widely known social groups into the public eye, while encouraging them to work together for common goals. The effects often reached far beyond an evening of music, dance, and drama.

What became *The Romance of a People* at first seemed like it would be just another ethnic day pageant at the world's fair. But from the start its organizers had in mind a more ambitious goal, especially after the rise to power of Adolf Hitler in Germany. The event became a seminal one for the country's Jewish community, and a test of Chicago's acceptance of ethnic and religious minorities. Jewish Chicago had a long history, but Jewish Chicagoans were less well accepted as part of the city's culture than were Christian Irish or German immigrants. *The Romance of a People* became a touchstone of Jewish pride and a spectacle reveled in by many Chicagoans, Gentile and Jew alike. Rather than promoting assimilation into America's melting pot, the event helped make pride in being Jewish more acceptable to non-Jewish Chicagoans and at the same time, helped define what being Jewish would mean for generations of American Jews.

American Jewish culture had a history of large public shows of solidarity dating back to the beginning of the twentieth century. In the early to mid-1930s, the growing Zionist movement, which advocated creation of a Jewish state, combined with the Nazi threat against German Jews to bring together elements of the Jewish community that previously had rarely worked in concert. *The Romance of a People* became the first, most public manifestation of this coalition and provided a catalyst for later collaboration. It also helped make the Zionist cause attractive to a new generation of Chicago-area Jews seeking a way to make sense of the growing horrors of Nazi Germany.[8]

Jewish Day at the fair was the brainchild of Meyer Weisgal, who until late 1932 had been the Jewish Agency for Palestine's executive director of Zionist activities for the Midwest. For the fair, Weisgal built on the success of a Chanukah pageant he had planned at the Civic Opera House while he was still with the Jewish Agency. Weisgal, a Polish emigrant who lived in Chicago when he was a boy, had returned in 1931 at the request of leaders who feared the Zionist movement was "dying on its feet." What was needed, he realized, was something that would appeal to Jewish audiences in the way that the often simple stories of operas did.

"This inspiration did not come out of the blue," Weisgal wrote in his 1971 autobiography. "A few days after my arrival in Chicago I attended a performance of *Aida* at the Chicago Opera House, and a train of thought was set in motion leading into the heart of my problem. If ridiculous stories and childish plots like *Aida* and *Carmen* could be turned into meaningful and moving experiences by music, color and action, what could not one do with a heroic theme like that of Chanukah?"

To help bring in more adults, Weisgal recruited hundreds of Jewish schoolchildren as extras. The opera house gave him the use of its machinery and props, including some from the production of *Aida*. It met with critical acclaim and was well-received by the Jewish community. It also proved its success in terms of one stereotypical Depression-era Chicago yardstick: racketeers printed thousands of fake tickets, only to have most of them confiscated—and their sellers jailed—when someone tipped off Weisgal's group.[9]

In the wake of the Chanukah pageant's success, and with the support of other Zionist leaders in Chicago, Weisgal approached the fair's president, Rufus C. Dawes, an industrial magnate and brother to former U.S. vice president Charles G. Dawes. Weisgal pitched the pageant as a way to educate visitors to the fair—Jewish or not—about the four thousand years of history of the Jewish people. Weisgal knew Rufus Dawes was "conservative, deeply religious, and loved the Bible," so he pitched him on the Jewish people's having a unique, deep history central to the development of Western civilization. Dawes told him that he would help in any way he could.[10]

Weisgal was able to rally a broad group of Christians and Jews to support the pageant, which was slated for July 3, 1933. Some supported it on principle, some in the hope that it would bring a bonanza of tourism dollars to Chicago. Weisgal worked with several collaborators in planning and orchestrating the pageant, chief among them Isaac Van Grove, the conductor of the Chicago Civic Opera.[11] The event would raise the profile of the Jewish community, raise money for the resettlement of European Jews in Palestine, and celebrate Jewish identity in the face of Nazism's rise. Perhaps most important, Weisgal hoped it would build on the success of the Chanukah pageant to promote Zionism in general.[12]

Recalling more than thirty years later the preparations for the pageant, Weisgal said that he became the chief planner for the event largely by default. "When plans were being made for the Century of Progress fair, the Jews of Chicago decided they should have something at the fair. They couldn't agree on what it should be so they called me in," he explained on a visit to Chicago in 1967, when he was president of Israel's Weizmann Institute of Science. Weisgal got seed money from Judge Harry M. Fisher, a Cook County judge and leading Zionist, and began planning a pageant on a much larger scale than the Chanukah celebration. Their plans were helped by the political calculations of the Chicago Democratic Party. By giving events like *The Romance of a People* a massive public venue, the party could both further its own ends and seem in the public eye to fulfill the good-government objectives of some of the stadium's original backers.[13]

In planning the event, Weisgal took inspiration from his brother and father, both cantors, using more than six thousand singers, actors, and dancers to depict Jewish holidays and history. Most of the cast came from Midwestern cities, but Weisgal also brought in Emma Lazaroff Schaver, the lead soprano of the Tel Aviv Opera. Van Grove used a variety of ancient Jewish musical forms in composing parts of the show. Weisgal had a hand in the initial script, but credited van Grove and others with producing the show.[14]

One of the aims of the pageant, van Grove said at the time, was to increase understanding among non-Jews of Jewish religious passion and belief in a compassionate God. Weisgal and Fisher, by then chairman for Jewish Day, emphasized even more than Weisgal had in pitching the idea to Dawes that Jewish history was the history of Western civilization.[15] The pageant preceded the construction of the Chicago Park District administration building at the north end of the stadium, so like the 1926 Eucharistic Congress, its stage had the Field Museum as a backdrop. The mammoth set built for *Romance* was unquestionably the most elaborate stage ever at the stadium. It was built on four levels, with the largest section 150 wide and 200 feet long, and at its south end had a flight of stairs 60 feet wide up from the stadium arena.[16]

As if the spectacle itself weren't enough, Weisgal decided he needed a Jewish celebrity to top the bill at the pageant. He recruited Chaim Weizmann, the longtime president of the World Zionist Organization, who at the time was living in England, to give a short speech at the beginning of the event, and promised Weizmann he would pay him $100,000 or the speech. Weizmann, later the first president of Israel, was known to many Jews as the man who had saved the world Zionist movement from splintering into national groups in the early 1920s. By 1921, Weisgal noted later, "In the eyes of . . . a large section of American Jewry . . . he was almost a Messianic figure."[17]

"Jewish Day in Chicago, till then of purely local concern, assumed the proportions of a national event," Weisgal wrote later.[18] By June, in part because of Weizmann's promised presence, Jewish groups nationwide signed on as sponsors. By the end of the month, the show had come together, and the cast was ready for a full dress rehearsal at Soldier Field. Ticket sales were brisk, with sixty thousand tickets sold by ten days before the event. Adding to the impact and success of the pageant was an American Zionist convention held the same week in Chicago. Speaking at the convention, Rabbi Stephen Wise of New York decried the months-old German Nazi regime and demanded a two-prong response to Hitler: condemnation by Christians, and the creation of a Jewish state in Palestine. Wise warned prophetically of the effects of Hitler's ideology: "The Jew is always ready to die for his country, but he is not ready to die at the hands of his country."[19]

The night of the pageant, July 3, 1933, authorities dispatched double the number of police officers originally assigned to the event to help with the crowd, which was among the largest ever at Soldier Field, probably trailing only the 1926 Eucharistic Congress and the 1954 Marian Year celebration among cultural events. In all, between 120,000 and 131,000 people crowded into the stadium, many seated on the grass of the arena. Much of the text for the pageant came from Jewish religious ritual and the Jewish Bible. It began with the Genesis account of creation: a single illuminated performer stood at an altar at the center of the stadium, turning the pages of a book, as a voice intoned, "B'reshith boro elohim es hashomaim v'es haorets" ("In the beginning, God created the heavens and the earth, and the earth was without form and void") and colored lights representing the rising sun illuminated the stage.

The pageant continued with hundreds of dancers in gray robes, chanting in Hebrew, "Adonai Echod" ("The Lord is One"). A benediction was sung and the scene changed as a pagan idol—"Brazen Moloch, vomiting fire"—was hauled onto the stage. A scene showing sexual predation and human sacrifices to Moloch, ending with a woman's screams, was followed by the story of Abraham and his willingness to sacrifice his son Isaac, ending with the voice of God telling Abraham to spare his son. From Israel's enslavement in Egypt and Moses confronted by the burning bush, to the building of Solomon's Temple and the sacking of the Second Temple, to the Diaspora in Europe and the immigration of Jews to the United States—all were part of the pageant.[20]

Public reaction to *The Romance of a People* was immediate and intense. "For once the Jews of America seemed to be acting in unison and harmony," Weisgal wrote. The pageant had indeed brought together American Jews as never before and, along with the Zionist convention, helped to spark a new era of pro-Israel sentiment among Chicago Jews. Meanwhile, the *Tribune* ("not particularly a pro-Jewish paper," as Weisgal put it) sponsored a second performance of the pageant at Soldier Field, bringing in as many as seventy-five thousand spectators, Jewish and non-Jewish. The production impressed the *Tribune* enough to cause Philip Maxwell to call Colonel Joseph Medill Patterson, Colonel McCormick's cousin and the founder of the *New York Daily News*, and urge him to sponsor performances in New York. Patterson agreed, and New York governor Herbert Lehman and other civic leaders lent their support to the show.[21]

The pageant was even more successful in New York than in Chicago, even though it had to be rescheduled from an outdoor venue to the Kingsbridge Armory in the Bronx. There it ran for a month and brought in about $450,000, turning a profit of about $150,000. Inspired by the response, Weisgal went on to produce another, even more elaborate show, *The Eternal Road*, in 1937, with music by Kurt Weill, and to manage the Palestine Pavilion at the 1939 New York world's fair.[22]

Whereas Jewish Day at the Chicago fair was successful and had a ripple effect on Jewish culture in the United States, the first day set aside for African Americans at the fair failed abysmally. After years of crusading to get an exhibit at the Century of Progress Exposition honoring Jean Baptiste Pointe DuSable as the founder of Chicago, not just of *black* Chicago, many Chicago blacks were hostile to the idea of a day set aside for members of one ethnic or racial group. But while there were complaints about discrimination against blacks at the fair throughout the year—discrimination fair authorities apparently tried to combat—the reason the pageant failed was that it was not organized with the help of local Chicago community groups or a national group with a strong local base.

Chandler Owen, a onetime socialist leader and editor of the *Chicago Bee* turned would-be Republican politician, took it upon himself to run the world's fair Negro Day events, but he was considered something of an outsider. Merely having the grand space of Soldier Field available was never enough. The stadium worked best when its events were woven into the fabric of Chicago culture. Owen brought in Andrew Dobson, a staffer at WJJD radio and an author, and Sammy Dyer, a theatrical producer and dance instructor, as writer and director of what they decided to call *Epic of a Race*. Dobson consulted with Carl Sandburg on the historical accuracy of the pageant's script and met with him for several hours to go over it. Renowned black actor Richard B. Harrison, who in 1930 had won an NAACP award for distinguished achievement, was booked as master of ceremonies.[23]

Though billed as an event that would draw two hundred thousand people, Negro Day on Saturday, August 12, 1933, saw overall fair attendance drop a hundred thousand from the day before. U.S. representative Oscar DePriest, a South Sider who was the first black congressman elected from a northern state, wrote a letter to the *Chicago Defender* a week before Negro Day to say he would not participate, in part because tickets to the pageant wouldn't admit people to the fair itself. But also, he complained, "I have not yet been able to ascertain where the money is to go if any is made."

Following DePriest's lead, black Chicagoans declined to participate. The South Side parade that preceded the Soldier Field event drew few "civic, fraternal and business groups which are the mainstay of Chicago's citizenry," the *Defender* noted. To be panned by the *Defender* was a death sentence for most black-oriented events of the time. At the time of the pageant, the paper was inspiring an entire generation of Southern African Americans to move north to industrial cities like Chicago, to forge a new life and a new identity. Though some mainstream newspapers wrote about the pageant and delegations that had come from as far away as New York and New Orleans, they refrained from touting attendance figures—a sure indication of a low turnout. the *Defender* called the parade and Negro Day "a flop" and said that "rather than depicting the progress of the Race for the past hundred years, it seemed to show we have retrograded in that time."

Epic of a Race followed the format that had succeeded for *The Romance of a People*. It made use of fifteen hundred performers and as many as three thousand singers, included music by the Eighth Illinois National Guard Regiment Band, and depicted eleven distinct historical episodes. But critics judged the sets sparse and small in the giant arena, the narrative muddled, and the movement of the cast inconsistent with the soberness of much of the storyline. Though the *Defender* said Owen was "well intended," it summed up the event as the day's "final fizzle." (Owen's status as a potential rival to a popular black politician and as editor of a competing publication may have skewed the *Defender*'s coverage; some mainstream newspapers, including the *Herald and Examiner*, were kinder in their assessments.) Dewey R. Jones, who wrote a regular column on the fair for the *Defender*, wrote that "I hope to forget 'Negro Day' as thoroughly and as completely as I have forgotten Caesar's Gallic wars in the original Latin."[24]

Soon after it was announced that the world's fair would be extended for a second year, members of Chicago's black community began discussing how it could be improved for 1934. Black Illinois legislators fought to make the fair more accessible to African Americans and to have them better represented. And a second black-oriented Soldier Field event was soon planned.[25]

Instead of being run by a relative outsider with connections to the less influential *Chicago Bee*, the 1934 pageant, *O, Sing a New Song*, was conceived of by Nahum Daniel Brascher, editor of the Associated Negro Press and a *Defender* columnist. The *Defender* and black community leaders backed the event fully, which helped ensure its success. Brascher enlisted Noble Sissle, coauthor (with Eubie Blake) of the most influential black musical of the 1920s, *Shuffle Along*, to act as general manager of National Auditions, Inc., the ad hoc group that would stage the production.[26] In a measure of Brascher and Sissle's influence, *O, Sing a New Song* attracted many of the most celebrated black musicians, writers, composers, and musical directors of the time. Onah Spencer, a correspondent with *Down Beat* magazine, collaborated with Sissle on the script. Other musicians who worked on the project included Harry Lawrence Freeman, whose *Voodoo* was the first opera written by a black man to be staged on Broadway; W. C. Handy, considered the father of the blues; and Major N. Clark Smith, a composer, bandleader, and music instructor who had organized Chicago's first black symphony orchestra. J. Wesley Jones, the longtime director of the Chicagoland Music Festival's black chorus, and James A. Mundy, another well-known Chicago choir leader, took charge of the choirs.[27]

Wesley Jones deserves more recognition than he receives today in the annals of Chicago music. The son of former slaves, Jones came to Chicago in 1906 at about age twenty-two after graduating from Walden College in Nashville, where he was sent by the director of the Tennessee Industrial School for Orphans. After pushing a wheelbarrow during the construction of Orchestra Hall and acting as a West Side correspondent for the *Defender*, Jones worked his way up from music director at a small West Side chapel to choir director at the South Side's large Metropolitan Community Church, a post he held for thirty-eight years. As the *Defender* noted in an editorial at the time of his death, Jones "was one of the men most responsible for keeping the traditional singing of Negro spirituals alive."[28]

Soon after the announcement of the pageant in March 1934, the *Defender* began a campaign to bring black musicians to Chicago for *O, Sing a New Song*. Brascher's usual column space became devoted to promoting the event. National Auditions planned contests throughout the country, similar to those for the Chicagoland Music Festival, to culminate in the Soldier Field event, with the aim being to bring the black musicians to the attention of the recording industry and Hollywood.[29]

Although the fair did better than in its first year, discrimination still continued in employment, and the exposition was not without the petty humiliations and slights against African Americans. Even as Chicago's blacks were pushing to be included fully at the Century of Progress, the *Defender* was waging a war to end lynching. On the day Brascher's first column on *O, Sing a New Song* appeared in the *Defender*'s national edition, the paper also carried an item about a Kentucky lynch mob.

Despite a number of obstacles to integrating the fair, Chicago blacks were able to enlist Mayor Kelly and Rufus Dawes to support *O, Sing a New Song*. Their photos appeared, along with Handy's, in the advertisement announcing the musical competition, which promised $3,000 in cash prizes (about $50,000 in 2008 dollars). "Music is the eternal heritage of the Negro!" the ad declared. "We have made good use of the heritage. The best is yet to come."[30] Brascher also enlisted white political leaders in cities such as Indianapolis to encourage participation in the event and secured seed money from the Julius Rosenwald Fund (which largely financed the creation of the Museum of Science and Industry).[31]

The hype in the run-up to the festival made it clear that many of the most prominent black musicians of the day were pitching in to help with the pageant.[32] Much of the early preparation of the script went on in New York, in meetings at Handy's offices. By July, Freeman, the opera composer, and others had journeyed to Chicago to complete the arrangements with Sissle and participate in rehearsals.[33] Rehearsals for the pageant's five thousand singers and thirty-five hundred dancers began in midsummer, with singers practicing at Wendell Phillips High School, the city's first predominantly African American high school. Groups were directed by musicians including

Freeman, Jones, and James A. Mundy, whose Mundy Choristers performed weekly concerts at the fair in both 1933 and 1934. In addition to his other duties, Sissle drilled two hundred men in military maneuvers at the 8th Regiment Armory for a scene in the pageant depicting black contributions to the U.S. military.[34]

To enhance publicity for the pageant, Sissle gave a preview to white backers. "Feeling that the great Negro composers should express themselves in telling the story of their race before they died, we interested the Rosenwald fund, which gave us a start," he told them. "Never before have the Negro people in America attempted a production of the magnitude and significance of this."

Though many notables came to Chicago to join in the pageant, few caused as much of a stir as a delegation of Zulus from South Africa, who arrived several weeks before the event. They arrived in full traditional dress, the men in beaded leather loincloths, eagle-feather headdresses, and hand-carved brown bead necklaces and the women in leather tops and short skirts decorated with colored glass, mirrors, and beads. They refused to let redcaps at LaSalle Street rail station carry the zebra-skin shields, war clubs, and war drums they had brought with them for the pageant, and caused a scene when they went into the station.[35]

In the last days before the event, special trains chartered from Memphis, Saint Louis, and Cincinnati brought visitors to Chicago for the festival. More than a hundred seamstresses put the finishing touches on five thousand green and brown robes to be worn in a scene in which dancers took the place of stalks of cotton. Bill "Bojangles" Robinson arrived the night before the pageant in time for the last dress rehearsal. Cast members and stage designers worked late into the night, rehearsing their parts and even weaving baskets as part of the scenery.[36]

The night of the pageant, about sixty thousand people filled the stadium. In imitation of the ceremony in which President Grover Cleveland had opened the 1893 Columbian Exposition by pressing a button at the White House to turn on the fairground's electric lights, President Franklin Roosevelt lit up Soldier Field by pressing a button at the White House. Smith—the festival conductor, himself the son of an African immigrant—Freeman, Will Marion Cook and J. Rosamond Johnson, and W. C. Handy each conducted a portion of the program based on their compositions. After a prologue that included part of Smith's "Negro Choral Symphony," with lead singer Lillian Jackson, came three acts depicting black experiences in Africa, under slavery, and in modern times. Richard B. Harrison, who also had acted as master of ceremonies for 1933's Negro Day pageant, served as narrator.

Although it was written by African Americans and included African tribe members as actors, the style of the pageant—storytelling through musical numbers, much like the operas Weisgal had used as his model—lent itself to the use of stock characters and situations. Tom-toms signaled dawn over an African village to start the first act. Warriors threw spears to kill a lion, then a human sacrifice was averted through the mercy of a tribal king. The act closed with Portuguese traders attacking the village and carrying the king and his tribe off to slavery. To lead into the second act, which started with a plantation scene, Harrison read a passage about black destiny in America. Wesley Jones led the *Tribune*'s festival chorus in several spirituals, including "Steal Away to Jesus," thought by some to be a song sung when slaves were planning to escape. The five thousand dancers in brown and green robes mimicked cotton plants, and a woman playing a white slave owner told the story of Moses. Alternating strains of "John Brown's Body" and "Dixie" played, then an actor portraying Abraham Lincoln came forward and read parts of the Emancipation Proclamation. The last act depicted the progress of African Americans since the Civil War, though it included a few passages we might today think clashed with that idea; after a scene featuring Booker T. Washington, the full chorus sang "Carry Me Back to Old Viginny," which includes these lyrics: "There's where I labored so hard for old Massa / Day after day in the field of yellow corn; / No place on earth do I love more sincerely / Than old Virginny, the state where I was born."

The third act also included a number by Sissle, "On Patrol in No Man's Land," about black soldiers' service in the Great War, and a medley of then-current songs from Harlem. Bojangles Robinson brought the crowd to its feet with his tap dancing, Handy conducted a piece based on his "St. Louis Blues," and the pageant ended with the entire cast singing Sissle's composition for the occasion, the title number for the pageant:

> O, let us sing a new song
> O, let us sing a new song
> Let's help each other,
> Sister and brother
> To sing a new song.[37]

What we might now think of as shortcomings in the pageant cannot detract from its lasting importance. African Americans came from all over the country to attend what was then one of the largest mixed-race gatherings ever held in a public place, if not the largest. (Reports indicate about a quarter of the audience was white.)

Unlike the annual Chicagoland Music Festival, *O, Sing a New Song* was a onetime event with no opportunity to build up a reputation for fostering young talent. Still, some winners of its national auditions did go on to professional music careers, including Clyde Winkfield, who came in third in instrumental music and in 1938 became the Detroit Symphony Orchestra's first black pianist.[38]

With most big happenings at the Century of Progress guaranteed to garner public attention, the event received some national coverage, including an Associated Press report carried by a number of newspapers (though the *New York Times* and several other papers only carried capsule versions of the story). At least part of it was also broadcast nationally. Albert G. Barnett, another writer for the *Defender*, gushed over the pageant: "Its value in the furtherance of interracial goodwill and understanding is one that cannot be overestimated."[39]

The event enhanced the professional reputations of those involved. But another long-term effect was to show to the rest of Chicago, and the country, that black entertainers were capable of putting on a stupendous, large-scale spectacle. In an era in which much of the country's white population still doubted African Americans' abilities to organize even a small business, Brascher, Sissle, and their collaborators were able to put together an event to rival the biggest and flashiest ever staged at Soldier Field. The stadium had once again fulfilled its purpose.

The Romance of a People and *O, Sing a New Song* were not the only show-cases of American cultural heritage held at Soldier Field over the years, or even during the Century of Progress Exposition. Apart from Negro Day, the fair's ethnic days often were among its most popular, and many included a pageant. While the Jewish and African American spectaculars may have had more lasting significance, *The Pageant of the Celt*, celebrating the history of the Celtic people—the Irish, Scots, Welsh, Manx, and Bretons—gained as much recognition nationwide at the time.

Produced with the help of both Irish actors and historians of Celtic culture, the pageant was held a few days after *O, Sing a New Song*. It too followed the formula for historical pageants, including a thousand-voice chorus. Its narrative began with a tremendous battle involving native Irish tribes and an invading force in 1700 BC—and of course included a scene about Saint Patrick. The pageant made good use of the vast Soldier Field arena, placing a Druidic ceremony attended by an Irish tribal king in the center of the stadium while the actor playing Saint Patrick lit an Easter fire in one corner of the arena. When the king had Patrick arrested, the saint went calmly and then used a shamrock to explain the Christian Trinity. The next scene showed the mythical queen and prince and other members of their tribe being baptized. Micheál MacLiammoir, the Irish actor who established the famed Gate Theater in Dublin, narrated the pageant, which was popular enough that its run was extended from one night to two.[40]

Throughout much of the stadium's history, groups that held celebrations of their cultures at Soldier Field were guaranteed a higher profile than would have been possible at any other venue. As a large downtown space owned by a secular, nominally neutral government body, it was extremely visible and relatively affordable. Though more spectacular and highly publicized than most comparable events over the years, the ethnic programs that took place during the Century of Progress Exposition are typical of Soldier Field's cultural pageants. Other such events included a 1937 pageant marking the accomplishments of Chicagoans of Polish origin, part of the city's hundredth anniversary party, which was attended by fifty thousand people. Yet Soldier Field primarily functioned as a sports stadium, and as sports palace it gave Chicago's families a grand if sometimes run-down place to bring their children.

9 *A Family Place*

Most Chicagoans today think of Soldier Field as the Chicago Bears' home stadium. But the Bears were not the first professional football team to make the stadium their home, much less the first professional athletes to perform there. For decades, in fact, professional sports other than football dominated the stadium's calendar.

The first professional sport presented at Soldier Field is one more associated with Texas than Chicago—rodeo. In the heyday of the city's meatpacking industry, many Chicagoans, including Richard J. Daley before he entered politics, worked as cowboys rounding up cattle at the Union Stock Yards.[1] Many of the men and women who participated in the earliest rodeos in Soldier Field were ranch hands rather than professionals on the rodeo circuit. But as Soldier Field came to prominence between the world wars, great changes were taking place in the sport. In that period, rodeo's popularity grew enormously, Wild West shows disappeared, and the first professional rodeo organizations were organized. Rodeo stars were becoming professionals, and in the years when rodeos were most popular at Soldier Field, similar shows were drawing as many as 250,000 people in New York.[2]

The Chicagoland Chamber of Commerce sponsored Soldier Field's first rodeo in 1925. The event was put on by John Van "Tex" Austin—the Rodeo King—one of the most influential promoters in the history of the sport. Born about 1888 in South Carolina or Texas, Austin—whose parents were Jewish and whose last name was a pseudonym—left home at age twelve, going west. A masterful horseman, Austin worked as a cattle hand and trader for more than two decades, and began promoting big-city rodeos after World War I. By the time his first Chicago Roundup was scheduled, Austin had staged rodeos in New York's Madison Square Garden and Yankee Stadium and at Wembley Stadium in London.[3]

Chicago's rodeo was part of a larger scheme to use Grant Park Stadium to attract tourists to the city. In announcing the event, the Association of Commerce cited the huge popularity roundups had in Western cities like Cheyenne, Wyoming, and Pendleton, Oregon.[4] The annual Madison Square Garden show—which Austin had founded but lost control of—was not yet considered the last stop on each year's national rodeo circuit, and Chicago businessmen hoped to make the city's rodeo the most important championship contest of the year. Performers in the nine-day contest would be independent contestants, rather than Austin's employees, as in a Wild West show, and would compete for prizes totaling $32,000. Their mounts would be steers and wild horses culled by Austin at his ranch. Austin promised the meanest-tempered horses in the world—the better to give the audience an authentic Western experience. "Not one is trained to buck," Wilbur D. Nesbit, an advertising executive who was helping to promote the rodeo told the *Tribune*. "He does it because he wants to. His cussedness is plumb natural."[5]

Although most comment on the rodeo was favorable, there were some protests because of concerns about animal cruelty. "This barbarous and cruel form of so-called entertainment is . . . an outrageous disgrace to our civilized community," wrote Dr. H. J. Streibert of the Anti-Cruelty Society in a letter to the *Tribune*. The Illinois Humane Society, however, dismissed his objection. "There are cranks in every line of endeavor," said George A. H. Scott, the group's secretary, who also happened to be the chairman of the American Humane Society's national committee on rodeos. Austin assured everyone that the rodeo would adhere to strict rules: no drinking of hard liquor, abusing livestock, or quarreling with other contestants would be tolerated. "We urge those who have heard the charges of brutality to witness the exhibition," he said, pitching tickets even as he answered his critics.[6]

With the Humane Society in his corner, Austin turned to attracting contestants. A number of champion cowboys, including husband and wife Mabel Strickland and Hugh Strickland and trick roper Chester Byers of Oklahoma, entered more than a month in advance. Also on the schedule were rodeo clowns and trick riders King Merritt (later a champion steer roper) and John Dixon "Red" Sublett, one of the earliest and most famous rodeo clowns. The city's newspapers fawned over the entrants, with the *Daily News* running a three-hundred-word story on cowboy slang and another declaring that the city had been "lassoed by cowgirl champs."

On the first day of the rodeo, August 15, seventy-five cowboys and fifty cowgirls rode through the Loop not on horses but on an open-topped double-decker bus. Back at the stadium, the saddles were polished and the horses combed to a shine. An eight-foot-high fence surrounded the contest area on

RED SUBLETT "SPARK PLUG" TEX AUSTIN'S RODEO,
(DOUBLEDAY) CHICAGO.

John Dixon "Red" Sublett, a popular early-twentieth-century rodeo clown who Tex Austin helped make a star. Note the open north end of Soldier Field, with the Field Museum in the background, ca. 1925. By permission of National Cowboy & Western Heritage Museum, Oklahoma City.

the field to keep the livestock from straying into the box seats and grandstands. U.S. vice president Charles G. Dawes was the guest of honor at the opening ceremonies, which began with a parade of the contestants and officials, including a director of the Anti-Cruelty Society, Chauncey McCormick of the McCormick Reaper manufacturing family. Streibert also was on hand to prevent any cruelty to animals, claiming that a horse "may not even get his feed" if its owner fails to win.

But Streibert sounded one of the few discordant notes that day. The competitors were enthusiastic about the amount of prize money and amazed by the large turnout. Spectators had come from as far away as New York and Oregon, and in large numbers from throughout the Midwest. After the 3:30 p.m. parade, contests began with bareback bronco riding, followed by fancy roping, relay races, calf roping, and other rodeo staples.[7]

While housed at Soldier Field, the five hundred animals Austin imported for the rodeo ate more than two hundred tons of oats, hay, and straw. In later years, the rodeo sometimes turned the animals loose in the stadium arena, where they grazed for several days before the start of the show. (Not something today's Bears would tolerate.) Austin used a special crossbreed of

Norman Mason, riding bucking bronco Hot Shot at Soldier Field, most likely in 1925. The full stands testify to the popularity of rodeo in Chicago at the time. By permission of National Cowboy & Western Heritage Museum, Oklahoma City.

cattle for his bull riding contests, a mix of humped Brahman cows from India and Mexican longhorns. For the steer-wrestling contests, he used longhorn Mexican cattle, considered at the time the most ornery breed.

The Chicago businesspeople who gambled on bringing the rodeo to town must have been pleased with Tex Austin's performance. Only about thirty thousand people showed up for the start of the event, but a hundred thousand people took in the two performances that day. By the third day, the *Daily News* was reporting that thirty-seven thousand Midwesterners had arrived in Chicago by train on one day alone, apparently drawn by the roundup. Daily attendance averaged between 50,000 and 70,000, and one day the number of spectators reported for two shows was 145,000. Among those who made the rodeo part of their summer visit to the city was a group of 150 prominent Mississippians who were traveling the country in a rented train to encourage tourism in their own state.[8]

One competitor at the rodeo was bronco rider Pete Knight, who won some events but not the overall bronco riding championship at the 1925 Chicago Roundup. Among the year's all-around winners were Louis Jones for calf roping, Tad Lucas for women's fancy and trick riding and for the women's relay race (in which she upset Mabel Strickland), and Rube Roberts for steer wrestling. Some corporate sponsors chipped in prizes in addition to the cash awards. For example, Edwin F. Carry, president of the Pullman Company, donated silver championship cups and solid gold belt buckles for the winners.[9]

Spurred by its first-year success, Austin's Chicago Roundup rodeo ran three more years at Soldier Field. Even on a rainy day in 1926, thirty-five thousand people turned out to see the show, watching numerous cowboys slip and slide through the stadium mud (two received minor injuries). Sublett, the Stricklands, and other stars returned for the 1926 event. Mabel Strickland, who had held the title of top rodeo cowgirl in the United States for six years before Lucas bested her at the 1925 Chicago Roundup, regained it, in part by winning the women's relay race. The rodeo that year drew as many as eighty thousand people in one day, and Chicago boys who won a roping contest got a free trip to Tex Austin's ranch as a prize. The 1927 rodeo was even more successful, drawing more than 350,000 people in its nine-day run. When it ended, however, the Association of Commerce announced that it would discontinue its sponsorship, passing responsibility for the event to City Hall, because the complexity of staging a rodeo each year got in the way of the association's primary mission. Tex Austin's contract with the association was canceled. But the next year, he was back anyway, with $33,000 in prizes. That year's roundup received less publicity in the newspapers than in previous years, despite the presence of movie stars Edmund "Hoot" Gibson, who spent several days there shooting scenes for *The King of the Rodeo*, and Tom Mix. It failed to match the successes of previous years, and it was not brought back to Soldier Field, although Austin did stage a smaller rodeo at the Chicago Stadium in 1929. Many traveling shows like circuses, Wild West shows and rodeos ended in the late 1920s and early 1930s, faced with economic hardship and the growing popularity of movies. Austin too met a sad fate, a decade after his last Chicago Roundup. Diagnosed with an illness that would leave him blind within six months, he committed suicide in his garage in New Mexico.[10]

The 1928 rodeo was not the last one held at Soldier Field, however. In 1933 a highly successful rodeo was staged in conjunction with the Century of Progress Exposition. The sport also had a brief resurgence there in the 1940s, with shows in 1941, 1942, 1943, and 1947. The later shows used celebrities to lure people in, with Gene Autry, a singing cowboy of movie and radio fame, starring in the 1942 rodeo. Several cowboys from Valparaiso, Indiana, competed in that show and had the thrill of talking to Autry, as well as Tex Cooper, a workhorse actor who acted in dozens of Westerns. Cooper, who looked like Buffalo Bill Cody, had played in Cody's Wild West Show in the late 1800s, and continued to perform in Western shows and attend rodeos long after he began movie acting.

Movie star Tom Mix with fans at the 1928 Chicago Roundup. Courtesy Chicago History Museum. Chicago Daily News archive, glass negative DN-0085660.

As in the 1920s, the shows attracted large crowds, almost filling the stadium for some performances. Like many of the most successful Soldier Field events, they were benefits—in this case, for the Veterans of Foreign Wars, which used the proceeds to send a carton of cigarettes to any serviceman fighting abroad whose family or friends asked for them. The 1942 show, which cost $40,000 to produce, included two hundred horses, two hundred cowboys and cowgirls, among other performers, and thirty Brahman bulls and steers. Although prizes were offered for competitors, the shows were more staged than those in the 1920s and also incorporated some circus acts.

The 1947 rodeo was also a fund-raiser, for an American Legion home for disabled veterans in Orland Park. In addition to traditional rodeo contests, that year's events included a beauty contest, in which nineteen-year-old Pat Varner, who had learned to ride on Chicago Park District bridle paths, was crowned Chicago rodeo queen. The 1947 rodeo, along with a midget auto race the night of one of the rodeo's championship performances, on July 20, was also among the first Soldier Field events to be televised. "Children were especially enthusiastic about the job the television station did on the rodeo at Soldiers' Field. The bucking broncos and bulls were extremely realistic," one report noted.[11]

Most rodeos in Chicago after 1947 were held at the Chicago Amphitheatre, which offered better facilities for animals and a guarantee that the shows wouldn't be rained out—a constant threat at Soldier Field. Rodeos were held at the amphitheater regularly until about 1981, a decade after the Union Stock Yards closed. Although rodeo stunts made a few appearances at Fourth of July shows and other events at the stadium, the last real rodeo at Soldier Field was in 1966, a few weeks before the yearly College All-Star Game. That event also included stunt-car driving to liven things up. Among the animals entered in the 1966 rodeo was a prize bull, Lippy Leo, owned by baseball great Leo Durocher, at the time manager of the Chicago Cubs. The show suffered from bad weather on the first of its five days, and while it was well received, appears to have failed to renew interest in rodeo in Chicago.[12]

The rodeo, as both the *Tribune* and the *Defender* noted, was an integrated sport well before 1966, but blacks were rarely top competitors. One of its pioneers, in the early twentieth century, was Bill Pickett, a black cowboy who invented "bulldogging"—that is, steer wrestling—as a rodeo sport.

As critics had pointed out, the rodeo contests included an element of danger. On the first day of the Chicago Roundup's 1925 debut, one cowboy, Jack Wilson, was gored in a steer-wrestling contest. Then, at a Friday performance in 1926, a rodeo bronco killed a cowgirl at the stadium. Louise Hartwig of Big Sandy, Montana, had a successful ride that night, but as she was about to be helped down from the horse, it threw her from the saddle and crushed her head under its hooves. Estranged from her husband, Hartwig had left her five-year-old son with her mother in Springfield, Missouri, before the rodeo, friends told reporters. Tex Austin announced he would pay for Hartwig's funeral, which was held two days later, on the morning of the rodeo's last day. Association of Commerce chief William Dawes, the vice president's cousin, gave a eulogy to the more than a hundred cowboys who showed up to pay their respects. Dawes—a banker and brother of the vice president—spoke about "the type of western womanhood the dead girl represented." Hartwig still appears to have been the only performer fatally injured at a Soldier Field event.[13]

Although rodeos were held at Soldier Field many times, boxing is one of the professional sports most associated with the stadium's early history. This stems exclusively from the famous 1927 fight between Jack Dempsey and Gene Tunney, the "long count" match that resulted in Tunney retaining his world heavyweight championship.

Raised in a Colorado mining town, the ninth of thirteen children, Dempsey struck out on his own at age sixteen, and began his fighting career in tavern matches. Famous for his aggressive style in the ring, he had dominated the ring since 1919, when he captured the heavyweight title, and he was also a presence on the big screen, dabbling in movies and marrying an actress. But by the time of his first meeting with Tunney, in 1926, he had neglected workouts and training, and the challenger took his title. Tunney also had a working-class background and was part of a large Irish American family, but he had grown up in Greenwich Village and gained national prominence after joining the Marine Corps and winning the Armed Forces light heavyweight title.[14]

Boxing promoter George "Tex" Rickard had tried to set up a match between Dempsey and Tunney in Chicago in 1926 after the New York State boxing commission had banned the fight from taking place there. Illinois had only just legalized boxing again after a three-year ban, and businessmen who made money off tourism, as well as politicians (and probably what were then known in the papers as "hoodlums"), were eager to have Chicago host a championship fight. With that in mind, Rickard traveled to Chicago in July 1926 and announced that the fight would be held there in September. Edward Kelly, at the time president of the South Park Commission, refused to comment on whether Soldier Field could be rented for the match. A few days later, though, newspaper headlines across the country screamed that Rickard's decision was wavering, and the fight might not be held in Chicago. What swayed Rickard is unclear. One account had it that "petty politicians" jammed Rickard's temporary office in Chicago the minute he announced the location of the fight, all demanding their cut of the presumed proceeds, causing Rickard to give up in disgust. A promoter tied to the Chicago Coliseum claimed to have a contract with Dempsey for a title fight. Others said Rickard's Chicago backers got cold feet about how little they might earn.

Dempsey's trainer and longtime confidant, Teddy Hayes, claimed in his autobiography that the match ended up in Philadelphia because he and Rickard bribed the wrong Illinois politician. Rickard might have known plenty about boxing, but in Chicago, knowing the right people has always helped. And pleasing the right politician could often make a difference between holding an event at Soldier Field or not. Hayes wrote that Rickard asked him to go to Chicago to negotiate a deal to hold the 1926 fight at the stadium. Rickard had been told that Len Small, the governor of Illinois, was the man to talk to—and the man to whom to give a $100,000 "campaign contribution" to secure Soldier Field. Through a longtime friend, Hayes set up a meeting with Jacob Kern, an attorney close to Small, and he brought the talk around to the money. Kern called Small, and Small arranged to meet Hayes the following Sunday at the governor's home, where he agreed to the arrangement. When

Rickard came from New York to Chicago to complete the deal, however, Kelly summoned him to his attorney's office and warned him that no one could arrange for a Soldier Field permit without his say-so. Rickard came out of the office "with a look on his face like a man gets when he has been cut out of the will," Hayes recounted. Kelly had told Rickard that, because Hayes had first gone to Small, it would cost $300,000 to get Soldier Field.

A *Tribune* reporter wrote the next year that Rickard had divulged to him reasons why it was impossible to hold the fight in Chicago. "Those reasons were so personal that they were not for publication. Furthermore, some of them would not look well in print." Circumstantial evidence for Hayes's account comes from Small's later indictment on corruption charges, although a jury acquitted him.[15] In any case, Philadelphia officials wooed Rickard, and Dempsey and Tunney fought in that city on September 23, 1926, with Tunney taking the heavyweight crown from Dempsey. One account has it that Small and Rickard sat next to each other at the Philadelphia fight. "Soldier Field will hold 200,000 people, more than any other stadium in the country," Small is said to have told Rickard. "Chicago is centrally located, easy to get to and a live town." Rickard needed little convincing. "Well, governor, the next big fight'll be held in Chicago," Rickard supposedly replied.

By the following June, Rickard again was rumored to be interested in bringing Tunney and a challenger—either Dempsey or another fighter, Jack Sharkey—to Chicago. On June 19 the news came out that Rickard had signed all three fighters and that the championship match likely would be held in Chicago in September. Democratic leader and South Park commissioner Michael Igoe, Kelly, and George Getz, representing Mayor Thompson, all traveled to New York City to meet with Rickard. Kelly and the others promised Rickard he would pay less than $150,000 to rent the stadium and that he would receive the full cooperation of Thompson and the South Park Commission. One Chicagoan who was at the meeting told newspapers that he believed "the deal was closed," despite pitches made that day by New York and Philadelphia. Kelly, however, said that he would wait for the people of Chicago to express their opinion for or against the bout. Apparently he decided Chicagoans wanted it badly enough, and backed the match. As one South Park official put it later in a memoir of the fight, "Upon the invitation of . . . Kelly, the citizenry expressed itself overwhelmingly in favor of the event."[16]

Politicians weren't the only pressure group Rickard had to deal with. Veterans had fully accepted Soldier Field as a war memorial, and the Dempsey-Tunney fight was one of the first instances of their attempting to prevent its desecration—something that would be echoed seventy years later in the fight over the 2001–2003 renovation. Members of the American Legion were incensed by reports that Jack Dempsey had dodged the draft during the Great War, despite the fact that a number of Legion posts—and a federal court—had determined the charges were false. In 1920 Dempsey had been charged in federal court with seeking to evade military service after his ex-wife, Maxine, accused him of what was known at the time as "slacking." The much-publicized trial, in San Francisco, heard testimony from the pugilist, whose real name was William Harrison Dempsey, that he had been the primary wage earner in his family since age fourteen and had asked for an exemption from the draft because his wife and family depended on him for support. During the war, Dempsey had worked in a shipyard in Philadelphia, as well as fighting a number of matches for military charities, he testified. A Navy lieutenant who met Dempsey while he was boxing at Great Lakes Naval Training Station, Lieutenant John Kennedy (apparently no relation to President Kennedy) told the court that Dempsey had asked him to get him released from his exemption so that he could return to Philadelphia and enlist. The permission came through in the fall of 1918, Kennedy testified, but it was rescinded when the armistice was signed ending the war. The jury took ten minutes to acquit.

Despite the trial's outcome, the charge of draft dodging haunted Dempsey throughout his career. Soon after the Dempsey-Tunney fight was announced, former Indiana congressman Frederick Landis urged his state's American Legion to oppose the Soldier Field fight. Delegates to the Indiana Legion's convention voted to urge Chicago to reject the fight, agreeing with Landis that "Dempsey is a slacker." A few days later, a Chicago attorney, J. Kentner Elliott, filed a taxpayer suit in Cook County Circuit Court to stop the fight on several grounds: allowing Dempsey to fight there would run counter to the stadium's purpose as a war memorial, he argued; moreover, the fight, a for-profit event, would produce no public benefit and thus should not take place in a taxpayer-funded facility. Perhaps the most stunning blow came when the Gold Star Fathers and Mothers, through Fred and Josephine Bentley, parents of one of the first U.S. casualties in World War I (see chapter 1), declared their opposition to the fight. "It will be an insult to the memory and glory of those who gave their lives for this country to allow this field to be the scene of a championship boxing match," Bentley told the South Park Commission, before it voted 4–1 in favor of renting the stadium to Rickard's representatives for $100,000.

Noise about desecration of the field continued for a while, with one local Legion post proposing that the Soldier Field name be removed from the stadium, and another proposing that the $100,000 be used to build a memorial there. (Something that the South Park Commission still had not done.) Kelly and the other board members, however, argued that the business community was in favor of the match because the tens of thousands of people who would come to Chicago for the match would spend at least $5 million. "The field was dedicated not only to the dead, but to the living," Kelly told Bentley, adding he thought the "boys" would have enjoyed the proposed match. As with the lakefront designs of the original 1909 Burnham Plan, the beautiful stadium also had a useful purpose, in this case, drawing boxing enthusiasts to Chicago to spend money. South Park vice president B. E. Sunny said that the $100,000 would "help meet the expenses" of the stadium. In the end, the terms of the agreement were especially generous to Rickard and his fellow investors. Rickard expected to take in almost $3 million from the match, $1 million of which would go to Tunney and about $500,000 to Dempsey. [17]

In preparation for the fight, the Illinois Athletic Commission adopted a new rule regarding knockouts, under which a boxer would be found to lose if he failed to stand up within ten seconds of being knocked down, as counted by the referee. The new rule, supposedly formulated by Dempsey supporters and agreed to by Dempsey, specified that the referee's count would not start until the fighter who was still standing had retreated to a neutral corner. The rule was designed to keep the standing boxer from hitting the downed boxer immediately if he stood up in less than ten seconds. Dempsey, who lived in Los Angeles at the time, moved to Chicago about a month before the fight to train at the Lincoln Fields racetrack in Crete, Illinois (now known as Balmoral Park). There, crowds of five thousand or more came out and paid to see him spar with training partners. Tunney, meanwhile, trained in upstate New York, and at a former estate on Fox Lake in Quincy, Illinois, that was about to be developed into Cedar Crest Country Club. Newspapers around the country tracked both boxers' every move, and reported whatever could be gleaned from their training about their condition.

More than a month before the September 22 fight, Rickard set up headquarters at the Congress Hotel and started selling tickets at prices ranging from $5 to $40 (about $63 to $500 in 2008 dollars). On one day alone he took in $200,000 and by early September $2 million. At that point Rickard released a list of who had reserved tickets, including the South Park Commission, which had twenty-five hundred, the Chicago press, with twelve hundred, and Mayor Thompson and Governor Small, with six hundred each. A week before the fight, Rickard released the names of many of those getting so-called front-row seats. Unsurprisingly, the select few included Kelly, who had three such tickets. George Brennan, the leader of the Cook County Democratic Party, was to be his guest at the bout.[18]

Over the years, the machinations surrounding the fight have become almost as legendary as its result. It was well known that Dempsey was friendly, if not friends, with Al Capone. Capone spent $50,000 on parties for Dempsey the week before the fight—according to some accounts, the same amount that he ended up losing in bets when Tunney won. In later years, Dempsey maintained that he had discouraged Capone from bribing someone to fix the match. Capone responded by sending flowers to Dempsey and his wife, with a card reading, "To the Dempseys in the name of sportsmanship." In a series on racketeer influence in boxing, Charles J. McGuirk—who later collaborated with Dempsey on a *Saturday Evening Post* article—alleged that Capone spent the evening before the fight with Dempsey at Lincoln Fields, along with Bill Duffy, another racketeer. But they weren't the ones who tried to influence the fight, McGuirk alleged. Another racketeer who also was a notorious gambler, and a politician close to the athletic commission, came to see Dempsey and told him he needed to pay them $100,000 in protection money to fix the fight. Dempsey sat for a minute, then replied, "I don't want no protection. I can whip Tunney without it." After Capone left, the rumor was, he put $150,000 on Dempsey. But at the same time, the other, unnamed racketeer put his money on Tunney. Some gamblers concluded the match was fixed for Dempsey, others that it was fixed for Tunney. "It never occurred to these 'smart fellows' that the fight might be on the level. It never does."[19]

The fight approached, with newspapers devoting as much as three or four pages to previewing it, often in deeply purple prose. Many newspapers, including the *New York Times*, considered Dempsey the favorite, but opinions varied widely, and the *Tribune* reported on the day of the fight that most boxing experts in Chicago for the bout favored Tunney. "At the end of ten rounds or less Jack Dempsey will be the new heavyweight champion of the world. That's my guess and I'm going to stick to it," wrote Paul Lowry, sports editor of the *Los Angeles Times*. Cowboy Tom Mix, a friend of Dempsey's and himself an attraction at a Soldier Field rodeo the next year, said he thought Tunney was scared of how much better shape Dempsey was in than he had been at the time of the 1926 bout. Damon Runyon, one of the most prominent sportswriters of the time, wrote, "The little torch of civilization sputters feebly tonight against the furious flares of human savagery. A great prize fight impends. . . . I would say that Dempsey's hope lies in the chance that the champion's insufferable ego may send him into the ring determined to show the world that he is a ripsnorting son-of-a-gun when he has the mind."[20]

The field was set up much the way it would be for later amateur fights, with a ring in the middle of the vast arena amid seats set up on planking, in addition to the regular seats in the stands. All over the country, people rearranged their furniture to listen in on the radio. The *Tribune* and six other Chicago newspapers and radio stations received special permission from the South Park Commission and Rickard to broadcast the fight, although NBC was sending it live to about sixty-five stations around the country. The *Tribune* even printed a cartoon scorecard so listeners could keep track of who landed how many punches when. Graham MacNamee was slated to broadcast, and in New York City at the 71st Regiment Armory, two boxers followed MacNamee's description of the fight. In a highly unusual move, the Illinois

Athletic Commission voted to reserve the right to make the final ruling as to who won the fight. Speculation ran rampant about who the referee would be, with many guessing it would be Walter Eckersall, the *Tribune* writer and close associate of Knute Rockne (see chapter 3). The commission said only that the referee would be announced to the public only five minutes before the match bell.[21]

Both boxers proclaimed their confidence in a win. "I think I am good enough now to finish Tunney inside of seven rounds," Dempsey, thirty-two, told reporters. "If he happens to last the limit, I am sure I will be far enough out in front to win the decision." Tunney said he had "reached the very peak of condition, and [was] without a bruise or hurt on the hour of battle. . . . I hope and expect our contest will be a fairly and cleanly waged battle, which will merit the attention given it by the greatest crowd ever gathered to see a sporting event." Dempsey's wife, Estelle Taylor, had a more peculiar take on things: "You know, I have always bragged that I am psychic. . . . I can only see success ahead for Jack when he enters the ring."[22] On the afternoon of the fight, Tunney drove to the Illinois Athletic Club in an armored car to be examined for the match. He weighed in at 190 pounds, Dempsey at 192½.

In the audience that night were movie stars like John Barrymore and musicians like George M. Cohen. Governor Small of course was there, as were the governors of five other states.[23] It was the first heavyweight boxing championship in Chicago, and although Rickard was not to get a full house—which would have been 163,000 because of the small area roped off for the ring—it would still end up as one of the best-attended sporting events in history. Starting around 7 p.m. the night of the fight, two and a half hours before the scheduled start time, thousands converged on the stadium. About thirty-five hundred police officers directed the crowd, ringing the stadium with police lines four blocks away.[24] As the crowds filed into the stands, peddlers outside Soldier Field barked, "Get your lunch here, only five cents," and offered small bags of peanuts, while others sold cushions to make sitting on the stadium's plank benches more comfortable. Hundreds of federal prohibition agents had combed the city in the days leading up to the fight, trying in vain to keep the city dry. Even so, "fans who carried hip pocket flasks or hollow canes into Soldier Field drank unmolested," one wire service reported.

The Dempsey-Tunney fight became perhaps the most debated sporting event ever at Soldier Field. What happened once the bell rang still stirs debate among historians of pugilism. With an estimated fifty million people listening in, one of the largest radio audiences ever up to that point, it was announced that Dave Barry, a longtime Illinois boxing referee, would oversee the main event. Radio listeners from coast to coast, including two men scheduled for execution the next day in San Quentin Prison in California, settled in to listen.

A set of four undercard matches, scheduled to start at 8 p.m., went off on time, although there were some technical problems with a microphone that had been wired to be used in the center of the ring. In the first professional fight at Soldier Field, Johnny Grosso fought "Big Boy" Peterson as the spectators were still entering the arena. Peterson dominated the fight, punctuated by a short burst of rain, winning the six-round match.

About 10 p.m., Dempsey, wearing white shorts and a white robe, entered the ring first. Tunney, in blue-black shorts with red stripes and a robe with a Marines logo on it, came in behind several politicians. Small, Thompson, and Robert Crowe, the state's attorney, all stood in the ring for a moment to soak in the cheers of the crowd. The pols shook hands with the two opponents, then cleared the canvas. The bell rang at 10:07. The fight started slowly, both Dempsey and Tunney "boxing conservatively," as MacNamee put it in his play-by-play, but Tunney landed the first blow—a shot to the left side of Dempsey's face. Tunney outboxed Dempsey in the second, hit more aggressively than usual to make up for several hits by Dempsey, and connected with rights to Dempsey's jaw, MacNamee told his listeners. In the third round, Dempsey landed several blows, perhaps illegal rabbit punches, that caused Tunney's seconds to protest, but both landed solid hits until they went into a clinch. The fourth and fifth rounds clearly went to the defending champion, as Tunney, red from Dempsey's blows, relentlessly attacked the challenger, landed a strong left to his face, and put the unsteady Dempsey on the ropes. The former champ appeared to recover in the sixth and "seemed to have Tunney bothered with his terrific short rights and lefts," MacNamee told the radio listeners.

The seventh round still lives in the minds of thousands of boxing fans, and still causes some to maintain that Dempsey was robbed of the title. Dempsey came at Tunney with both gloves, but as the two boxers dropped apart, Tunney's right grazed Dempsey's face. Tunney hit Dempsey with his left three times, then Dempsey came back with a rain of blows, knocking Tunney down by the ropes on the west side of the ring. "Dempsey was like a cat—just like a cat!—the way he pounced," recalled H. A. "Jimmy" Jones, a racehorse trainer who was in the audience. "After chasing Tunney all night, Dempsey finally got a whack at him. And he whacked him good!" The timekeeper, Paul Beeler, started his count at "one," then looked back at the ring and saw Dempsey in his own corner, near Tunney, looking, as one reporter put it, "foolishly serious," and stopped the count. In the film of these crucial moments, it appears it took Barry almost five seconds to get Dempsey to understand he could not hover over Tunney but had to go to a neutral corner, as specified by the new rule that he himself had agreed to. Only after Dempsey went to a neutral corner did Beeler and Barry resume counting. These extra few seconds gave Tunney time to recover and stand up just as

Barry's hand began to descend to count ten. "Some say it was a good twelve, but that is something to be argued later in columns upon columns of comment," Runyon wrote. "It seemed a long time even to a neutral." Associated Press writer Alan J. Gould wrote, "It unquestionably was a 'long count.'" As Tunney got up, cheers from the crowd increased in pitch and turned from a roar into an ear-splitting scream. Tunney came back swinging, but Dempsey continued to dominate the round, laughing and urging Tunney to fight before apparently losing his temper and hitting Tunney with a one-two to the head, dazing him before the round ended.

In the eighth, Tunney downed Dempsey with a right to the jaw, but Dempsey jumped back up, only to be pummeled by Tunney as the bell rang. In the ninth, the crowd booed as Tunney retreated from Dempsey's attacks, but then he engaged Dempsey, hitting the challenger with a sharp right, and blood gushed from around Dempsey's left eye. The round ended with several more hits to Dempsey's head, and the challenger returned to his corner unsteady on his feet. At the start of the last round, the two shook hands; at the end, Tunney almost sent Dempsey to the mat with a left and right to the jaw as the bell rang. The fighters apparently didn't hear the bell, and kept on hitting until Tunney's seconds entered the ring. Tunney won on a unanimous decision.

Following the match, Tunney told reporters, "Dempsey fought a much better fight tonight than a year ago. He was much tougher, punched cleaner, harder and was faster on his feet. He's a game warrior, one of the greatest battlers in the history of the ring." Tunney said the long count knockdown was "my own fault," because he failed to heed his second's advice between rounds to continue to move to Dempsey's right and avoid his left hook.

If Dempsey had gone straight to a neutral corner and the count had finished before Tunney rose, Dempsey would have won. Instead the long count and the decision gave sports fans a controversy they argue about to this day— but then, sometimes sports fans prefer an engaging argument to a clear-cut decision. "He beat himself by being slow in getting back to his corner," said department store owner George Lytton, one of the judges who awarded the fight to Tunney. "In my opinion Tunney would have been counted out if the ex-champion had moved away faster."[25]

Newspapers played up the cultural impact of the match for days afterward. The official attendance figure was 150,000, although later accounts indicate that number was a few thousand high. The AP and the *Tribune* reported a number of deaths among fans listening at home who apparently found the excitement too much to handle. Detroit factory worker James J. Dempsey, the *Tribune* said, "fell dead while arguing over the defeat of his namesake."[26]

The South Park Commission got a pittance compared to the eventual gate from the fight—the $100,000 amounted to less than 4 percent of Rickard's

$2.6 million in ticket sales, well below the 10 or 15 percent the commissioners usually charged for-profit enterprises. To be fair, no previous Soldier Field event had charged as much for tickets as Rickard did. At the time, annual income for the stadium was generally less than $100,000; in 1928, for example, tickets brought in just $60,000 and concessions another $12,000, while expenses totaled more than $115,000. So the $100,000 Rickard did pay (about $1.2 million in 2008 dollars) was a windfall for the parks. It's no wonder that for several years, city officials kept pushing for a repeat of the Dempsey-Tunney fight. Kelly, however, in his capacity as South Park president, insisted that the city benefit even from charity bouts fought at Soldier Field, and other fights proposed in the next decade—a high point for boxing's national popularity—went nowhere.[27]

RACING, SOLDIER FIELD'S LIFEBLOOD

Although Soldier Field will forever be associated with professional boxing because the of the Dempsey-Tunney fight, the stadium's most popular attraction almost every year for three decades will likely never again take place there: auto racing. Driven by the need to keep the stadium financially viable and to justify the large crews assigned there, the Chicago Park District began looking to auto racing as a new source of revenue in the mid-1930s. Before the stadium became a regular venue for midget auto racing and stock car racing, the International Motorcycle Association held a month of motorcycle races there, starting July 4, 1934. Despite plans for more, it appears the only motorcycle races at Soldier Field after that year were part of police meets and thrill shows.

Auto racing got a tentative start at Soldier Field the following May, at the end of an indoor midget auto racing season that had run that winter and spring in the 124th Field Artillery Armory at 52nd Street and Cottage Grove Avenue—the first such season in the Chicago area. The first race at Soldier Field drew twenty thousand people. Marshall Lewis of Los Angeles, the winner of three races that day, clinching the Midwest midget auto crown, was a regular on the circuit in the 1930s and 1940s. When they created a quarter-mile cinder track for what were known as doodle-bug cars, park district officials apparently had little idea how popular the sport could be. Another race wasn't held at the stadium until 1939, when races were held throughout June, with ninety thousand people attending. More races were held in May 1941, when about forty-five thousand people attended a championship event, and in 1942, but then took a hiatus until after the war. Then, in 1946, auto racing at Soldier Field really took off, with numerous midget, stock car, and other races, including a few demolition derbies, on the schedule every year from then until 1968, except for 1959, the year of the Pan Am Games.

As popular as they were in their day, events like rodeos, auto races, and boxing matches other than the Dempsey-Tunney fight are almost forgotten as part of Soldier Field's story. Instead, one single professional sport dominates the stadium—a sport that at the time Soldier Field was built was considered a distant second to its college version: professional football.

Ever since the 1926 Army-Navy Game, Soldier Field has been known as a football stadium, and professional football started there early on, after some hesitation on the part of the South Park commissioners. When Thomas R. McCarthy of Chicago asked on October 30, 1924, for permission to stage a series of football games at the stadium in the fall of 1925, the South Park Commission referred the matter to J. F. Foster, its general superintendent, asking him to evaluate whether holding professional games at a public facility was appropriate. McCarthy was asking for eleven Sundays and Thanksgiving Day—a large number of dates from any one applicant. Foster reported on November 19 that he thought professional games would be all right: "It is very probable that the demand for the use of the Stadium for such purposes will be very great, so that it will be found desirable to grant the privilege for creditable exhibitions in the sporting line, even though conducted for profit." He went on to suggest that the rental fee for such events should be much higher than it ended up being—and many times higher than it is today for the Bears: "I believe . . . remuneration should be more than ten percent—probably in the neighborhood of twenty-five percent."[28]

Today, after the complete revamping of Soldier Field of 2001–2003, it's taken for granted that the stadium had never before been suitable for football games. At the time it was built, however, almost everyone, from South Park officials to architectural experts, considered it the height of modern design for sports, including football. In his memoir of the stadium, South Park chief engineer Linn White wrote:

> In determining the width of the arena, careful consideration was given to sight lines, sight distances and the uses to which the arena could be placed. Consideration of a baseball diamond was eliminated owing to the impracticability in such stadiums. The athletic requirements of the arena were decided upon with the assistance of Avery Brundage of the Chicago Athletic Club and A. A. Stagg of the University of Chicago. The football field is centered on the center line of the main east and west stands in section two, thus all seats are of nearly equal value in that section.

One of the architects at Holabird and Roche who helped design the stadium wrote an article for the *American Architect*, boasting that the builders' use of modern engineering principles regarding the elevations of seats ensured good sightlines throughout the stadium.[29]

Football fans would quickly come to disagree. And several professional football teams' attempts to play there seem to endorse their view. The first professional football game at the stadium appears to have been an Armistice Day game in 1926 between the Chicago Bears and the Chicago Cardinals. Like all Cardinals-Bears matches at Soldier Field until the Bears moved there in 1971, it was played for charity—in this case, to fund the building of Rosary College in River Forest. Almost every crucial Cardinals player had suffered an injury the previous weekend, so the team had little chance of winning against the Bears. The team's bad luck continued in the opening minutes of the game, with halfback Red Dunn breaking his leg above the ankle. John "Paddy" Driscoll, the Bears quarterback who from 1920 to 1925 had played for the Cardinals, threw a forty-yard pass to Duke Hanny for the only touchdown of the game in the second quarter—and the first touchdown by a Bears player at Soldier Field. Driscoll then kicked for the extra point, and scored again with a field goal later in the same period.[30]

The Cardinals played another regular season game at the stadium later that month. The most notable professional game of the year, however, came on December 19, 1926, when the Bears met the Green Bay Packers for the first time at Soldier Field, with the stadium counting as their home field. The game benefited a charity near and dear to the hearts of Chicago's Irish Democrats: the P. J. Carr Christmas Fund. Carr, the Cook County treasurer, had died suddenly in November, just after being elected county sheriff. The game could have determined the NFL championship for the year if Phila-delphia's Frankford Yellow Jackets had lost their last game of the year. But the Yellow Jackets won, clinching the title, and the Bears and the Packers played to a 3–3 tie, with the Packers' three points scored by quarterback Pid Purdy, also a White Sox player.

The Cardinals played at the stadium occasionally from 1926 on, and the Bears and other professional teams started playing the annual College All-Star Game there in 1934. But the first professional football team to adopt Soldier Field as its regular home stadium was the Chicago Rockets, part of the new All-American Football Conference that started in 1946. The Rockets played four seasons at Soldier Field, changing their name to the Hornets for the 1949 season. At first, it seemed that the AAFC might succeed in winning over fans from the older National Football League. The Rockets' home opener against the Cleveland Browns drew just shy of fifty-two thousand fans, more than had attended any Bears conference game up to that point. The Rockets lost, however, 20–6, an unfortunate portent of things to come. The team never had a winning season. In 1947, and again in 1948, it lost thirteen games and won only one. Although the Rockets' fans included state senator, and future mayor, Richard J. Daley, attendance dropped sharply, with the last Soldier Field games of 1946 and 1947 each drawing only about five thousand spectators. The name change in 1949 did not prevent the team from having another lousy season; the Hornets closed it out with a loss to the Cleveland Browns and a record of four wins, eight losses. The conference overall did not fare much better, and on December 9, 1949, conference officials hammered out an agreement that allowed the more popular teams—Baltimore, Cleveland, and San Francisco—to join the NFL. There was brief talk of the Hornets franchise being bought by a Houston businessman, but that soon faded.[31]

The Cardinals used Soldier Field as their home stadium for one season, in 1959, following the Pan Am Games. The Chicago Park District spent about $120,000 to renovate the field and put in temporary north stands that created a bowl at the south end of the stadium—very similar to the configuration made permanent by a major renovation for the Bears twenty years later. The Cardinals also insisted that some of the bleacher-style seats, which had dominated the stadium since it first opened, be fitted with backs. The changes created a bowl with a capacity of about 53,600, making possible single-game ticket sales of about $180,000. The move to Soldier Field did not, however, improve the Cardinals' record. Since being named NFL champions in 1925, the team had only played seven winning seasons, and 1959 was not one of them. That year the South Siders had a dismal 2–10 record, playing only four games at Soldier Field, the last being a 31–7 loss to their North Side rivals, the Bears. In March 1960 the Cardinals ownership announced that the team was moving to Saint Louis. Lauding this removal of a local rival, Bears founder and owner George Halas said, "It is the best thing that has happened to St. Louis since Lindbergh." Later that year, the Cardinals paid the Chicago Park District $110,000, after receiving $500,000 from the NFL as incentive money for moving.[32]

In 1974 the ill-fated World Football League, a summer conference, fielded the equally ill-fated Chicago Fire football team. The league's first day of play went well, with nearly two hundred thousand spectators at five games, including forty-two thousand at Soldier Field. The Bears were coming off a disastrous 1973 season in which they won three and lost eleven, and Chicago football fans were ready to embrace a better team. But the Fire wasn't that team. It played a losing season and lost its owner $300,000 more than the $500,000 in red ink he had planned for. The next year, the Chicago Winds replaced the Fire in the WFL, but they too called it quits after one season.[33]

Until the Bears started using Soldier Field as their home stadium in 1971, professional football at the stadium usually took the form of a charity game. Several times the Bears played the Cardinals in the Armed Forces Game, an annual contest, originated by Halas in 1946 at Wrigley Field, that

JOE FARACI—
ARTIST

The Chicago Tribune Charities, Inc. presents its

14ᵗʰ Annual All Star Football Game
COLLEGE ALL-STARS vs CHICAGO BEARS
SOLDIERS' FIELD AUGUST 22, 1947 • OFFICIAL PROGRAM 50c

Cover of program for the 1947 College All-Star Game. Courtesy Chicago Tribune Charities.

was played until 1970, when the Bears moved to Soldier Field full-time. (The Cardinals were not always the Bears' opponent; the first game in the series was played against the New York Giants.) Halas first thought of starting the game, which benefited the four armed forces relief funds, while serving as a naval commander in the Pacific during World War II. Created with the cooperation of General Dwight Eisenhower of the Army, Admiral Chester Nimitz, and General Ira Eaker of the Air Force, the game over the years raised $1.2 million, Halas estimated. The Bears' cosponsor was originally the *Herald-American*, then, after 1955, the *Sun-Times*, and later a consortium of Chicago newspapers. The first Armed Forces Game at Soldier Field in 1947 saw the Bears win, 28–0, over the Washington Redskins. In many ways, the game supplanted the military shows that had preceded World War II at the stadium, bringing military units to parade at Soldier Field and providing a cheap recreational outlet for military personnel. From the start, the stadium's tradition of patriotic spectacle melded easily with professional football, as Halas and others involved with the NFL cultivated the Americanness of their sport[34]

Like the Armed Forces Game, the College All-Star Game was a once-a-year series. Conceived by *Tribune* editor Arch Ward the year after he started the Major League Baseball All-Star Game at Comiskey Park, the College All-Star Game usually served as a fund-raiser for Chicago Tribune Charities, which before World War II divided the profits among three charitable organizations: Catholic Charities, Jewish Charities, and United Charities of Chicago.[35]

During World War II, Soldier Field served the war effort in many ways. In 1942 the All-Star Game was the culmination of a months-long campaign to raise money for the families of dead or wounded servicemen. The *Tribune*, always eager to draw its readers into any cause it supported, used the game to bring them into the war effort. "A nation at war, with its industries and military forces girding for ultimate victory, today begins further assault on the axis thru the medium of the All-Star football game," Arch Ward wrote a month and half before the game, looking forward to "the greatest single effort for war charities in the history of American sport."

More than two hundred newspapers and radio stations helped conduct the all-star ballot, with the *Tribune* casting readers' participation as almost a patriotic duty: "Many of last year's collegiate football headliners are now in the armed forces. Some already are in foreign service. Fans are urged to vote for any man they think deserves a place on football's honor team, regardless of his whereabouts. He is entitled to that recognition." And Ward pitched the game hard: "Football's great charity drive for Army Emergency Drive has reached the scoring zone. A few more power plays will bring a $100,000 touchdown. . . . Every penny of the $100,000 fund will be turned over to Army Emergency Relief." Of course, while the game's boosters promoted the hope that their donations would help bring success in the fight against the Axis powers, anyone who bought tickets also anticipated seeing the most hyped—if not the best played—football game of the year, the equivalent of the Super Bowl in the years before color television.[36]

Over the years, the professional teams won most of the College All-Star Games, although the collegians played the Bears to a scoreless tie in the first

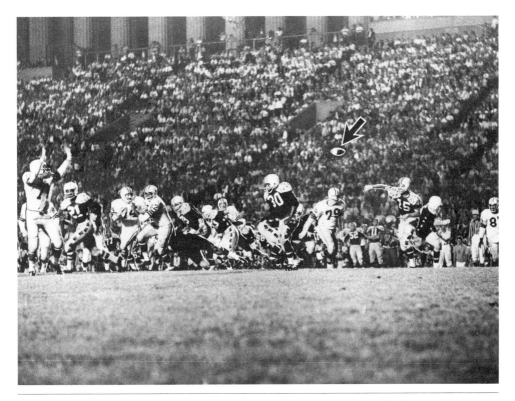

Ron VanderKelen of the College All-Stars passes to Pat Richter in a game against the Green Bay Packers, the last the All-Stars won, 20–17, August 3, 1963. Courtesy Chicago Tribune.

game in 1934. The first win by the All-Stars came in 1937, when Sammy Baugh of Texas Christian University passed forty-seven yards to Gaynell Tinsley of Louisiana State for the only score of the day; the 6–0 upset of the Green Bay Packers took place in front of almost eighty-five thousand fans. The biggest crowd to see the game was in 1948, when more than 101,000 people watched the Chicago Cardinals beat the All-Stars, 28–0. The last time the All-Stars won was in 1963, when the collegiate squad again defeated the Packers, 20–17, in an exciting game that saw the lead change repeatedly. After that, however, the professionals won game after game. Finally, in 1976, with the Pittsburgh Steelers leading, 24–0, the game was ended early because of a torrential rainstorm—and the fact that many in the crowd of fifty-two thousand streamed onto the field, where they played in the rain and tore down both goal posts. And that was the last College All-Star Game. Overall, the collegians won nine of forty-two contests to the pros' thirty-one, with two ties.[37]

Already, before the All-Star Games ended, college and amateur football at Soldier Field had been eclipsed by the Bears' move to the stadium. As television influenced Americans' choice of entertainment and Chicago-area college programs declined in strength, the Bears became the dominant football team in the Chicago area. Soon the team would also become the dominant presence at Soldier Field, as television—the same medium that helped kill pageants, music festivals, and cultural events—linked the stadium indelibly with the Chicago Bears. Before that happened, however, Soldier Field had a few more landmark events to host.

10 New Religious and Political Movements in a Classic Space

Soldier Field rose as a monument to Chicago's war dead, a great altar at which they could be mourned and the living culture of the city celebrated. Among the constituencies that the popular new venue helped bring together were religious groups, and as American worship changed, religious events at Soldier Field changed as well. A few popular gatherings—including what may be the largest single event in the stadium's history—focused on the traditions of established religious groups. But the most noteworthy events since the election of Mayor Richard J. Daley in 1955 have focused on figures who challenged old alliances of religion and politics, using new methods to bring people together.

In the 1940s, at the same time that the Catholic Holy Hour was growing into a popular yearly event, many Protestants who had helped initiate the stadium's Easter sunrise service in the 1930s were joining a new evangelical movement that would help propel the Reverend Billy Graham to fame. In Chicago, this trend derived some of its popularity from its high-profile events at Soldier Field—which it expanded in the mid-1940s, partly as a response to the Catholic events.

Graham belonged to a movement among evangelical Christians called Youth for Christ, at first made up of loosely affiliated groups in New York, Washington, D.C., and other cities. In 1944 Torrey Maynard Johnson founded Chicagoland Youth for Christ, and Graham, later the national group's first employee, spoke at its first major rally, at Orchestra Hall on May 27. Johnson wrote, in a book intended to foster the movement's growth, that he initially felt reluctant to start the Chicago-area group. But "God seemed to say" that if Youth for Christ could be successful in other cities, "don't you think I am sufficient for Chicago?" From the beginning, Johnson tried to make Youth for Christ a mass movement, exploiting its leaders' experience in radio, large evangelical gatherings, and—to keep people connected between larger events—smaller prayer groups.[1]

After its initial meeting, Chicagoland Youth for Christ used Orchestra Hall every Saturday night for about twenty weeks, sometimes holding two meetings a day. The "excitement" of downtown Chicago and Michigan Avenue helped attract people to the rallies, with some coming from fifty to a hundred miles away, much to Johnson's surprise.[2] The group soon organized formally, with offices on Wells Street. The evangelical movement was then dwarfed by mainline Protestant churches, but many of its younger leaders saw potential for converts in the rootless youth of the era and potential for growth in the use of mass media. At the beginning, some established churches viewed Youth for Christ as an interloper, Johnson said. Will Houghton, head of the Moody Bible Institute, had been one who refused to cooperate in cultivating the movement. But by the stint at Orchestra Hall, Houghton had decided to help "whole-heartedly and gave us the use of his radio [station] to do the broadcasting."[3]

To cap its twenty-week campaign, the group held a rally in the Chicago Stadium. About twenty-five thousand people—ten thousand of them teenagers—attended. "High school youth of bobby-sox age are demonstrating once again that Christianity really works," Johnson told one interviewer before the event. From early on, Youth for Christ made a point of having sports celebrities who had accepted Jesus as speakers, a practice that Graham himself adopted. (Johnson himself was a former Wheaton College football player.) Gil Dodds, a track and field champion later known as "the flying preacher," spoke at the Chicago Stadium rally, which garnered positive publicity for Youth for Christ as an alternative to the purported debauchery of popular culture. ("Bobby-soxer" referred to the fashionable young female fans of musicians like Frank Sinatra—as great a threat to public morals in the 1940s, from some perspectives, as rock 'n' rollers would be in the 1950s and punk rockers in the 1970s.) Several high-profile Chicagoans wrote to Johnson to commend him on the outcome of the rally.[4]

The following spring Youth for Christ held a first-anniversary rally at Soldier Field the weekend of Memorial Day. Two decades after the stadium's opening, Chicagoans associated it more than ever with all things patriotic, and the members of Youth for Christ sought to suffuse their rally with that aura. The event's organizors, Johnson later said, aimed to "demonstrate our patriotism to our country, to show to show that Evangelical Christians are also loyal Americans, that there could be no mistake about that." To underscore that point, they decided to sell war bonds at the meeting, and brought in Army chaplain Robert P. Evans, a Wheaton College graduate who had been at the Anzio beachhead in Italy in 1944, as a spokesman for evangelicals in the military. They also hoped to show up the Catholics, whose annual Holy Hour was scheduled for the following weekend.[5]

In the months leading up to the rally, Johnson and other leaders of the group worked feverishly to recruit evangelicals to attend. Johnson sent letters to eight thousand leaders of local youth groups, asking for their "sacrificial and prayerful support." Meanwhile, various committees ramped up publicity for the event. The head of the radio committee, C. J. Ulrich, wrote to stations to ask for public service announcements about the rally. Charles Palmquist, chairman of the publicity committee, wrote to group members, asking them to help blanket the city with posters.[6]

In early May, "Gospel Teams" from Chicagoland Youth for Christ traveled around the Midwest, bringing news of the rally to evangelical audiences. Graham, for example, went to Princeton, Utica, and Pekin, Illinois, as well as other towns. On May 10 Johnson wrote to Chicago-area pastors, telling them, "We have been challenged to fill Soldier Field on Memorial Day, May 30, with 125,000 people for a great testimony to the Saving Grace of our Living Saviour." The letter made reference to the Holy Hour the following week as one might to a rival team. For the Catholic event, "Soldier Field will be packed in all probability. Therefore, every Protestant should rally to this Memorial Day meeting." Soldier Field had become a center of competition not just among sports teams, but for the souls of the city's believers.

The nationalistic tone struck in preparation for the rally helped ensure its success. As many as a hundred thousand people from forty cities within three hundred miles of Chicago attended the event, which started with a three-hundred-piece band and a choir of five thousand performing popular military music. After a few religious hymns, Charles Templeton, who would later tour with Billy Graham on Youth for Christ missions in postwar Europe, introduced Johnson, the evening's master of ceremonies. The rally included a short military exercise and ceremonies honoring members of the military and Gold Star parents. Howard Jones of Milwaukee Youth for Christ then played taps as the sun went down. Immediately after, the group appealed to the audience to buy war bonds.

The main speaker for the rally was the Reverend Percy Crawford, known as the pastor of the *Young People's Church of the Air*, a national radio program. Graham spoke, but only for a short time, as one of five speakers representing China, India, Russia, Africa, and the United States. Graham called for a new "great revival," like the one that had brought fundamentalist Christianity to the forefront of American culture in the early nineteenth century.[7] During the event, excerpts of notes from Governor Dwight Green and Mayor Edward Kelly were read from the podium. In his letter, written on stationery that advised the reader to "buy war bonds," Kelly said that he was glad to hear of the plans for a Memorial Day Mass Meeting at Soldier Field. Movements such as this are bound to have a decisive influence on the lives of young people and indirectly on the City as a whole. . . . Demonstrative efforts such as this are certain to be reflected in the betterment of the City record of crime and juvenile delinquency.[8]

Reaction to the event was overwhelming, and helped convince Johnson and others that Youth for Christ could succeed on a grand scale. The event was "the beginning, not the climax, of a great crusade," Johnson told the *Protestant Voice*, a weekly religious newspaper.[9]

Graham had become the first employee of the national organization loosely tying together the Youth for Christ groups from around the country (he earned $75 a week). In July 1945, inspired by the success of the Soldier Field rally, the group that had met in 1944 to organize Youth for Christ nationally gathered again at Winona Lake, Indiana, and created Youth for Christ International. A few months later, Johnson and Graham were telling reporters about how they planned to bring the movement's message to a war-torn Europe. Graham, described in one article as "a boy evangelist," though he already had been a full-time pastor at a church in Western Springs, Illinois, was at first overshadowed in news accounts by Johnson, the president of the group.[10] In March 1946 Graham, Johnson, Templeton, and others left for a series of evangelical rallies in Europe, touring from London to Copenhagen to Berlin. In May they returned to the United States for a five-week series of Saturday crusades, culminating in another well-attended Soldier Field rally on Memorial Day, at which Johnson and others reported on the European trip.[11]

Youth for Christ's mass rallies reflected a shift in evangelical Protestant culture toward one that embraced a more public role for religion. The World War II period had seen the development of what we know today as "youth culture." Many observers remarked that here was a different kind of young person. With the Soldier Field rallies, Johnson provided them a context in which to demonstrate their patriotism. Much of the press coverage, however, emphasized how members of Youth for Christ were simultaneously enjoying life and devoting their lives to Jesus, in contrast, reporters implied, to hedonistic bobby-soxers and jitterbugs.[12]

In many ways, Youth for Christ looked like a new way of finding religion. Its roots, however, grew from a long tradition of American religious revivalism. Like the Progressives and City Beautiful adherents, the leaders of Youth for Christ spoke as part of an American discourse on moral reform. For more than a century, Protestants in small towns throughout the expanding country had used revival meetings to bring people to belief in the Gospel. Groups like Youth for Christ built on that tradition using the new media of radio and motion pictures, meeting in concert halls and stadiums instead of tents or local theaters. Youth for Christ used Soldier Field each year for several more years, and these rallies gave Graham a model for mass meetings in large venues on which he based the rest of his career.

Before Graham returned to Soldier Field as a world-famous preacher instead of a barely known suburban pastor, the stadium hosted two other momentous religious events, both in 1954: an international gathering of Protestant and Orthodox Christian denominations and a celebration of the Catholic Marian Year, often cited as the lakefront stadium's largest event ever.[13]

The first meeting of the World Council of Churches had taken place in 1948 in Amsterdam, with Billy Graham attending as an observer. Mainline Protestant and Orthodox denominations in Europe and North America had agreed to create the group in 1937, as part of a growing liberal ecumenical movement, but the group had not jelled until after World War II. Then, even as conservative fundamentalist Christianity grew in influence, the World Council and, within the United States, the National Council of Churches, brought together disparate denominations in a more politically liberal coalition. Conservative elements within the National Council, however, welcomed the second meeting of the world body as an opportunity to reverse some of the anticapitalist sentiments of the organizing statement the group had issued in 1948. This political conflict provided the backdrop as the World Council of Churches planned its meetings in Chicago and adjacent Evanston for two weeks in August 1954.

The World Council held its opening ceremony, the Ecumenical Festival of Faith, at Soldier Field on August 15. By three days before the event, eighty-three thousand people had gotten tickets. Four hundred churches had been enlisted to host a dinner and reception for sixteen hundred delegates in the Soldier Field exhibition halls in the hours before the program. The festival itself, with the theme "Christ, the Hope of the World," was narrated by the Reverend George E. Johnson of the Oakton Community Church in Evanston. Although the Marian Year festivities a few weeks later would upstage it, the festival was one of the last large-scale urban pageants of the sort that had been so popular in the first half of the twentieth century. More than twenty-five hundred singers from two hundred churches and a cast of as many as four thousand people rehearsed for weeks a drama scripted by Helen Kromer, who at the time specialized in Christian-themed plays.

Henry P. Van Dusen, president of the New York Union Theological Seminary, called the World Council of Churches gathering "the most widely representative, most truly 'ecumenical' assemblage of the followers of Christ who have ever met 'in one accord in one place.'" Newspapers compared it to

Soldier Field convention halls laid out for an event, as they would have been for the 1954 Festival of Faith dinner. Courtesy Chicago Park District Special Collections.

the 1926 Eucharistic Congress. Delegates came from four countries behind the Iron Curtain, Yugoslavia, East Germany, Czechoslovakia and Hungary. Notably absent were Russian Orthodox leaders, as well as any representatives from Christian churches in China. Despite some pushback by conservatives, the council intended its show of ecumenical force to support what many religious leaders in the group considered more responsible government action. The group's 1948 declaration committed the gathering to backing what the *Tribune* described as "welfare statism," but the Chicago-Evanston assembly also issued a statement warning that "centralized government power cannot be extended indefinitely without destroying freedom."

The day of the opening ceremonies began with a service in the First Methodist Church in Evanston, where more than sixteen hundred delegates participating in a solemn religious ceremony. The Festival of Faith, that evening, began at 7:30 with a procession into the stadium of delegates and church officials. After some singing and a short prayer, Mayor Martin Kennelly, one of the few Catholics at the event, greeted the crowd of about 125,000. The program continued with music by a twenty-two-hundred-voice chorus, the dramatic pageant, and an interpretive dance with the theme "Jesus Christ Is the Hope of the World," interspersed with periods of prayer and narration of Bible stories. After the Soldier Field event, the meeting continued for two weeks and included an address by President Dwight Eisenhower, who asked the group to pray for peace because "there is no true and lasting cure for world tensions in guns and bombs."[14]

A few weeks later, Chicago's Catholics held a massive Holy Hour service at the stadium, the culmination of a number of celebrations of the 1954 Marian Year. Since the 1926 Eucharistic Congress, Catholics had gathered at Soldier Field several times for Holy Hour services, most notably on September 22, 1946, to celebrate the newly proclaimed sainthood of Mother Frances Xavier Cabrini. Cabrini, the first American-born saint, spent years in Chicago ministering to Italian Catholics; a seventy-five-foot-tall portrait of Cabrini watched over the hundred thousand gathered to hear Cardinal Samuel Stritch proclaim, "Of course, a saint is in a real sense something of the whole world, of all history. But she is Chicago's saint." In 1954 Stritch again led Chicago's Catholics in a great display of their faith, celebrating the Marian Year that Pope Pius XII had proclaimed in honor of the hundredth anniversary of Pius IX's pronouncement of the Immaculate Conception as an infallible teaching of the church. (The doctrine holds that Mary, the mother of Jesus, was herself conceived without original sin.)

Catholics prepared for the September 8 celebration for weeks in advance. A sixteen-foot-tall statue of Mary and a modernist high altar for the mass dominated the north end of the field. Where the baldacchino towering over the altar at the Eucharistic Congress had replicated a famous neoclassical structure in Rome, the one over the plain 1954 altar was impressive mainly for its size and the giant white crucifix sheltered under its red, white, and gold cloth. The comparative austerity of the setting, however, did nothing to dampen people's enthusiasm for the event. Parishes throughout the archdiocese organized groups to attend. Church groups chartered more than twelve hundred buses, and the Illinois Central Railroad alone carried more than twenty thousand people to Soldier Field.

The gates opened at 4 p.m. At 6 p.m. forty-five thousand people already were in the stadium. By 7 p.m., when choirs began singing devotional music and chimes began ringing to signal people to take their places on Soldier Field's wooden benches, the crowd had swelled to about a hundred thousand. Fifty police controlled the crowd outside, while another fifty worked inside. Meanwhile, the fire department had three ambulances, a rescue squad, and two engine companies at the stadium, while more than seven hundred firefighters helped out as ushers and helped direct the crowds. Priests stood

Souvenir color print from the Marian Year celebration at Soldier Field, 1954. Courtesy Chicago Park District Special Collections.

at each of the stadium's first aid stations and intermingled throughout the crowd, in case anyone collapsed and required the last rites. By 8:15 there were about 180,000 people inside the stadium and another 80,000 outside listening to the services on loudspeakers.

The program began with patriotic gestures: the American flag was raised, the Pledge of Allegiance said, and the crowd rose to sing "The Star Spangled Banner." After a saying of the Rosary, members of the Knights of Columbus and other lay organizations, dressed in formal, quasi-military garb, marched to the flagpole to the strains of "God Bless America." A parade of people dressed in the costumes of immigrants to Chicago—German, Irish, Croatian, Chinese—followed the knights from the south entrance into the arena. The crowd sang the responses to the Litany of the Blessed Virgin, and then Cardinal Stritch and other clergy entered the arena and processed to the altar.

A high Latin mass started just before 9:30, with forty seminarians chanting the responses for the Feast of the Nativity of the Blessed Virgin Mary. The reason for the gathering, Stritch told the assembled, was to make known "our deep, filial love for the mother of God and to beg her to intercede with

Crowd shot of the Marian Year celebration at Soldier Field, 1954. Courtesy Chicago Park District Special Collections.

her Divine Son for us and for all men in our miseries and necessities." A spotlight lit the center of the altar, clearly outlining the cardinal's consecration of the Eucharist. At the end of the Mass, the congregation sang the "Salve Regina," a traditional prayer to Mary, and then "Holy God, We Praise Thy Name." Following the end of the closing hymn, just before 11 o'clock, the crowd dispersed peacefully, and the area surrounding Soldier Field was almost empty by 11:30.

Those who attended the Marian Year Holy Hour thought of it as proof of the strength of Chicago's Catholic community. "Soldier Field is one of the world's largest gathering places, but it is not large enough for our people when they want to express publicly their love and devotion to our Blessed Lady," Cardinal Stritch wrote the week after the event. But the crowd of a quarter million had come together not just as followers of a particular faith but also as Chicagoans. It hearkened back to the City Beautiful disciples' vision of the stadium as part of a larger effort to integrate new citizens into the full life of the city. Soldier Field was to stand "in decided contrast" to college football

The Reverend Thomas McGlynn, of Raleigh, North Carolina, a Dominican sculptor, assembles a sixteen-foot statue of the Virgin Mary at the north end of Soldier Field in preparation for the Marian Year observance. Monsignor William Gorman looks on. Courtesy Chicago Tribune.

stadiums, one South Park official wrote soon after the Army-Navy Game. It existed to foster "something greater and finer of which [Chicagoans] will be proud."

The question remains whether the Marian Year Holy Hour or the first day's events at the Eucharistic Congress attracted more people. The 1954 event is usually cited as the largest event ever held at Soldier Field, but this is mainly because its attendance can be more reliably verified. The basis of this greater certainty is curious, if not ironic: the Chicago Civil Defense Corps—then headquartered at Soldier Field—had decided to use the Holy Hour to plan the evacuation of Chicago in case of a nuclear attack. The city was busily doing its part in the larger Cold War, which pitted the forces of godless communism against the Christian democracies of the West—or at least that's how many Chicagoans saw it.

Based on a training exercise held June 14 and 15—part of a national exercise with the premise that three atomic bombs had exploded over Chicago—the Civil Defense Corps concluded that its traffic plan for evacuation of the city was inadequate. It decided that the Marian Year event "would present an opportunity for study from a civil defense viewpoint, not only of the mass dispersal but of mass concentrations and of the various logistical, sanitary and psychological factors involved" in bringing together and dispersing a large crowd. The corps studied the World Council of Churches gathering and worked with the planners of the Marian Year event as they made their preparations. When it came time for the gathering itself, the corps had about eight staff members on hand, keeping track of the crowd's movements and the effectiveness of the transportation arrangements. The corps's coordinator for the project, Pat Kelly, observed that movements into and out of the stadium went very smoothly and concluded that the logistics of bringing twelve hundred chartered buses, several hundred CTA buses and numerous taxis and private cars into the area were relevant to how people responding to a nuclear attack might be gathered and dispersed. But, he cautioned, it was unrealistic to think that the serenity that prevailed at the Marian Year event would be present in people fleeing an enemy attack: "The people concerned were in a tranquil mood resulting from a great spiritual experience. Therefore, there was a total absence of the irritability sometimes evident in dispersals from assemblies related to sports events, etc., and of course, there was no hysteria or panic."[15] The lasting impact of the Marian Year Holy Hour had nothing to do with its lessons for civil defense, of course. Like the Eucharistic Congress, it showcased Chicago Catholicism flexing its muscles. It became the event against which all others at Soldier Field—and indeed anywhere in Chicago—were measured. Not until Pope John Paul II's visit to the city in 1979 would Chicago's Catholics come together in such numbers.

In the meantime, U.S. evangelicals had made stadium events an ever more important facet of Protestant religious life. And no one used such rallies as a tool for conversion or took better advantage of the mass media than Billy Graham. After more than a decade, during which he established himself as an evangelical leader worldwide, Graham returned to Chicago in 1962. Planning for the revivals began in 1959, with Graham announcing that he would come to Chicago only if local clergy invited him. From the start, Graham and his organizers decried the extent to which Chicago had purportedly turned away from God.

When Graham's organization, in the late summer of 1961, announced definite plans for a Chicago event, the *Tribune* compared Graham to another famous fundamentalist preacher who tried to reform Chicago, Billy Sunday. Sunday, a former player for the Chicago White Stockings, converted to fundamentalist Christianity in 1886 at the old Pacific Garden Mission on East Van Buren Street. In 1918 he led a famous series of revival meetings, declaring, "The whiskey gang, the infidels, and all of hell's outfit will fight me, but take it from me, I am ready for a fight." More than fifty years later, Graham and his fellow evangelicals fought on. Sunday held his revival meetings in a giant tent with a sawdust floor; Graham planned his for the McCormick Place convention center, ending with a service at Soldier Field. Herbert J. Taylor, chairman of the Club Aluminum Company, headed the group sponsoring the revivals. [16]

In three years of planning for the events, Taylor and three successive Chicago Park District general superintendents, including George W. Dunne (later president of the Cook County Board) haggled over whether Graham's followers could solicit donations at the event. The Billy Graham Evangelistic Association usually raised a third to half of the money needed for a crusade in the years or months leading up to the events, and the rest during the crusade itself. Despite Graham's connections to President John Kennedy, the park district would not budge, and organizers had to find other ways to raise money. Instead they asked for donations from churches around the Midwest that planned to send members, and appealed to Graham's strong base of support in the Chicago area.

By 1962 Graham was in constant demand, looking for converts all across the world and driving himself to the point of exhaustion. In the months prior to the Chicago crusade, he had traveled to South America, where despite his friendship with Kennedy, the first Catholic U.S. president, he was greeted in several cities by Catholic protesters. In Chicago, by contrast, the newspapers helped Graham's advance team to publicize the upcoming crusade. And local churches came through with donations, helping Taylor and others to raise about 75 percent of the $500,000 needed for the crusade to begin.

When the crusade opened on May 30 in McCormick Place, about 33,500 people attended the first meeting to hear Graham rail against "the greatest moral crisis in the history of mankind," represented by racial conflict, communism, and nuclear weapons. That first night, about 450 people approached the stage when Graham asked audience members who wished to be saved to come forward. Over nineteen days, at events that drew an average daily attendance of about 37,000, Graham's organizers boasted that almost 16,500 people stepped forward to accept Jesus Christ. The culmination of the crusade was Graham's Soldier Field event on June 17. More than 116,000 people from at least fifteen states attended, the largest crowd Graham had ever drawn in the United States. A choir of three thousand voices sang under a blazing sun. Graham told the crowd that they faced a stark choice: "The great question of our time [is] will we be motivated by materialistic philosophy or by spiritual power? Will we be led by God or by Satan?" He went on to compare the United States to the decadent Roman Empire: "The historian Gibbon said Rome fell because of its high divorce rate and its taxes. You know about America's divorce problem, about the movie stars who seem to believe that the more husbands or wives they have, the more of a box office attraction they will be."

Many in the crowd had attended other meetings during the crusade and trekked to the Soldier Field event to hear Graham one last time. "We are so impressed every time we have come," said Lee Getschow, who had attended six of the McCormick Place sessions with his wife, Diane. "The crowd in Soldiers' Field is the greatest we have ever seen. It is a tribute to God and Christianity that so many persons spent a hot Sunday afternoon in a religious atmosphere." Others pointed to what they thought would be the benefits of having Graham come to Chicago. "Dr. Graham has had a tremendous and wonderful beneficial effect on the people of Chicago in these troublesome times," said the Reverend Alvin Bray, a chaplain at Cook County Hospital, who brought his wife and sons to Soldier Field to hear Graham.[17] Graham himself was greatly pleased with the results of the crusade, telling the crowd he considered himself an honorary Chicagoan. "It is here that I got an education. It is here that I found my wife, and it is here that I had my first church," Graham said. "Therefore, my heart belongs to Chicago in a very peculiar and unique way."[18]

DR. KING AT THE STADIUM

Even as Graham exhorted Chicagoans to eschew worldly behavior, another group of religious and political leaders strove to improve material conditions in the city's poorest neighborhoods. And the Chicago civil rights movement, long one of the most active in Northern cities, galvanized its supporters in 1964 with the help of a Soldier Field rally led by the Reverend Martin Luther King Jr. Leaders in Chicago's black community had pressed for change in the city since before Soldier Field first rose from the lake. Starting in the early 1950s, civil rights groups, particularly the Chicago branch of the National Association for the Advancement of Colored People, applied further pressure to members of the city's political establishment, particularly black machine politicians like U.S. representative William Dawson, on issues of racial equality.

In the decade preceding King's arrival in Chicago, the city experienced major racial upheavals, starting with the 1953–1954 integration of the Trumbull Park Homes, a public housing project in the city's Deering neighborhood. Although the murder of fourteen-year-old Chicagoan Emmett Till, while he visited family in Mississippi in 1955, reverberated throughout the country, it especially roused the black community in his hometown. The bus boycott in Montgomery, Alabama, begun the same year, also stoked the Chicago civil rights movement while simultaneously establishing King's leadership of the nationwide movement.[19]

By the time King proposed coming to Chicago, the Chicago civil rights movement had been pressing for school desegregation for several years, with Chicago Board of Education superintendent Benjamin Willis as a focal point for protests. In early 1963 a group of South Side families had begun a small boycott of a school in a converted industrial building that they labeled the "Willis warehouse."[20] As the result of a court settlement, the board of education announced plans to allow high-achieving students to transfer to any high school they chose. Willis opposed the plan, prompting calls by numerous city groups—most of them black—for his resignation.[21] But when Willis did threaten to resign over the policy, the board of education voted to limit the transfer option to only a few schools. That precipitated the first large-scale school boycott by black students, with more than 224,000—about half the Chicago Public Schools' student body—staying out of class on October 22, 1963. In the end, however, little changed. In December, as black students pressed their case in court, the board of education voted against integration.[22]

While the Chicago desegregation movement was already gaining strength in 1963, some involved with the actions that year credit the King rally at Soldier Field the following year with bringing together a broader coalition and ushering in an era of greater activism in the Chicago civil rights movement. In a way that its builders probably never imagined, the vision of the stadium as a uniter of the city was fulfilled by the King rally of 1964, better than by almost any other event after the 1940s.

Billed as an interfaith gathering for racial equality, the Soldier Field rally had a range of sponsors that included the Church Federation of Greater Chicago, the Chicago Interracial Council, B'nai B'rith, and the Chicago Urban League. The Chicago Park District board, which included Colonel Jacob "Jake" Arvey, a Democratic National Committee member who controlled much of the West Side in the Edward Kelly years, voted to give the group free use of the field.[23] The rally came only two days after the U.S. Senate passed the 1964 Civil Rights Act. Just before the rally, King held a press conference to announce that as soon as President Lyndon Johnson signed the legislation, civil rights leaders would launch legal drives to test the limits of its public accommodations provisions.[24]

Despite its national and local importance, the rally drew a smaller crowd than expected. Some estimate that about fifty-seven thousand people showed up, others say seventy-five thousand.[25] Either number is respectable, even when compared with some of the stadium's most notable events, but organizers had predicted that a hundred thousand people would attend. Most of the blame for the lower turnout, however, goes to the organizers themselves. The most successful Soldier Field events had months of publicity; some were trumpeted as must-see happenings as much as a year in advance. Only about five weeks of planning and publicity preceded the 1964 civil rights rally, and the staff of about twelve was a mix of people from the various organizing groups. But like all significant events at Soldier Field, the rally was more than just what its organizers intended. In this case, it helped to coalesce a group of people behind a social movement that still has an effect on Americans' daily lives today.[26]

On the day of the rally, King entered the stadium in a white convertible (even though President Kennedy had been assassinated while riding in a similar car less than a year before) as the crowd erupted in a cheering welcome. A few picketers outside the stadium carried signs warning "Don't Be Led into Red Slavery by Martin Luther King" and "King Is for Racial War." Most attendees ignored them, but police arrested one black man when he got too close to the protest area while carrying a hammer.

Inside the stadium, King launched into his speech:

> To all of my freedom-loving friends of Chicago. This afternoon I come to Chicago . . . to join with you in what I consider one of the greatest civil rights rallies ever held in the history of this nation. After this rally, I am sure that everybody in Chicago will realize that the Negro in this community is determined to be free.

The just-passed Civil Rights Bill, King said, was no "panacea," and demonstrations should continue to "get rid of subtle segregation in the North and de facto segregation in the South." King predicted there might be more violence from opponents of the Civil Rights Bill, however, because of anger over having "lost the legal and moral battle."[27]

Many religious leaders attended the Soldier Field rally in a show of support for King and the civil rights movement. The Reverend Theodore Hesburgh, president of the University of Notre Dame, also spoke, telling the crowd that "equal opportunity is meaningless unless Negroes use it with great persistence and effort and pride," but that white Americans had the responsibility first of ensuring that blacks have equal opportunity.[28]

Despite criticism in the *Defender* regarding the relatively low turnout, leaders involved in the 1964 rally said they considered it a success. King's subsequent Soldier Field rally, held in 1966 as part of the Chicago Freedom

Movement, is more often cited by historians of the stadium and of the area's civil rights movement. But some who were involved in the movement say the 1964 rally did more to further the cause of civil rights in the city. It sent a signal that national civil rights leaders considered Chicago a key front in the movement's struggle, at a time when much of the national focus remained on changing the legal status of black Americans in Southern states.

"We always thought it was a very powerful statement, to make it at Soldier Field," Archbishop Arthur M. Brazier, a leader of the South Side's Apostolic Church of God who acted as master of ceremonies for the 1964 rally, said in a 2003 interview. The event, he felt, marked the beginning of a much more active and united civil rights movement in Chicago. "I think it really gave energy to people on those issues. There were a lot of people in the city who were opposed to Dr. King. But I think that everyone thought that there would be some significant changes . . . in racial attitudes in the city."

Though the Civil Rights Act's passage was a focus of many of the speeches at the 1964 rally, many who attended felt the energy it generated among activists to work harder for civil rights in the Chicago area held more significance. "It was a very exciting air there, because Dr. King, who was the real national leader of the civil rights movement, was there," Brazier explained. "Just his dynamic presence and speaking ability gave real legitimacy to everything that people here in Chicago were doing in regards to civil rights."[29]

A year and a half later, the civil rights movement was going through tumultuous change when King came once again to Chicago, this time to work with the Coordinating Council of Community Organizations, of which Brazier was a founder, in the Chicago Freedom Movement. The CCCO was then the city's leading civil rights group. The Freedom Movement began in June 1965, a year after the first Soldier Field rally, when the Chicago Board of Education tried to prevent black children in Chicago from boycotting classes in another demonstration against Willis. Though the movement's initial focus was on the city's public schools, the involvement of a large coalition of groups set in motion a broadening of its agenda. King lent his support early on, announcing that the Southern Christian Leadership Conference (SCLC) would make Chicago the target of its first northern campaign.[30] In July 1965 King's brother, the Reverend A. D. King, spoke at a Grant Park rally that was unremarkable except for the number of arrests that ensued (twenty-seven) and the fact that A. D. King admitted, in remarks to reporters before the rally, that there were "undoubtedly" communists in the civil rights movement, as Mayor Richard J. Daley had claimed.[31] That same summer, Martin Luther King spent three days on a quick tour of the Chicago area, speaking at rallies throughout the city, including at housing projects such as Altgeld Gardens, and even in suburban Winnetka, before leading twenty to thirty thousand people in a march on City Hall.[32]

In the summer of 1965 the Freedom Movement was cohesive, well-organized, and vital. King and the SCLC were planning a campaign in Chicago, a prominent and highly segregated northern city, and following the 1965 school boycotts, they began strategizing with Brazier's CCCO. King "realized that it was, in a sense, harder for northern blacks to pinpoint their grievances," Coretta Scott King wrote two years after her husband's assassination. His move to Chicago was part of a "pilot project designed to dramatize the issues and focus the attention of the nation on the despair, hopelessness, and desperation of ghetto existence."[33]

Finally, on January 5, 1966, King came "secretly" to the Chicago area to meet with local civil rights leaders at the Sahara Inn in Schiller Park, just south of O'Hare Airport. In attendance were the heads of the CCCO, the Chicago Urban League, and CORE, the Congress of Racial Equality, which had pioneered nonviolent protests against legal discrimination starting in 1942. By that time, the national civil rights movement had gained momentum from its victories at the federal level but had splintered as some radical elements criticized what they saw as conciliation on the part of leaders allied with establishment political forces in cities like Chicago. King was planning an extended stay in Chicago and advocated what the *Defender* called an "intensive, non-violent rights drive" that would focus, an aide said, on combating discrimination in Chicago housing, education, and employment.

Two days after arriving, King held a press conference, announcing the aims and strategies of what he called "the first significant northern freedom movement ever attempted by major civil right forces." King announced that he would spend two or three days of each week in Chicago, living in a West Side apartment meant to symbolize "slum lordism." He said he would spend the late winter working to bring as many clergy as possible into the movement, with a particular emphasis on involving Roman Catholics. King also used Chicago as a base to organize in other cities, and he spent a good deal of time elsewhere over the next several months.[34]

King's efforts met with some skepticism from the white press, and with hostility from Mayor Daley, though Archbishop John Cody and other religious leaders made common cause with him. A few days after King's first visit of the year, the *Tribune* editorialized against his plans, even claiming that it was "an open secret" that King's priorities clashed with those of civil rights leaders in Chicago. Chicago leaders wanted to emphasize better education; King planned to fight against slums. This aim was "absurd," the *Tribune* said. By replacing old neighborhoods with $390 million in public housing, Chicago had already worked harder to combat slum conditions than to solve almost any other city problem. (Former residents of the now-demolished Henry Horner or Robert Taylor homes, the fruits of these "slum clearance" policies, might be forgiven for questioning how well postwar urban renewal worked.)[35]

Despite such criticism, and some from South Side preachers with close ties to the Democratic machine, King pressed on to make Chicago "the beautiful city of brotherhood that it is called to be." In January, the King family moved into an apartment in Lawndale.[36] With King settled in on the West Side, the Freedom Movement gained momentum through the first half of 1966, although its broad agenda sometimes made its efforts hard to track. Early on, King organized Operation Breadbasket, a series of boycotts designed to pressure employers to hire blacks. (The Reverend Jesse L. Jackson headed the operation and used it to establish himself in Chicago.) King met with police brass, including Superintendent Orlando W. Wilson, who opened their meeting with a reference to how Alderman Leon Despres had researched King's genealogy and found that King had Irish ancestors. King pledged that any demonstrations during his time in Chicago would be nonviolent and went on a tour of police headquarters. In March King led a Chicago Freedom Festival at the International Amphitheatre, packing the house with almost fourteen thousand people, including Mahalia Jackson, Sidney Poitier, and Harry Belafonte. But more was needed, and organizers hoped Soldier Field would be the place to forge citywide change out of the movement's activism. Organizers knew that no other Chicago venue could bring attention to their cause the way Soldier Field would.[37]

In May 1966 the Freedom Movement truly crystallized, with King announcing a late June rally at Soldier Field (later moved to July 10 so as not to conflict with demonstrations in Mississippi following the shooting of James Meredith, the first black student admitted to the University of Mississippi). "Every church must turn out that Sunday and bring all the members to Soldier Field. . . . Chicago will have a long hot summer, but not a summer of racial violence. Rather, it will be a long hot summer of peaceful nonviolence," King said.[38] A few days later, the Freedom Movement released its list of demands of city leaders—especially Daley—"for creating an open city." They included full school integration by September 1967, a city income tax, a $2-an-hour minimum wage (about $13.50 an hour in 2008 dollars), and a redistribution of city population to create more integrated communities. The Soldier Field rally and a subsequent march to City Hall were part of the movement's overall strategy to advocate for these goals, and organizers expected 125,000 people.[39]

Whatever the 1964 rally's virtues, the 1966 Soldier Field rally gained the backing of a much broader coalition and benefited from much tighter organization. By 1966 many Chicagoans had been involved in civil rights work in the South, had gained experience working with their own local groups, and had built up a more solid core of activists. King and many others publicized the event nonstop for a month, while members of the CCCO and the SCLC reached out to religious leaders in neighborhoods throughout the city.[40]

Chicago-based national groups, such as the National Association of Social Workers, and locally focused groups like the Catholic Interracial Council urged their members to attend the rally. In addition to a mass mailing from the Episcopal Diocese of Chicago to all its area churches, the Episcopal bishop wrote personally to all clergy urging them to attend.

Like Edward Kelly and Patrick Nash in the early days of Soldier Field, the organizers made every effort to fill the house. But unlike those machine operations, the Freedom Movement relied heavily on unpaid helpers. Volunteers and members of the SCLC and CCCO staffs distributed thousands of leaflets to churches, housing projects, businesses, and neighborhoods throughout the city, one staff member of the CCCO wrote in a memo on rally publicity.[41] Organizers placed advertisements on local radio stations, and King sent telegrams to local clergy. On Monday, July 4, King led nine smaller rallies to urge people to go to Soldier Field the following Sunday. Then, two days before the event, King and other leaders held a press briefing, with King emphasizing that while northern racism "never featured lynchings," it "relegates the Negro to an inferior and second class status."[42]

Some dissension appeared among black leaders in Chicago as the Freedom Movement gathered strength. A few days before the rally, King spoke against the Black Power campaign of the Student Nonviolent Coordinating Committee and weathered the attacks of the Reverend Joseph H. Jackson, president of the National Baptist Convention. Jackson, who supported Daley, refused to endorse the rally and said King's nonviolent approach sowed the seeds of violence. King also had had little success in converting youth gangs into nonviolent activists, although some members of the Blackstone Rangers joined the movement.[43]

Coverage in the *Tribune* stressed the number of black groups that were not planning to send their members to the rally, but by the day of the event, it appeared King had inspired legions of people to join the Freedom Movement. By the time the rally occurred, the Freedom Movement's original target, Benjamin Willis, was set to retire at the end of August. Though the slums were still there, City Hall appeared to have responded by sending out more building inspectors and rat exterminators to black neighborhoods. Outreach to people on welfare had helped increase payments for some of them to the full eligible amount.[44]

Organizers had predicted a hundred thousand people at the rally. But the weather that week was witheringly hot, and though the thermometer only hit eighty-seven at Grant Park the day of the event, the heat did not bode well for a great turnout. Still, organizers estimated that as many as sixty-five thousand people made it to the stadium for the 1966 rally. The setup for the rally was spartan, with a stage at the north end of the stadium, close to the stands leading up to the Chicago Park District administration building. Anticipating trouble if people surged onto the arena, the park district installed crude wire fencing to keep attendees off the field (other photos from the era show no such fencing at events like the Mum Bowl). Those arriving early sat in areas shaded by the colonnades, and many others used umbrellas to keep the sun off.

After the stadium opened at noon, attendees enjoyed entertainment that included Mahalia Jackson, Peter, Paul and Mary, and ten singing nuns from Mundelein College. Before the speeches, there was also a song celebrating the rally itself, with some dancing to the music on the arena grass and in the aisles. West Siders Milton Ray, his wife Barbara, and their two-year-old son, Bryant, came to see King because Ray felt the rally marked a turning point for civil rights in Chicago. Despite all the hostility King had faced that summer, many Chicagoans like Ray felt the Freedom Movement had been a long time coming. "I'm a World War II veteran, and when I came out of the service, I couldn't even get my old job back," Ray told the *Sun-Times*.[45]

The main speakers arrived in a forty-car motorcade about 3:15 p.m., just a few minutes late. A half dozen speakers preceded King, including Albert Raby, the head of the CCCO. While calling for the election of civil rights–friendly aldermen to help create an "open city," Raby attacked Daley's administration as "socially and morally bankrupt." Other speakers, including James Meredith, who was still recovering from his shooting the month before, appealed for unity. "There is enough room in this movement for everybody," Meredith said, to fight against the "system of white supremacy." Floyd B. McKissick, the national director of the Congress of Racial Equality, tried to reconcile the idea of Black Power with King's message of nonviolence. "Black power is not hatred. It is a means to bring the black American into the covenant of brotherhood," McKissick said.

To introduce King, auxiliary Bishop Aloysius Wycislo read a statement from Archbishop John Cody. Cody praised King highly, as "a man who has become a symbol of all this (civil rights, racial, human freedom) to America and to the world," and endorsed many of the Freedom Movement's demands. "This man has awakened the conscience of a nation. This man has taught us that wherever there is segregation, no man can be truly free."[46]

King then took the podium to a "deafening" roar. His remarks laid out the rationale for the rally, and for what needed to be done in Chicago, including having those at the rally "decide that our votes will decide who will be the mayor of Chicago." He continued:

> We are here today because we are tired. We are tired of being seared in the flames of withering injustice. We are tired of paying more for less. We are tired of living in rat-infested slums and in the Chicago Housing Authority's cement reservations. We are tired of having to pay a median rent of $97 a month in Lawndale for four rooms while whites in South Deering pay $73 a month for five rooms.

Group carrying a "Black Power" banner at the 1966 civil rights rally at Soldier Field. Courtesy Chicago Park District Special Collections.

King criticized those who, like J. H. Jackson, had boycotted the rally as too confrontational:

> We have also come here today to remind Chicago of the fierce urgency of now. . . . Now is the time to make real the promises of democracy. Now is the time to open the doors of opportunity to all of God's children. Now is the time to end the long and desolate night of slumism. Now is the time to have a confrontation in the City of Chicago between the forces resisting change and the forces demanding change. Now is the time to let justice roll down from City Hall like waters and righteousness like a mighty stream.[47]

King reiterated the Freedom Movement's fourteen demands, saying, "We must not wait for President Johnson," the Supreme Court, or Mayor Daley "to free us. These forces will only respond when they realize we have a powerful inner determination to be free." King then criticized the Black Power movement.[48] Though Black Power had already been debated in Chicago, some mark the 1966 rally as a turning point in its popularity in the city. Before the speeches began, members of the Blackstone Rangers paraded a bedsheet

Crowd members dancing at the 1966 civil rights rally, before speeches by the Reverend Martin Luther King Jr. and others. Courtesy Chicago Park District Special Collections.

with "Black Power" emblazoned on it around the field. Others carried a sign with a drawing of a submachine gun and the caption "Freedom Now," while chanting, "Black Power."[49] King, however, did not relent in his criticism of the idea that armed violence could win the day: "We must work passionately and unrelentingly for first class citizenship, but we must never use second class methods to gain it." Only nonviolence had made a climate for progress possible, King emphasized.[50]

King ended his speech by repeating the phrase "We shall overcome" several times, then led several thousand people—one organizer estimated as many as 80 percent of those at the stadium—from Soldier Field up Columbus Drive, then east through the Loop to City Hall. Between Soldier Field and State Street, King rode in an air-conditioned car; then, flanked by Coretta Scott King and McKissick, he made his way to City Hall, where the crowd surrounded the building. Marchers joined arms in a wide circle around King to keep people back about twelve yards. In imitation of his namesake, who in 1517 had nailed a list of criticisms of the Catholic Church's doctrine on indulgences to the door of the castle church at Wittenberg, Germany, King taped a copy of the Freedom Movement's demands to City Hall's brass doors.[51]

The next day, Daley met with King and other leaders for three hours.

Daley complained to King that he was ignoring "massive programs of the city" that addressed slums, poor housing, and unemployment, and after the meeting, told reporters he had asked, "'What would you do that we haven't done?' They had no answers." For his part, King said Daley had made no specific commitments. He proclaimed the meeting unsatisfactory and said demonstrations would continue for the rest of the summer.[52]

The day after the meeting, riots erupted on the West Side following the shutoff of an open fire hydrant and continued for several days. (At the time, it was common—and still is, in some Chicago neighborhoods—for children in poorer areas to open fire hydrants to create cool fountains on sweltering summer days.) Daley blamed members of King's staff for the riots, while the head of the Chicago Urban League said King's demands "may have motivated" them.[53] Before the riots even started, the *Tribune* said that King's marches and demonstrations had "become tiresome."[54] The *Daily News*, however, firmly backed many of the Freedom Movement's demands, and King himself. Neither King, "locked in a leadership struggle with the 'black power' people," nor the city, could "afford to settle for less than deeds," the *Daily News* editorialized.[55]

King stayed on in Chicago through the end of the summer, marching through several white neighborhoods. In Marquette Park, he said, "I can say that I have never seen, even in Mississippi and Alabama, mobs as hostile and as hate-filled as I have seen in Chicago." In August King met again with Daley, along with a large group of others, including Archbishop Cody, and reached an agreement on open housing. "Never before has such far-reaching and creative commitments been made and programs adopted and pledged to achieve open housing in a community," King said after the meeting. The agreements promised a nondiscrimination policy by area real estate concerns, equal opportunity loans, the end of concentrated public housing, and work toward integration of white neighborhoods. King announced the end of the neighborhood marches but pledged to hold the city to its promises.[56]

The results of the Freedom Movement were mixed. It helped put integration on the agenda in Chicago and initiated a number of changes in housing policies that are still under way today. After 1966 Reverend Jesse Jackson moved to the city permanently, where he became a focal point for both civil rights action and criticism of the movement's methods. King continued to press the demands of the movement, but just two years later he was assassinated. It would be another twenty years before black leaders again united around a single cause—the election of Harold Washington as mayor—as they had in the days of the Freedom Movement.

The 1966 rally marked the last large-scale political event at Soldier Field for a while. Some still tried to use the stadium as a place to draw attention to their causes, but all were rebuffed.[57] Soon after the King rally, the Ku Klux Klan again tried to get a permit for the field, and again was denied. In 1968 the Chicago Park District denied a permit for antiwar protesters who wanted to hold a rally for what they claimed would be "half a million people" at the stadium during the Democratic National Convention.[58]

Religious events, too, were less common at Soldier Field as the 1960s wore on. Not until the 1990s, just after a major renovation of the stadium for the World Cup briefly brought it new life, would its popularity as a religious venue revive. In 1996 the stadium hosted the Promise Keepers, a conservative Christian men's group that drew about sixty-nine thousand people for its main event. On June 24, 2000, Chicago's Catholic archdiocese held a celebration of the start of the third millennium—part of a Holy Year proclaimed by Pope John Paul II—at Soldier Field. It was the largest gathering of Catholics in the city since John Paul II visited in 1979, but still drew only about thirty thousand people. Timed to coincide with the feast of Corpus Christi, the event echoed the much larger Catholic events held at Soldier Field between 1926 and 1954, as a choir of 250 children and several parish choirs and musical ensembles performed, but it also gave Catholics a chance to reflect on how life had changed for them since the Eucharistic Congress. "In 1926 much of the church was immigrant, working-class. Now a third of the Fortune 500 CEOs are Catholic," the Reverend Wayne Prist, one of the event's organizers, told the *Tribune*.[59]

The relatively low numbers at the 2000 event reflected more than just a decline in Catholic church attendance. In the seventy-five years since the Eucharistic Congress, Chicago's broader culture had also changed. For years, the stadium had lived up to the dreams that Chicagoans had invested in it, becoming the premier place for any coming together of the city's religious communities. In the new millennium, religion may still play a large role in many people's lives, but large-scale outdoor gatherings for anything other than entertainment have become far less common. Sporting events remain big draws, but rallies like King's and Graham's have disappeared from the stadium.

In one of the few political events at the stadium since the Vietnam War era, advocates of legalized marijuana held the Windy City Weedfest in the Soldier Field parking lots in 1996, but Chicago Park District officials said they would deny any future permits because of illegal drug use at the festival. When they did so the following year, Weedfest organizers took them to court. In a decision reminiscent of the Illinois Supreme Court's ruling against Father Coughlin in the 1930s, the U.S. Supreme Court sided with the Park District, saying that "to allow unregulated access to all comers could easily reduce rather than enlarge the park's utility as a forum for speech."[60]

The decline of Soldier Field's role as a center of religious and political life in the 1960s came as Chicagoans began to view its crumbling edifice more as a reminder of the city's hastening decline, and less as a symbol of its possibilities. Residents in the city's burgeoning suburbs looked less and less to the city as a pivotal place. As an older Chicago faded, private developers, and suburbs such as Rosemont started building modern venues to compete with the increasingly dilapidated Soldier Field, Coliseum, and Amphitheatre. At the same time, city leaders across the country began to think of new sports stadiums as catalysts for urban revitalization. Many traditions at the stadium soon became mere entries in yellowing scrapbooks, reminders of a city's faded glory.

PART 3

THE FALL AND RISE OF SOLDIER FIELD

11 Celebrations in an Era of Decline

The success of events like Billy Graham's crusade and Martin Luther King's civil rights rallies masked somewhat Soldier Field's inevitable decline. The stadium's builders had followed the City Beautiful vision of creating a gathering place for all Chicago. Its architects had used the most advanced approaches available in designing the arena, including a then-innovative technique to determine how high each row of seats should be above the ones in front of it. But by the 1950s fewer and fewer of the cultural events popular in the time of the City Beautiful movement still appealed to modern audiences. As Chicago and American culture and politics changed, many of the popular events at the stadium faded or died. Some traditional events saw brief postwar revivals, and a few continued into the 1970s, but all eventually gave way to cheaper or flashier alternatives.[1]

FIRE AND POLICE SHOWS: A BRIEF REVIVAL

Few events showed the oddball streak of Soldier Field happenings like the fire department show. After more than a decade's hiatus, the department revived its show in 1958, with a three-hour program staged by about a thousand fire-fighters. Antique and modern firefighting vehicles paraded, and firefighters put out fires in building facades constructed on the field and performed stunts on ropes hanging from the eighty-five-foot ladders of six hook-and-ladder trucks. The next year, the police brought back their own Soldier Field show, by then more of a circus than an athletic event.[2]

Civic spirit helped bring back the shows. The police and fire meets always functioned as fund-raisers for the departments' benevolent associations

Firefighting demonstration with mock building, at the 1962 Chicago Fire Department thrill show. Courtesy Chicago Park District Special Collections.

and so were a tangible way for ordinary Chicagoans to honor fallen police officers and firefighters. Even after the shows stopped in the 1940s, other fund-raisers continued. The police fund, for instance, used stock car races at the stadium as its chief annual moneymaker from the mid-1940s through the mid-1950s.[3] The revived police and fire shows proved popular, but over time tastes in entertainment changed. So too did the way Chicago provided for the survivors of those killed in the line of duty. In the case of the police meet, attempts to clean up the police department also contributed to the show's demise.

In 1960 the Summerdale Scandal—in which a crew of police officers from the Summerdale District (a now-defunct North Side station) turned from catching burglars to burgling—shocked the city. The scandal disturbed Mayor Richard J. Daley enough that he brought in Orlando W. Wilson, an expert on policing at the University of California–Los Angeles, to reform the department.[4] Almost immediately, Wilson confronted a dilemma. On the one hand, if they were to remain above suspicion, police officers could

The queen of the police stock car races with Mayor Richard J. Daley (right), 1957. Courtesy Chicago Park District Special Collections.

not be soliciting money from citizens; on the other, the Police Benevolent Association had always relied on officers' selling tickets to its fund-raisers to bring in money. "I was told I couldn't maintain the integrity of the police benevolent fund unless I permitted policemen to sell tickets to these fine events," Wilson said. To solve the problem, he enlisted the city's five daily newspapers and a host of other organizations to sell the tickets instead. After much cajoling by the newspapers and Daley's political organization, about ninety-three thousand people turned out to witness two performances of the 1960 Soldier Field show, headlined by television talk show host Jack Paar. After Wimpy the Clown, an acrobat called Bettina, and the auto stunts of the Trans-World Airdevils entertained the crowds, Stanley R. Sarbaneck, president of the benevolent association, pronounced himself "pleased and proud" of Chicago's support for its police officers.[5]

Though the fire show was held again in 1962, Wilson decided against allowing the police show to continue, and the Police Benevolent Association switched to mail solicitations to raise money. The final police and fire thrill show came nine years later, as part of a Lakefront Festival that also included the Air and Water Show. Thirty-eight thousand attendees, including Mayor Daley and fire commissioner Robert Quinn, saw firefighters put out a blaze in a mock-up of the Merchandise Mart and laughed at a group of clowns dressed as women firefighters.[6]

The 1971 show, while a nostalgic revisiting of a tradition that thrived from the 1920s to the 1940s, reflected larger changes in Chicago culture—and in the use of Soldier Field. It was part of a larger city-run festival that did not benefit a private group. No admission was charged—not unusual for religious events and some political and social rallies, but not the norm for cultural events held at Soldier Field. But thanks in part to the increasingly popular Air and Water Show and events such as Venetian Night, both created under Richard J. Daley, Chicagoans were getting used to "free"—that is, taxpayer underwritten—lakefront and downtown festivals. They were no longer willing to pay to be part of a larger cause that also included entertainment. At the same time, many of the middle-class and blue-collar white families that had filled the Soldier Field stands for earlier events had left the city. As Chicago, always a patchwork of disconnected neighborhoods and suburbs, fragmented even more after World War II, the City Beautiful idea of uniting its citizens through happenings at Soldier Field became even harder to realize. And as urban decay spread through the South and West sides on Richard J. Daley's watch, Chicago's downtown became associated more with danger and decline than with entertainment and celebration. [7]

THE END OF THE CHICAGOLAND MUSIC FESTIVAL

Soldier Field's longest-running nonsports event also fell victim to these changes in the 1960s. The *Tribune*'s Chicagoland Music Festival had endured through the Depression and World War II, and even thrived in the television age as it attracted Hollywood stars. Honors were extended to well-known musicians and composers; in 1956 Richard Rodgers and Oscar Hammerstein were special guests, driving into the arena to a medley of their own show tunes.[8] And even nationally known people with little connection to the entertainment industry, such as aviator "Wrong Way" Corrigan, who sang at 1938's festival, also helped raise the event's profile. [9]

The *Tribune* regularly touted its own stars, singers and conductors known from their appearances on the newspaper's WGN radio and television stations. In later years, as WGN Radio became less of a musical powerhouse, one of the station's star hosts, Wally Phillips, became a frequent announcer at the festival. And in 1963 Bob Bell—Bozo the Clown—and other cast members of *Bozo's Circus*, a WGN-TV favorite that went on the air in 1961, entertained young people at the start of the festival.[10] The festival featured more than

In addition to stars, small bands, and massed choruses, local marching bands, such as this one, performed at Chicagoland Music Festivals. The photo was most likely taken in 1957. Courtesy Chicago Park District Special Collections.

just locally based performers, however. In 1954, when Liberace headlined the show, Jack Webb appeared in connection with the premiere at the Chicago Theatre of a movie based on his television show *Dragnet*.[11]

Patriotism seemed to be the one common theme for all Soldier Field events over the years, and any longtime employee of the *Tribune*'s superpatriotic Colonel McCormick was expected to play up nationalism at every chance. Sometimes the festival's director, Philip Maxwell, used the choice of music, with frequent renditions of the national anthem, Sousa marches, and such less-familiar pieces as "Invincible U.S.A.," by Francis A. Myers, a prolific Sousa protégé.[12] Once, in 1958, the show featured a reenactment of one of the Lincoln-Douglas debates, with about 250 audience members dressed in period costumes. During World War II the festival favored military bands, and in 1942 also featured a number by a thousand female dancers wearing red, white, and blue ballet costumes. More common were spectacles such as 1946's Dutch wedding dance, performed by hundreds of Chicago-area women and girls wearing colorful dresses, fabric tulip hats, and giant cloth tulips on their wrists and 150 wooden-shoed dancers from Holland, Michigan. In 1950 the park district enlisted six hundred young people to ride bicycles—including a collection of antiques—around the field.[13]

Until the 1970s the park district usually charged the organizers of cultural and religious events that charged no admission—such as the Easter sunrise service and some of the festivals at the Century of Progress Exposition—only the cost of opening the stadium. For events that charged admission, even fund-raisers for charitable groups, the fee for years was 10 percent of ticket sales up to $100,000 in tickets, plus the cost of running the field. Correspondence between park officials and event organizers makes it clear the district also expected a certain number of free tickets for most events. Park district officials always took full advantage of their positions as de facto owners of Soldier Field, operating the stadium in some ways as a private arena aimed at currying favor with other political leaders. For the 1957 Music Festival, for example, Erwin "Red" Weiner, then head of special services for the district, asked for 145 free tickets—45 for commissioners and administrative staff, plus 100 for employees working the event (who would have gotten in in any case with their event badges). "This is the same arrangement as in the past; the complimentary tickets will go to our Building & Facilities Operating, Electrical, Landscape, Mechanical, Repair and Traffic Section personnel who are assigned to work your event," Weiner wrote to Maxwell, the *Tribune*'s director of the music festival.[14]

The music festival wound down in the mid-1960s, as Maxwell's career at the *Tribune* came to a close. Attendance had fallen at many privately organized public festivals in other big cities as urban populations declined and Americans increasingly turned to television for their entertainment; large public events had begun to seem, in an odd sense, less intimate than those on TV, with it false sense of closeness. The 1964 festival had a successful run at Soldier Field. But the elaborate event cost too much to stage, and in 1965 Tribune Charities decided on a smaller festival at the Arie Crown Theater. The 1965 festival honored Eubie Blake and Noble Sissle, who had directed *O, Sing a New Song*, the African American pageant at Soldier Field during the 1933 world's fair (see chapter 8). In 1966, instead of the festival itself, the paper held only a luncheon that had previously run in connection with the festival. Maxwell retired in January 1967, and with his exit the Chicagoland Music Festival ended its four-and-a-half-decade run.[15]

FIREWORKS FADE TO BLACK

Soldier Field had risen on the lakefront as a place for grand civic spectacles, especially patriotic gatherings to commemorate the sacrifices of war. The

American Legion, founded in the aftermath of the same war that inspired the stadium's builders, used the stadium for one of its original purposes for four decades: to bring Chicagoans together in celebration of their country. Until changes in the city's political landscape and the expectations of its citizens made a rival fireworks show into a tradition, the Legion's display at Soldier Field proved the most popular in Chicago. Over the years, attendance at the show fluctuated, although it rarely dipped below thirty thousand until the early 1970s. In 1972 the show's chairman raised the possibility that increased liability concerns might snuff out the Legion show. But fifty thousand people still showed up that year for the fireworks, circus acts, and the Chicago Fire Department's clown band.[16]

What did extinguish the Legion's show was Chicago's Bicentennial celebration and the tradition of city-sponsored fireworks it sparked. Before 1975 the city had only occasionally put on fireworks displays. That year, however, Mayor Daley, who had supported the Legion show in the past, planned a fireworks show in Olive Park (north of Navy Pier), getting an early start on the celebration of the United States Bicentennial by commemorating Paul Revere's 1775 ride. The Legion held its fireworks show as usual that year, but in 1976, when the city repeated its display, the Legion canceled its event. "It will be the first time in at least 37 years that we have not scheduled it," said James Lissner, spokesman for the Legion's Cook County Council. "It would be foolish to try to put on two shows."

In 1977 the Legion resumed its shows at Soldier Field. But attendance dwindled to eighteen thousand in 1978 and fifteen thousand in 1979. The city's display had two major advantages: free admission—in the early 1970s the Legion charged $1.50 for general admission, $2 for reserved seats (about $11 in 2008 dollars)—and more elaborate pyrotechnics.[17] In 1973 the Legion show used about $6,000 worth of fireworks; the city, in 1978, spent about $20,000, plus it was able to launch its rockets from barges on Lake Michigan. Its Soldier Field show could still be billed as the "world's largest fireworks extravaganza"—the show's total budget, including the cost of the circus acts and bands, was higher than that for the city. But ultimately the Legion couldn't compete. If the first Mayor Daley, who had addressed the Illinois Legion convention in 1973, had not died in 1976, it's possible the city might have ended its display after the Bicentennial. But his replacement, Mayor Michael Bilandic, had several conflicts with the Legion's Cook County leaders—and also likely wanted to take credit for the city's tax-supported show.[18]

Over the next few years, the Legion's show continued to decline, its audience drawn away by the growing city fireworks. In 1978 the municipal show relocated from Olive Park to Grant Park and returned to a tradition dating to the 1800s of having fireworks displays on July 3, with July 4 reserved for more dignified remembrances. That year 350,000 people watched the July 3 fireworks and concert in Grant Park, while attendance at the Legion event hit an all-time low of 15,000. The nadir came in 1981, when the Legion made the disastrous decision to couple its fireworks show with a Chicago Fire football game. The Fire (unrelated to today's Chicago Fire soccer team) was an unsuccessful team in the unsuccessful American Football Association. On July 4, 1981, the team won, beating the Shreveport Steamer, 24–15, but even with the fireworks, only about sixty-nine hundred people showed up.[19] The next year, about half a million people attended the Taste of Chicago, at the time a relatively new downtown festival, on Saturday, July 3, the day of the city fireworks. On Sunday, July 4, some of the two hundred thousand people who showed up at the Taste also expected fireworks. But the Legion's forty-six-year tradition was dead.[20]

The end of the Legion show also marked the death of one of Soldier Field's original missions: as not just a sports stadium but a center of civic life. Veterans Day memorials have once again become a regular occurrence at the new Soldier Field, but they are small gatherings. And except for an Easter egg hunt and several fund-raising races, the stadium hosts no longer hosts any annual musical or cultural events.

THE LAST PAGEANT

Even as the Chicago tradition of grand happenings at Soldier Field faded, the city marked a few momentous occasions at the stadium. Some few of them followed in traditions that the stadium's builders would have found familiar. The last real theatrical pageant at Soldier Field was the 1966 commemoration of a thousand years of Christianity in Poland. Held at the height of the Cold War, the event highlighted the Chicago Polish community's commitment to the Roman Catholic Church, which though legal in Communist Poland was restricted in its activities and its ability to proselytize. In Poland that year, the government threw up as many roadblocks as possible to an open celebration of the anniversary, scheduled for May 3, scheduling road repairs and disrupting train traffic throughout that week. At the same time, the state was waging an anti-Catholic propaganda campaign, branding Catholic leaders as neo-Nazis. Although Polish-born Catholics from Chicago journeyed to their homeland for some celebrations, Archbishop John Cody and other Catholic prelates, as well as many laypeople from outside the Eastern Bloc, were barred from traveling there.[21]

In this Cold War climate, Chicago-area Poles and the Archdiocese of Chicago held a series of commemorative events, culminating in an August 28 mass and celebration at Soldier Field. As with the 1954 Marian Year Holy Hour, and in contrast to the 1926 Eucharistic Congress, the altar constructed for the event was of modernist design, a hundred feet wide

Workers construct a space-age altar for the 1966 celebration of the Polish Millennium of Christianity. Courtesy Chicago Park District Special Collections.

and forty feet tall, at the center of the stadium. The Polish government barred Cardinal Stefan Wyszinski, the primate of Poland, from attending, but Wladyslaw Rubin, the auxiliary bishop of Gniezo, Poland, was able to come in his stead.

People began arriving by 11 a.m., almost filling the stadium by 5 p.m., an hour before the program was to start. The event began with a parade of people dressed in the traditional costumes of countries influenced or ruled by Poland over the centuries—Czechs, Ukrainians, and Latvians, in addition to Poles—all of which were then under communist rule. As many as ninety thousand people watched as actors, dancers, and singers dramatized the broad sweep of Polish history, beginning with the baptism of Mieszko I, the ruler of Greater Poland, in 966, a year after his marriage to the Bohemian princess Dobrava. A twelve-hundred-person choir sang, accompanied by a fifty-piece orchestra, as 125 people performed traditional Polish dances—the mazurka, the polonaise, the krakowiak—all popularized during the nineteenth century. The pageant ended with Poland's regaining its independence as a nation-state in 1918 and a dramatization of Polish contributions to science and world culture. Archbishop Cody praised Poles who had immigrated "to Chicago to find freedom and have remained steadfast to their faith." Mayor Daley and Governor Otto Kerner Jr. spoke, both asserting that Poland would soon be free.

Archbishop Cody was the main celebrant of the mass. At the beginning of the religious ceremonies, he and the other priests processed on a red carpet from the south entrance to the arena to the altar, flanked by Knights of Columbus in red-trimmed black capes and white-plumed naval hats. Instead of celebrating the mass in Latin, Cody sang in Polish, which he had been studying for the preceding year for the occasion. Then, at the end of the mass, the priests walked to the north end of the arena to venerate a twenty-two-foot-high picture of Our Lady of Czestochowa.[22]

PURE ENTERTAINMENT—WITH A FEW MISSTEPS

Many recurring events at Soldier Field included circus acts, and the Chicago Park District held its own circus event in 1936, but for twenty years, beginning in 1931, the stadium and its parking lots were also the site of the Greatest Show on Earth: the Ringling Brothers and Barnum & Bailey Circus. For more than a decade before its move to Soldier Field, Ringling Brothers had taken over a large swath of Grant Park in the middle of each summer, an early instance of the park district's renting out public land for private entertainment. (For a few years, elephants had bathed at the downtown lakefront every morning when the circus was in town.) Once it relocated to Soldier Field, the circus usually set up its big top in the parking lots east of the stadium after unloading its train on the nearby Illinois Central tracks, and newspapers—which customarily received many free tickets to visiting circuses—touted Ringling Brothers' "old time circus." The show skipped Chicago in 1933 and 1934, during the Century of Progress world's fair. Then in 1935 and 1936, it set up inside Soldier Field itself; with the north end of the stadium still open, crews could easily bring large equipment like a circus tent into the arena. When construction began, in 1937, on the Chicago Park District administration building, which closed off the north end, the circus returned to the east parking lots.

Circuses of the early Soldier Field era were much larger than they are today and included a greater variety of entertainments, although they already had begun to consolidate and decrease in size. The 1935 edition featured 150 clowns and a thousand animals, as well as the traditional sideshow with "Major Mite, the world's smallest man . . . Miss Weight, the world's fattest woman, [and] Sky High, the world's tallest human being."[23]

The years Ringling Brothers performed at Soldier Field were troubled times for the circus, as it competed with radio, movies, and eventually television and the cost of putting on a show skyrocketed. In 1939 Ringling Brothers announced that it had jazzed up many of its acts but streamlined its show to avert "the dinosaur's trail to extinction." The circus tent was redesigned and even air-conditioned.[24] In 1944 the circus returned to the Soldier Field arena for one season, following a July 6 fire in Hartford, Connecticut, in which almost 170 people died in a tent that Ringling Brothers had failed to fireproof adequately (in part because the U.S. Army at the time refused to allow civilian use of a new fireproofing compound; following the fire, the Army released more of the compound for civilian use). That year, the audience at the show's first Soldier Field performance was made up almost entirely of people who had bought war bonds through their employers and received free tickets as a reward.[25]

Despite a friendly relationship with the newspapers and local charities, the circus sometimes ran afoul of park officials. When, in 1943, the park district contended that Ringling Brothers owed it $874.79 after the season's performances, the circus asked the board to reconsider the amount, contending in part that the free passes given to park employees and political supporters should count toward the outstanding bill. This attempt to whittle down the bill angered the board president, Robert J. Dunham, who wrote a scathing letter to James A. Haley, Ringling Brothers' representative in Chicago: "We do not ask and do not wish a permittee who pays for the use of any of our facilities to figure that the issuance of passes to anyone in any way diminishes the amount of compensation" due the park district.

In 1945 Ringling Brothers and the park district got into a spat, this time about how much the circus should pay to set up in the stadium parking lot. The circus proposed to pay a flat fee, but the park board demanded its usual 10 percent share of gate receipts. The circus's new management, put in place after the 1944 fire, rejected the arrangement, and Ringling Brothers bypassed Chicago that year. But the circus was back in 1946, apparently on its old terms, and continued at Soldier Field until 1955.[26] Red Weiner, at the time in charge of the stadium, bragged that 1954 was one of the best years ever for the stadium, and specifically cited the almost 160,000 people who attended the circus.

In the mid-1950s, most likely 1955, someone—possibly Weiner—wrote up a list of problems the park district had had with the circus. The three-by-five-inch index card listing the grievances ticks off problems ranging from poor housekeeping to leaking women's toilets and allegations of crimes committed by performers and others, including murder, rape, and slaughtering horses. While it's uncertain whether these complaints turned into a serious point of contention, after 1955, Ringling Brothers took a three-year hiatus from Chicago. And

In the 1940s and 1950s Soldier Field sometimes hosted two large events at once, with happenings like the circus or this 1947 General Motors car expo set up in tents in the stadium's east parking lot. Courtesy Chicago Park District Special Collections.

when it returned, in 1959, the circus settled in at the Chicago Amphitheatre, a private, indoor facility that was air-conditioned.[27]

The Chicago Park District tried to bring other circuses to Soldier Field over the years, with limited success. In the summer of 1958 the Christiana Brothers Circus took over the stadium's east lots for seventeen days of performances. The stadium saw no more full-fledged circuses for almost two decades. Then the last circus in Soldier Field came in 1975, as part of an effort by parks general superintendent Edmund Kelly to get new uses out of the stadium's north end, which the park district had closed off by erecting temporary bleachers to form a bowl for football games at the south end of the field. The Emmett Kelly Jr. Circus was booked for a stint starting June 14, and Mayor Daley urged each Democratic ward organization to buy a thousand tickets. Emmett Kelly Jr., the son of one of the most famous circus clowns in history, had decided in 1960 to follow his father's lead and adopt the persona of "Wearie Willie," the hobo clown his father made famous in Ringling Broth-

The Emmett Kelly Jr. circus performed in Soldier Field's north end in 1975. Chicago Park District general superintendent Edmund Kelly attempted during that period to make use of a section of the stadium cut off when the Bears installed the north stands. Courtesy Chicago Park District Special Collections.

ers performances. In 1972 the younger Kelly created his own European-style one-ring circus, which toured for about a dozen years, but played only the one year at Soldier Field.[28] Since then, no circuses have appeared at the stadium. In big cities like Chicago, only the biggest or most elaborate circuses have remained able to compete with movies and television.

MUSIC AT THE STADIUM

Soldier Field has also hosted a number of onetime concerts and other musical events. Most have featured popular music, especially from the 1970s on (on rock concerts at the stadium, see chapter 14), but some were decidedly highbrow. There was a 1933 production of *Aida*, with an all-Texan cast, presented as part of Texas Day at the world's fair, and the Chicagoland Music Festival always included at least a few operatic numbers. But the mid-1940s marked the height of opera's popularity at the stadium. For several years beginning in

1941, the Chicago Opera Company tried to pull itself out of a Depression-era financial slump by performing summer operas and concerts in Soldier Field. In 1942 the company presented Bizet's *Carmen*, as well as a concert, both for military servicemen, who got tickets from Mayor Kelly's servicemen's welcome center. Critics, including the *Tribune*'s Claudia Cassidy, were generally positive in their reviews of the Soldier Field operas—in one case, Cassidy noted that Chicagoans could see a $4 opera for only $2 at the stadium—and the performances attracted as many as thirty-two thousand people. But the appeal did not last, and by 1944 the Chicago Opera Company was struggling so much that it brought in the San Carlo touring company as a substitute at the stadium. By 1947 there was no full-time opera company in the city at all.[29]

High culture made few appearances at Soldier Field after the end of the Chicagoland Music Festival. But popular culture continued to thrive, even in Soldier Field's worst years, the late 1960s. Probably the oddest event at Soldier Field in modern times was the Mixed Breed Dog Show, held September 10, 1967; the event, a show for mongrels, was organized by longtime Chicago newspaper columnist Mike Royko as a spoof of the Westminster Dog Show. Over the years, newspapers had sponsored everything from patriotic events to sports games at the stadium. As one of the last newspaper-sponsored events at Soldier Field, Royko's tongue-in-cheek dogfest was emblematic of big papers' withdrawal from the active role they took in Chicago civic life in the first half of the century.

Not every event at Soldier Field came off perfectly. After many events the stands and concourses were strewn with rubbish—including, on occasion, a surprising number of newspapers (see the photo on page 41). Bad weather marred many events, especially football games and other fall programs and Easter celebrations in the spring.

Sometimes chaos erupted at the stadium when organizers underestimated the crowds their events would attract. If anyone in the twenty-first century thinks of bobby-soxers at all, it's probably as an icon of a more innocent America, one in which a teenage kiss in public constituted scandalous behavior. One of the most out-of-control events ever staged at Soldier Field, however, was a jitterbug concert put on August 23, 1938, by Chicago's New Century Committee, a City Hall–backed group that organized events to celebrate the beginning of Chicago's second century. The swing jamboree featured a battle of fifty amateur bands and "some of the city's leading dance orchestras," with three fifty-by-one-hundred-foot dance floors in the stadium arena and no admission charge. Bands participating included those led by Jimmy Dorsey, big band jazz leader Tommy Dorsey's older brother; Earl Hines, who had been the main jazz pianist at Al Capone's Grand Terrace Cafe for a decade; and Shep Fields, whose band won a 1938 Academy Award for the song "Thanks for the Memory."

Organizers apparently did not realize how young crowds, inspired by the nascent celebrity culture, would flock to Soldier Field for a free show, and certainly did not anticipate how they would act once they got there. But young people who usually could only afford to listen to music stars like Dorsey or Hines on the radio saw the event as a great opportunity. The "jolly but uncontrollable crowd" of at least a hundred thousand—estimates ranged as high as two hundred thousand—overwhelmed the stadium an hour before the program was scheduled to start at 8 p.m. News accounts described the event as "run riot," partly because when police ordered the gates of the stadium closed at 6 p.m. because all the seats were filled, the fans forced them open again. Swing dance enthusiasts, or "jitterbugs" (named for a Cab Calloway song, about heavy drinking and the resulting "jitters," that typified the fast big band dance style of the 1930s), crowded the south end of Grant Park, surrounding a group of twenty-one thousand people gathered for a classical music concert at the Chicago bandshell north of the Field Museum and causing police to close Lake Shore Drive. When there was no room left in the aisles or on the colonnades in Soldier Field, fans flooded the arena itself, even forcing the bands off one of the stages. The announcers, Ken Ellington and Paul Luther of CBS Radio, pleaded for the youngsters to leave the stages, to no avail.

In the end, the music from the stages stopped, but the jitterbugs kept on dancing, some bringing out their own instruments and bottles of liquor (alcohol would not be allowed at the stadium until more than forty years later). Throngs of teenage boys and girls clasped hands and danced in long, snaking lines. But even when some young men found a fifty-foot rope and began cutting through the masses with it, bowling people over, there appeared to be little anger from the crowd. "Some of the things that are happening here tonight could cause real trouble in any other kind of crowd," said Captain Michael Hayes, in charge of the police at Soldier Field that night. "Thank heavens they seem so cheerful about everything." The crowd calmed down a bit when the city's corporation counsel, Barnet Hodes, called off the amateur band contest and announced that the music would be limited to the professionals. The bands and would-be dancers finally left Soldier Field around 1 a.m. "The whole thing got away from us," Hodes said afterward, lamenting that the group would probably have to pay $40,000 to have the arena resodded.[30]

Nothing like it would be seen at Soldier Field again until the 1970s, when Edmund Kelly began booking mammoth rock concerts at the stadium. In Soldier Field's waning years, fluke successes like Grateful Dead concerts became more common than the amateur sports the City Beautiful dreamers hoped would fill the stadium. As the sports it was designed for changed or lost favor, Soldier Field's decline came more quickly than almost anyone might have expected.

12 *Amateur Sports Founder at a Fading Stadium*

UP AND DOWN WITH THE PREP BOWL

In time, reformers came to associate Soldier Field less with instilling civic virtue and more with Mayor Edward Kelly's corrupt political machine, and that contributed to the decline of sports at the stadium. For a few years in the early 1950s, and then again in the 1970s and 1980s, it looked like the Prep Bowl, made famous by Mayor Kelly and embraced as his own by Mayor Richard J. Daley, would entirely disappear from the city.

Under reform mayor Martin Kennelly, whose two terms followed Kelly's and preceded Daley's, attendance at the Prep Bowl mostly hovered below thirty thousand. With fewer strong Democratic ward organizations and a more hands-off mayor, city employees and union members were under less pressure to buy and sell tickets. But in 1954 the numbers rebounded, reaching almost forty-seven thousand for a game in which Fenger beat Mount Carmel, 20–13. Beginning in 1955, the newly elected Mayor Daley again pushed attendance at the game.

As ward heelers again peddled tickets, Erwin "Red" Weiner worked with radio stations to make certain the game made it on the air. With these efforts, the early 1960s marked the last glory years of the game, as highly competitive high school playoffs drew some of the largest crowds ever for high school football games. The 1961 game between Weber and Lane Tech was one of the most dramatic, with Weber claiming a last-minute win after Lane fumbled the ball deep in its own territory with only minutes left to play. But the third-highest attendance ever at a Prep Bowl, more than ninety-one thousand, came in 1962, when undefeated Fenwick blasted Schurz, 40–0,

The 1963 Prep Bowl at Soldier Field. Red Weiner claimed the Chicago Park District originated the now-common practice of painting the sidelines with slogans or team names. Courtesy Chicago Park District Special Collections.

with the Friars' Jim Di Lullo scoring 5 times. In 1963 Saint Rita, also undefeated, beat Chicago Vocational, 42–7, with halfback John Byrne scoring five touchdowns and six extra points. Vocational returned to the Prep Bowl in 1964 and 1965, but lost again, first to Weber High School and then to Loyola Academy. Though in 1968 *Tribune* writer Ralph Leo wrote that the Prep Bowl had "reached unprecedented success" under Daley, by the early 1970s when Saint Laurence had a three-year winning run, attendance had dwindled to forty thousand or less.[1]

The 1970s saw major changes in high school sports throughout Illinois. The Illinois High School Association created a new playoff system, and the Prep Bowl no longer always matched the best teams of the Catholic and public leagues—the Catholic League had started sending runners-up rather than league champs to the game. Other factors also worked against the Prep Bowl: the decline of Chicago's downtown from the 1960s through the 1980s made events there less attractive; the Democratic machine and its workers again became less of a force in the city; and a reliable source of boosters dried up as neighborhoods changed, Catholic schools closed, public schools became more African American, and alumni's ties to their old schools weakened. At the same time, Chicagoans' allegiances were shifting more toward professional sports. After 1977, as the stadium became more and more identified with the Chicago Bears, the game struggled to attract even five thousand spectators.

One controversy in the late 1980s symbolized how much the Bears' professional concerns had eclipsed the original uses of the stadium. Since 1986 the Prep Bowl had taken over Soldier Field on the Friday after Thanksgiving. In 1988, after several years using artificial turf, the Chicago Park District returned the arena to natural grass. Because of the relatively fragility of the grass, the park district and the Bears added a clause to the team's lease that barred any sports on the field with forty-eight hours of a Bears game. Because of this clause, park district officials announced their intention to move the 1988 Prep Bowl from Soldier Field to Gately Stadium on the South Side. "We don't want to risk any damage to the grass. . . . Because the Bears and our landscape department have expressed reservations, we felt it was the prudent thing to do," park district executive vice president Jesse D. Madison said after the decision became public.

After a city council uproar, Mayor Eugene Sawyer announced that the game would indeed be played at Soldier Field, but on the Monday after Thanksgiving, a day after the Bears played the Green Bay Packers. Despite the added publicity from the controversy, only about twenty-five hundred people saw Loyola beat Julian, 21–6. Still, the mystique of the Prep Bowl remained, and Loyola coach John Hoerster said, "This is the experience of a lifetime. I'm really thankful for the people who worked so hard—the media, too—to ensure this game would be at Soldier Field. You could never reproduce this feeling anyplace else." It wasn't just the idea of a large crowd cheering on the teams; the stadium itself had become an intimate part of the Prep Bowl rivalry.[2]

From the late 1970s on, commentators frequently raised the possibility of ending the Prep Bowl. In the late 1990s, however, it saw something of a resurgence, as Chicago Public Schools CEO Paul Vallas, other Board of Education officials, and Mayor Richard M. Daley worked to rekindle interest in the game. By 1999 between twenty-five thousand and thirty-five thousand fans saw Hubbard defeat De La Salle, 20–13. The game moved temporarily in 2002 while the new Soldier Field arena was under construction, but it returned in 2003, with Loyola winning, 22–14, over Simeon. Since 2005 the Kickoff Classic, played at the beginning of the prep season, has given high school players another chance at playing at Soldier Field, matching high-ranking prep teams against one another and at least packing much of the lower deck stands of the new stadium.[3]

COLLEGE FOOTBALL BACK, THEN GONE AGAIN

College football too lost ground at the stadium as Chicago changed, although Richard J. Daley fought to bring it back. The 1950s saw few college games at the stadium, with the College All-Star Game and the Prep Bowl the highlights of the football season. In the late 1950s and early 1960s, Daley and park officials including Erwin "Red" Weiner pushed to use the stadium more, and lobbied to get another armed forces game. In January 1962 Daley, at the peak of his national political power, announced that the Army–Air Force Game, which had its first showing in 1959 at Yankee Stadium, would come to Soldier Field the following year. In scenes reminiscent of the frenzy that greeted the 1926 Army-Navy Game, Daley and his special events director, Colonel Jack Reilly, planned receptions and a ball for the cadets (again recruiting thousands of young women to dance with them). As with the 1926 game, the city ran up substantial expenses bringing the cadets to the city. Reilly also planned a motorcade for President John F. Kennedy, who was to attend the game and toss a coin to decide who would kick off.[4]

In a configuration first used by the Chicago Cardinals in 1959, the park district put up special bleachers at the north end of the playing field for the game. The newspapers noted that the only member of the Air Force team from Chicago proper was linebacker and center Pete Mitchell, a 1960 graduate of Fenwick who had played in two Prep Bowls for the Oak Park school. The two teams' records were well-matched: Army had won five of its first six games, and Air Force had won four of six. Though the Air Force Academy was in only its eighth season playing football and had not yet beaten either Navy or Army, the Falcons gave the Army's Black Knights a game. Army led throughout the contest, but Air Force stayed within four points. But Army halfback Ken Waldrop scored two touchdowns, including one in the last quarter that clinched it for the Knights.[5]

Daley lobbied to make Chicago the home every other year for the Army–Air Force Game. He did not succeed, though the game did return in 1965. Daley, a staunch supporter of President Lyndon Johnson, directed that the city set aside game day, November 6, to honor Americans serving in Vietnam. Wounded Vietnam veterans were to be guests of honor at the game, Daley told reporters. Again, the city prepared a number of parties and a dinner dance for cadets, this time at the new McCormick Place.

In an echo of the Army-Navy Game forty years before, a fifty-round howitzer salute in Grant Park preceded a parade including cadets from both academies, marching bands, and the Medinah Temple Black Horse Troop. Police estimated that two hundred thousand people lined the parade route from downtown to Soldier Field, applauding as the servicemen passed. At Soldier Field, Air Force outgunned Army from the start, keeping the Knights outside Air Force's 45-yard line throughout the first half. The only touchdowns of the game came on a five-yard run and a twenty-seven-yard pass by Air Force quarterback Paul Stein, while Army was held to a single field goal.[6]

The last armed services game at the old Soldier Field was the 1968 Navy–Air Force Game. Both teams had fared poorly that season; Navy came into the game at 0–3, Air Force at 1–3. Though some predicted Navy could upset the Falcons, Air Force ended up with a 26–20 win. About fifty-one thousand people attended, a decent crowd but smaller than those drawn by previous military academy games. Daley and Reilly again campaigned to get the game on a regular basis, but it never did return.[7]

The low point for college football at Soldier Field came after the Navy–Air Force match. As part of Daley and Weiner's attempt to fill Soldier Field more regularly, they signed the University of Illinois at Chicago to a contract to play at the stadium. The school's Near West Side campus, then commonly known as Chicago Circle, was Daley's controversial pet urban renewal project. UIC started playing football at Soldier Field in 1966, the year after the new campus opened. A decade or two earlier, the venue itself might have attracted fans. By the late 1960s, however, Soldier Field added little to an event's mystique—and events like the 1950s ski jump and faltering auto races likely tarnished the stadium's reputation. Without an established alumni following and with apparently little backing from the university, UIC football never really took off. The team attracted crowds of six to ten thousand at first and had a winning season in 1967. But its fortunes declined into the 1970s, so badly that by 1972 the team was playing to fewer than a thousand people. The school's administration decided to cut the sport, despite feeble protests from boosters. In their last home game at Soldier Field, on November 3, 1973, the Chikas, as UIC teams were known at the time, lost, 53–6, to the University of Wisconsin–Platteville.[8]

The Chicago Urban League tried to revive black college football at the stadium with an annual benefit game between historically black colleges. The series started out well in 1971, as thirty-three thousand people Grambling College played Alcorn A&M in a stadium recently renovated to accommodate the NFL's Bears. Chicago's black businesspeople supported the game heavily its first year, with many buying blocks of tickets. The response encouraged black leaders. "Initially, it introduces the possibility that thru the proceeds of big sports events, black-oriented organizations may raise most of their finances other than by relying heavily on the charities of big foundations," wrote columnist Vernon Jarrett. But, Jarrett warned, "This is not a new idea. The problem has been in the area of promotion." The game received front-page coverage, with newspapers trumpeting Grambling's easy 21–6 win over Alcorn. But trouble started to brew at the 1973 game between Morgan State and Alabama State, when the halftime show took fifty minutes, more than three times as long as NCAA regulations allowed for regular season games. Worse, attendance had slumped to about twenty thousand people, filling less than half the stadium. In 1974 the Urban League ended its sponsorship of the game, citing falling attendance and mounting expenses. Other groups tried to revive it a few times in the 1970s but failed.[9]

From the mid-1970s to the early 1990s college football was driven away from Soldier Field by restrictions on game dates due to the Bears, higher rental costs, and the stadium's physical deterioration despite repeated renovations. Since 1992, however, and especially since the 2003 renovation, things have been looking up. Notre Dame played Northwestern there in 1992 and 1994, and Northwestern played Oklahoma in 1997. And Soldier Field has once again become a destination for black colleges thanks to the Chicago Football Classic. The group promoting that series was started in 1997 by African American executives including Larry Huggins of RiteWay Construction, a prominent black-owned construction company that was involved in the Millennium Park project. In 2006 about forty thousand people attended a match that saw Mississippi Valley best Arkansas–Pine Bluff, 10–0. Also in 2006, the NCAA announced that the Iowa Hawkeyes would play the Northern Illinois University Huskies at Soldier Field, the first NCAA Division I-A football game at the stadium since it reopened in 2003. Unlike the UIC Chikas, both teams command large fan bases: sellout crowd saw the Hawkeyes whip the Huskies, 16–3, on September 1, 2007.[10]

Although its designers never envisioned football as the primary sport to be played at Soldier Field, from its earliest days most Chicagoans have associated the stadium with gridiron contests. But Soldier Field football has done more than just provide another Saturday afternoon diversion for Chicagoans. From the Prep Bowl to games between black colleges regular-season public school games, the stadium has been over the years a place where Chicagoans and their guests—or rivals—can come together with pride. For years, the stadium's status as a unique gathering place could magnify the importance of even some of the most mundane games. At the same time, the popularity of amateur games such as the Prep Bowl ensured that they would be used by the city's Democratic machine for its own ends. Nonetheless, as the stadium began to look less like a sports giant and more like a white elephant, and as Chicago began losing population in the 1960s, the sport suffered a decline at Soldier Field.

NO LONGER AN OLYMPIC DREAM

About the same time that the Prep Bowl went through its first decline, amateur athletics—track and field—all but disappeared from Soldier Field. The decline of athletic competition coincided with a new Chicago Park

District policy requiring most events, except those sponsored by a favored few organizations, to cover their own expenses. The district adopted this policy by 1945, replacing an earlier one that simply required groups to pay a percentage of their gate receipts. An "event in the structure should pay its own costs, where people are charged admission to the structure," V. K. Brown, the park district's director of recreation, wrote in a 1945 letter to the Los Angeles recreation superintendent, replying to a query about the stadium. Park officials "do not think the taxpayer should contribute to the cost of an event and then be denied admission unless he pays a fee for entrance." The district made exceptions for high schools but not for college events and track meets. Such events generally charged admission, but attendance at most would not have been sufficient to pay the costs of operating Soldier Field. The stadium therefore became a less popular destination for meets. Meanwhile, as athletic events became less visible as spectacles, young people turned to more hyped spectator sports like baseball, football, and basketball. Long-distance running has seen some revival since the rise of marathons in the 1970s, but other athletic events like those Soldier Field was designed for rarely rate even a mention in the newspaper, let alone a a television sports show—with the exception of the Olympics.[11]

The only successful athletic events after World War II had ties to the Democratic political machine that Mayor Daley inherited from Mayor Kelly, after it survived the Kennelly years largely intact. On September 15, 1956, the city held an International Folk and Sports Festival at the stadium to raise funds for the U.S. Olympic team and honor members of the team. The festival showed off the music, dancing, and athletics of numerous Chicago ethnic groups, with more than five thousand performers and athletes, including some members of the U.S. Olympic team. "The Olympic games are the highest type of competition," Daley told the seventeen thousand who attended. "They are won on the playing fields and not on the battle fields." The mayor's citizens' committee, headquartered in City Hall, donated more than $10,000 earned from the festival to the U.S. Olympic Committee.

Before its current bid for the 2016 Olympics, Chicago tried several times for the games. In their 1960 bid, written in 1954, city boosters argued that Chicago could be ready to host almost immediately: "No stadiums need be built here. Soldiers' Field, Chicago Stadium and [the] International Amphitheatre, and various parks for the cross-country competition, already are available." But by 1957, when the city looked at trying to get the 1964 or 1968 games, the suitability of Soldier Field as an Olympic venue seemed dubious, and the possibility of building a new stadium arose. In 1966 the city put forward a bid for the 1972 Olympics, with Olympian Ralph Metcalfe, by then a Chicago alderman, among those making the city's presentation. Metcalfe, well aware of the stadium's history of athletic competitions, pointed to Soldier Field as suitable for Olympic ceremonies and track and field events, if a running track were reinstalled in the field. (By the mid-1950s, the original running track had been replaced with an asphalt track used for stock car racing. Contracts with the racing company stipulated that it would restore the running track if Chicago hosted the Olympics.) By 1977, when Mayor Michael Bilandic tried to get the U.S. Olympic Committee to make Chicago the U.S. candidate for the 1984 Olympics, Soldier Field was in such disrepair and so out of favor that it was almost taken for granted that the stadium would be replaced. Regardless, the city lost out to Los Angeles—and its Memorial Coliseum, built around the same time as Soldier Field for about one-tenth the cost—for a second time.[12]

Although Chicago never lured the Olympics to Soldier Field, the stadium did host the 1959 Pan Am Games. The last great athletic competition at Soldier Field also was the highest-profile international sporting event held in Chicago prior to the 1994 World Cup. The games came to Chicago partly as a result of the city's aspirations to host something like the Olympics, partly because of attempts by Mayor Daley and Chicago Park District officials to breathe new life into Soldier Field, and partly due to a fluke. The Pan Am Games, discussed since the early 1930s, had first been held in 1951, after delays caused by World War II. The 1959 games were to be the first held in the United States, and Cleveland was on the verge of hosting them, but in spring 1957 the U.S. Congress voted against a $5 million appropriation to defray the costs of holding the games there, placing the U.S. hold on the games—and the games' very existence—in jeopardy. When Chicago and Philadelphia advanced bids to take over for Cleveland, Metcalfe, the U.S. Olympic Committee, and several Latin American consuls in Chicago threw their weight behind Chicago's bid, and the president of the Pan Am Games, Douglas Roby, decided that "it would appear that we will recommend Chicago." On August 3, the Pan-American Games committee, meeting in San Jose, Costa Rica, voted 13–6 in favor of Chicago's bid. The decision may have prevented the Pan Am Games from falling into obscurity. Although the competition—like track and field more generally—is no longer prominent in the United States, it is highly regarded in most Latin American countries and remains an important part of international track and field today.[13]

The games were scheduled for late August and early September 1959, giving Chicago two years to prepare. Sites for the various competitions were set almost a year in advance, with Soldier Field playing a major part in track and field competitions, and other venues spread across the city and a few suburban locations. In October 1958 Red Weiner brought in an English expert to consult on the stadium's new running track. The English-made compound selected for its running surface was said to be better than any other surface then available in draining moisture—and producing record-fast runs. Work on the $100,000 track started in early December, and newspaper accounts promised that it would be the envy of track teams everywhere, and that, by putting Soldier Field once again on a par with the most advanced athletic fields in the world, it should help bring other track and field events to Soldier Field. And while city officials did not get anywhere near the amount of money Cleveland had hoped for from the federal government, they did finagle $500,000 from Congress, at least paying for the athletes' housing. Throughout its preparations, Chicago played up comparisons to the Olympics, blatantly suggesting that success with the Pan Am Games—nicknamed "the Olympics of the Americas"—should qualify it to host the more prestigious worldwide competition. In November 1958 Chicago Park District officials joined Princess Sophia of Greece in a brief ceremony in which she mixed earth from the Soldier Field arena with soil from the Greek village of Olympia, where the first Olympics were played sometime around 776 BC.[14]

Daley pushed hard to get business leaders to support the games, starting a drive to sell $250,000 in $5 sponsorship tickets to Pan Am events almost nine months before they opened. Regular admission tickets started at $1, with only tickets for the opening and closing ceremonies and a few other events priced above $3. To broaden the appeal of the games, organizers announced a twenty-four-hundred-mile torch relay by Boy Scouts, from Mexico City through Laredo, Texas, to Chicago, and planned a discount day for high school groups at Soldier Field. The city also planned a Festival of the Americas that would coincide with the games, including exhibitions of Latin American art, musical performances, and a screening of a South American–themed Donald Duck cartoon at the Field Museum. High school and college girls from the West Side tried out at Columbus Park to be part of a dance number at the games' opening ceremonies. Crews erected a giant torch attached to the scoreboard at the south end of the field. And Jesse Owens made a brief return appearance at Soldier Field, running on the new track with athletes from the University of Chicago.[15]

The opening of the games drew visitors from throughout the western hemisphere and brought out immigrant Chicagoans to cheer on athletes from their home countries. In the Pan Am Games, the stadium achieved more than just its goal of bringing together all of Chicago: as with the 1926 Eucharistic Congress, the games brought together people from far beyond the borders of the United States. The day was exceedingly hot for late August in Chicago, topping ninety degrees—so hot that the *Tribune* ran a feature about female athletes and audience members at Soldier Field who complained about the discomforts of wearing makeup and hose in the heat. Daley said the athletes were "not only champions of athletic achievement, but the true champions of the Pan-American spirit which is symbolized by the slogan on the Pan-

Workers install a giant torch next to Soldier Field's original scoreboard for the 1959 Pan American Games. Courtesy Chicago Park District Special Collections.

American shield: 'America, espirito, sport, fraternite,' the American spirit of friendship through sport." Fifteen-year-old Boy Scout Ronald Rodriguez of Chicago then circled the new running track with the torch; at the end of his run he touched the flame to an electronic trigger, which lit the giant torch next to the scoreboard, where it would burn throughout the games. A parade of the more than twenty-two hundred athletes followed, Jesse Owens and Ralph Metcalfe marching with the U.S. team, and hundreds of white doves flew overhead as the competitors gathered on the field. Estimates of the crowd at the ceremony ranged as high as forty-seven thousand.

The competitions started the next day, with eleven events at nine locations. Women's track and field was first on the schedule at Soldier Field. Among the outstanding athletes who competed there were Lucinda Williams and Wilma Rudolph, Tennessee State University teammates who in 1960 would be part of the U.S. team that won the Olympic 400-meter relay. Williams and Rudolph each won three gold medals at the Pan Am Games, with Williams narrowly defeating Rudolph in the 100-meter dash. Another standout

Alphonse Cahue of Mexico City at the opening ceremonies of the 1959 Pan Am Games. Courtesy Chicago Tribune.

was Earlene Brown, described by the *Defender* as "the brown bombshell" and by the *Los Angeles Times* as "the Compton housewife." Brown, who had participated in the 1956 Olympics and went on to the 1960 and 1964 Olympics, won two gold medals. (Retiring from track and field following the 1964 games, she continued her athletic career for several years on a Los Angeles roller derby team.)[16]

Not every aspect of the games went as smoothly as the opening ceremonies. In the first day of track and field competition at Soldier Field, judges had to recalibrate the hammer throw results because they had measured them wrong. And the steeplechase, which combines running and an obstacle course, was postponed for an hour after officials, making a final check of the course, discovered that someone had stocked the water obstacles with fish, which then had to be removed. Despite such glitches, the United States dominated the competition. In the track and field contests held at Soldier Field, the United States won eighteen of twenty-two men's gold medals and eight of the ten women's. Overall, the United States won 121 gold medals,

A high jumper competes during the 1959 Pan Am Games at Soldier Field. Courtesy Chicago Park District Special Collections.

including the last gold medal awarded at the games, for an equestrian event at Soldier Field that preceded the closing ceremonies.[17]

Although the Pan Am Games succeeded overall, some of the Soldier Field events attracted extremely small crowds—only four thousand people for the first day of competition. So regardless of the attention they garnered for Chicago, the games failed to generate a resurgence of athletic events in the city—or at Soldier Field. In the wake of the games, there was briefly talk of holding a Big Ten track meet at the stadium in May 1960, but it went to Michigan State University instead. Sadly, the Pan Am Games became the wrong kind of turning point for Soldier Field. In a sense, they marked the end of the stadium's golden age: it was only after they failed to generate new interest in the stadium that discussions began in earnest about replacing it.

THE SKI JUMP REVIVED

The ski jump has assumed almost mythical status at Soldier Field. But when people talk about it, they often are thinking of the less successful 1950s ski jumps rather than the successful earlier ones. In 1954 the Chicago Park District and the Norge Ski Club had a 184-foot-tall ski tower built off the

The Norge Ski Club ski jump at Soldier Field, 1954. Courtesy Chicago Park District Special Collections.

east stands of the stadium. The jump itself was a long wooden slide and the landing area, streching across the width of the stadium arena, a snowy slope and a length of hay. The Norge club hoped to capitalize on a trend of warm-weather ski jumping that had started in Los Angeles and Portland, Oregon. Its meet, held over three days starting September 17, drew several champion skiers, including Matti Pietikainen, a Finnish tinsmith and that year's world ski jumping champion, and Erling Erlandsson, a Norwegian who was then the ski jumping champion of Sweden. A U.S. Olympic skier, the University of Denver's Bill Olsen, won the first day's contest before a crowd of fifteen thousand, and Harald Hauge of Seattle placed first overall in the three-day meet, doing an airborne somersault in front of twenty thousand people on the third day.

After that, Soldier Field went skiless for a few years, although it hosted a few winter ice skating shows. But in May 1957 the park district awarded a five-year concession to Winter Wonderland, Inc., headed by Lake Shore Drive attorney Oscar A. Brotman. Brotman convinced Weiner that a ski jump could generate needed revenue during months that Soldier Field had usually been idle. Winter Wonderland used twelve compressors to make artificial snow at a rate of three tons a minute, covering the stadium's arena and parts of the stands with twenty-six inches of snow and allowing for both skiing and tobogganing. Brotman advertised the ski jump with the slogan "There's snow business like snow business," and offered hay rides and sleigh rides as additional attractions. Early reactions were positive, and by early January the *Tribune* included Soldier Field, along with more traditional ski resorts, in its snow cover reports, reporting in mid-February that the slope had an eighteen-inch base and eight inches of new snow. But the odd circumstances of the ski jump seem to have put some people off. "I took three ski lessons in Chicago's Soldier Field, where I slid down the icy west stands, covered with machine-made snow, and came to rest on the 50-yard line," wrote *Tribune* travel editor Alfred Borcover almost twenty years later. "That was so much fun that a decade passed before I took another lesson." Although some people did find the skiing enjoyable, inconsistent weather—either too cold for all but the most committed skiers or too warm to bring people out—appears to have doomed the endeavor. Brotman lost $40,000 on his first and only season and concluded that "Soldier Field is good for one thing—bullfighting." As the years wore on, more Chicagoans began to agree with him, but first one last successful amateur event used Soldier Field to show off the achievements of Chicago Park District athletes in the way the South Park commissioners had hoped the stadium would.[18]

THE SPECIAL OLYMPICS

By the late 1960s few amateur athletic events other than the Prep Bowl took place at Soldier Field with any regularity. In fieldhouses throughout the city, the Chicago Park District was trying to recapture an earlier era's enthusiasm for athletics, but its most prominent facility had offered athletes participating in park district programs no opportunity to show off their skills since the 1930s.

In the mid-1960s the district had started programs for mentally disabled young people, the first of which were run by Anne McGlone (later Illinois Supreme Court justice Anne Burke) at two South Side parks. "Teaching retarded children isn't an 'Everybody-line-up-on-this-side' proposition," McGlone told the *Tribune* in 1966. "They are too active to stand still in a group. You can't even say 'Form a circle,' because they don't know what a circle is." When McGlone had the idea in late 1967 for a citywide track meet for the children she was working with, she asked Weiner and park district board president William McFetridge for permission to create it. The Joseph P. Kennedy Foundation had funded the initial programs, and Weiner and

McFetridge believed Eunice Kennedy Shriver would be willing to fund such a meet. So in early 1968 McGlone wrote to Shriver, proposing the idea, and within days received an enthusiastic letter back:

> Thank you so much for your letter . . . informing me about your plans to initiate a National Olympics for retarded children through the Chicago Park District. Both Mr. Shriver and Dr. Hayden have spoken to me about your project and I think it is a most exciting one. I sincerely hope that you are successful in launching it. This is certainly a large undertaking and we know that you will need a great deal of assistance of many kinds.

Shriver continued:

> This is bigger than just Chicago. With Chicago behind this program, it can succeed as a national event. The Kennedy foundation will help with $10,000, and I'll be there personally.[19]

For help in organizing the Special Olympics, McGlone turned to Dr. William H. Freeberg of Southern Illinois University, an expert on recreation for children with disabilities. Around the same time, McGlone married Democratic Party regular Edward M. Burke and took his last name. Now Anne Burke, she also enlisted the help of Dan Shannon, the vice president of the park district board, as well as Edmund Kelly, then McFetridge's assistant. Burke convinced the International Olympic Committee to allow the event to use the Olympics name and logo and to light a torch at the south end of the stadium by the scoreboard, much as the Pan Am Games had.

The event took shape quickly, and it became more clearly national and even international in character, with children from twenty-three states, Canada, and France traveling to Chicago to participate. Once in Chicago, the athletes ate their meals and trained with athletes from the International Olympics, including gold medalists Jesse Owens and Rafer Johnson, who had won the decathlon at the 1960 Olympics. Other athletes, such as hockey stars George Armstrong, captain of the Toronto Maple Leafs, and Stan Mikita, the Chicago Black Hawks' center, also came to Soldier Field to act as coaches.[20]

Meanwhile, Shriver had flown in from Paris, where her husband, Sargent Shriver, was the U.S. ambassador. And seventy college student volunteers who had worked on the presidential campaign of Shriver's brother, Senator Robert Kennedy (who had been assassinated less than two months earlier), traveled to Chicago to act as guides for the athletes. Soldier Field's immense size allowed it to house almost all of the Special Olympics, with a swimming pool and skating rink set up inside the stadium.[21]

The first-ever public games for people with intellectual disabilities opened

The skating rink set up inside Soldier Field for the first Special Olympics, 1968. Courtesy Chicago Park District Special Collections.

with the familiar torch lighting and parade of athletes. As Mayor Daley stood with Eunice Kennedy Shriver at the reviewing stand, he was visibly moved by what he saw. Turning to Shriver, he said, "Eunice, the world will never be the same." "The Chicago Special Olympics prove a very fundamental fact, the fact that exceptional children—children with mental retardation—can be exceptional athletes, the fact that through sports they can realize their potential for growth," Shriver said during the opening ceremonies. The athletes participated in many of the events held at the International Olympics, such as the broad jump, foot races, and the high jump. The participants competed against others of similar age and skill, and six hundred medals were awarded.[22]

The first Special Olympics set in motion a movement that is still growing, and Soldier Field has played an ongoing part in the games. The stadium hosted the second International Special Olympics in 1970, and since then has regularly been one of the sites for Chicago, Illinois, and Midwest Special Olympics events. Although Shriver often gets credited with creating the

Sargent Shriver Jr. (left), U.S. attorney general Edwin Meese III (fourth from right), and Chicago mayor Harold Washington (right) with Special Olympics athletes at Soldier Field for the beginning of the a law enforcement torch run for the International Special Olympics, July 30, 1987. At right in the background mural is Richard J. Daley. Courtesy Chicago Park District Special Collections.

games, she herself acknowledges that Anne Burke played the largest role in their creation. "When the history of the Chicago Special Olympics is written," Shriver said in a letter to Burke soon after the event, referring to the first Special Olympics, "there will have to be a special chapter to recount the contributions of Anne Burke. You should feel very proud that your dedicated work with retarded children in Chicago has culminated in an event of such far-reaching importance. We all owe you a debt of gratitude."[23]

Not too many people outside of the families of the children involved and the organizers realized the games' importance at the time, although having them at Soldier Field helped raise their profile. David Condon, an early advocate for the games who wrote the *Tribune*'s "In the Wake of the News" sports column, chastised Chicago television stations for running only short clips from the event. By 1970, when the next International Special Olympics came to the stadium, the event received much more publicity. That event drew

Harold Washington joins others outside Soldier Field for the start of the 1987 Special Olympics torch run. Courtesy Chicago Park District Special Collections.

more than twenty-five hundred athletes from forty-five states, France, Canada, and Puerto Rico and, like subsequent Special Olympics, was open to adults as well as children. Burke and Shriver watched as Linda Wach, a Chicagoan who attended Saint Rose Day School, carried the torch into the stadium. Texas athlete Perry Clegg ran a mile race in 4 minutes, 54 seconds.

Burke's and Shriver's hope that the games would have a lasting impact has been realized. In addition to publicizing the abilities of cognitively disabled people, they have given rise to local Special Olympics organizations throughout the world, encouraging people with intellectual disabilities to participate in sports and athletics. Burke and Shriver always maintained that recreation for people with mental disabilities would result in not just better health but a greater sense of self-worth, and studies of participants have confirmed that belief. At a twenty-fifth anniversary celebration of the Special Olympics in Orlando, the final torchbearer was Kevin O'Brien, who took part in Burke's first special recreation programs at West Pullman Park, across the street from his family's home, and competed in swimming and track and field at the first Special Olympics—an experience he recalled as "happy. A good time. I was enjoying myself." O'Brien has since won hundreds of medals in Special Olympics competitions, worked a full-time job for most of his adult life, and participated in his church. And he has become a role model for other mentally challenged athletes. "He would pull people in and help teach them things," Jackie Guthrie, O'Brien's coach at the time, said in 1998. "If someone was lazy and didn't want to try something, he would seek them out and get them to try."

The Illinois and Chicago Special Olympics continue to hold regular events at Soldier Field. In fact, it's one of the few events connected to the original purpose of the stadium that is still held there, in part because the new arena built in the 2001–2003 renovation is too small to hold a standard running track. The reasons behind this shift have little to do with the amateur sports originally envisioned for the stadium. They have everything to do with professional sports, which are the main reason Soldier Field still exists.[24]

13 *Professional Sports in a Changing Era*

Long before the Bears dominated fall Sundays at Soldier Field, fans of another professional sport reveled in matches that included some of the best players in the world. Professional soccer has a long but tortured history at the stadium and only became truly successful in Chicago after the 1994 World Cup. Before then the most successful professional and semiprofessional soccer games at Soldier Field had been exhibition games, in which foreign teams with large Chicago followings sometimes played other foreign teams and sometimes what were essentially local amateur all-star teams.

In 1926 Sparta AC, from Prague, drew an audience of thirty thousand for a game against a local all-star team; its match a few days later against Toronto Ulster United brought out only fifteen thousand fans and ended in a draw. In 1933, in one of many world's fair–related sporting events, the Toronto Scots, that year's champion of Canada's professional league, played Saint Louis's Stix, Baer and Fuller team, the U.S. champs, for the North American soccer title. The Scots won, 2–1. Although amateurs played foreign professional teams several times in the 1930s and 1940s, the stadium apparently did not see another match of two professional teams until May 7, 1954, when the West German Dortmund Borussia beat England's Plymouth Argyle, 4–0, before about thirteen thousand people.[1]

In the early 1960s the Chicago Park District, under president James Gately and general superintendent Erwin "Red" Weiner, made yet another push to keep Soldier Field relevant. Chicago newspapers had started agitating for a modern stadium and an increasing number of people were calling the existing one a "white elephant." Starting in 1961 the stadium hosted a series of international soccer games. It kicked off July 28, with a double bill:

an amateur game between a Chicago all-star team and the Saint Louis Kutis, the national amateur champions, followed by a benefit game for the March of Dimes between Vienna's Rapid team and Español of Barcelona. Almost eighteen thousand people watched as the Chicagoans walked away with the opener, with the surprisingly high score of 6–0, and Vienna beat Barcelona in another high-scoring game, 5–4. The first year's games were well enough attended that in 1962 the park district scheduled international matches throughout the spring and summer, featuring members of the International Soccer League, which had started in 1960. The Friday night matches started with America FC of Rio de Janeiro squaring off against Palermo of Italy, with the Brazilians winning, 3–2. While some games drew only about five thousand fans, others brought out fifteen thousand; about fifty thousand people watched International Soccer League games at the stadium that year.[2]

In 1963 the International Soccer League played nine games at Soldier Field, including the first game of a two-game championship series (the second was played in New York). Again, most games attracted ten or twelve thousand people—not necessarily a failure, but nowhere near the number that came out for other sports. The low attendance figures at the professional games came in spite of opening matches featuring relatively popular Chicago amateur and all-star teams. The story was much the same the next year, except there were only four games. A separate invitational tournament promoted by local amateur teams included three other international soccer matches, with a Liverpool team winning what was dubbed the Governor Otto Kerner trophy. The International Soccer League lasted only one more year, with the first game of the 1965 season at Soldier Field drawing only about nine thousand spectators. In 1966 the international games were largely exhibition games played by touring teams.

The next year the Chicago Spurs played at Soldier Field as part of the National Professional Soccer League (NPSL)—a league that lasted only one season. In their first game, on April 16, the Spurs beat Saint Louis, 2–1, with Chicago native Willie Roy scoring both Chicago goals, but fewer than five thousand people saw them play. Attendance remained dismal throughout the season, with only a few thousand people showing up for each game. By December, with losses in Chicago alone at $400,000, the NPSL merged with the United Soccer Association (USA), which was sanctioned by FIFA, the world governing body for what every other nation calls football, to form the North American Soccer League. The USA had its own Chicago team, the Mustangs, which played at Comiskey Park, so the terms of the merger agreement required that the Spurs relocate. (The Mustangs folded after the 1968 season.)[3]

Chicago's next resident professional soccer team was the Sting, which joined the North American Soccer League in 1975. The NASL had foundered initially, but attendance crept up in the mid-1970s, and by 1975 the league had expanded to twenty active teams. The Sting started out playing at Soldier Field, making the playoffs in its second year; the postseason ended with a second-round overtime loss, on its home field, to Toronto, which went on to win the league championship. Attendance was better than for the Spurs and Mustangs, building slowly from an average of forty-one hundred a game in 1975, but even in the team's best seasons was often less than ten thousand people.

In 1977, following its first playoff season, the Sting went on a losing streak and attendance fell, not even bouncing back for the last Soldier Field appearance of Pele, perhaps the sport's greatest player. At the end of the year, the team announced that half of its subsequent home games would be played at Wrigley Field. The following year, having again made the playoffs, it announced that it would no longer play at Soldier Field. Officials with the team claimed that the poor condition of the stadium itself kept fans away. While playing elsewhere, the team won the league championship in 1981, drawing crowds of about twenty-five thousand for its playoff games.

In 1983 the Sting returned to Soldier Field. Owner Lee Stern said the move was motivated by a "remarkable" renovation and a need to give the team a more distinctive permanent home. By that June, however, the team was making noises about moving to Milwaukee because of poor attendance and dissatisfaction with the team's performance on Soldier Field's artificial turf. The team averaged almost eleven thousand fans per game and again made the playoffs, but its last playoff game at Soldier Field—which it won—drew fewer than six thousand fans. In 1984 the team switched back to Comiskey and Wrigley, then moved to an indoor soccer league before folding in 1988.[4]

Around the time that the Sting folded, the United States for the first time won the right to host the 1994 FIFA World Cup Finals. The World Cup has been played every four years since 1930, except 1942 and 1946, due to World War II, each time growing in international popularity. It features the best national teams in the world, selected through nearly two years of qualifying matches. In 1994, there were twenty-four teams in the finals. As a condition of awarding the games to the United States, FIFA required the formation of a new professional soccer league. When Chicago began lobbying to host some of the World Cup games in late 1989, a proposal to create a new domed stadium was under consideration, but it soon became clear that that would doom the city's bid. FIFA officials visited the city in April 1990, pronounced themselves impressed by Soldier Field, and said only minor renovations would be needed to bring the stadium up to FIFA standards (the games came only a decade after the overhaul that had lured back the Sting). The sixty-thousand-plus capacity of the stadium at the time made it big enough to host any World Cup event. In October 1992 FIFA announced that Soldier Field would host five matches, including the first, between Germany, the reigning champions, and another team.

The city went all-out for the World Cup. In 1992 Mayor Richard M. Daley announced that the Chicago Park District and the city would build a $1 million indoor soccer facility for practices that would be converted to a youth soccer venue after the tournament. Just as when Soldier Field was being planned, Chicago's leaders tied the project rhetorically to the ideal of physical fitness for the city's youth. But the structure never materialized. Still, the World Cup was the first big step in a rehabilitation of Chicago's image that began early in Daley's tenure and culminated in the 1996 Democratic National Convention. Just before the tournament opened, a spokesman for the mayor expressed what always seemed to be in the back of Daley's mind in his first decade in office: "Sadly in some parts of the world, as incredible as it may seem, we're still trying to live down the Al Capone image." The Cup was one of the old Soldier Field's last acts on behalf of polishing the image of a Democratic mayor and his allies: when the matches opened, President Bill Clinton and Daley played roles in the opening ceremonies. Republican Illinois governor Jim Edgar—never a favorite of Daley's—did not.

By June 1994 the stadium had gotten a $20 million facelift, including the installation of copies of twenty-four acroteria—a sort of architectural ornament—that had sat atop the colonnades in the stadium's early years. Officials thought at the time that the originals had been taken down during the preparations for the Pan Am Games, but a 1971 *Sun-Times* report indicates that the ornaments, each weighing as much as a ton, were actually taken down in October 1971, using a helicopter.[5]

Chicago's unpredictable weather made the June 17 opening ceremonies less than ideal. Temperatures soared to ninety-three degrees Fahrenheit, although they were back down to eighty-three by game time. Forty-five people had to be treated for heat exhaustion. Still, two thousand volunteer dancers filled the field, carrying colored plastic tubes and forming the World Cup logo. President Dwight Eisenhower's brother had opened the Pan Am Games. In the United States of the 1990s, television dominated like no other cultural force, and the city put forward a television celebrity as its ambassador: Oprah Winfrey welcomed the world to Chicago. The official welcoming was followed by music from Diana Ross and music and folk dancers from the twenty-four countries with teams in the competition. It was, soccer enthusiasts hoped, the turning point for the sport in the United States. "Our time has come," said Alan Rothenberg, World Cup chairman and CEO, during the opening ceremonies. "Welcome, world, to the United States of America."[6]

The stadium, said one sportswriter, had never looked better. Bolivia had drawn the slot to oppose Germany, the defending champion, in the first match, and U.S. residents with roots in the South American country traveled to Chicago to see the game. Bolivians chanted their country's name as they walked to Soldier Field, singing as they strode past the Chicago Park District headquarters and toward the stadium gates. "Bolivia has never accomplished anything like this before," said Ivan Duran, a Maryland resident who, with his brother Fernando, had flown their father from their native country for their team's first appearance in the World Cup in forty-four years. Unfortunately, the match did little to dispel the American idea of soccer as boring. "The 1994 tournament began—in keeping with ancient tradition—with an insufferably dreary and low-scoring match," wrote the *London Guardian*'s Matthew Engel. Minor mishaps made the play even less stellar. Players slipped on the stadium's new grass—the worst slip being by Bolivian goalie Carlos Trucco, who fell on his back trying to block what became Germany's winning goal, and the only tally of the game.[7]

The German team had good luck at Soldier Field, winning two of the three games it played there and tying Spain 1–1 in the third. In the other two games at the stadium, Bulgaria overwhelmed Greece, 4–0, and the Bolivians lost again, to Spain, 3–1. In the final match at Soldier Field, Germany beat Belgium, 5–2, to advance to the quarterfinals. Average attendance at the Chicago games topped sixty-two thousand for each of the three first-round matches, and crept slightly higher for the two second-round matches. Celebrities who attended included Placido Domingo, a fan of Spain.[8]

Some of the earliest calls for a stadium like Soldier Field—even before World War I—had come from businesspeople who hoped to boost tourism. In the 1990s that remained part of the justification for spending tax money on events at the stadium. Organizers had predicted that the World Cup would bring in about 400,000 out-of-towners. As it turned out, it drew about 250,000, no more than half of them from other countries. Still, those visitors are thought to have pumped about $200 million into the local economy. And regardless of the economic impact, the hosting the World Cup helped to project a new image of the city, and of Mayor Daley, to the world. "Forget the dollars and cents, because money can't buy the breathtaking image of Chicago that was beamed to a billion people around the world from the June 17 opening ceremony," the *Tribune* wrote after the German team, the last to leave the Chicago area, moved on to a New York match July 10.[9]

A more tangible result of the World Cup was that the Chicago area regained a full-time professional soccer team, the Chicago Fire—one that appears headed for long-term success. (The team has no relation to the short-lived American football team of the same name; see chapter 14). The team's owners announced its creation in October 1997, after months of back-and-forth with sportswear giant Nike, which, for reasons unknown, wanted the team to be named the Rhythm. The Fire roared to a start in 1998, although the park district officials running Soldier Field had not allowed the players to practice at the stadium before their first game there. Nonetheless, in their home opener they beat Tampa Bay, 2–0, before more than thirty-six thousand fans. That first year at Soldier Field, the team averaged almost eighteen thousand fans a game, a figure that rose to twenty-two thousand for the playoffs. They ended the season by winning both the U.S. Major League Soccer championship and, in a tournament involving both professional and amateur teams, the U.S. Open Cup. Since then, the team has won the U.S. Open Cup three more times, although only once more—in 2000—while playing at Soldier Field.

The effect of the Fire on soccer's popularity in Chicago has been electric. The team's viability shows that more Chicagoans have become soccer fans in the years since the Sting's demise but also demonstrates the vibrancy the city still derives from the immigrant populations Soldier Field was built to help Americanize—Polish and Mexican immigrants having been a key part of the fan base. But the team could never fill Soldier Field and worked with southwest suburban Bridgeview to build a 20,000-seat stadium it could fill profitably. Despite a decent season in 2006, attendance at the team's new venue, at 76th Street and Harlem Avenue was down from the Soldier Field figures, perhaps a sign that despite its reputation as a football stadium, the lakefront venue still can help draw fans to an event.[10]

AUTO RACING: SOLDIER FIELD'S REAL FAMILY SPORT

Soccer's popularity at Soldier Field pales in comparison to that of auto racing, which drew sizable crowds well into the 1960s. For several years after stock car racing followed midget racing to the track, starting in 1946, the first race of the season benefited the Chicago Park District Police Benevolent Association fund. Races regularly drew thirty thousand people or more.

One well-known racing family that helped popularize auto racing at the stadium was that of Anthony "Andy" Granatelli and his two brothers, Vince and Joe. The Granatelli brothers raced at Soldier Field from the mid-1940s until the mid-1950s, and Andy Granatelli first raced at the Indianapolis 500 in 1946. In the 1960s he purchased a small company and became a millionaire by making STP motor oil a household name. In 1969 his company's car, driven by Mario Andretti, won the Indy 500.

In 1947 midget, stock car, or hot rod auto races ran at the stadium almost every weekend from the start of June through late September. In one week in August, racing events drew more than fifty-five thousand spectators, including some twenty-four thousand people who attended a day of hot rod races sponsored by Granatelli. Well before any of the racers on the circuit attained

"Flat Out" Fagan.. ANNOUNCES
3 BIG DAYS
AT
SOLDIER FIELD
THIS COMING FRIDAY NIGHT

★ JULY 23RD ⚠ MIDGETS
100 LAP NATIONAL CHAMPIONSHIP

★ ★ ★ ALL THE STARS ★ ★ ★
★ TONY BETTENHAUSEN
★ DUKE NALON

★ ART CROSS	★ JIMMY KNIGHT
★ MIKE NAZUREK	★ CAL NIDAY
★ FRANK BURANY	★ JOHNNY ROBERTS
★ ROY NEWMAN	★ JACK BATES
★ GENE HARTLEY	★ PLUS MANY OTHERS

ADULTS $1.50   CHILDREN 25c

★ SUNDAY NIGHT, JULY 25TH HURRICANE STOCK CARS

MID-SEASON CHAMPIONSHIP
RAIN DATE SUNDAY NIGHT, AUGUST 1st

10 BIG EVENTS

★ TROPHY DASH	★ SENSATIONAL BACK-UP RACE
★ ELIMINATION EVENTS	★ DOG RACE
★ MEN'S AMATEUR	★ 50 LAP FEATURE EVENT
★ LADIES RACE	

ADULTS $1.50   CHILDREN 25c

★ FRIDAY NIGHT, JULY 30TH CIRCUIT OF CHAMPIONS

NATIONAL CHAMPIONSHIP
LATE MODEL STOCKS
120 LAP FEATURE RACE
6 EVENT PROGRAM
ALL LATE MODEL SHOWROOM CARS
JUST LIKE YOU DRIVE, INCLUDING
BOB PRONGER'S '54 CADILLAC AND
PAT KIRKWOOD'S '54 OLD'S
MANY MANY OTHERS!

ADULTS $2.00   CHILDREN 25c

NOT JUST A FEW LATE MODEL CARS BUT ALL!   THIS IS THE ONLY GENUINE
LATE MODEL STOCK CAR SHOW ON ¼ MILE TRACK, DON'T BE FOOLED!

Circular promoting stock car racing at Soldier Field, 1954. Courtesy Chicago Park District Special Collections.

fame at the Indianapolis 500, the popularity of the Soldier Field events made the races extremely lucrative. Jim Rathmann, who started racing at Soldier Field in 1948 and won the Indy 500 in 1960, recalled years later what happened one time when he was careless with his winnings. After an early race, he stuffed some cash in his jacket and got back on the track for another run. Then during the main race, the rushing air started plucking bills out of his

Families arriving for the Tournament of Thrills, 1964. Stock car racing and stunt shows were among the many family-oriented events held at Soldier Field over the years. Note the deterioration of the stadium in this photo, taken five years after a major renovation. Courtesy Chicago Park District Special Collections.

jacket. "I knew people was pickin' it up, but I couldn't stop. After, I figured I was about 900 short."[11]

In December 1953 the Chicago Auto Racing Association requested thirty-three dates, all Fridays and Saturdays, between May and September of the following year. The organization even maintained an office at Soldier Field's Gate 8. The gates for evening races opened at 6:30 p.m., and ticket sellers remained on duty as late as 10 p.m., with the last race usually ending about 10:30. American flags, Chicago flags, and Chicago Auto Racing pennants decorated all the flag posts from Gate 0 to the colonnades. Both tourists and locals attended, as the racing association struck a deal with the Conrad Hilton Hotel for free admission to the races for the hotel's guests.

On the afternoon of May 16, 1954, the park district's Police Benevolent Association sponsored its ninth annual Gold Trophy race. The bill promised "8 exciting, thrilling events" and "many famous drivers," eighty-one cars in all. More than thirty thousand tickets sold, most at $1.50 but twenty-four

One of the motorcycle stunts that lured families to the 1964 Tournament of Thrills. Courtesy Chicago Park District Special Collections.

hundred at 25 cents, generating $32,872 for the widows and orphans of officers killed in the line of duty.

There were slow days; records show that the races on June 25 attracted only 4,327 paying adults and 699 children—organizers took in $6,368, of which the park district received its standard $750 "minimum charge." And ten days earlier, just under six thousand people had come out to see the "Irish" Horan Lucky Hell Drivers. An ad for that show boasted that "'Irish' Horan's automobile thrill show has been using Dodge cars *exclusively* since 1935. You'll know why when you see the terrific punishment they take." Along with Horan, the show starred Bill Vukovich, who had just won his second consecutive Indy 500.

But many racing days attracted more than twenty thousand people, not enough to fill the stadium but enough to make money for both the park district and the race promoters. Families were a prime market, and many who attended as children grew up to be racing fans. "Dad took me to the midget

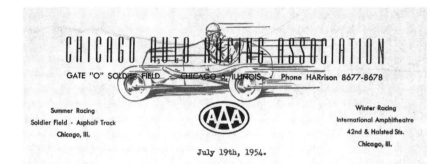

CHICAGO AUTO RACING ASSOCIATION

GATE "O" SOLDIER FIELD   CHICAGO, ILLINOIS   Phone HARrison 8677-8678

Summer Racing
Soldier Field - Asphalt Track
Chicago, Ill.

Winter Racing
International Amphitheatre
42nd & Halsted Sts.
Chicago, Ill.

July 19th, 1954.

Mr. Erwin Weiner,
Director of Special Events,
Soldier Field,
Chicago, Illinois.

Dear Mr. Weiner:

As per your request, we are enclosing herewith
advertising material relative to dates and events to
be held by Chicago Auto Racing Association at Soldier
Field, which is self-explanatory.

Please excuse the delay in mailing this material
to you.

Sincerely yours,

CHICAGO AUTO RACING ASSOCIATION

Anthony Granatelli, Pres.

A^G;dp

Letter to Erwin "Red" Weiner from the Chicago Auto Racing Association, giving as a return address "Gate 'O' Soldier Field"—an indication of how important auto racing was to the stadium. Courtesy Chicago Park District Special Collections.

---

races at Soldier Field when I was 11. I was hooked," Dan Cotter, then the head of True Value Hardware, told a *Sun-Times* reporter more than twenty years after racing had ended at Soldier Field.

Safety inspections each racing night apparently protected the drivers and the public to a great extent. Two cars did catch fire during a tag race on May 2, but a track crew quickly extinguished the blaze. And on June 6 a car hit a barricade and knocked some timbers loose. But park district records report no injuries or damage to property during the 1954 racing season.[12]

On July 21, 1956, Soldier Field hosted the Grand National NASCAR 100, presented by the National Association for Stock Car Auto Racing. Glenn "Fireball" Roberts won by a single car length after passing Jim Pascal in the

194th lap of the 200-lap, 100-mile race. The following year, Soldier Field hosted two NASCAR races: a fifty-lap NASCAR Grand National race on June 15 and a hundred-lap NASCAR race on June 29. (The June 15 event does not appear in lists of NASCAR Grand National events for that year, but it was advertised as one at the time.) Bill Brown of Chicago's Roseland neighborhood won the shorter race, and Glen Wood of Stuart, Virginia, the longer one. As with any popular Soldier Field event at the time, Chicago politicians made sure they were seen at the races. Mayor Daley was on hand at the May 28, 1955, Police Benevolent Association race to hand out the trophy. [13]

But in the 1960s, other tracks started to steal Soldier Field's thunder. Most, if not all, of the top Indy 500 racers showed up for one June 1962 race, but Granatelli dropped out of promoting races at the stadium races or recruiting drivers for them, and the 1963 season sputtered because of bad weather on many racing nights. In the mid-1960s, N. Perry Luster, who had been involved in U.S. professional racing as an insurance broker for a decade, took over the racing card at Soldier Field. Within a few years, "fans were staying away in droves," one profile said. In 1967, a racing sanctioning body warned Luster to change the usual Soldier Field racing dates to keep from conflicting with other races. He tried a number of ways to keep people in the stands, increasing advertising, and even having a new, longer track installed in the stadium, in addition to the existing half-mile track. Luster held races at the stadium for one more year, then gave up.[14]

The very last auto races in Soldier Field were drag races held as part of the American Legion's Independence Day celebration in 1970. Later that year, the auto track came out so that the arena could better accommodate a professional football field. The Bears were taking over.

14 *The Bears, the Stadium's Savior*

By the late 1950s, less than forty years after Big Bill Thompson first proposed building a stadium as a monument to Chicago's war dead, Chicagoans were starting to look at other cities and wonder why they couldn't have a sports palace better than Soldier Field. Discontent about the stadium dated back to its earliest days. The architects had insisted that Grant Park Stadium was beautifully designed and well built, but the shoddiness of some aspects of its construction became apparent even before it was finished. The design too came under attack, with critics decrying the stadium's unusually narrow plan and poor sightlines.

The design would indeed become a major hindrance to the stadium's long-term viability. But in its early years, Chicagoans preferred to see Soldier Field as a potent symbol of what their city could accomplish. It was at the time the largest concrete structure ever built and could claim to be the largest stadium in the world, at least in terms of capacity. Yet even before it opened, Grant Park Stadium had physical problems. A dispute between the lead contractor, Blome-Sinek, and the South Park Commission over damage to support columns during the first phase of construction was settled and the damage mended. But from that time on, the need for repairs was almost constant, providing frequent headaches for the Chicago Park District but also a continual flow of jobs and contracts for the politically connected.

When the Century of Progress Exposition ended in 1934, crews took down the Sky Ride that towered over the stadium from just south of Gate 0 to Northerly Island. In the process, large pieces of steel fell and hit the stadium's walls, tearing holes in their veneer. Repairs cost about $50,000 ($700,000 in 2008 dollars).[1]

In the mid-1930s, repairs became enough of a problem that the park district issued another round of stadium bonds. The $800,000 thus raised would most likely have been enough to repair the twelve-year-old stadium, but Robert J. Dunham, Mayor Edward Kelly's park district president, had other ideas. Dunham proposed to apply for a $2 million Works Progress Administration grant to renovate the stadium and build a new Chicago Park District administration building that would close off the north end of the stadium, eliminating the open view of the Field Museum but adding new, permanent seats. Harry Joseph, the former head of the West Park Commission and vice president of the merged Chicago Park District, pointed out that the park district already had a headquarters building, the administration building from the world's fair. Plus, Joseph said, "The million-dollar Lincoln Park headquarters, and the two million dollar West Parks headquarters are going to waste. I'm in favor of improving Soldier Field, but we don't need a new administration building for the parks. The taxpayers' load is getting too big."[2]

Dunham, however, pointed out that the fair's administration building was not meant to be a permanent structure. The plans would, he said, complete the stadium, making it a better venue for pageants. Not everything should be judged on the basis of economy: "If we operated the parks on the basis of saving every possible dollar, we would not be justified in going ahead with any of our governmental programs." Dunham prevailed, and Soldier Field soon changed from open-ended to entirely enclosed, like most modern stadiums.[3]

In its early years, the South Park Commission insisted that Soldier Field make a good deal of money, or at least do better than cover its ongoing expenses. There was some thought early on that the stadium might even recoup the money spent to build it. In 1927, following three years of operation, the *Herald and Examiner* declared, "Soldier Field promises to be a money-maker." Already, the stadium had made back about 8 percent of construction costs, it gushed, including $100,000 from the Dempsey-Tunney fight alone. But paying back the public appears never to have been a priority. Instead, as tax dollars paid for construction costs, the commissioners quickly came to think of the money the stadium made beyond its day-to-day expenses as "profits." In all, from 1925 through 1927, stadium rentals brought in $183,287.92 (about $2.3 million in 2008 dollars).[4] By 1930 stadium rentals were steady and high, with more than $112,000 in rental fees and another $12,400 in concessions, against just more than $101,000 in expenses. The Depression cooled things at Soldier Field, as everywhere else, and changes in park district policy intended to bring in more money appear to have backfired. From 1937 through 1944 the stadium had only one year in which it made back its operating costs. That year, which included a war bonds show, Soldier Field brought in a little more than $185,000 and spent $129,000. Even that surplus was less than the cost of depreciation in the value of the stadium and the cost of its bonds. Over the whole period, with interest and depreciation figured in, the stadium lost more than $470,000 (about $7 million in 2008 dollars). Attendance over the years varied wildly, from about 400,000 in 1934 to a peak attendance of more than 2.6 million in 1955, after which the number of people attending events declined to an average of a few hundred thousand, rebounding to about seven hundred thousand after the Bears moved in in 1971.[5]

The park district seems to have discouraged use of the stadium over the years by its policy of making many events pay for themselves. Although the South Park commissioners had always tried to use the stadium to bring in money, they were content to let it run a modest deficit many years, as long as the events that cost money were for charitable causes or involved recreation or sports for schoolchildren or college athletes. But during the Depression, the rule against losing money seems to have become more inflexible. In early 1944, only twenty years after the stadium opened, the *Chicago Daily News* ran the first article calling Soldier Field a "white elephant." Harold L. Baker, the park district's chief accountant, had released figures on the stadium's expenditures, which showed that only once in the previous four years had the stadium brought in more than it spent. "At its inception, Soldier Field was considered a perfect revenue maker, especially from sports events," wrote reporter Harry Sheer. "Boxing, track and football have been the big moneymakers in the past, but in 1943 it took the War Show to keep the park board from marking Soldier Field figures in the red again." The article went on to criticize the district for getting greedy; instead of just trying to recoup costs the district had, in the mid-1930s, started trying to bring in money on larger events.

Few events other than local football games were being held at the stadium in those years, and the *Daily News* blamed the park district's attempts to hike revenue. For example, the stadium had lost a 1937 boxing match between Joe Louis and Jim Braddock when the district asked to get 25 percent of the gross receipts. Even the *Tribune*'s long-running College All-Star football game had taken a one-year hiatus in 1943, with the *Tribune* citing "excessive charges levied against the game by the park board" as the primary reason for moving it to Northwestern University's Dyche Stadium. In 1945 the *Daily News* ran another article and an editorial critical of the park district's policies, this time siding with the chairman of the Illinois Athletic Commission, who had written a letter to the park board criticizing it for overcharging, in violation of the stadium's original purpose. "There is no doubt that many championship fights and other sports events, which would bring a lot of money to Chicago, would be held here if the field could be obtained at a reasonable figure," wrote the chairman, Sheldon Clark. "The Park Board apparently would rather have the field lie idle than see this money come here." The decision

Marketing brochure for Soldier Field, ca. 1952. Courtesy Chicago Park District Special Collections.

of the Ringling Brothers and Barnum & Bailey Circus to bypass Chicago in 1945 because of disputed fees was also cited as evidence the park board was getting greedy (see chapter 11). Voters who had authorized the bonds for the stadium, the *Daily News* argued, "were led to believe that Soldier Field would provide an unexcelled setting in which local groups could stage athletic and recreational events, pageants, religious and cultural gatherings and public meetings." Those uses had declined, as had the use of Soldier Field for larger events that could help Chicago attract tourists, the newspaper argued. Park district policies should change to make Soldier Field part of reviving the city's fortunes rather than driving away tourists and their dollars.[6]

This criticism came, however, at a moment when the stadium was actually experiencing an upsurge in popularity. From 1941 to 1955, annual attendance rarely dipped below a million. In the 1950s, after Evan Kelly's ignominious departure from the stadium, Erwin "Red" Weiner brought attendance figures back up. Despite some of the difficulties he had filling the stadium in his later years at the Chicago Park District, for the rest of his life Weiner was justifiably proud of the innovations he made at the stadium. Weiner kept track of entertainment culture and advertised the stadium's availability in *Billboard* magazine. Weiner's efforts paid off in 1955, when events at the stadium drew more than 2.6 million people, still apparently a record. (In the new Soldier Field, annual attendance had reached about two million by 2004, although since the Chicago Fire soccer team moved to its own stadium, numbers have dipped a bit.) Weiner, a close friend of legendary Chicago gossip columnist Irv Kupcinet, succeeded in planting items about the stadium in trade magazines like *Variety*, bragging, for example, that he expected 1958 to be a banner year for Soldier Field. But in subsequent years, as Weiner came into conflict with other parks officials, attendance went into precipitous decline, falling as low as 223,201 in 1970—the equivalent of fewer than four sold-out Bears games today.

To make the field useful when it lacked events, the park district put it to work in several different ways. In 1936 it installed a shooting range for park police under the stands, near Gate 30 north of the east colonnade. The stadium also served as park police headquarters for many years. Starting in 1947 a traffic court annex operated in a few of the many offices under the stands. In addition, some of the stadium's workshops, originally used to construct stages and scenery for pageants, had by 1955 been used to build moorings for the park district's seven harbors. Although the stadium was part of the larger Chicago Park District system, its function as the center for park program championships, one of its original missions, survived only in high school football games—other sports held their tournaments elsewhere.[7]

The stadium's steadily deteriorating condition, and some bad renovation decisions, also contributed to the lack of use. As the park district poured more money into the stadium, more and more people began calling for its replacement. Each successive renovation brought improvements but also sacrificed some amenities and details of the original stadium. Particularly noteworthy was the diminished access to restrooms that accompanied the conversion, in the early 1980s, of the original arena into a field better suited for football. Early architectural plans of the stadium show many more restrooms than were available after about 1950, and even fewer were accessible to the public after the Bears moved in.

In 1958 the Chicago Park District and the *Chicago Sun-Times* fired the opening volleys in what was to become a forty-two-year war over the fate of the Holabird and Roche landmark. In a weeklong series titled "Chicago's Sports White Elephant," the paper mustered every complaint, criticism, and conflicting proposal about what could or should be done with the stadium. In the first article in the series, reporter Edgar Munzel raised the possibility of demolishing some of Soldier Field's south stands to make room for a regulation baseball diamond. Foreshadowing the Chicago Bears–driven plans that would come to fruition more than forty years later, Munzel noted that the proposal would require double-decking some of the stands, increasing the number of good seats from about twenty thousand to about sixty thousand. The full proposal, put forward by parks general superintendent George T. Donohue, would only be revealed if approved by the park district board, but assuredly it "would be a very costly venture," Donoghue told the *Sun-Times*, before clamming up. The stadium, the paper argued, "always has been considered a white elephant insofar as a sports stadium is concerned. Seating capacity is listed at 85,000 permanent seats with temporary seats boosting the total to 110,000. However, many complain the seats are too far removed from the action. . . . For football only approximately 22,000 of the permanent 85,000 seats are between the goal lines." The owners of professional sports teams had always considered Soldier Field an inadequate venue, the *Sun-Times* series claimed, and would have preferred to erect an entirely new stadium.[8]

The *Sun-Times*'s sister paper, the *Daily News*, joined the anti–Soldier Field choir, as did the *Tribune*. (Forty years later the Chicago papers would sing a very different tune, joining preservationists and park advocates in a fight with Richard M. Daley and the Chicago Bears to retain the stadium's historic structure.) But Richard J. Daley's push for the 1959 Pan Am Games seems to have scuttled the idea of replacing the stadium, at least for a few years. In early February 1958, when the park board met to discuss its options regarding the stadium, Robert A. Black, the district's chief engineer, told the members that adding an upper deck to allow for baseball games would cost about $2.5 million (about $19 million in 2008 dollars). But nothing could be done until after the Pan Am Games. Instead, on top of $300,000 for improvements in 1956, the district decided to spend $100,000 to renovate Soldier Field's running track and tens of thousands more on other renovations. Even so, in January 1959 Mayor Daley announced that he and park district officials had been talking about building a new, multipurpose sports stadium on the lakefront. Soldier Field would still have a place in Chicago, Mayor Daley declared, because it remained an ideal place to host opening ceremonies for a Chicago Olympics. After that announcement, talk of replacing Soldier Field faded for a few years, as civic leaders held out hope that the Pan Am Games would restore some of Soldier Field's fading glory. The *Daily News* touted the possibility that the stadium was "ready to change colors . . . from red ink to black."[9]

Despite Weiner's and Daley's best efforts, however, the games had no long-term effect on the stadium's popularity as a venue. In 1959 the park district spent another $120,000 to set up the stadium for Cardinals football, but the money went to waste when the team moved to Saint Louis after only one year of poorly attended games at Soldier Field. At the same time, the arrangement with the Cardinals had cut off high school games at the stadium, except for the annual Prep Bowl and the Mum Bowl, another public school football game. The professional team hadn't wanted high school teams sullying its playing

Players pinning flowers on their mothers at the 1967 Mum Bowl. The championship game for Chicago Park District football teams is a vestige of the South Park Commission's practice of using Soldier Field to showcase talent developed in its fieldhouse programs. Courtesy Chicago Park District Special Collections.

field, and Park District officials didn't want to spend the money to open the stadium for games that would only attract a few thousand people.[10]

Forrest Lull, Weiner's successor as head of special services at the Chicago Park District, bragged in early 1963 that the previous year the stadium had seen more events than the Rose Bowl. But that year, the number of people who visited the stadium declined slightly, a slide that continued until the 1970s.[11] By 1964 it was clear that the efforts to enhance Soldier Field's marketability were not paying off, and talk about replacing the stadium began in earnest—talk that was to continue almost unabated until the announcement in 2000 of a deal to renovate the stadium.

In the 1960s the city came up with several schemes to replace Soldier Field. Mayor Daley took a page from the *Sun-Times*'s 1950s plans by proposing a revamp that would accommodate baseball and football, and bring both the Bears and the Cubs to the lakefront. Then in February 1964 he appointed a blue-ribbon committee to study the possibility of building a new stadium.

By then, the Chicago Park District was estimating the cost of renovating the stadium at $4 million, or $12 million with a dome. In his first nine years as mayor, Daley had established himself as another builder mayor, ready to follow in the footsteps of Thompson and Kelly. Already he had instituted grand schemes to clear slums, build huge housing projects, and remake large swaths of the city. He soon took to criticizing anyone opposed to replacing the stadium. "Nothing is done of significance without tremendous opposition," Daley said. "You will recall the opposition to the University of Illinois [at Chicago] when it was being planned. Now everyone is saying it is a great thing."[12]

Though in the early 2000s the *Tribune* would try mightily to dissuade Mayor Richard M. Daley from plans for a drastic renovation of Soldier Field, in the 1960s it called upon his father to demolish the structure. The paper began 1964 by proclaiming, "The old stadium . . . was designed about as badly as any structure intended for viewing spectator sports and spectacles could be." Soldier Field "should be razed without further delay and a new Soldiers' field located to the south of it in what is now a large parking area. . . . We trust that civic officials will get going on the realization of a project which could be of inestimable benefit to Chicago."[13]

Later that year, a *Tribune* editorial pointed out that Chicago was falling behind cities like Philadelphia, where voters had approved a $25 million bond issue for a new stadium for the Phillies and the Eagles. "When cities like Philadelphia and Houston move ahead of Chicago, it is time to ask what has happened to this city's much vaunted spirit," the paper concluded. A few weeks later, Daley's blue-ribbon committee finally issued a report on building a new stadium, which it had hired out to a group called the Real Estate Research Corporation. The report urged that a new stadium be built using general tax bonds and pointed to three possible sites: that of the present Soldier Field; the Near South Side, between Harrison and Roosevelt west of State Street; and the Near West Side, between Madison Street and the Eisenhower Expressway. In each case, construction would cost about $22 million (about $156 million in 2008 dollars), not including acquisition of land. Tearing down Soldier Field and building a new stadium on land the city already owned would be the cheapest option, bringing the total cost to about $34.5 million, while buying and demolishing existing buildings at the other two sites would essentially double the price tag. Mayor Daley endorsed the report with one important qualification: he wanted to see the new Chicago arena built using revenue bonds—that is, future revenues from the stadium—rather than taxpayer money.

Reaction to the proposal was swift and positive, especially among most members of the mayor's committee. George Halas, the owner of the Chicago Bears, called the building of a new stadium "inevitable." In a meeting of the committee in late December 1964, Halas told Daley that the city's ballparks were "more than 50 years old and cannot be brought up to modern standards by alterations or repairs without major expense. . . . Chicago needs a new stadium, and Chicago has everything required to make the new stadium an outstanding success." The lone holdout on the committee was Arthur C. Allyn, the owner of the White Sox. Allyn objected to the idea of building the stadium with taxpayer money for "the benefit of a few private industries" (an ironic stance, given the tax support his team would receive to renovate its new stadium twenty-five years later as part of the 2000 Soldier Field deal).[14]

Civic groups whose ideological predecessors had backed the stadium's creation and whose successors would oppose its renovation in the 2000s began to get on the bandwagon to demolish the field. In late 1965 the Daniel Burnham Committee and the Chicago Heritage Committee asked for the demolition of Soldier Field, McCormick Place, and Meigs Field to clear the lakefront for parkland. The greatest effect of the two groups' testimony at a Chicago Plan Commission hearing on December 1, 1965, was to lend credence to the idea that a new stadium was a better alternative than renovating Soldier Field. The *Tribune* kept up the drumbeat for Soldier Field's destruction for years. In 1967 the paper published an editorial under the title "Will Chicago Be Left Behind?" that urged Daley to move forward with plans for a domed stadium: "Houston, Atlanta, Pittsburgh, Philadelphia, New York, Los Angeles, Boston, St. Louis, Kansas City, and now Detroit have all recognized the desirability and need to build such structures. Is Chicago to be the last of the major league cities to drag itself into the modern age?"

As the debate stormed, Chicago felt the rumblings of the unrest and white flight that would remake much of the city over the next decade. Daley was busy putting out political fires, and had little time to concentrate on the stadium, especially after the riots that followed the assassination of the Reverend Martin Luther King Jr. and, also in 1968, the disastrous Democratic National Convention.[15]

Indeed, Chicago wasn't standing still. In contrast to the era in which civic leaders first debated building a stadium, Chicago was starting to empty. Between 1910 and 1930 the city had grown from 2.2 million people to 3.4 million; between 1960 and 1980 it lost almost half a million residents. That, combined with an exponential increase in television watching, seems to have sealed the fate of many of the traditional events at Soldier Field. As calls for a new stadium continued, a section of stands gave way under a stress test during an engineering review in June 1970. About a third of the seats in Section 26, in the east stands above the north 10-yard line, collapsed in sandbag tests ordered because the area "was definitely the worst section," park district president Daniel Shannon said. Shannon said the damage would be repaired within a few weeks, but meanwhile spectators at a soccer game between Poland and

The 1970 stress test of Soldier Field stands convinced some that the stadium needed to be entirely rebuilt—or replaced. Courtesy Chicago Park District Special Collections.

Portugal, a few days after the test, all had to sit in the west stands. The next week, Shannon pointed to the collapse as further evidence of the need for a new stadium, and ordered more tests on the building's structural integrity. Shannon called the failure of the stands a "death knell" for Soldier Field. (The park district would later claim that the tests did not demonstrate serious structural flaws. Engineers, they claimed, had loaded the stands with much more weight than they were designed to hold.)

Meanwhile, the Chicago Bears continued to play at Wrigley Field, as they had for decades, but their days at the North Side stadium were numbered. As television increased attendance at NFL games across the country, the league decided that the Bears' arrangement for home games, using temporary stands at Wrigley Field, wouldn't do and demanded that the team find a larger venue. The team already had a history at Soldier Field. Its Armed Forces Game, an annual event from 1946 through 1970, had often been played at the stadium.[16]

Soldier Field wasn't the ideal place to see a game, but it was built with football in mind. Its single-deck, classical design mirrored that of storied football stadiums around the country: the Yale Bowl and Soldiers Field, Harvard's football stadium, as well as other early-twentieth-century venues. By making the lakefront arena their home, the Chicago Bears ended up preserving that model, and postponing Soldier Field's day of reckoning, for thirty years.

The Bears at first had wanted to go to Dyche Stadium, Northwestern University's football stadium, where they had played their first home game of 1970. By 1971 it appeared that another major renovation would be necessary to make Soldier Field suitable for NFL games, and Halas's opinion that it was an inferior stadium was well-known. In February 1971 Halas announced that the Bears were moving to Dyche, and as part of its contract with Northwestern, the team canceled that year's Armed Forces Game in favor of a benefit game for the city of Evanston. For a few weeks it seemed that 1971 would be the first year in decades with no Bears games at Soldier Field. Then the Big Ten Conference rejected the deal with Northwesten. A few months earlier, the athletic conference had given its approval for professional teams' playing at member schools' stadiums, but only before and after college teams' seasons. The Bears' lease overlapped the Northwestern season. The Chicago Park District, recognizing a chance to sign prestigious tenants that fit better with Soldier Field's original mission than stock car racing, jumped at the chance to bring the Bears there.[17]

It appeared at first that the Bears might return to Wrigley Field for another year, although P. K. Wrigley, whose family company owned both the Cubs and the ballpark, wasn't keen on having them back. Halas, Wrigley said, had a sense of entitlement to the venue because of how long the Bears had been playing there. The Bears owner had long tried to cram in as many fans as possible, rearranging the seats, which weren't bolted down, so he could fit eight people in where six would sit for a baseball game. When the Cubs decided to bolt down the seats, Halas got angry. "One of the things that upsets him the most is the way he keeps losing attendance as we continue to modernize the ballpark," Wrigley said. Northwestern, meanwhile, tried desperately to convince the Big Ten that it ought to be allowed to rent to the Bears, but its efforts failed. A few days later, it came out that the Chicago Park District was, according to its president, Dan Shannon, "very much interested" in bringing the Bears to the stadium.

By April, the Bears and the Park District were close to an agreement, and newspapers were writing about possible configurations for the field if the Bears moved in. Shannon said that it would be possible to seat sixty-seven thousand people if games were played at the north end of the field. The park district, however, preferred the configuration used for the Cardinals a decade earlier: moving the playing field sixty to ninety feet south from where it traditionally had been when football was played at Soldier Field. The Bears would bring with them the temporary stands they had used in the Wrigley outfield to close off the north end of Soldier Field. That would all add up to about fifty-three thousand seats, but that was seven thousand more than could be seated at Wrigley. Lastly, the park district would install Astroturf, which would not get torn up during non-Bears games and so would allow for more such events at the stadium.

Shannon and other parks officials insisted that taxpayers wouldn't foot the bill for the renovation; the Bears were to pay a rent equal to 10 percent of their ticket sales and to cede parking and concession revenue to the Park District. In May came the announcement that the Bears would move to Soldier Field for at least three years, with an option for two more. If the team decided after two years not to renew the lease, then it would have to pay for the improvements to the stadium. The park district expected to bring in enough money to run a surplus of about $100,000 for the first three years of the contract. Halas said that the renovation was sufficient for the moment, but that he hoped a new stadium could be built within three years.

A new stadium was going to be a hard sell to taxpayers—but Bears fans sided with Halas on the idea of replacing Soldier Field. The team had been doing poorly for a few years, and some fans were skeptical about the tired old stadium. "I'm contemplating giving up my season tickets, and I think I will," Niles electrician Tim Harahan told the *Tribune*. "The parking there is bad, and getting to and from there is bad. Once you're there, it's a poor place to watch a game. And the climate is bad. I've been there on October nights watching the Rockets or Hornets and it's miserable with the wind off the lake and nothing to shelter you."[18]

Even before the contract was signed, the Bears' aborted move to Evanston and Halas's talk about a new stadium got Daley's notice, and he once again formed a special committee to look at the possibility of building a new arena. Daley's Stadium Site Committee moved forward with a full evaluation of Soldier Field's viability and in May 1971 proposed five possible sites for a new stadium, including the current Soldier Field site and a spot just west of the stadium on land owned by the Illinois Central Railroad. Two months later Daley and the citizens committee announced a plan to tear down the old stadium and build a new one just to the south. The $55 million structure would seat seventy-five thousand people and have an "open dome" design, with the stands covered but the playing arena open to the elements. Halas was overjoyed, calling the proposal "a mark of progress."

But Halas wasn't to have the last word on this, or any other, stadium proposal. Chicagoans thought of Soldier Field and the lakefront as their own, and many thought the idea of another lakefront building violated the spirit of the Burnham Plan. The Metropolitan Housing and Planning Council was among those opposing the lakefront location. "A sports arena is not a public facility but a private corporate facility for putting on events to which an admission charge is required. The economic advantages of this facility should not take precedence over preservation of the lakefront," said Dale O'Brien, the president of the council. One of those on the stadium committee was Marshall Field V, who also opposed putting a new stadium on the lakefront. His papers, the *Sun-Times* and the *Daily News*, came out against the proposal, and his and other city newspapers pointed out that a new stadium likely would need taxpayer support. Earlier proposals for financing a new stadium using gate revenue had counted on revenue from Cubs or Sox games, or both, and the teams weren't going to be part of the newly proposed arena. A new levy by the park district or the city seemed like "the most logical way" to get money for the project, agreed Robert W. Christensen, head of the city's Public Building Commission.

Daley wasn't pleased with the opposition. He claimed at the time that calls and letters regarding the new stadium were two-to-one in favor of it, but appears to have worried about a backlash against raising taxes in an already shaky economy for the benefit of the Bears. Taxpayers wrote scores of letters to newspapers, and papers such as *Chicago Today* trumpeted objections to constructing a football-only stadium that would cost as much as stadiums built in other cities for both football and baseball. Times were lean in Chicago, and whites on the West and South Sides were fleeing the city for the suburbs. "A lakefront stadium is the kind of structure Chicago needs least," wrote Henry Metzger, in response to a *Daily News* appeal for readers' letters on building a new stadium. "Even if not one cent of public funds were involved, it would be inconceivable for the city to accept a structure so esthetically and socially offensive when so many real needs of the city parks and other open spaces are unmet."

Even though he'd just been reelected for a fifth term with 70 percent of the vote, Daley wasn't keen on adding to taxpayer burdens. *Chicago Today* aired plans for possible uses of the stadium other than football, a list as long as that the South Park commissioners had come up with in the early 1920s—including many items that never materialized or occurred only a few times. People weren't convinced, however, and still worried about the cost of the proposed new stadium. *Chicago Daily News* columnist Mike Royko weighed in, ridiculing Daley in a column written in stereotypical "injun" dialect. Native Americans had occupied an abandoned Nike missile site near Belmont Harbor and asked that it be made into a Native American housing complex; After about two weeks, police ousted some fifty people from the site. Royko compared the city's treatment of the protesters with what was certain to be a windfall for Halas: "Oh, Great White Father, you speak with forked tongue," he began. "Same day you throw Indian off people's land, you call big powwow. You say at powwow that you make treaty to give people's

In the stadium's early years, the parking surrounding Soldier Field was touted as a public amenity; in later years, the parking lots were criticized as monopolizing too much lakefront land. This photo of the east parking lot was taken April 20, 1941. Courtesy Chicago Park District Special Collections.

land away. But you not give land to Indians. You give land to Papa Bear. You say you give 75,000 seats to Papa Bear, on same day you give kick in seats to 50 Indians. You put Indian bucks in jail. But you put taxpayer's bucks in Papa Bear's pocket."

With the protests ringing in his ears, a few days after the initial stadium report Daley appointed a five-member architectural committee to see if Soldier Field could be renovated. Bringing Soldier Field up to modern standards "would be half the price" of building a new arena, Daley said. His site committee would hold off pressing for a new stadium until after the architectural committee figured out if Soldier Field could be saved. In any case, the city's Public Works Department had decided that the stadium was structurally sound enough for use, even without major renovations, for several years. "I don't like to see Soldier Field torn down," Daley said. "It is possible it would cost $150 million to build a place like it."[19]

Lakefront protection advocates who took Montgomery Ward as their guiding light were skeptical even about keeping Soldier Field. In her classic study of Chicago's lakefront, *Forever Open, Clear, and Free: The Struggle for Chicago's Lakefront*, Pulitzer Prize–winning editorial writer Lois Wille derided Daley's plan to renovate the stadium. Cars dominated the lakefront whenever the Bears played, Wille pointed out, spilling over from the forty-one acres of parking lot around Soldier Field onto every available open piece of asphalt in the area, and even the lawns surrounding the Field Museum. At the same time, Edmund Kelly believed that the leadership of the three museums near the stadium—in addition to the Field, the Shedd Aquarium and Adler Planetarium—had themselves agitated for the stadium's replacement, in the mistaken belief that the Bears games next door decreased their attendance on fall weekends.[20]

As the city debated the long-term merits of keeping Soldier Field, the park district went ahead with a $700,000 renovation of the stadium, including $206,000 to replace the arena's natural grass with Astroturf. All the costs were to be recouped from the Bears' rent—10 percent of the team's home game receipts for three years—although the initial outlay came from bonds backed by tax revenues. In the renovation, the stadium's owners continued the slow transition from the plank benches that had long dominated the field, installing backs on another thirty-four thousand seats. To give some Bears fans a closer view of the action, the park district installed new temporary box seats along the stadium running track. (The presence of the boxes ensured that the running track would be removed in the stadium's full-scale renovation in the early 1980s, and also made it impossible to run stock car races at the stadium.)

The company that won the contract to place the asphalt that underlay the Astroturf was a longtime city contractor, Rock Road Construction, which only a few years earlier had been implicated in a major city contracting scandal. In 1966 a *Tribune* investigation had found that Rock Road, one of two major suppliers of asphalt to the city, was charging Chicago more than 30 percent more per ton than it charged the state of Illinois for exactly the same asphalt. It appeared that the company had overcharged the city about $400,000 over several years—almost $2.2 million in 2008 dollars. A few months after it got the Soldier Field asphalt contract, Rock Road, which by 1971 had moved its headquarters from the city to Des Plaines, became embroiled in another fraud investigation. In that scandal, federal prosecutors determined that state transportation secretary William F. Cellini Jr. had given out millions of dollars in road contracts without bids, including some to Rock Road, by breaking them up into subunits of a size that would not have to be competitively bid. A few years later, Rock Road's president, William Nanini, was implicated in yet another scandal and federal investigation, this time involving bid rigging in state contracts.[21]

Most Chicagoans who cared, however, focused on the physical changes at the stadium and the possibility of renovating Soldier Field. The architectural committee made its initial report at the end of July and followed up with a full report later in the year, along with a contractor's study of the concrete used in the original construction. In July the group met with Daley to tell him they believed it was possible to increase capacity in the south half of the seating area and make the stadium viable long-term. The stadium could be permanently divided into two arenas, with the north end hosting events like tennis, soccer, and Little League baseball, Public Works Commissioner Milton Pikarsky, head of the architectural committee, told reporters. Halas reacted favorably to the report but said he still wanted an entirely new stadium. "I am very happy with the arrangement, which means that if we have to play in Soldier Field longer than our three-year lease, I will be willing to do so," Halas said.

As the stadium committees studied the matter further, the Bears and the Chicago Park District negotiated a final lease for 12 percent of the Bears' ticket revenues, with a minimum payment of $788,827 over their three-year lease. (This minimum, only about a third of the cost of the renovations, did not include parking and concessions revenue.) The 12 percent figure, formalized at a park board meeting the week before the first Bears game at the stadium, matched what Halas had agreed to pay Northwestern University when the Bears had tried to move there. In October, tests determined that the stadium stands could be repaired, or as Pikarsky put it, made "as good as new." Late that month, the architecture committee put the minimum cost of renovation at $12 million—or up to about $22.3 million, if the work went beyond structural rehabilitation and included new mechanical, plumbing, and lighting systems. The committee also estimated costs for adding an upper deck or canopy to protect spectators in bad weather. The plans then languished for several years. Meanwhile, Soldier Field's crumbling condition remained a constant source of ammunition for Halas and other critics of the stadium.[22]

One revelation in the architectural committee's study is particularly notable for what it said about the contractors who built the stadium in the 1920s. The consulting firm Erlin, Hime Associates evaluated the original concrete and found that support columns below ground level contained chemical compounds that indicated "exposure of poor quality concrete to ground water." Some of the concrete had "variable" water-to-cement ratios—too much or too little water—a sign that crews had "probably ineffectually mixed" it before pouring it. The tests helped explain why Soldier Field had needed so many renovations over the years to keep it viable. Instead of building the best stadium in the world, the politically connected South Park contractors had apparently used shoddy work to enrich themselves. Ironically, they had also enriched successive Democratic administrations who reaped the political benefits of contracts for the almost constant renovations. Arguably, if Soldier Field had been as well built as originally envisioned, while it still would have provided work for politically connected park district employees, much less cash would have flowed to contractors over the years.[23]

Meanwhile, the Bears moved in. As one columnist put it, the first game at their new home, against the Pittsburgh Steelers on September 19, 1971, appeared to be a good omen. With little more than four minutes left in the game, the Steelers were up, 15–3. Then Bears defensive lineman Ed O'Bradovich hit Steeler Warren Bankston, forcing a fumble. Bear linebacker Ross Brupbacher grabbed the ball and ran for a touchdown. A few minutes later, Dick Butkus blitzed the Steelers, causing another fumble, and O'Bradovich picked up the ball to score, winning the game. The rest of the season was less successful—the Bears played some good football but, as many said at the time, not good enough. Butkus saved the day again on November 14 when he caught a pass in the end zone in the fourth quarter, giving the bears a 16–15 win over the Washington Redskins and a 6–3 record for the season. But the team went on to lose its five remaining games, and Halas replaced coach Jim Dooley with Abe Gibron—dubbed by *Tribune* writer Cooper Rollow, the "jowled jester of Dooley's staff."[24]

Gibron was talkative, funny and convivial, and helped keep the team popular even as its record got worse. His teams were plagued with injuries and overwhelmed by losses. Both Gayle Sayers and Butkus had to leave the team—and leave football—because of insurmountable injuries in Gibron's first two years. In his postgame talks with reporters, Gibron often had to put a good spin on bad ball.[25]

As the Bears struggled, the park district labored to keep the stadium viable. Edmund Kelly, after several years as assistant general superintendent and a park board member, was elevated to general superintendent in 1972 and immediately became Soldier Field's biggest public advocate, working hard to try to bring new events to the stadium. In late 1973 Kelly touted the configuration of the stadium that resulted from putting the Bears' Wrigley Field bleachers at the north end of the stadium. Renovations for the north end alone cost about $600,000, while more was spent rebuilding some crumbling stands at the southeast end of the field. (Meanwhile, Patrick L. O'Malley, the president of the park board, had promised the Bears a $15 million to $20 million renovation that was subsequently postponed.) Park officials had also successfully argued that the Chicago Fire, a member of the short-lived World Football League, should be allowed to play over the summer at Soldier Field, despite an exclusivity clause in the Bears' lease. The NFL gave its blessing, and the Fire, owned by businessman Tom Origer, play its sole season at the stadium.

Lloyd Bridges was one of several celebrities at the 1974 International Festival of Tennis, held in the north end of Soldier Field. Courtesy Chicago Park District Special Collections.

Kelly also pushed to bring tennis and other events, such as the Emmett Kelly Jr. Circus (see chapter 11), to the north end of the stadium. Kelly dreamed of bringing the Davis Cup to Chicago, and envisioned a 1974 Chicago International Festival of Tennis as a way to prove to tennis promoters that the city was worthy of hosting one of the world's most prestigious championships. "This stadium at the north end of Soldier Field is the best in the world, and I've played 'em all," former tennis champion Grant Golden told *Today.* "We can seat 20,000, and there isn't a bad seat in the house." Meanwhile, national reporters declared the Soldier Field courts the best in the country. Would-be tennis stars and celebrities alike showed up for the first year of the tennis fest. Although the matches failed to attract as many spectators as Kelly had hoped, with only about twenty thousand people attending the almost week-long tournament, Kelly and some of the players declared them a success. But the charities that sponsored the matches lost money. The next year, another field of up-and-coming tennis stars, including former River Forest resident Billy Martin, headlined at the International Festival of Tennis. Roscoe Tanner, who would go on to win the Australian Open in 1977 and lose to Björn Borg in the Wimbledon Finals in 1979, won the tournament and a $9,000 purse. But attendance was even poorer than in 1974; the quarterfinals drew two thousand people, while another five thousand watched a Sting soccer game in the south end of the field. Kelly wasn't ready to give up, however. He still wanted the Davis Cup—and didn't want to think the renovation of the north end of the stadium would come to naught. But despite continuing talk of bringing tennis back to the stadium for the next decade, it never happened.[26]

ROCK 'N' ROLL COMES TO SOLDIER FIELD

Kelly was more successful in establishing a new tradition of rock concerts at Soldier Field, one which persists to this day. The *Tribune*'s Chicagoland Music Festival had left the stadium a decade before, and Kelly thought that large-scale musical events should once again become a drawing card at the stadium. In early 1975 Kelly announced that Aretha Franklin would be the first headliner of a Soldier Field rock concert, and that other musical acts would follow. The park district board following a disastrously aborted Sly and the Family Stone concert in Grant Park in 1970. But Kelly, who saw the successes that Comiskey Park was having with events like the World Series of Rock, featuring Aerosmith, KISS, and Peter Frampton, kept pressing for them through the 1970s. In the end, Franklin did not perform in 1975, but Marvin Gaye did, in the stadium's north arena. He was well-received, despite complaints that the opening acts took too long and Gaye didn't take the stage until after 11:30 p.m. The next few years would be the golden age of Soldier Field rock concerts and festivals.[27]

After Gaye's 1975 concert, the next really big rock event at the stadium was a concert featuring Emerson, Lake & Palmer on June 4, 1977. Promoters billed the event, in a conscious allusion to the Comiskey Park series, as the Super Bowl of Rock. Tickets sold for $10 to $11.50, and eighty thousand people showed, some as early as 9 a.m., six hours before bands began playing. Kelly knew he'd gotten the park district hooked on concerts: the one-day take for the parks was about $150,000, more than the stadium had brought in over three months the previous year. But while park board members were pleased with the results, the lucrative new venture also brought new allegations of corruption. The week after the Emerson, Lake & Palmer concert, the *Sun-Times* reported that concert promoters who got Soldier Field permits tended to have as their attorney Victor Cacciatore, a lawyer who had hired Edmund Kelly's son Robert Kelly.Cacciatore's three clients got the first three dates at Soldier Field. And Jerry Mickelson and Arny Granat of JAM Productions, who hadn't hired Cacciatore, said they had been unable to get a booking.

The Rolling Stones play Soldier Field, 1977. Courtesy Chicago Park District Special Collections.

Park board president O'Malley deflected the criticism, saying, "What is important is that we had a successful concert—the city made money and the Park District made money." Instead of responding to demands by the Better Government Association to competitively bid concerts, the park board added a Peter Frampton concert to the Pink Floyd and Ted Nugent dates already on its calendar. Three years after the Emerson, Lake & Palmer concert, three of the promoters involved, Bruce Kapp and brothers Carl and Larry Rosenbaum, as well as the treasurer for the Super Bowl of Rock concerts, were indicted on charges that they had defrauded the city, the park district, and the bands involved. All of them pleaded guilty, and Knapp was sentenced to six months of prison work release. Neither Kelly, his son, nor the Cacciatores were ever accused of wrongdoing.[28]

Despite questions of corruption, concerts became a significant part of the public image of Soldier Field after the mid-1970s. One of the most memorable was the Rolling Stones' first concert at the stadium, on July 8, 1978. The concert began half an hour early, at 11:30 a.m., after more than forty thousand people rushed the field when police opened the gates at 7:30 a.m. The three opening acts, Southside Johnny and the Asbury Jukes, Peter Tosh, and Journey, warmed up the crowd before the Stones' two-hour set.

Fans came from all over the Midwest to see the band, on its first tour of the United States in three years. Its act opened with the release of hundreds of pink balloons and ended with fireworks. Mick Jagger "went through his standard prancing paces with alacrity. From the far end of the stadium the visual effect was somewhat akin to viewing a trained mouse, but his music was unmistakable," wrote the *Tribune*'s Lynn Van Matre. The one sour note was the death of a Stones fan who fell thirty feet from a walkway at the stadium. David M. LaFollette, twenty-seven, of Michigan City, Indiana, was dead on arrival at Mercy Hospital that afternoon.

The accidental death at Soldier Field, only the second on record there, did nothing to stop the parade of concerts. That same summer, Funk Fest, with headliners Parliament Funkadelic and Taste of Honey, packed the stadium; part of that show's proceeds were donated to the United Negro College Fund. Rock concerts became a mainstay of the stadium, and a significant, if not always reliable, source of revenue for the park district. Several citywide festivals took place at the stadium in the years Jane Byrne was mayor, but most of the concerts were purely for profit. Performers as diverse as Bruce Springsteen, Madonna, and the Grateful Dead all played there over the next twenty years. The last Grateful Dead concert, the final stop on the band's 1995 tour, turned out to be its last show ever, when the group's fabled leader, Jerry Garcia, died a month later. As a result, the show has become legendary among Deadheads, the band's followers.

Where people from throughout the Midwest had once flocked to the city for events like the Chicagoland Music Festival and the Bears' Armed Forces Game, organized mainly for charity, massive crowds now came together at the stadium almost exclusively for for-profit ventures. As the culture changed, large-scale events meant to edify and uplift the citizenry had fallen by the wayside. Ethnic events, when they were still held, were on a much smaller scale. Religious gatherings were at times larger but were held less often. It wasn't that massive cultural events became extinct—although pageants like *The Romance of a People* were almost unheard of by the 1960s—but Soldier Field no longer came to mind when most groups were thinking of a place to hold a gathering, and McCormick Place had taken all the stadium's convention business. Before the Bears moved in, the park district regularly brought in less than $100,000 in revenue from stadium rentals each year, sometimes much less. So few other large events were being held there that, as the 1970s wore on, Soldier Field came to be thought of more and more as a football stadium, with a few soccer games and rock concerts as sidelights.[29]

As Kelly tried his hand at concert promotions, Soldier Field's football teams tried to get on their feet. Abe Gibron was fired from his post at the Bears only two days after his last game, finishing with a record of eleven wins, thirty losses, and one tie. The next summer, a new World Football League team, skippered by Gibron, tried to compete with the Bears. But the Chicago Winds played only two preseason games and five regular-season games before folding. Their only win came before 3,502 fans in driving rain, against the Portland Thunder. Despite what was known as the Jim Finks Housecleaning, for the new general manager's wholesale firings that season, the Bears didn't do much better than under Gibron in 1975. In fact, under new head coach Jack Pardee, they managed exactly the same 4–10 record.[30]

But in the 1975 NFL draft, the Bears had gained someone who would define the franchise for the next generation: Walter Payton. Payton and three other players drafted January 28, 1975, were "expected to run, block and tackle the Bears out of their misery." That didn't happen overnight, as the record shows, but the team started to show glimmers of success. Payton, whom Pardee called a "big little man," for his ability to "run big" despite being only five-foot-ten, came to the Bears a known quantity among football scouts, if not the general public. In his native Mississippi, he had stood out first as a high school player, then broken an NCAA touchdown record by scoring sixty-five times at Jackson State University. In 1975 he scored only seven touchdowns for the Bears, but in his second season the team improved to a 7–7 record, as Payton ran for 1,390 yards and scored thirteen touchdowns. And 1977 showed what the Bears and Payton could do. The team improved to 9–5 and made the division playoffs for the first time since its last NFL championship in 1963. Payton pushed hard to beat O. J. Simpson's 1973 rushing record of 2,003 yards in a single season and, although he fell short, hit what was to be his career high of 1,852 yards. The high point of the season was the November 20, 1977, game against the division champion Minnesota Vikings. Payton played with flu symptoms but still rushed for 275 yards in forty carries, beating a single-game record Simpson had set the year before. More than forty-nine thousand fans filled the stands, as Payton smashed record after record, leading the Bears to a 10–7 win. In the days that followed, Payton came into his own as an NFL star, with a request from the Pro Football Hall of Fame for the jersey he'd worn that day, an appearance on the *Today Show*, and a conference call with seventeen national sportswriters. The Bears made it to the playoffs, but fell to the Cowboys in Dallas in a 37–7 rout.[31]

Even as fans cheered the resurgent Bears, Halas, Kelly, and a parade of politicians starting with Richard J. Daley continued their dance over whether to build a new stadium or rehab Soldier Field. In early January 1975 the executive director of the Public Building Commission put forward the idea that the city spend at least $35 million completely remodeling Soldier Field, while Daley floated the idea of razing Soldier Field and building an entirely new stadium. "Who does Daley think he is? Julius Caesar? Give 'em circuses when the people want schools and the ability to walk down the

Chicago Bears star rusher Walter Payton (top right) is stopped by the Minnesota Vikings at the 1-yard line, November 20, 1977. Courtesy Chicago Tribune.

streets without fear," scoffed mayoral candidate Alderman John Hoellen (47th Ward), Daley's eventual Republican opponent in his last reelection campaign. Daley later contradicted the aide who had said that City Hall's preference was to tear down Soldier Field. A rehab of the stadium was being considered more seriously than a $150 million new stadium, and "you can say the mayor definitely is not for building a new stadium on the present site," Daley told reporters.

"When Richard J. was alive, we had over 13 different stadium designs," Kelly said just before demolition began on the old stadium in 2002. "And there was one that we finally came up with that was gorgeous, and that's the one that I think that the mayor really wanted to do."

The back-and-forth went on and on, with Halas pushing the city toward doing something about the state of Soldier Field by flirting with moves to the suburbs. Halas knew what football fans who had attended games at Soldier Field had known since the beginning: that whatever the grandeur of the stadium, the sightlines and the distance of the seating from the field were inferior to many other football stadiums. As the city, the park district, and the Bears wrangled over the stadium, Kelly and those in charge of Soldier Field struggled to keep it viable. "Hell, there were times that people were walking around, they had bricks and pieces of the stadium falling on them," Kelly said. "I told [Daley], and that's when the mayor was concerned too."[32]

Things seemed to come to a head when Halas revealed his plans for a northwest suburban stadium to Chicago sports reporters. Reports that the Bears had decided on a particular location were "a damned lie," he said, but in subsequent months, the idea of an Arlington Heights stadium picked up steam. Throughout his quest for a new stadium, Halas had made it clear he would prefer a government-subsidized building project, although often discussions focused on government-floated bonds to be paid back through ticket sales. Daley, for his part, denounced Halas's threats to move the team. In one red-faced, angry press conference, the mayor told reporters, "If the Bears were to move they could not use the name 'Chicago.' If they try, they'll get the biggest contest they ever had." Daley is supposed to have called Halas and told him in more sarcastic terms:

> I think that's fine, George. You're a businessman. Do what you have to do. I'm a businessman, too. I think moving out there would be a fine thing for you, George— if you wanna call yourselves the Arlington Heights Bears. Our lawyers say you just can't take the name Chicago with you out there to the suburbs. We'd have to take you to court. That could take years. Besides, I wonder how many people will come out to see the Arlington Heights Bears, George. . . . You make the call.

Even after Daley's threats, Halas persisted, attending a meeting of the Arlington Heights Village Board where he declared that he would move to a stadium near Arlington Park "if the people of Arlington Heights welcome us." Residents asked for a referendum, but it never came to that. By October 1976 Halas revealed he had committed to staying in Soldier Field through 1977. In what was to be Daley's last year in office, it looked like the mayor was going to back a long-term plan to add an upper deck at Soldier Field as well as a hundred skyboxes, which news reports at first called "VIP rooms." The $35 million to $50 million full renovation was to come on top of a $1.3 million sprucing up done in 1976, and supporters hoped it would do for Soldier

Field what the renovation of Yankee Stadium did for that ballpark—turn it again, at least for a time, into a viable, modern building.

The day he died, Daley opened a new fieldhouse with the park district's Kelly, and the two talked about renovating the stadium as they went back downtown together in Daley's car. Kelly was worried that a renovation of the stadium, which he had grown to love despite its being a "white elephant," would not be approved by the Public Building Commission—in other words, that Daley would instead choose to build a new stadium: "The renovation was a must. Otherwise you would have had to close the stadium down. Regardless of the Bears or anyone else. You've got to have a tenant there." The Bears wouldn't stay without major revamp, Kelly said, recalling the situation. Daley, who in the past had defended the stadium's sightlines and said it would be a shame to tear it down, told Kelly that he would get the money to renovate. The Bears might have to move to Comiskey Park for a year, but after that, they would have a fully renovated, almost new stadium to call home.[33]

But when Daley died before the plan could go forward, the full-scale renovation became much less of a sure thing. The mayor's replacement, Michael Bilandic, previously the alderman from the 11th Ward, said he wasn't sure whether the stadium should be renovated or a new facility built. In any case, he said, "Soldier Field can't stay the way it is. The city of Chicago needs a sports facility." Bilandic hesitated, however, to move forward with the renovation plans that Kelly says Daley had approved. Early the following year, Bilandic put together yet another stadium panel, this one headed by former Illinois governor Richard Ogilvie. Ogilvie quickly set about knocking down the idea that Soldier Field could be renovated. The plan Kelly backed was "not adequate or appropriate for the City of Chicago," he said. Ogilvie went so far as to disparage the stadium's condition as he and other stadium committee members toured it with Kelly in May 1977. The Bears locker room looked "pretty crummy," he said, comparing the stadium's outfitting unfavorably to that of any high school he'd ever visited. Kelly gave committee members two renovation options, one priced at about $25 million, the other at almost $61 million. Bilandic told reporters the more expensive one was unlikely to pass muster, because it would require shutting the stadium for twenty-one months or more.

During 1978's episodes of stadium speculation, park board president O'Malley told a city council committee that one option on the table was using the shell of Soldier Field as the frame for a new stadium—a plan similar to the one eventually adopted in 2000. Parks and city officials were considering that option because it was thought to be less expensive than building a new stadium for $200 million, O'Malley said. (The $200 million stadium of 1978 would have cost about $528 million in 2000, about 22 percent less than the actual 2001–2003 Soldier Field project cost of $675 million.) In

Aerial photograph of Soldier Field in 1948, showing the stadium's configuration before the renovation under Mayor Jane Byrne and parks superintendent Edmund J. Kelly. Courtesy Chicago Park District Special Collections.

December 1978 Bilandic agreed with Kelly to start a $3.5 million stopgap renovation that would replace the temporary north stands with permanent ones, add two thousand seats, replace the artificial grass on the field, and put new carpeting in the locker rooms. Halas said he would be all right if the Bears had to play in the old stadium for two seasons, adding, "I hope it's 20" more seasons. (In his autobiography, published in 1979, Halas hints at his complaints about Soldier Field by saying that it's "vast," but then calls it

North stands under construction, 1979. The addition permanently closed off the north end of the stadium, after which it was used primarily as a parking lot for park district employees. Courtesy Chicago Park District Special Collections.

an "architectural gem.") Then Jane Byrne, Bilandic's opponent, was elected mayor, and Soldier Field was saved.[34]

Byrne had derided the idea of a new taxpayer-funded stadium and criticized Ogilvie's stadium committee, which had visited stadiums in several other cities. "It doesn't seem to have done much but travel around," Byrne said in one interview. "I think it was a campaign gimmick from the beginning to get bipartisan support." In another interview, she said that she opposed tax funding for a stadium, calling it "a low priority" in comparison to the city's other needs. Almost immediately after she came to power, then, Byrne helped revive Kelly's less expensive renovation plan. When Byrne held a celebration of her forty-fifth birthday, complete with a giant birthday cake from the Palmer House and music by the Shannon Rovers bagpipe band, she talked up renovation. Saying that she didn't "think there's a lot of money floating around to build a new stadium," Byrne gave her blessing to a $30 million renovation plan for Soldier Field. The Bears weren't entirely pleased, but general manager Jim Finks seemed resigned to playing in the old stadium for a few years. "In the long run, renovation is not right, but if that's the way it has to be, it's better than we have right now," he said. Ironically, park advocates who at the time would have liked to see the stadium torn down for green space were tacitly backed by Patrick G. Ryan, head of Ryan Insurance (who, with his friend Andrew McKenna Sr., would buy a 20 percent stake in the football club a decade later). "We could build a dome-type stadium and make money from it," Ryan wrote in a letter to the *Tribune*. "We could build the new stadium south of the Loop in the old railroad yards and name it 'The Mayor Daley Memorial Stadium.'"[35]

As haggling over whether to build a new stadium faded, Bears fans adopted Soldier Field as their own, with some feeling a certain affection for the building, even as others racked up reasons why it deserved dynamiting. Traditions developed in reaction to the peculiarities of Soldier Field. One reason Chicago football fans are among the NFL's best tailgaters is the moralistic laws that govern the use of Chicago Park District facilities, laws that are still largely in effect but began falling when the district realized that making exceptions to its rules could bring in money. Many fans may not know or remember why the Soldier Field parking lots are such storied spots for pregame festivities: The South Park Commission, and the Chicago Park District after it, banned alcohol sales at the stadium until 1981. So Bears fans used to drinking at Wrigley Field, the team's old haunt, had to smuggle in booze or get their fill before the game. For years, Bears fans complained that they'd prefer to warm themselves up in the stadium legally. Then in 1980 the park district for the first time opened up its concessions for bidding, finally breaking an almost fifty-year monopoly by two companies that were vestiges of the old park systems that had merged to form the Chicago Park District in 1934. State law still banned the sale of beer and other alcoholic beverages in any park district, but Edmund Kelly knew that such sales could make the concessions more attractive—and bring in money for the park district.

As part of the bidding, park district president Raymond Simon said the district would, for the first time, ask the state legislature to allow beer and liquor sales at Cafe Brauer in Lincoln Park and at Soldier Field—though he told reporters he had "mixed emotions" about selling beer at the stadium. "We do need the revenue increase we might realize from this, but then there's the question of fan behavior," Simon said, going on to opine that maybe Bears fans wouldn't really want to drink that much, anyway, because of the cold weather conditions at games.[36] Within a few months, the state Senate passed a bill allowing the park board to OK liquor sales at specific park locations. The initial sites would be those two and the former South Shore Country Club.

The possibility of beer sales came at the same time that the Bears and the Chicago Park District were negotiating a new contract for the use of the stadium. In June 1980 Simon warned that if the Bears failed to renew their lease for Soldier Field, it most likely would be closed. The team wanted a twenty-year lease, and although Simon and other parks officials left the impression the situation was dire, Halas played down the possibility that the Bears would leave for another venue. The differences would "be resolved and we will play in Soldier Field," he declared to reporters. As they would twenty years later, Bears officials pressed hard to pay as little as possible out of their own pockets to put the stadium in playable shape. The proposed renovation of Soldier Field, which eventually would cost about $32 million, would be paid for largely through $20 million in real estate taxes over the life of the renovation (that is, until 2000). At first, the Park District said it wanted the Bears to pay 30 percent of the cost by adding a 50-cent surcharge onto each ticket. The Bears offered to pay a rent of $1 per ticket and 12 percent of gross receipts. (Tickets at the time started at $9.50, the equivalent of $25 in 2008, or a little more than half the cost of the cheapest Bears tickets in the 2003 season at the new Soldier Field.) For several months, the team and the district stood at an impasse, hardly moving until the issue of beer sales seemed to sweeten the pot a bit for the park district.[37]

The park district, however, decided it didn't need the beer sales immediately, once the terms of the new lease were agreed to. Instead of increasing the ticket surcharge, the Bears had agreed to finance the $3 million building of fifty-four skyboxes at the top of the grandstands in conjunction with the proposed renovation of the stadium. By the late 1970s the stadium finally was profitable again, after years of running deficits. In 1977 the park district brought in $1.2 million from Soldier Field events, and spent $400,000 on operations and maintenance. But the renovation would send those figures back into deficit, at least at first. The new lease only brought down the deficit, from $1.26 million to about $750,000 annually.

Even with the $32 million renovation assured, Halas left the door open for the construction of a new Chicago football stadium. "If somebody comes up with the financing for a stadium, we could try to buy out of the Soldier Field contract. Whatever happens, the Bears are here for many years to come," he said.[38]

Despite the new-found amity between the Bears and the Park District— Simon, not Kelly, spoke on behalf of the board during the final stages of the negotiations—beer sales weren't part of the final deal. "Paying for the security and the required dram shop insurance would cut our profits down to perhaps $15,000," on beer sales, Simon said. "There's no great urgency. We're interested in liquor sales for restaurants run by the Park District, because making them profitable without cocktails is almost impossible. But the Soldier Field situation can wait." The state law allowing beer sales didn't go into effect until 1981, in any case, and when Volume Services, Inc., received a contract to run concessions at Soldier Field and in Grant Park, a provision of the document required another vote by the park board before the start of beer sales.

Finally, in the summer of 1981, Volume Services president Vincent J. Pantuso told a park district committee that the district could make an extra $1 million over five years from beer sales. The next week, the park district board unanimously approved the sale of beer at Soldier Field during Bears games on a one-year provisional basis. "The main thing is to let the fans enjoy and protect them from anybody who becomes drunk and obnoxious," park commissioner Sydney Marovitz said. The park district was on the hook for about $50,000 more for security from then on—essentially cutting into the extra $1 million from the Bears by $500,000, if the district's figures are to be believed. The first game at which fans could buy beer legally at Soldier Field came on August 8, 1981, a 23–7 loss to the New York Giants. Sales were slower than expected that first day, a result John Fernandes, the district's general manager of the stadium, attributed to the loss, as "beer sells better when the home team is winning."[39]

When the renovation program of the early 1980s began, the shoddy work-manship of the stadium's original construction was finally dealt with in a way that those involved thought would keep the structure usable for decades to come. According to one of those involved, G. J. Klein, "The tread-and-riser system of the stands had deteriorated due to reinforcement corrosion and cyclic freezing and thawing of the non-entrained concrete. Also, ground water fluctuations accelerated the deterioration of the highly permeable concrete at the base of the columns." The rehab "included several new amenities—new seats, scoreboards locker rooms. . . . The crux of the rehabilitation effort was strengthening and repairing the stadium's structural system. [A] completely new tread-and-riser system was constructed using the old stands as a stay-in-place form." New box seats were set closer to the field, and the seating section closest to the field was sloped differently. New "stadium-style" seats were installed, with rows staggered so that no one would be directly behind someone else. In addition to the skyboxes, the renovation also created new restrooms, although not enough to replace those done away with in earlier renovations. There were also new refreshment stands, new ramps, and new elevators up to the skyboxes.[40]

The renovation also required the removal of several historic architectural details. With the construction of new, permanent box seats, the original wall that separated the grandstands from the arena was removed. The old wall had been topped with a decorative molding and also had metal rings to attach bunting. The rings were a minor detail but an important one. Provision for hanging bunting was one of the requirements of the original

Soldier Field architectural competition. The rings represented the idea of the stadium as a place to bring together the whole city for celebratory events, the climax of parades, and patriotic pageants—a function that had almost entirely disappeared by the end of the 1970s. A new concrete wall, plain and purely functional, was put in closer to the field. Despite the elimination of a few such details, Kelly and others thought the renovation had saved Soldier Field for the ages. "Supposedly, the conditions after the renovation meant it would stay usable for 50 years," Kelly said in 2002.[41]

As the renovations finally began, the Bears started to look like they might actually deserve a refurbished arena. After Pardee was fired, the team had a bang-up 1979 season under Neill Armstrong, achieving their best record since 1963, with ten wins and six losses. The team won both its games against the Green Bay Packers, their home opener and a December 9 contest at Green Bay, though by only a few points. They lost, however, in the wild card playoff and limped home to Chicago. The next two years went poorly, as Armstrong failed to inspire his team to winning records. Then on January 19, 1982, Halas, back in charge after the death of his son, George Halas Jr., who headed the Bears from 1963 to 1979, announced that Mike Ditka, a former Bears player who had clashed with Halas while he was on the team, would become the new head coach. After the 1981 season, Halas had called Ditka and brought him to Chicago, where they worked out a deal at Halas's kitchen table to pay Ditka $100,000 for his first year. From the first, Ditka told his players that he wanted them to go to the Super Bowl, trying to do away with what he saw as a "defeatist attitude."

As the season opened with a fully renovated stadium, it appeared the Bears might be headed back to their glory days. Fans' hopes for a new era were delayed, however, by a players' strike, which began in September after two regular-season games and shortened the season by seven games. The first win for Ditka's team didn't come until November 21, against the Detroit Lions. The team racked up only three wins against six losses that year, and blew a 20–6 lead in its last game, against Tampa Bay, losing not only the game (in overtime) but a chance to make the playoffs.

In 1983 Chicago saw the full-blown Ditka, as his hot-tempered, high-pressure style started to grate on his players. During a home game against the Minnesota Vikings that the team lost, 23–14, Ditka lost his cool and dressed down quarterback Jim McMahon as well as Jimbo Covert, a rookie offensive tackle, and fullback Matt Suhey. A few days later, he admitted he needed to change, saying, "I've got to relax, and I will." On Halloween, after a long bout with cancer, Halas died, and Michael McCaskey, his grandson, soon took over the Bears organization. The team finished with an 8–8 season, putting them second in the NFC Central.

In 1984 the team got off to a good start, winning its first two at home, then besting the Packers in Green Bay. Ditka felt one of the highlights of the season was the game against the Los Angeles Raiders, the reigning Super Bowl champions. Payton scored two touchdowns, leading the team to a 17–6 win, which buoyed the players' spirits. "It's a blessing," safety Todd Bell told reporters. "I think we'll get more respect around the NFL. The sky's the limit now." It wasn't, though, at least not yet. The Bears won their first playoff game, in Washington against the Redskins, but with McMahon lost to injury they failed to get past the 49ers, and the San Francisco team went on to win the Super Bowl.[42]

Meanwhile, the Chicago Park District and architectural preservationists got into a tussle that would help define park advocates' and good-government activists' views of Soldier Field for the next twenty years. As Ditka made the Bears his own, Kelly bandied about the idea of eventually putting a dome on Soldier Field. Kelly's talk of a $20 million dome angered architect Harry Weese, who had helped to preserve the Glessner House, an 1885 Prairie Avenue home. So in 1983 he and a colleague nominated Soldier Field for designation as a National Historic Landmark. More exclusive than the National Register of Historic Places, which includes tens of thousands of buildings and historic sites, the landmark list is reserved for places that have played a pivotal role in American history and that are still largely preserved in their original state. Kelly opposed the landmarking, but it was approved.

For the 1985 Bears, a 38–28 win in their home and season opener against the Tampa Bay Buccaneers started a twelve-game winning streak. "We emphasized playing with a chip on the shoulder," Ditka recalled in his autobiography. "Everybody knew what their role was, and I think that's why we were as close as we were," wide receiver Dennis McKinnon said a few years later. "And I think that started at the top and Walter set the tone as far as [to] how we approached the game." "The Bears have always played what coach Ditka has referred to as 'Bear Football,'" said punter Maury Buford. "That is hard-nosed, tough defense and very good, precision offense and good special teams."

As the season chugged along, certain players became legendary. Ditka introduced William "Refrigerator" Perry, a 310-pound defensive player, on offense in a game against the 49ers in San Francisco as a way to settle a score, but Perry performed so well in the position that Ditka kept him on offense. Perry's celebrity grew when, in a Monday night game at Soldier Field against the Packers, he scored a touchdown. As the fall wore on, Chicago fans grew giddy with anticipation of the team's possible Super Bowl trip. Their only loss was at Miami on December 2. The next day, however, about twenty players, including Payton, Perry, Richard Dent, and Gary Fencik showed up at a recording studio to shoot a music video, "The Super Bowl Shuffle." Along with the hype surrounding the song, the wind-whipped stadium became a

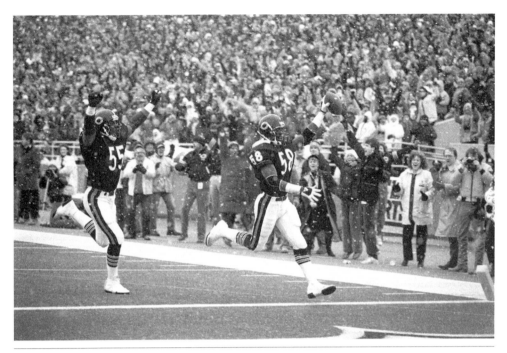

Snow falls as the Bears' Otis Wilson (55) accompanies Wilber Marshall (58) into the end zone in the fourth quarter of the teams January 12, 1986, win over the Los Angeles Rams. Courtesy Chicago Tribune.

dominating force in the team's playoff games that year, as Chicago players and their opponents were tested by what had come to be known as "Bears weather." Fans watched from barstools and even hospital delivery rooms as the Bears dominated the New York Giants, 21–0, in their first playoff game at Soldier Field, on January 5, 1986. A week later, the team held the Los Angeles Rams scoreless in a game that ended with a snowstorm that Ditka attributed to the otherworldly intervention of George Halas. The team went on to win the Super Bowl against the New England Patriots, 46–10, the greatest margin of victory in a Super Bowl up to that time.[43]

The Bears' success emboldened McCaskey, the new Bears president, to try another push for a new stadium. Over the next several years, as the team charged ahead under Ditka—with occasional stumbles—McCaskey pressed three successive mayors for a solution to the team's stadium quandary. The Bears rankled under the lease Halas had signed, which gave the park district the profits from parking and concessions. But McCaskey was not to see the team in a new stadium until after he handed stewardship of the Bears over to Ted Phillips, a professional who had no connection to the McCaskey family, Halas's heirs.

Soldier Field had been saved when the Bears moved there, but the Chicago Park District had gone with the cheaper of two renovation options. Much was improved by the $32 million renovation, but the stadium still lacked many of the amenities football fans were coming to expect. As the stadium declined relative to its peers, the Bears' management hungered for the sightlines and the ticket revenues other team owners enjoyed. Yet at the same time, football fans from around the country became used to seeing Soldier Field's colonnades on television, enhancing the stadium's reputation as a historic part of the Chicago landscape. Two decades after Kelly thought he had saved Soldier Field, the Bears' desire for new revenue and a better stadium would clash with the desire to save the historic look of the stadium—and result in a compromise that sparked heated debates throughout the country.

15 *A New Century, a New Stadium*

The Bears and local politicians had proposed so many new stadiums and renovation plans over the years that many Chicagoans may not have believed Soldier Field would really be overhauled until the night in January 2002 when the Bears' postseason ended, Tom and Trevor Kay stepped onto the empty field to play catch, and wrecking crews began tearing out the stadium's seats. Over the forty years leading up to that night, scores of proposals had been floated and some even approved by governmental bodies. Architect Benjamin Wood, whose firm collaborated with Chicago-based Lohan Caprile Goettsch on the design that was eventually implemented, had himself devised at least seven stadium schemes in his six years working with the Bears.

Throughout its history, Soldier Field's fate depended on the political calculations of those who controlled it. Mayor Richard M. Daley often cited the many proposals to build a new stadium, some dating to before the Bears' move to Soldier Field in 1971. Early in his own tenure, a deal to build a domed stadium fell through when the recalcitrant Jim Edgar replaced his more deal-friendly fellow Republican James Thompson as Illinois governor. Beginning with the failed dome and continuing through to the final renovation, Daley turned to a trusted adviser, Edward Bedore, to lead all negotiations on stadium issues. Bedore had been Richard J. Daley's budget director until the elder Daley's death in 1976, and again held that position under Mayor Michael Bilandic and early in the younger Daley's administration. In 1993 Bedore took early retirement and almost immediately received a six-month, $32,000 consulting contract from Daley. He worked steadily on city consulting jobs from then on, forming his own firm, E. B. Enterprises/Illinois, Inc., with Michael Daley, the mayor's brother, as its registered incorporation agent.

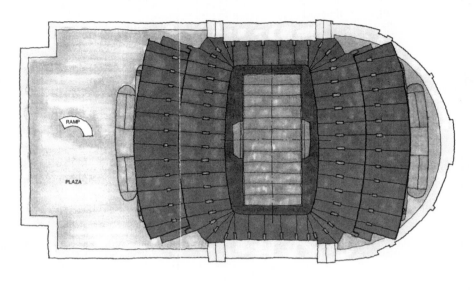

PLAN NORTH SCALE: 1:100 SK-1
sketch
10 MAY 1991

SOLDIER FIELD RENOVATION

This 1991 plan for Soldier Field proposed tearing out the original stands and rotating the playing field 90 degrees. Courtesy Chicago Park District Special Collections.

The first of many failed deals under the new Daley administration was a 1989 proposal for a multipurpose domed stadium adjacent to McCormick Place, a plan put together under John Schmidt, a former Daley aide who at the time chaired the Metropolitan Pier and Exposition Authority. The first McDome, tied to an expansion of McCormick Place that did get built, got as far as a signed lease for the Bears. But the project needed the approval of the Illinois General Assembly, and when it failed to secure it in the fall of 1990, many observers say, the proposal's chances of ever passing decreased, because a few months later Edgar succeeded Thompson. Daley and Edgar never got along, nor did Daley and Bears president Michael McCaskey. Moreover, Daley, who some describe as fiscally Republican, wasn't enthusiastic about creating a stadium solely for the Bears. A political hangover from the 1988 deal to build a new Comiskey Park for the White Sox further muddied the waters.

In 1989 McCaskey stood with NFL commissioner Paul Tagliabue at a press conference to warn that federal authority for tax-exempt bonds for a Chicago stadium, included in a 1986 tax reform bill shepherded by Chicago congressman Dan Rostenkowski, was soon to run out. Daley responded, "You cannot stand here today and say you can build a new stadium for eight [football] games," the number of regular-season Bears home games.[1]

Schmidt said in 2002 that Thompson's departure from office doomed the domed stadium at McCormick Place."My sense of it was that if Thompson was still there, it would have gotten done. He had an enthusiasm for big projects of this type that Edgar never did. And Thompson and Daley had a very good relationship. Edgar and Daley were just like oil and water."[2] In the end, Edgar, Daley, and McCaskey never got close enough to strike a deal. That first failure kicked off a pattern of negotiations that continued throughout the 1990s. For ten years, it seemed that every few months another stadium plan would surface, but each proposal foundered because of personality conflicts among political players.

In the meantime, the Bears' fortunes ebbed and flowed as they struggled to recaptur the glory of their 1985–1986 season. In 1989 the team had its first losing season since 1982, Ditka's first year as head coach. In 1990 and 1991 Ditka pushed a new crop of players to 11–5 records, and made the playoffs each year. Then in 1992, after a 2–2 start, the team and Ditka seemed to implode during a game against the Minnesota Vikings. When a Viking player intercepted a Bears pass and ran for a touchdown, Ditka lost his temper, and the team lost the game, 21–20. The Bears played a few more good games, but ended the season with five wins, eleven losses, and dissension between the coach and his players. Ditka was also making noises about quitting if McCaskey interfered with hiring decisions. Early in January, Ditka was gone.

The Bears tried to get a venue built southeast of Chicago in Gary, employing Wood as architect for the first time, but elected officials in Lake County, Indiana, refused to create a new income tax to fund the project. Several other projects also foundered quickly, including a proposal to install a retractable dome over Soldier Field that Daley said would "be the envy of the National Football League." On September 13, 1996, Daley, who wanted control of any new building and a hand in guiding its construction, met with McCaskey and Edgar to present the $375 million proposal ($175 million of which was to come from Bears revenues). Later that month, the retractable dome plan, called "Soldier Field House," was announced at a City Hall press conference. Daley spoke first, then stood near the podium, fidgeting with a model of the stadium, pushing its miniature retractable dome in and out, as the architects summed up the plan's benefits. McCaskey and Edgar, it turned out, had about as much interest in that plan as Daley did in what others were saying at his press conference. The McCaskey family rejected it outright: it would cost them far too much. Daley underestimated the cost by at least $45 million according to McCaskey—and perhaps as much as $140 million, according to an analysis by an engineering firm that regularly worked for the board that

This 1996 proposal by Mayor Richard M. Daley would have added a movable dome to Soldier Field. Courtesy Chicago Park District Special Collections.

runs McCormick Place, Chicago's government-run convention center.[3] The back-and-forth continued, with several more plans offered just in the fall of 1996. When the dome plan failed, Daley summed up the frustrations of all involved in characteristic style: "Nothing is dead, and everybody is alive."

One of the Bears' standing objections to renovating Soldier Field was that the stadium was too small—the distance between its historic colonnades too narrow—to accommodate enough seats along the sidelines. (The stadium's dimensions had been dictated by the South Park Commission, which wanted it to harmonize with the Field Museum.) When Wood, the Bears' architect, raised the possibility of renovating the structure, the team told him, "We would love to renovate Soldier Field, but we've been told by every major sports planner that it's not possible."

Then, in the fall of 1998, about six months before Ted Phillips took over from McCaskey as Bears president, Wood (then based in Boston) was in Chicago and decided to take another look at Soldier Field's dimensions. Using an electronic range finder to measure the distance between the colonnades, he determined that if the old seating bowl were removed, a new, modern seating bowl could fit. "I set out to prove it wasn't possible, and in my firm and my team trying to prove it wasn't possible, we actually discovered it might be possible," Wood said later. After meeting with the Bears and getting the go-ahead to design a retrofit of Soldier Field, Wood's firm incorporated ideas his team had created for previous stadium proposals. Most crucial to fitting the bowl within the narrow shell was the idea of putting all the high-priced skyboxes on one side and all the club seats on the other. Wood began working with Chicago architect Dirk Lohan's firm to get rid of some of the unsightly parking lots surrounding Soldier Field and transform the area into a more parklike setting. The creation of new green spaces, it was thought, would appeal to park advocates and other reformers steeped in the traditions of Burnham and Ward.[4]

Lohan presented the proposal to Daley. By May 1999 Phillips was confirming that the Bears had come up with a way to save the stadium's columns while creating a new arena, and by July Daley was making friendly noises about it.

The Bears charted a careful public relations course that most press reports followed until well after the plan passed the Illinois legislature. A public relations firm had recommended changing the focus the debate from public financing for the Bears to preserving Soldier Field and creating new lakefront parkland. And for months thereafter, many media reports did indeed emphasize the parkland that would be created by the revamp. The Bears also used an NFL commitment to loan any team building a new stadium $100 million to pressure legislators to agree to the plan. Political insiders say it was around this time that horse-racing magnate Richard Duchossois hosted a cruise for Governor George Ryan on Lake Michigan, and the new Soldier Field deal was born. About twenty people were aboard, including Patrick Ryan, at the time the head of insurance giant Aon Corporation and a part owner of the Bears. Before buying a stake in the team, Pat Ryan had opposed the early 1980s renovation of the stadium. But at the governor's birthday party, as the boat was rounding Navy Pier, Pat Ryan is said to have strolled up to the the governor as he sat on a lower deck and asked, "When are you going to do something about Soldier Field?" After that conversation, the stadium deal got done.[5]

For the architects, a key piece of the puzzle involved figuring out how the stadium had been put together, but original blueprints couldn't be found. The Bears hired V3 Companies, an engineering firm based in the Chicago suburb of Woodridge, to survey the support columns and beams underlying the stadium. At first they worked in the dark, beneath the stands, using flashlights to locate each of fifteen hundred columns precisely. "We didn't know what we were getting ourselves into," Chris Bartosz, V3's director of surveying, told the *Daily Herald*. But two weeks into the survey, they found one of the many hidden offices built under the main structure. Inside was a drafting table—and in one of its drawers was a blueprint with the location of each of the columns clearly marked. The discovery allowed the project to move forward behind the scenes, while the Bears and Bedore worked on coming up with a political deal to make the new stadium a reality.[6]

For a while, the tax money dedicated to the project appeared limited. In August 2000, with cost of the entire project estimated to be $587 million, city and Bears officials proposed that the team and the NFL pony up $350 million, and asked state legislators for only $150 million in tax subsidies. By November 2000, when Daley and Phillips stood together to announce the end of thirty years of haggling, the private contribution had shrunk to $200 million and the tax contribution had ballooned to about $400 million. With the full cost of issuing the bonds for the project, the final public subsidy stood at $432 million. Crucially—and in contrast to the stadium's original construction—there was no need to go to voters to approve the bonds, so the proposal was a go.

"After years of false starts, we finally have a plan that works for Chicago taxpayers, children and families, the museums, the Park District, the Bears and their fans—and it won't cost the people of Chicago a penny," Daley said in the press conference announcing the deal on November 15, 2000. Emphasizing the need to respect the Burnham Plan and beautify the lakefront, he also played up the parkland that would replace some Soldier Field parking lots. The Bears would help fund their share by selling naming rights to the field, Daley said. A few weeks later, Daley said of the Bears, "I think they finally realized, because of Wrigley Field and also the ballpark in Baltimore, how people like older fields. There's something magic about it in a relationship, as compared to a new stadium that has no character, no identity." In a *Sun-Times* op-ed the same day, Daley wrote that the deal protected ordinary Chicago taxpayers by using only hotel taxes collected for the Illinois Sports Facilities Authority to repay the bonds. The Bears were paying more than a third of the upfront cost and would end up paying 70 percent of the cost over the life of the stadium, Daley asserted. The city had agreed to cover any shortfalls in the hotel taxes with sales tax revenues, but Chicago would be reimbursed in future years, Daley said, ensuring that regular taxpayers would never pay a dime. Critics pointed out, however, that the Bears were actually paying a very small portion of even the $200 million in private funds. In reality, $70 million was to come from the sale of seat licenses, $100 million from revenues from visiting teams, and only about $30 million from the Bears directly. In the final reckoning, the Bears ended up paying about $50 million more when the final bill ballooned from $612 million to more about $675 million.[7]

Some familiar with the negotiations say that with Phillips and George Ryan in place and a feasible renovation plan finally available, Bedore saw a chance to put together something that would keep the Bears paying rent to the Chicago Park District for years to come. "I think Ed was in it to try

Illinois secretary of state George Ryan, who would later become governor (second from right), at an antidrug event with Chicago Bears athletes, circa 1991. Courtesy Chicago Park District Special Collections.

to get a deal done," said one source. "There was a lot of times, even on the dome, he wanted to get it done. Daley didn't want to do a deal with Edgar, either; he didn't want to give him credit." Barnaby Dinges, a spokesman for the project, said that what came together was a mutually beneficial deal for the park district and the Bears, a deal that didn't require new taxes. David Doig, the park district's general superintendent at the time, noted that the district's ability to retain the Bears as a rent-paying tenant, renovate Soldier Field without spending any of its own money, and get new parkland at no cost to the district made the renovation worthwhile.

Opponents took the 1983 National Historic Landmark nomination as their guide, playing up the architectural significance of the stadium, as well as the numerous historic events that had taken place there. They argued that the approval process was a sham, and that the deal handed control of the stadium, a public building, to the Bears—a private company—shortchanging the public. Those seeking to preserve Soldier Field emphasized all of its historic uses. Chicagoans remembered triumphant events like the 1966 civil rights rally and the 1926 Eucharistic Congress. But many of the events re-called during the renovation debate, such as the great pageants of the 1930s, had long outlived their relevance. Preservationists overlooked Soldier Field's constant need for renovation, which stemmed from the essential shoddiness of its construction. They ignored the Bears' role in preserving Soldier Field in the early 1970s, which likely saved the stadium from the fate of buildings like the Coliseum, the International Amphitheatre, and Chicago Stadium, all demolished between 1982 and 1999. Renovation proponents emphasized Soldier Field's longstanding defects and pre-NFL design—its shortage of restrooms and bad sightlines got mentioned most often. Meanwhile, they discounted the possibility that fundamentally altering the stadium's design might erase its historic nature. Everyone romanticized its history, paying little heed to the debates over its designation as a memorial and its role in building and maintaining the Kelly and Daley machines.

The plan to transform Soldier Field passed the state legislature quickly, with only a few false starts, and Ryan signed the bill on January 5, 2001, in a ceremony at Soldier Field. From the moment the proposal went before the Chicago Plan Commission in March 2001, however, controversy raged—although in retrospect, the course was already set. Park advocates filed two lawsuits against the tax-backed project's legality, one attacking the approval of the proposal by the Plan Commission, the other challenging the $406 million in tax-backed bonds for the project. The latter suit eventually reached the Illinois Supreme Court.

Opponents enlisted several economists who were skeptical that the benefits of remaking Soldier Field as a modern football stadium would extend beyond the shareholders in the Bears organization. The University of Chicago's Allen Sanderson had long contended that team owners win out with tax-financed stadiums while cities see little added economic activity. Arguments over the economic benefits of redoing Soldier Field echoed similar civic disputes in other cities—and earlier debates in Chicago.

Richard J. Daley, from his earliest mentions of replacing Soldier Field, had always looked for a way to finance a new multipurpose stadium without dipping too deep into the city's coffers. A 1964 mayoral commission report reached possibly one of the most honest conclusions ever by a government-sponsored study about government-owned stadiums: modern sports stadiums aren't profitable. Every major one built up to that time had required public subsidy. As George Halas, and later his heirs, pressed for a new stadium, their allies always touted the economic boon to the city. Richard J. Daley and his successors embraced other, similarly massive public works projects, but for years the argument that tax money should not subsidize wealthy sports team owners helped scuttle each stadium plan.

The first sign of a changing political environment came in the mid-1980s.

As the White Sox threatened to move to Florida, Chicagoans debated whether building a new Comiskey Park using money from a new hotel tax made sense. Mayor Harold Washington embraced the idea, and his successor, Eugene Sawyer, worked with Republican governor James Thompson to create the new tax—and the Illinois Sports Facilities Authority—during the fall session of the state legislature in 1988. Hotel operators tried to derail the tax, contending it would drive away conventioneers and tourists, but failed.

By the late 1990s hotel tax revenues had grown enough to allow a new bond issue. So when it came time to propose the Bears' new Soldier Field plan, Richard M. Daley and his allies could claim that no money for the project would come from Chicago taxpayers. With the country's attention fixed on the disputed 2000 presidential election, Daley and Ryan pushed through the Soldier Field renovation with little debate. Only well after Ryan signed the legislation did opponents of the plan wake up to the full meaning of what had happened.

Their battle really began at the Chicago Plan Commission in March 2001, and proceeded to the city council and the park district board. But critics of the plan failed to sway any of those bodies: Daley controlled them all. On the day the park board considered the proposal that summer, Daley joked about park advocates' claims that the new Soldier Field would violate the Burnham Plan. "Did they talk to him yesterday?" Daley asked. "Only they can talk to Daniel Burnham." His point was clear: park advocates hold no monopoly on interpreting Burnham. After all, as the history of Soldier Field shows, except for the South Park Commission under Edward Kelly the mayors of Chicago since Big Bill Thompson can claim far more credit for realizing Burnham's plan than any reformers.

Meanwhile, at the park board meeting that authorized the renovation, dozens of renovation foes who turned out to denounce it failed to realize they had to sign in to speak. Because of the mix-up, the board approved the proposal without discussion and without comment. "They didn't tell us we had to sign in," said Marius "Scotty" Gallagher, one of many World War II veterans who opposed the renovation in part because of the Bears' scheme to sell naming rights to the field (scuttled after the September 11, 2001, attacks). "I don't think they were really honest."

The old Soldier Field found defenders in some unlikely places. The *Tribune*'s editorial board in the 1960s and 1970s had campaigned for a new stadium, in 1975 calling Soldier Field "the great white elephant by the lake." In the 2000s the board—which plays no part in the coverage of news at the paper—looked askance at the economics of sports palaces and the aesthetics of the Bears–park district proposal. At the same time, the newspaper's reporting staff wrote about those questioning the project and reported on some of its political intrigue and possible drawbacks. Newspapers sometimes report civic conflict relentlessly, yet in this case there had been little conflict to report until after Ryan signed the bill. It's not clear what caused opponents' delayed reaction: whether they failed to see the full implications of the plan, were distracted by the national distraction of the 2000 election, or were inattentive to what was happening in Springfield. Not until early 2001 did Chicago preservationists and longtime Daley allies begin denouncing the renovation—and not until then did Chicago newspapers start paying attention to their objections. Understandably, backers of the project, who had thought their work selling the plan largely done, reacted angrily.

The lawsuits against the plan failed. One revealed in court that the Bears expected to triple their profits at the stadium, from about $11 million a year in 1999 to about $33 million in 2003, the first season in the new stadium. The judge in the lawsuit challenging the bond legislation hinted he found the economic arguments against it persuasive, but said they were immaterial to the legal case.[8]

As the court cases and appeals dragged on, the park district moved out of its headquarters at the north end of Soldier Field, and demolition of the building began late in the summer of 2001. When terrorists flew hijacked planes into New York's World Trade Center and the Pentagon on September 11, 2001, the NFL season was delayed two weeks. The Bears resumed the season playing better than expected, and after winning a playoff berth against the Philadelphia Eagles, the last Bears game at the old Soldier Field was scheduled for January 19, 2002. By then, crews had already demolished the concrete bleachers at the north end of the stadium, where Edmund Kelly had hoped to establish a tradition of championship tennis, and where Emmett Kelly's circus elephants had paraded. The Bears lost to the Eagles, and after a quick cleanup, wrecking crews began uprooting seats in the north stands. "They were ripping out seats as soon as people stood up and started to walk away," said Ed Stogenson, who worked for electrical contractor Siemens on the renovation. Fans grabbed whatever they could get as souvenirs. Some lamented the old stadium's passing, and others bid it good riddance. Many agreed with Bill Warner of Spring Grove, who said he had no nostalgia "at all" about the stadium: "We need something new."[9]

The latest renovation at Soldier Field echoed the script of prior ones: rewarding politically connected businesses in a selection process hidden from public view. The primary contractors, including the companies that made up the joint venture that oversaw the project, signed their pacts without any of the usual government contracting procedures or openness. But about $340 million in work was bid out, with about $120 million worth of contracts going to minority- and women-owned businesses. A few of those contractors became embroiled in controversies of their own. Most prominently, Monterrey Security Consultants, co-owned by Santiago Solis, the brother of Daley ally

The Chicago Park District administration building, seen from the top of the 1979 north stands in 1999, just after the plan that became the 2001–2003 renovation was first floated. Courtesy Chicago Tribune.

Alderman Danny Solis, won a $1 million contract to guard the construction site, as well as stadium security work after the renovation. Just before Monterrey was awarded the contract, state regulators hit the company with a $22,000 fine, in part because it hired as an armed guard someone who lacked state authorization to carry a gun. Monterrey later received city certification as a minority-owned firm even though Santiago Solis and his partner violated a city ordinance by running the company while working for the city.

The project started off a month behind schedule and ran over budget almost from the beginning. The contractors made up for most of the time lags, however, so it finished more or less on time. And no wonder: any contractor that caused a delay faced a $4.5 million fine for each game canceled if the stadium didn't open on September 29, 2003.

When demolition started, crews discovered that the stadium contained more asbestos than originally thought, and cleanup costs escalated while work to remove the material ate up time. Then, when the main demolition ended, the city's Buildings Department required National Restoration Systems, tasked with repairing the remaining concrete, to do a full-scale reassessment of all the concrete in the stadium. The contractor found four times as many defects as expected, and renovation slowed for two months while they repaired more than sixty thousand square feet of exposed concrete.[10]

Despite the delays, by October 2002 contractors had almost completed the old structure's renovation, and the area inside the rising walls of the new seating bowl looked like a modern football stadium. Crews worked twenty hours a day, pouring concrete, fitting the glass skin of the east side of the arena to its metal skeleton, and getting set to turn on the new stadium's electricity. They raced to install enough glass to allow work to continue through the winter.

At that point, the project had required about $13.5 million in change

Demolition work had already chewed through most of the north stands less than two weeks after the last game at the old Soldier Field in early 2002. Courtesy Chicago Tribune.

By the end of 2002, construction on the skeleton of the new south side of the stadium by the main gate, Gate 0, had already commenced. Courtesy Chicago Tribune.

orders for unexpected work. During excavation work for the field, workers found a few artifacts of old Soldier Field and Chicago's past, including druggist bottles and broken china from Chicago hotels, project manager Alice Hoffman said. Work was back on schedule overall, and crews installing the glass walls of the east side of the stadium—the side with the skyboxes—were about a month ahead of schedule. Only small parts of the steel structure remained to be placed, including supports for the two giant video screens at the north and south ends of the field. Meanwhile, though, the Bears weren't doing as well. Playing during the construction at Memorial Stadium at the University of Illinois at Urbana-Champaign—another Holabird and Roche building—they finished 4–12 for the 2002 season, completely out of the running for a playoff berth.

By April 2003 critics began to see a monstrosity rising on the lakefront. "I called it earlier 'post-modern neoclassical junk.' Metal and glass clash with cement pillars," said Chicagoan Paul Knudtson, as he walked along Burnham Harbor with his wife Nicole a few months before the new stadium opened. But "as long as the product on the field is better than that which surrounds it, it will all come out in the wash." Others were more approving but questioned whether the new Soldier Field could really be as good for fans as advertised. "It's a beautiful building, but I wonder who can afford the tickets," said James Cotton, of the south suburbs, after visiting the nearby Field Museum. "I wonder if the average person is going to be able to afford to see a game there." While most critics focused on aesthetics, those who looked forward to the completed overhaul concentrated on more mundane aspects, including new parking garages.

Chicago's architectural community also stood divided: many prominent architects were displeased, but growing numbers spoke out in favor of the new stadium. One outspoken critic was Robert Cassidy, the editor in chief of *Building Design & Construction*, a trade magazine for the construction industry. In a 2002 editorial, Cassidy wrote that "just looking at it makes me sick." Readers reacted strongly; some two hundred responded, with about 60 percent siding with Cassidy. "If this were elsewhere, I might have less concern, although not undiluted concern. But it's a real effrontery to the public and to our distinctive architecture here," Cassidy said. Project architect Lohan defended the stadium in Cassidy's magazine, comparing Soldier Field to the John Hancock Building: Chicagoans criticized the Hancock when it rose in the early 1970s, he noted, but most now consider it an icon of the city. Although many attacked the stadium design, Lohan and his collaborators received support from some prominent city architects. One was Sarah Dunn, of the Chicago firm Urban Lab, who said she felt the contrast between old and new worked. "If they were able to tear down, we would have gotten a typical retro thing," Dunn said. But "the way it just squeezes in, there's sort of a nice tension between the new and the old."

Later that summer, a group of former Bears players touring the new stadium as part of a press event to promote a charity flag-football game also raved about it—or at least, its insides. Jim McMahon seemed taken aback by the look of the new arena inside the shell of the old stadium. "That was a little strange. I guess that is modern art. But all the players are worried about is the field and the condition of the field."[11]

Although the *New York Times* gave the stadium a good review, many others weren't so kind—except when it came to actually watching a game there. One of the most merciless commentators was the *Daily Herald*'s Barry Rozner. Dripping sarcasm, he asked: "Look, for $630 million, how could you not have cushy seats, clean bathrooms and edible hotdogs? I'm not sure that's cause for celebration. . . . It remains inexcusable that the Bears and Mayor Daley conspired to desecrate a war memorial by dropping a spaceship inside the colonnades, and then stuck the public with a $430 million bill." The Bears remained unfazed by the criticism. "Fans are going to be really wowed by the intimacy of the building, the sight lines, all the state-of-the-art amenities. At the same time it's going to have a little bit of the old feel because of the colonnades, and also because of the cantilevered sections. You have overhangs now. Not many new stadiums have that," Phillips said as the first reviews were coming in.[12]

With the construction team having overcome all delays, the new Soldier Field hosted its first event on September 17, 2003, more than a week before it opened to the public. In a fitting reminder of the stadium's original City Beautiful purposes, the Soldier Field Kick-Off Gala benefited a group devoted to expanding the recreational and work opportunities of Chicago's young people—and one with tight connections to Edward Kelly's successor, Richard M. Daley. The fund-raiser, its coffers packed by companies with city and Soldier Field contracts, raised $3 million for After-School Matters, a youth tutoring and mentoring program founded by the mayor's wife, Maggie Daley. In a less homespun echo of the children's dedication of the original stadium, the Percy Julian High School marching band and other teen groups performed. The following week, on Saturday, September 27, 2003, the renovated stadium opened with a rededication ceremony.

Unlike the old stadium, the new Soldier Field saw only two real opening days: the day of the rededication, and the Bears' return to play the Green Bay Packers two days later. The Saturday rededication ceremony began with music by the Great Lakes Navy Band. Parks superintendent Doig then began the solemnities. After praise from Brigadier General Randal Thomas, head of the Illinois National Guard, JROTC students from Benito Juarez and Eisenhower High Schools raised the flags, and members of the U.S. Army's 178th Infantry shot off a salute. Daley unveiled a refurbished statue of an American World War I soldier—a doughboy—that now stands inside the entrance to the stadium. After the event, Daley proclaimed the renovation "an awful success. . . . Architecturally, I think it's just as good as any other, better than any other field."

Dedication day was also "Meet Your Seat Day" for all the Bears ticket holders who had been waiting twenty months to see how the new stadium would turn out. Jim Paulus and his fiancée Sharon Coleman climbed to the top row of stadium seats. "You have to be a very big fan to sit that high up, especially in 20-degree weather," said Paulus, "but the view should be great." The extended rededication ceremony annoyed some fans, who had expected to get in to see their new seats promptly at 11 a.m. Once inside, though, many gushed over the new arena. The restrooms gleamed. All the seats had good sightlines. The doughboy and other new memorial features honored America's war dead in a new and impressive way. And the massive television monitors at each end of the stadium looked stupendous. "For all those naysayers who say it looks like a spaceship or a fruit bowl, I say just come inside and look at it," said Kathy Voss.

Two days later, on Monday evening, fans jammed the stadium to its new capacity of 61,500 to see the Bears face off against their archrivals, the Green

Aerial photo of the new Soldier Field on opening night, September 29, 2003, showing the extent to which the old structure is overwhelmed by the new. Courtesy Chicago Tribune.

Bay Packers. After more solemn words, the game started with a spectacular fireworks show. But the Bears lost, despite all the hype, 38–23. And in an echo of the first football game ever at Soldier Field, between Austin High School and Louisville Male High School, a player from the visiting team, Ahman Green, scored the first touchdown.[13]

The old Soldier Field's use as a venue for trade shows, conventions, and private meetings in addition to games and public gatherings had mostly gone by the wayside by 1971, giving way to sports games and rock concerts. When the Bears proposed the $675 million renovation project, watchdogs such as Friends of the Parks said it would be better to build a new stadium for the Bears elsewhere and turn Soldier Field into a venue for other public events. City and park officials countered that keeping the Bears as a tenant helps subsidize other park district operations and that the new stadium, while designed with football in mind, would be able to accommodate other uses. (A $3.5 million yearly subsidy from the hotel tax helps keep the stadium financially viable.) The Chicago Park District and SMG, the private managers of the field, had little trouble booking events once the stadium opened. Along with six soccer games, two days of high school football were played in the fall of 2003, including a Mum Bowl playoff game for park district football teams and the Prep Bowl.

Part of the new arena doubles as a publicly owned banquet hall, with views

The Packers' Ahman Green, pursued by Bears Warrick Holdman (53) and Mike Green (43), during the opening night game at Soldier Field. Green scored the first touchdown at the new stadium, and the Packers went on to win, 38–23. Courtesy Chicago Tribune

of Lake Michigan and the original east colonnade. On game days, the new field's club lounge is only to open fans with club or suite tickets, but as soon as the renovation finished it started renting out for everything from charity fund-raisers to wedding receptions. In addition to the eight Chicago Bears games in the fall of 2003, by the end of the year the stadium saw about fifty other events, partly due to the lounge's popularity. Jerry Gerami, AT&T's regional vice president for business sales, organized a meeting of the company's Illinois salespeople there in fall 2003. More than 150 attended, and many thought having the event at the lounge was "exciting," Gerami said.

Officials started bringing public festivals to the surrounding parkland a few months after the stadium reopened, beginning with a winter festival the week after Christmas that included a snowman-making contest, taking advantage of snowmaking equipment purchased for the sledding hill southeast of the field, said Tim LeFevour, manager of Soldier Field for SMG. A snowboarding competition was held the same winter at the sledding hill, and in early 2004 many charity walks and runs that in the past had started out in Grant Park kicked off in Burnham Park near Soldier Field. "I think we've just begun to touch the tip of the iceberg of how the stadium, the club and the rest are going to be used," said Barnaby Dinges a few months after the Bears settled in. [14]

One promised benefit of the stadium was delayed until the weekend after Thanksgiving 2003, largely because of ongoing minor construction work. For years, skyboxes had blocked public access to the historic colonnades, but in the stadium's new incarnation anyone can walk among the iconic columns, except on game days.

Some concerns remained. Although the remodeled stadium has up to three times as many restrooms as the old Soldier Field, male fans—who substantially outnumber women at Bears games—still complained of long lines during the first season. [15]

A bigger, if less visceral, failure involved the project's budget. Throughout construction, project and Chicago Park District officials had regularly insisted that work was progressing "on time, on budget." But in the end, the renovation went about $63 million over. Despite the project manager's vow that contingency funds would cover increased costs, the overruns were paid for by the Bears. Final spending documents generated by the park district and the Illinois Sports Facilities Authority, which financed the project, put the total cost at around $695 million, including $31 million in bond financing. Aside from Soldier Field, its parking lots, and the surrounding parkland, the budget also included $21 million for renovations at U.S. Cellular Field (the new name for the new Comiskey Park)—a political sweetener that helped ease the revamp plan through the legislature. The *Tribune* reported that the work had entailed $72 million in change orders, charges resulting from changes in the scope of work specified in contracts.

Phillips later said that several things contributed to the rising costs, including meeting Chicago's building code, which does not have stadium-specific guidelines, and fitting the new arena within the shell of the 1924 stadium. "Where the buildings connect, they had to be very precise, and it was literally impossible to know up front exactly" the cost or extent of the work, he explained.

Some extra costs were apparent early in the project, but others came to light just before the new arena opened. In March 2002 the *Tribune* reported that costs for asbestos removal at the field had increased from an originally budgeted $4 million to $14.5 million. The final bill ran to almost $18 million. Smaller items also swelled the tab, including $1 million to create a team store. Moreover, the actual charges for some basic construction items ran much higher than contract estimates, including costs for electrical power and lighting work—up from $20.8 million to $32.9 million. Marc Ganis, president of SportsCorp Ltd., a Chicago-based stadium-consulting firm, nonetheless expressed surprise about the overruns, given the large cushion built into the budget in anticipation of increasing prices.[16]

One thing that the large budget did allow for was finally putting several tangible memorials at Soldier Field, something veterans groups had been seeking since the days of Edward Kelly. At a Veterans Day 2003 ceremony at the north entrance to Soldier Field, Mayor Richard M. Daley and others unveiled a new bronze bas-relief sculpture, *Chicago's Tribute to Freedom*, by husband-and-wife sculptors Jeffrey Varilla and Anna Koh-Varilla. The bas-relief, depicting modern-day members of the armed forces standing in front of the Chicago skyline with their families, was the last of several memorials at the renovated stadium to be completed. "Before, Soldier Field was just a name. Now it's a memorial to the men and women who have served our nation," said 11th Ward alderman James Balcer, a Marine Corps veteran of the Vietnam War. [17]

The National Park Service was less sentimental. In the 1980s the federal agency had added the stadium to the prestigious list of National Historic Landmarks. Now it looked skeptically at the stadium renovation. Even before the park district approved the renovation, the National Park Service wrote to Doig, warning that "the scale and massing of the original building will be substantially altered by the proposed new construction," endangering its landmark status. For four years, the Daley administration lobbied to keep the designation, arguing that the plan would "preserve Soldier Field's historic colonnades" and reinvigorate a building that had fallen into such a state of disrepair that it was practically unusable. (Through all the public discussion of the 2001–2003 renovation, the more than $80 million the park district had already put into refurbishing the stadium during the Bears' tenancy hardly rated a mention.) Daley continued to hail it as a great achievement for the city. "Our goal was to include all the best features of a modern stadium, while preserving and enhancing some of the features that made it historically significant," he said in a speech in August 2004 to the Association for a Better New York.

Finally in 2006, after much wrangling, the Park Service rendered its verdict: whatever its virtues, the new stadium could no longer be considered the same Soldier Field. Project spokesman Dinges continued to argue that the stadium was now "an even greater historic place." But in 2003 visitors could no longer look out over the grand arena where Billy Graham and Cardinal Mundelein had once addressed their flocks, Charles Lindbergh had beckoned Chicago to take to the air, and Martin Luther King Jr. had exhorted his followers to forge a new city. The plan "crossed the line in terms of too much renovation," a Park Service spokesman said. Whatever might be written about the stadium from then on, it was a new Soldier Field, reinvented for a new Chicago that the old stadium had helped create.[18]

ACKNOWLEDGMENTS

This book had its origins in chats I had with my wife, Ann Weiler, and my editor, William Savage, as I covered the reconfiguration of Soldier Field. Without Bill's constant encouragement and Ann's constant support, it would not have been written. My editors at the *Tribune* during the stadium revamp, particularly William Rood and Bob Secter, as well as Jim O'Shea, encouraged and counseled me. John Kass, who guided me through difficult times just before I took up the parks beat and my Soldier Field coverage, deserves my undying gratitude. My mother, Penny Ford, and my sister, Dolores Rose Ford, provided invaluable research assistance.

Many people helped get this project off the ground and into print, especially Robert Devens, Emilie Sandoz, Anne Goldberg, and Joel Score of the University of Chicago Press. No government body in America probably has a more helpful and thorough historian than Julia Bachrach of the Chicago Park District, who along with other district staffers assisted mightily in research for this book. Archivists who take pride in the vital history they preserve receive too little credit for their work, and Julia deserves great praise for hers. Staffers at several other archives also deserve thanks, including those at the Newberry Library, the Art Institute of Chicago's Burnham and Ryerson Libraries, the Billy Graham Center at Wheaton College, the University of Illinois at Chicago's Richard J. Daley Library, the Chicago Public Library's Harold Washington Library Center, the Chicago History Museum, and the National Cowboy & Western History Museum. Unfortunately, some staffers at the *Chicago Tribune*'s own reference and archive library who assisted in my initial research and helped gather photographs for this book have since lost their jobs.

The public officials and private people I interviewed in the course of my coverage of the 2001–2003 debate and renovation all deserve special thanks. Despite our disputes over the years, former parks general superintendent David Doig and spokeswoman Angie Amores always let bygones be bygones. Edmund Kelly and Erwin "Red" Weiner provided valuable insights into the district's use of Soldier Field over the years, although Weiner and I were unable to complete a formal interview before his death. I thank my father's longtime friend Joseph A. Morris for providing an introduction to Weiner. Chicago's Graham Foundation provided a generous grant that allowed us to add twenty-eight illustrations and increase the size of this book. The Friends of the Parks and the Landmarks Preservation Council of Illinois also gave invaluable help.

This book depended on the work of countless other reporters, editors, and photographers. It is a cliché to say that newspapers write the first draft of history. Reading numerous yellowed and brittle clippings in the *Tribune*'s morgue gave me a new appreciation for Soldier Field's history and sparked my interest in its place in twentieth-century Chicago. Especially worthy of praise for their work on Soldier Field are my colleagues Andrew Martin, Laurie Cohen, Gary Washburn, and Blair Kamin, as well as the *Tribune*'s football reporters and David Mendell and Jon Yates. Martin, Washburn, Cohen, and Mendell are no longer at the *Tribune* and are missed.

Finally, my love of Chicago's history comes from the long bond my family shares with the city through my grandparents John Edward Ford and Helen Cranley Ford. My grandmother's family first came to Chicago in 1857 or before, and her father survived the Great Fire. My wish to share that history comes from the storytelling of my mother's parents, journalists Margaret Triggs Ziemer and Paul Henry Ziemer, who served as a corporal in the U.S. Army Air Corps. This book is dedicated to their memory.

NOTES

Many of the newspaper articles cited in this book were accessed, in PDF format, either at http://www.proquest.com or http://www.newspaperarchive.com, which provide photographic reproductions of earlier microfilm records. I have noted the URLs and access dates only for online articles accessed in other formats. Other articles are from the *Chicago Tribune*'s clip files or the personal clip file I accumulated while covering the 2001–2003 renovation of Soldier Field.

ABBREVIATIONS

Newspapers

CA   *Chicago American (Daily or Evening)* and *Chicago's American*
CD   *Chicago Defender (national edition)*
CDD *Chicago Daily Defender*
CDN *Chicago Daily News*
CDT *Chicago Daily Tribune*
CHE *Chicago Herald and Examiner*
CO   *Chicago Today*
CST *Chicago Sun-Times*
CT   *Chicago Tribune*
LAT *Los Angeles Times*
NYT *New York Times*
WP   *Washington Post*

Wire Services

AP   *Associated Press*
UP   *United Press*
UPI *United Press International*

Archives

BGC/PTMJ   *Papers of Torrey Maynard Johnson, Billy Graham Center, Wheaton, Illinois*

CPD/SF   *Soldier Field collection, Special Collections, Chicago Park District Headquarters*

CUL   *Archives of the Chicago Urban League, University of Illinois at Chicago Daley Library*

PSPC   *Proceedings of the South Park Commission, Special Collections, Chicago Park District Headquarters*

INTRODUCTION

1. Rudyard Kipling, "Poor Chicago Kipling-Struck," in *Selected Works of Rudyard Kipling*, vol. 3 (New York: Peter Fenelon Collier, 1900), 275–77.

2. Charles Dwight Willard, "Chicago the Giant," *LAT*, Sept. 1, 1893.

3. Lambert Tree, "Chicago: Some of Its Merits and Demerits," *CDT*, Oct. 14, 1900.

4. "Anarchist Starts Murder Mission," *CDT*, June 2, 1904; "Seals Lips of Emma Goldman," *CDT*, Oct. 3, 1901.

5. James L. Merriner, *Grafters and Goo Goos: Corruption and Reform in Chicago, 1833–2003* (Carbondale: Southern Illinois University Press, 2004), 95–96.

6. William H. Wilson, *The City Beautiful Movement* (Baltimore: Johns Hopkins University Press, 1989), 54–62.

7. See, for example, Charles Zueblin, *A Decade of Civic Development* (Chicago: University of Chicago Press, 1905), 59–82.

8. John Coleman Adams, "What a Great City Might Be: Lessons from the White City," *New England Magazine*, n.s. 14 (March 1896), 3–13, http://www.library.cornell.edu/Reps/DOCS/adams.htm (accessed March 13, 2005).

9. Kevin Mattson, *Creating a Democratic Public: The Struggle for Urban Participatory Democracy during the Progressive Era* (University Park: Pennsylvania State University, 1998), 16–20; Wilson, *City Beautiful Movement*, 78–86; "For a Paris by the Lake," *CDT*, Feb. 11, 1897.

10. Lois Wille, *Forever Open, Clear, and Free: The Struggle for Chicago's Lakefront* (Chicago: University of Chicago Press, 1991), 73.

11. "Plan for New Park," *CDT*, Oct. 11, 1896.

12. John E. Findling, "Chicago Loses the 1904 Olympics," *Journal of Olympic History* 12, no. 3 (Oct. 2004): 26–27.

13. Julia Snyderman Bachrach, "Park Districts," in *The Encyclopedia of Chicago*, ed. James R. Grossman, Ann Durkin Keating, and Janice L. Reiff (Chicago: University of Chicago Press, 2004) 601–2.

14. Daniel H. Burnham and Edward H. Bennett, *Plan of Chicago* (Chicago: Commercial Club of Chicago, 1909), 10–29.

15. See, for example, Laurence C. Gerkens, "Community Aesthetics and Planning," *Planning Commissioners Journal*, no. 7 (Nov./Dec. 1992), http://www.plannersweb.com/wfiles/w461.html (accessed May 13, 2005).

16. Burnham and Bennett, *Plan*, 1.

17. Burnham and Bennett, *Plan*, 110; "Seek Park Site for Big Museum," *CDT*, Feb. 9, 1911; "Ask Site in Park for Big Museum," *CDT*, March 14, 1911.

18. Howard Gray Brownson, "A History of the Illinois Central Railroad to 1870," University of Illinois Studies in the Social Sciences 4 (1915), 337–39; "I. C. Must Pay Up; State Wins Taxes," *CDT*, Oct. 29, 1910; Wille, *Forever Open*, 26–37; "People to Own the Shore; Field Museum at 12th Street," *CDT*, Dec. 12, 1911. Wille identifies the 1910 decision as the key one involving the IC's rights to the lakefront. Although the U.S. Supreme Court's *Illinois Central R. Co. v. Illinois*, 146 U.S. 387, probably was more important for the lakefront as a whole, the state court's decision on the IC's tax payments appears to have spurred the deal that led to the Field Museum getting the railroad's land between Roosevelt Road and 13th Street, including the north end of the Soldier Field site.

19. Charles H. Wacker, "Little Ballot 'Yes' Means New Era for Chicago," *CDT*, Nov. 2, 1914.

20. "Business Men to Revivify Chicago Spirit," *CDT*, May 28, 1915.

21. Douglas Bukowski, "Big Bill Thompson: The 'Model' Politician," in *The Mayors: the Chicago Political Tradition*, ed. Paul Michael Green and Melvin G. Holli (Carbondale: Southern Illinois University Press, 1995). On Thompson and the Chicago Plan, see pp. 38–40, 67–68; on his antiwar stance, 64.

22. Lloyd Wendt and Herman Kogan, *Big Bill of Chicago* (Indianapolis: Bobbs-Merrill, 1953), 150–53, esp. 150; Bukowski, "Big Bill," 40.

23. Wendt and Kogan, *Big Bill*, 310–11; Douglas Bukowski, *Big Bill Thompson, Chicago, and the Politics of Image* (Urbana: University of Illinois Press, 1998), 131. Inflation in this book was calculated using the calculator at the U.S. Bureau of Labor Statistics Web site, http://data.bls.gov/cgi-bin/cpicalc.pl.

24. "Citizens Today Start Plan to Honor War Dead," *CDT*, July 2, 1918.

25. "Obelisk for Hero Memorial," *CDT*, Dec. 2, 1918.

26. "Hero Memorial," *CDT*, March 9, 1919; "3 Grant Park Sites Discussed for Memorial," *CDT*, July 16, 1918.

27. "'Reconstruction' Platform of Chicago Plan Commission," *CDT*, Dec. 14, 1918; Everett Brown, letter to South Park Commissioners, Feb. 11, 1907, CPD/SF; "Thompson in Pulpit Puts Youth First," *CDT*, April 12, 1915. Though the *Tribune* and Thompson often butted heads in later years, and Thompson and *Tribune* publisher Robert R. McCormick are remembered as enemies, in the early months of his administration at least, Thompson often received positive coverage from the paper.

28. Oscar E. Hewitt, "Vast Stadium as Memorial to Heroes Pictured," *CDT*, Feb. 23, 1919.

29. "Engineers Vote for $10,000,000 Hero Memorial," *CDT*, March 22, 1919.

30. Bukowski, "Big Bill," 66.

31. Hewitt, "Vast Stadium"; PSPC, May 26, 1919.

CHAPTER 1

1. See, for example, Lloyd Wendt and Herman Kogan, *Big Bill of Chicago* (Indianapolis: Bobbs-Merrill, 1953), 100–115; "Mayor Admits Defeat," *CDT*, March 12, 1919; "Business Men Compare Mayor with Sweitzer," *CDT*, March 16, 1919.

2. See, for example, John R. Schmidt, "William Dever: A Chicago Political Fable," in *The Mayors: the Chicago Political Tradition*, ed. Paul Michael Green and Melvin G. Holli (Carbondale: Southern Illinois University Press, 1995), 84–87.

3. "$10,000,000 Memorial by Soldier Labor!" *CHE*, May 4, 1919; "Cities Deciding on War Memorials," *American Architect* 115, no. 2249 (Jan. 29, 1919): 176; "An Editorial Suggestion," *CHE*, May 4, 1919; Louis Allen, "Westward the Course of Stadia Takes Its Way," *Overland Monthly and Out West Magazine* 78, no. 6 (Dec. 1921): 21.

4. "Victory Concourse for Chicago to Heroes' Memory," *CDT*, March 1, 1919.

5. "Plan Big Stadium for Grant Park," *CDT*, May 28, 1918.

6. "A Stadium for Grant Park," *CDT*, May 24, 1919.

7. "How Chicago Will Benefit," *CDT*, July 22, 1919.

8. "Mayor Asks Chance to Plead for Huge Stadium," *CHE*, May 2, 1919.

9. Western European and American culture often emphasized modern Western civilization's connections with, and superiority to, ancient Greek and Roman culture. Dead (and especially assassinated) American presidents were commonly depicted in togas, their heads adorned with laurel wreaths. When the era of the modern stadium began, with the Yale and Harvard bowls, there were frequent and favorable comparisons to the sports stadiums of Greece and Rome.

10. "How Lake Front Will Look," *CHE*, April 18, 1921.

11. "Chicagoans, Get Together," *CA*, June 23, 1919.

12. PSPC, May 26, 1919.

13. "Chicagoans, Get Together for the Building of the Athletic Stadium in Grant Park," *CA*, June 23, 1919.

14. PSPC, June 4 and June 25, 1919.

15. "Plans Stadium to Seat 150,000 in Grant Park," *CDT*, May 1, 1919.

16. Dwight H. Perkins, letter to South Park Commissioners, July 18, 1919, CPD/SF.

17. See letter from secretary, South Park Commissioners, to competitors in stadium competition, Aug. 11, 1919, CPD/SF; also "The Competition Program," *American Architect* 117, no. 2304 (Feb. 18, 1920): 206.

18. "'Beauty First' Is Keynote for Stadium Plans," *CDT*, Aug. 22, 1919.

19. Ibid.

20. Zachary T. Davis and William F. Kramer, "Competition for a Stadium on the Lake Front, Chicago, Part II," *American Architect* 117, no. 2305 (Feb. 25, 1920): 241.

21. Lois Wille's *Forever Open, Clear, and Free*, for example, mentions that the stadium was designed to fit, physically, with the Field Museum. It appears that a primary source for this was a comment by Park District general superintendent George T. Donoghue, quoted by the *Sun-Times* in a February 1958 article that was part of a series decrying the stadium as "Chicago's Sports White Elephant."

22. Dwight H. Perkins, letter re: stadium competition, Sept. 20, 1919, CPD/SF.

23. Grant Park Stadium competition jury, letter to the South Park Commission re: competion winner, Dec. 1, 1919, CPD/SF; John A. Holabird Jr., "Should Soldier Field Be Saved? The Answer Is No," *Crain's Chicago Business* Aug. 30, 1999; Paul E. Sprague and Edmund L. Kelly, "Submission to Illinois Historic Sites Advisory Council," Sept. 6, 1983, 6–7, Ryerson and Burnham Libraries, Art Institute of Chicago.

24. Holabird & Roche, "Description Submitted with Design for a Stadium on the Lake Front, Chicago," *American Architect* 117, no. 2304 (Feb. 18, 1920): 208–210.

25. "Ward Gives His 'O.K.' to Stadium Project," *CA*, June 1, 1911.

26. "Thirty Members of the University Sail with Ambulance Unit Today," *Harvard Crimson*, May 19, 1917; "Chicago Honors Bentley as Her First War Dead," *CDT*, Sept. 24, 1917; "Son of Chicago Pastor Killed in War Airplane," *CDT*, Sept. 17, 1917.

27. "Paul Bentley's Friend Tells How He Died," *CDT*, July 27, 1918.

28. "End of War Still Far Off," *CDT*, Oct. 14, 1917.

29. "Let Stadium Be Dedicated to Heroes—Legion," *CDT*, Oct. 16, 1924.

30. See, for example, "$20,000,000 Bond Issue Stake in Primary," *CDT*, March 7, 1920; "Approve the South Shore Bonds," *CDT*, Feb. 21, 1920; "Big Bill Is the Big Bunk," *CDT*, July 26, 1920; Oscar Hewitt, "Lundin's Eye on Parks as Fresh Party Pastures," *CDT*, Aug. 21, 1920.

31. Arthur M. Evans, "Voters Asked to Put Life in Dream of City," *CDT*, Feb. 19, 1920.

32. "Civic Societies Unite in Urging Bonds for Park," *CDT*, Feb. 23, 1920.

33. "Park Bonds Win," *CDT*, Feb. 25, 1920.

34. PSPC, Dec. 30, 1919, July 22, 1920, and Oct. 21, 1921. The stadium model, for which sculptor Joseph Dux was paid $454.15, was destroyed—intentionally—less than two years later.

35. PSPC, April 21, 1920.

36. Linn White, "Soldier Field in Chicago," unpublished bound manuscript (1936), 9, CPD/SF.

37. PSPC, April 21, Sept. 22, and Oct. 20, 1920; James Doherty, "$78,953 Cost of Lowden Fight," *CDT*, June 24, 1928; Arthur M. Evans, "Builders List $100,000,00 in Waiting Work," *CDT*, April 7, 1921; Col. H. C. Carbaugh and J. L. Nolan, "The History and Achievements of the South Park Commissioners," unpublished carbon copy manuscript (1932), 25, CPD/SF; George Castle and Stuart Shay, *Wrigley Field: The Unauthorized Biography* (Dulles, VA: Brassey's, 2004), 35; "High Bids Halt Grant Stadium," *CHE*, Feb. 16, 1922; White, "Soldier Field," 11–12. On Blome-Sinek being a pioneer in concrete construction, see, for example, R. S. Blome Co. advertisement, *American Architect and Building News*, June 3, 1908, 14.

38. "Park Bonds Win," CDT, Feb. 25, 1920; "Work Started on Grant Park Stadium" (photograph), CDT, July 20, 1922; White, "Soldier Field," 7–8; PSPC, July 7, Aug. 16, Aug. 30, and Oct. 16, 1922. Much of the information regarding the progress of construction comes from three volumes of construction photographs by the Chicago Architectural Photographing Co. and other, unnamed contractors, taken between September 12, 1922, and November 24, 1926, CPD/SF. "I.W.W. Tie Up Millions in Building Jobs," CDT, June 28, 1923; "Building Tieup to Be Extended to North Side," CDT, June 29, 1923; "'Outlaw' Strike Leader and 25 Arrested in Riot," CDT, June 30, 1923; "'Rebel' Strikers to Be Back on Job Tomorrow," CDT, July 1, 1923.

39. "Pay Roll Robbers Get $30,000; One Bandit Captured," *CDT*, Aug. 12, 1923; "Good Cement Output," *NYT*, Dec. 30, 1923.

40. PSPC, Dec. 19, 1923, and Jan. 22, April 4, and April 16, 1924; "Cold Wave Fails to Halt Work on City Stadium," *CDT*, Jan. 2, 1924; contract between Rudolph S. Blome and William J. Sinek and the South Park Commissioners, April 24, 1924, CPD/SF, stadium construction folder.

41. Soldier Field construction photographs, CPD/SF; PSPC, various dates including July 16, 1924; White, "Soldier Field," 11–12.

42. Walter Eckersall, "Police Games to Open New Chicago Stadium," *CDT*, Sept. 5, 1924; "Chicago Police Field Day," *Sullivan's Englewood Times*, Aug. 8, 1924; "1,200 March to Dedicate Stadium," *CA*, Sept. 6, 1924; Walter Eckersall, "Traffic Cop Wins First Police Event," *CDT*, Sept. 6, 1924.

43. "South Side Business Men to Attend Song Fest in New Stadium," *CDT*, Sept. 9, 1924; "30,000 Voices to Dedicate Stadium in Song Pageant," *CDT*, Sept. 10, 1924; "50,000 Expected at Huge Civic Pageant," *CD*, Sept. 10, 1924; "Elephants in Parade of Greatest 13 Ring Circus," *CDT*, Sept. 21, 1924; Mana-Zucca (pseud. of Gisella Augusta Zuckerman), *The Big Brown Bear* (New York: G. Schirmer, 1919); "Ogden Park Activities," *Sullivan's Englewood Times*, Sept. 19, 1924; South Park Commissioners, memorandum (unlabeled) on the "first free use" of the stadium, n.d. [1924], CPD/SF, speeches folder.

CHAPTER 2

1. Douglas Bukowski, *Big Bill Thompson, Chicago, and the Politics of Image* (Urbana: University of Illinois Press, 1998), 162–63.

2. Richard Norton Smith, *The Colonel: The Life and Legend of Robert R. McCormick* (New York: Houghton Mifflin, 1997), 111 (citing Jack Alexander, "The World's Greatest Newspaper," *Saturday Evening Post*, July 26, 1941).

3. "60,000 to See Chicago Fire Pageant," *CDT*, Oct. 4, 1924; "Look Out Firemen: Mrs. O'Leary's Kin Meets Kin of Famous Cow," *CD*, Oct. 8, 1924; "Chicago's Day Recalls 53 Yrs. of City Growth," *CDT*, Oct. 9, 1924; "60,000 Voice City's Spirit at Stadium Fete," *CDT*, Oct. 10, 1924; "Re-enact Fire for Chicago Day Crowd: 10 Veterans of '71 Run with Old Fire King," *CDN*, Oct. 9, 1924; "Chicago Stadium Has Latest Devices," *Decatur Review*, Sept. 25, 1924.

4. A memo on the meeting between a South Park Commission official and Holabird and Roche calls the proposed monument a "quadriga"—a different type of structure from what the architects included in their original design. A quadriga is a four-horse chariot of the ancient world, commonly depicted in triumphal sculpture; one of the most famous is atop the Brandenburg gate in Berlin. Design renderings as well as newspaper and periodical depictions of the stadium plans almost all show a structure resembling a Greek or Roman temple but topped with an obelisk.

5. Unknown author, memorandum on costs of stadium, Dec. 26, 1919, CPD/SF, construction folder.

6. Linn White, memorandum to South Parks acting general superintendent George T. Donoghue, Sept. 17, 1924, CPD/SF, construction folder.

7. "$3,000,000 Issue to Be Asked to Finish Stadium," *CDT*, Sept. 18, 1924; PSPC, Sept.

17 and Oct. 11, 1924; "Vote for Stadium Bonds," *CDT*, Nov. 1, 1924; "Gold Star Fathers Hit Stadium Bonds," *CHE*, Nov. 1, 1924; "Civic Groups Confuse Voters on 8 Proposals,"*CDT*, Nov. 2, 1924; "Kelly Makes Plea for Stadium Bonds," *CHE*, Nov. 2, 1924; "Stadium Bond Issue Urged," *CHE*, Nov. 4, 1924; "Little Ballot Proposals Look Like Winners," *CDT*, Nov. 5, 1924.

8. PSPC, April 4, April 15, May 5, July 15, and Aug. 19, 1925.

9. PSPC, April 14 and Aug. 19, 1925; "New Bridge to Link Up Outer Drives," *CDT*, Aug. 20, 1925; Louise Overacker, *Politics and People: The Ordeal of Self-government in America* (MacMillan Publishing, 1932; reprint, New York: Arno Press, 1974), 37; Carroll Hill Wooddy, *The Chicago Primary of 1926: A Study in Election Methods* (University of Chicago Press, 1926; reprint, New York: Arno Press, 1974), 90.

10. "Everything Wrong Here," *CDT*, Oct. 21, 1925; "This Is Going to Be Soldiers' Field If It Takes the 1st Division," *CDT*, Oct. 22, 1925.

11. "City Renews Pledge to Hero Dead: 10,000 Take Part in Dedication Rite," *CDN*, Nov. 11, 1925; William A. Simonds, *Kamaaina, a Century in Hawaii* (Honolulu: American Factors, 1949), 80; UP, "Fear Naval Plane Lost off Hawaii," in *Middleton* (NY) *Daily Herald*, Sept. 2, 1925; UP, "Five Men aboard Trans-Ocean Plane Now Thought Lost," in *Middleton* (NY) *Daily Herald*, Sept. 2, 1925; Chelsea Curtis Fraser, *Famous American Flyers* (New York: Crowell, 1942; reprint, New York: Arno Press, 1980), 106–22; John A. Rodgers (AP), "Plane Chief Tells Story of Hardship," in *Helena Independent*, Sept. 12, 1925; "Gen. Harbord Sees Peril in Volstead Law," *CDT*, Nov. 12, 1925; Wayne S. Cole, *America First: The Battle against Intervention, 1940–41* (Madison: University of Wisconsin Press, 1953), 21; AP, "Lowden Dedicates Chicago's Stadium," in *Decatur Review*, Nov. 11, 1925; "City Dedicates Soldiers Field," *CA*, Nov. 11, 1925; Edward J. Kelly, Soldier Field dedication speech, Nov. 11, 1925, CPD/SF, dedications folder. A handwritten note on the copy of the Kelly speech in this folder labels it as being "Probably delivered by Ed Kelly, president of the South Park Commissioners, Nov. 26, 1927." The text of the speech, however, matches quotations from Kelly in news accounts of the 1925 Armistice Day event (albeit not exactly; it is likely either that Kelly deviated slightly from his written speech or that reporters misquoted him slightly); the fact that events such as the 1926 Eucharistic Congress are not mentioned also points to the speech's having been given on the earlier date.

12. Thomas B. Littlewood, *Soldiers Back Home: The American Legion in Illinois, 1919–1939* (Carbondale: Southern Illinois University Press, 2004), 60; "100,000 Seat Stadium Bait for Admirals," *CDT*, Dec. 29, 1925.

13. "Chicago Happy as Army-Navy Game Is Landed," *CDT*, Jan. 23, 1926; "Talk of Political Influences," *NYT*, Jan. 23, 1926.

14. "Bond Fight on Stadium Perils Cadets' Game," *CDT*, April 20, 1926; William E. Furlong, "Voice of the People," *CDT*, Feb. 9, 1926; "Taxpayers' Suits: A Survey and Summary," *Yale Law Journal* 69, no. 5. (April 1960): 895–924; "Renew Fight to Save Old Fine Arts Building," *CDT*, Oct. 29, 1925; *William E. Furlong vs. the South Park Commissioners*, no. 16786, Supreme Court of Illinois, 320 Ill. 507; 151 N.E. 510, April 23, 1926.

15. L. M. Nulton, commander of the Naval Academy, letter to Edward J. Kelly, June 6, 1926, CPD/SF, Army-Navy Game folder.

16. James O'Donnell Bennett, "110,000 to See Game Today," *CDT*, Nov. 27, 1926.

17. Ibid.; Genevieve Forbes Herrick, "Cadets Dance, Cheer, Sing at Ball at Drake," *CDT*, Nov. 27, 1926; Sarah Brown, "Girls Make Cadet Ball a Success," *CA*, Nov. 27, 1926. See also, for example, A. W. Moore, general manager, the Parmalee Co., letter to Mr. G. T. Donoghue, Nov. 23, 1926, and George T. Donoghue, general superintendent, letter to Herbert Sobel, Dec. 6, 1926; both in CPD/SF, Army-Navy Game folder.

18. W. G. Brown, general passenger agent, Baltimore & Ohio R.R. Co., Chicago office, letter to George T. Donoghue, general superintendent, South Park Commission, Oct. 16, 1926; A. H. Shaw, general passenger agent, the Pennsylvania R.R., Chicago office, letter to Donoghue (with attached cost memorandum), Oct. 14, 1926; H. E. Holt, comptroller, the

Palmer House, letter to Mr. Bender, secretary to the treasurer, South Park board (with attached bills and documents), Feb. 24, 1927. All in CPD/SF, Army-Navy Game folder.

19. "The Weather," *CDT*, Nov. 27, 1926; Jimmy Corcoran, "Snappy Chicago Weather Freezes Army Mule and Chills Navy Goat," *Lincoln* (NE) *Star*, Nov. 27, 1926; "Secretary Wilbur Heads Navy Contingent to Game," *CDT*, Nov. 27, 1926; "Drill to Field Just before Big Game," *CA*, Nov. 27, 1926; "Here Is Official Army-Navy Game Program for Today," *CDT*, Nov. 27, 1926; Ted Patterson, *Football in Baltimore: History and Memorabilia* (Baltimore: Johns Hopkins University Press, 2000), 30–31; "100 Extra Tickets for Game on Sale," *CA*, Nov. 27, 1926; Paul T. Gilbert, "City Turns Out to Welcome Army and Navy," *CA*, Nov. 27, 1926; Kenneth D. Fry, "Army and Navy Locked in Great Annual Battle," *CA*, Nov. 27, 1926; Don Maxwell, "News Bits of the Game the Army and the Navy Played to a 21–21 Draw," *CDT*, Nov. 28, 1926; Chicago Tribune Press Service, "Coolidge Drops Work to Listen in on Grid Tilt," *CDT*, Nov. 28, 1926; "Fur Wrapped Society Joins Football Crowd," *CDT*, Nov. 28, 1926; James Crusinberry, "Players Glad Foe Was Held to a Tie Score," *CDT*, Nov. 28, 1926. Among those who consider the 1926 match the teams' best was sports historian Gene Schoor. See Schoor, ed., *100 Years of Army-Navy Football: A Pictorial History of America's Most Colorful and Competitive Sports Rivalry* (New York: Henry Holt & Co., 1989), 74–76.

20. Patterson, *Football in Baltimore*, 30–31; James L. Merriner, *Grafters and Goo Goos: Corruption and Reform in Chicago, 1833–2003* (Carbondale: Southern Illinois University Press, 2004), 109; Col. C. H. Carbaugh and J. L. Nolan, "The History and Achievements of South Park Commissioners," unpublished carbon copy manuscript (1932), 25 CPD/SF; Linn White, "Soldier Field in Chicago," unpublished bound manuscript (1936), 29, CPD/SF.

21. See, for example, "Local Republican Politics," *CDT*, Feb. 1, 1923; "New South Park Board Holds First Session," *CDT*, March 20, 1924.

22. Justin H. Forrest, "Kelly Brings Back Ideas for South Side Parks," *CA*, March 26, 1927.

23. Edward J. Kelly, "White Vision Coming True in 10 Years," *CHE*, Aug. 29, 1925.

24. "From Buggy to Motor Depicted by Ride in Park," *CDT*, Aug. 5, 1926.

25. Ibid.

26. "Kelly Favors Park Board's Contractors," *CHE*, undated 1933 clipping in *Tribune* clip files.

27. James Doherty, "Pointed Query: What'd You Get for 6 Billions?" *CDT*, Oct. 28, 1946.

28. "Ward Leaders Pledge to Help Christmas Fund," *CDT*, Oct. 21, 1938; "Pressure to Buy Tickets Arouses City's Teachers," *CDT*, Nov. 8, 1941.

29. J. Leonard Reinsch, oral history interview, March 13–14, 1967, 23–24, Truman Library, http://www.trumanlibrary.org/oralhist/reinsch.htm (accessed July 24, 2004).

30. Guy Gentry, "700,000 Tickets Out for F.D.R. Rally Tonight," *CDT*, Oct. 28, 1944.

31. "Record Crowd in Chicago Hears President Give Peace Program," *CD*, Nov. 4, 1944.

32. Willard Edwards, "F. D. R. Promises New Deal No. 2; Dewey Hits at War 'Credit' Claim," *CDT*, Oct. 29, 1944.

33. Roosevelt, Franklin Delano, "Campaign Address at Soldier Field, Chicago," Oct. 28, 1944.

34. Willard Edwards, "F. D. R. Promises New Deal No. 2; Dewey Hits at War 'Credit' Claim," *CDT*, Oct. 29, 1944.

35. Franklin Delano Roosevelt, campaign address at Soldier Field, Oct. 28, 1944, in AP, "Postwar Goal: 60 Million Jobs," in *LAT*, Oct. 29, 1944.

36. David M. Kennedy, *Freedom from Fear: The American People in Depression and War, 1929–1945* (New York: Oxford University Press, 1999), 767–769, 774–775.

37. "Record Crowd in Chicago," *CD*, Nov. 4, 1944.

38. Carl Wegman, "Keep U.S. Mighty—Truman," *CDT*, April 7, 1946; "Text of Truman Speech Given in Soldiers' Field," *CDT*, April 7, 1946.

39. "Chairman Puts Bite on Party Workers for Democrat Picnic," *CDT*, July 28, 1949; "Democrats Pay $10,000 to Hear President Talk," *CDT*, July 20, 1949; "Shriners' Parade Dazzles Chicago," *NYT*, July 20, 1949; Donald S. Dawson, oral history interview, Aug. 8, 1977, 26–27, Truman Library, http://www.trumanlibrary.org/oralhist/dawsond.htm (accessed Oct. 10, 2008); AP, "Truman Hints New Trouble Faces Stalin," in *LAT*, July 20, 1949; John McCutcheon, "500,000 Watch Gay Parade of 15,000 Nobles," *CDT*, July 20, 1949; Anton Remenih, "100 Man Hours Used to Put Truman on Air," *CDT*, July 31, 1949; Edward T. Folliard, "President Rejects 'Inevitable' War in Shrine Address; Warns of ERP Cut," *WP*, July 20, 1949.

40. "58,000 at 'Shrinerama'; Hear Truman at Dinner," *CDT*, July 14, 1955; UP, "Mr. Truman Tells Shriners to Back U.N. Peace Efforts," in *Holland* (MI) *Evening Sentinel*, July 14, 1955; "Ex-President Reviews Parade," *CDT*, July 13, 1955.

41. Parke Brown, "Plan House of Glass for Al in Speech Here," *CDT*, Oct. 6, 1928.

42. "Glass Cage Not Smith's Idea of Speaker's Stand," *CDT*, Oct. 14, 1928. Smith may have said "Soldier Field," but the *Tribune* stuck to its idiosyncratic spelling regardless.

43. James O'Donnell Bennett, "Al Calls G.O.P. 'Do Nothings,'" *CDT*, Oct. 20, 1928.

44. "Refuse Permit for Al Smith Parade in City," *CDT*, Oct. 21, 1936.

45. "Kennelly Acts to Push Merger of Parks, City," *CDT*, Nov. 10, 1948.

46. "Wife Wins $300 from Kelly's Brother," *CDT*, May 26, 1950.

47. "32 Fountains Running," *CDT*, Aug. 16, 1949; "Maude Bennot Is Suspended at Planetarium," *CDT*, Jan. 11, 1945.

48. "Feuding among Ex-Mayor Kelly Kin Gets Rough," *CDT*, July 11, 1950; "Evan Kelly Hearing Stars Fights, Charges—and Kellys," *CDT*, July 12, 1950.

49. "Kelly and Boss Deny Stadium Has 'Love Nest,'" *CDT*, July 13, 1950.

50. "Evan I. Kelly Resigns $8,000 Park Position," *CDT*, Aug. 10, 1950.

51. "Hoellen Sees Democratic 'Politics' in Service Game," *CDT*, Oct. 10, 1963.

52. Robert Wiedrich, "City to Welcome 5,000 Cadets," *CDT*, Nov. 1, 1963; Charles Bartlett, "72,000 to See Air Force and Army Clash," *CDT*, Nov. 2, 1963.

53. "Pageantry on a Grand Day for Football," *CDT*, Nov. 3, 1963.

54. Frank Blatchford, "Johnson's Visits to Chicago: War Often a Theme," *CDT*, Jan. 23, 1973.

CHAPTER 3

1. South Park Commissioners, Division of Playgrounds and Sports, "Stadium Uses—Outdoor" (list of possible uses for Grant Park Stadium), Feb. 15, 1923, Chicago Public Library Special Collections.

2. "Austin Preps Meet Kentucky Team Saturday," *CDT*, Oct. 2, 1924 ("It will be the first football game to be played in the new structure"); "Austin Again Loses to Louisville High," *CDT*, Oct. 5, 1924; "Oak Park Trims Austin, 13–0, to Dedicate Stadium," *CDT*, Sept. 28, 1924. I am indebted to Scott Griggs of Louisville, Kentucky, who was able to confirm that Norman's name was misspelled in Chicago accounts of the game and supply proof of both Norman and Ford's first names. (First names were routinely left out of news accounts of sporting events of the time.)

3. Chicago Park District, ninth annual report (1943), 256, CPSC; "Place to Play Is Problem of Prep Gridders," *Southtown Economist*, Sept. 8, 1925.

4. My argument regarding the mainstreaming of Catholic culture in relation to the Prep Bowl is in part drawn from from Gerald R. Gems, "The Prep Bowl: Football and Religious Acculturation in Chicago, 1927–1963," *Journal of Sport History* 23, no. 3 (Fall 1996): 284–302. On the Catholic League football group forming, see "Catholics to Form League," *CDT*, Oct. 3, 1912; "Mt. Carmel and Schurz Groom Aerial Plays," *CDT*, Nov. 30, 1927; Lloyd Wendt and Herman Kogan, *Big Bill of Chicago* (Indianapolis: Bobbs-Merrill, 1953), 257–61, 267.

5. "Mt. Carmel Seen Victor over Schurz," *Suburbanite Economist*, Nov. 29, 1927, 9–10;

"Mt. Carmel and Schurz Battle for Title Today," *CDT*, Dec. 3, 1927; "Mt. Carmel and Schurz Groom Aerial Plays," *CDT*, Nov. 30, 1927.

6. On Brosseau's college career, see, for example, UP, "Are Sent through Second Scrimmage," in *Oshkosh* (WI) *Daily Northwestern*, Sept. 19, 1930. Brosseau was barred from playing in 1931 because of poor grades, according to AP, "Marquette Athletes Declared Ineligible," in *Modesto News-Herald*, Feb. 7–8, 1931; see "Sports Flashes," *Suburbanite Economist*, May 22, 1931; Gems, "Prep Bowl," 287–89.

7. "Preps Gird for Title Combat," *CA*, Dec. 4, 1928; Charles Bartlett, "20,000 Watch South Siders Take Crown," *CDT*, Nov. 23, 1930; Gems, "Prep Bowl," 289; Wilfrid Smith, "Harrison Overwhelms Mt. Carmel, 44 to 6," *CDT*, Dec. 6, 1931; "Aid Is Sought from 45 Editors in Relief Drive," *CDT*, Sept. 4, 1931.

8. "Fathers Halt Plans for Prep Charity Game," *CDT*, Nov. 22, 1932; "Charity Game Chances Fade; Parents Firm," *CDT*, Nov. 26, 1932; "Prep Charity Game Plans Are Canceled," *CDT*, Nov. 29, 1932; Gems, "Prep Bowl," 290.

9. "Mt. Carmel to Get Another Title Chance," *CDT*, Nov. 24, 1933; "Mt. Carmel Is Ready for New Title Bid," *CDT*, Dec. 2, 1933; "Mount Carmel Defeats St. Rita in Title Game," *CDT*, Dec. 4, 1933; Gems, "Prep Bowl," 290–91.

10. Charles Bartlett, "Lindblom Defeats Leo, 6 to 0; Takes Prep Title," *CDT*, Dec. 2, 1934; Gems, "Prep Bowl," 291.

11. Charles Bartlett, "Music Aplenty Assured at Prep Football Final," *CDT*, Nov. 30, 1934; Charles Bartlett, "Leo Plays Lindblom Today for Prep Title," *CDT*, Dec. 1, 1934; Gems, "Prep Bowl," 292.

12. Charles Dunkley (AP), "High School Grid Star Amazes Fans," in *Reno Evening Gazette*, Nov. 15, 1937; AP, "Bill De Correvont Holds the Spotlight in Chicago Game," in *Stevens Point* (WI) *Daily Journal*, Nov. 27, 1937.

13. "Austin All Set to Bring Foot Ball Title Here," *Garfieldian*, Nov. 25, 1937.

14. "Seat Sales for Title Prep Game Exceed $80,000," *CDT*, Nov. 16, 1937; David Condon, "In the Wake of the News," *CT*, May 28, 1966.

15. Edmund Kelly, telephone interview with author, Jan. 17, 2002.

16. "Award $1,477,192 Building Job at Soldiers' Field," *CDT*, May 25, 1938; Jerry Shnay, "50 Years and 120,000 Fans Ago," *CT*, Nov. 27, 1987; Edward Burns, "Austin High Conquers Leo, 26 to 0, before Record Crowd," *CDT*, Nov. 28, 1937.

17. Edward Burns, "Austin High Conquers Leo, 26 to 0, before Record Crowd," *CDT*, Nov. 28, 1937; special to *NYT*, "120,000 Thrilled by Boy Wonder in Chicago School Gridiron Final," *NYT*, Nov. 28, 1937; Jerry Shnay, "50 Years and 120,000 Fans Ago," *CT*, Nov. 27, 1987.

18. Charles Bartlett, "C.Y.O. to Honor Prep Stars at Stadium Bouts," *CDT*, Nov. 30, 1937; James Segreti, "De Correvont Injured after Score; Austin Triumphs, 13–0," *CDT*, Dec. 12, 1937; AP, "Austin Star Hurt as Team Wins, 13–0," in *NYT*, Dec. 12, 1937; "Famed Chicago Prep Visits Southland," *LAT*, Jan. 1, 1938; AP, "Chicago Preps Down Arizona Stars, 9–6," in *LAT*, Jan. 2, 1938. Gems says that the Chicago prep all-stars visited both Los Angeles and Arizona over the Christmas holidays, but he appears to be confusing two years' all-star trips. The Chicago all-stars played in Arizona on Jan. 1, 1938, and a different all-star team, not made up of DeCorrevont contemporaries, lost to a Los Angeles team Dec. 30, 1938, almost a year after DeCorrevont had graduated.

19. Edward Burns, "Fenger Beats Mt. Carmel for Title, 13–0," *CDT*, Nov. 27, 1938.

20. For further information on the history of the Prep Bowl, see http://prepbowl. tripod.com, which includes, under "Past Prep Bowls," a list of scores from 1934 to 2004 (accessed Nov. 18, 2006), and Jerry Shnay, "The Tired and the Rested," *CT*, Dec. 2, 1983. See also Gems, "Prep Bowl," 295, and newspaper reports of the games, which, after 1938, were played the Saturday after Thanksgiving. On record attendance at Illinois football games, see http://www.ihsa.org/activity/fb/records/agen.htm (accessed Nov. 18, 2006).

21. James Segreti, "Fenger Whips Leo, 18–0, for City Prep Title," *CDT*, Dec. 1, 1940; James Segreti, "Leo Crushes Tilden, 46–13, for City Title," *CDT*, Nov. 30, 1941; Edward

Burns, "Leo Defeats Tilden, 21–14, for Prep Title," *CDT*, Nov. 29, 1942; Frank Norris, "St. George Beats Phillips, 19–12, for Title," *CDT*, Nov. 28, 1943; David Condon, "Tilden Beats Weber for City Title, 13 to 7." *CDT*, Dec. 3, 1944.

22. David Condon, "Austin Beats Leo, 13 to 12, for City Title," *CDT*, Nov. 30, 1947; Robert Doherty, "Lane Indians Find Caravan Much Too Strong for Ambush," *CDT*, Dec. 3, 1950.

23. Hal Foust, "Police Charity Fervor Scares Sunday Drivers," *CDT*, Nov. 16, 1936; James Segreti, "Prep Game Forecast: Warmer; Ticket Pressure Chills Police,"*CDT*, Nov. 29, 1940; "Kennelly Hands Out $70,000 to 5 Grid Game Beneficiaries," *CDT*, June 24, 1948.

24. Joseph Ator, "City Christmas Fund to Benefit 85,000 Children," *CDT*, Nov. 20, 1935; James Segreti, "Prep Game Forecast: Warmer; Ticket Pressure Chills Police," *CDT*, Nov. 29, 1940; "Turn Around, Alderman," *CDT*, Nov. 28, 1949.

25. "Grid Teams to Play Sunday for High School Benefit," *CDT*, Nov. 21, 1926, 24; "Marquette and St. Louis Renew 30 Year Rivalry," *CDT*, Oct. 9, 1936; "Rites Monday for Nun Who Set Up Forum,"*CDT*, July 11, 1959.

26. "St. Viator May Meet Columbia in Grant Park," *CDT*, Sept. 23, 1924; Riley Murray, "St. Viator and Columbia Fight to 0–0 Draw," *CDT*, Nov. 12, 1924; "St. Viator's and Columbia in Tie Game, 0 to 0," *CA*, Nov. 11, 1924. Examples of the Notre Dame–Northwestern game of 1924 being mistaken for the first college game at Soldier Field include Andrew Bagnato, "2 Games in 3 Days Recall Era When Stadium Was Showplace," *CT*, Sept. 1, 1994, and "Northern Illinois–Iowa Football Game at Soldier Field in 2007: Hawkeyes to Play Football in Chicago," press release, University of Iowa, June 5, 2006, http://hawkeyesports. CSTv.com/sports/m-footbl/spec-rel/060506aab.html (accessed Oct. 21, 2006), as well as "Stadium in a Park: The Lakefront Redevelopment Project," press release (information sheet), Chicago Park District, http://www.chicagoparkdistrict.com (accessed about Dec. 1, 2003).

27. Murray Sperber, *Shake Down the Thunder: The Creation of Notre Dame Football* (New York: Henry Holt & Co., 1993), 167–69; "Notre Dame Is Winner," *CDT*, Oct. 28, 1899; "Big Ten Season Closes Tomorrow: All Elevens Swing into Action on Grid," *Decatur Review*, Nov. 21, 1924; Walter Eckersall, "Grid Titles Decided in Today's Battles," *CDT*, Nov. 22, 1924, 17; Wallace Abbeyn, "Dame Held to 13–6 Win by Purple," *CDT*, Nov. 23, 1924.

28. On Rockne and Eckersall's relationship, see Sperber, *Shake Down the Thunder*, 259–61. Irving Vaughan, "Mayor Calls On City to Dress Up for Big Battle," *CDT*, Nov. 26, 1927; "4,000 Trojans on Way Here," *CHE*, Nov. 25, 1927; Walter Eckersall, "117,000 See Notre Dame Win: Trojans Fall 7 to 6; Drury, Flanagan Star," *CDT*, Nov. 27, 1927; Walter Eckersall, "City Welcomes Irish, Trojans Today: Pop Dearborn Dresses Up for Grid's Big Treat," *CDT*, Nov. 25, 1927; Walter Eckersall, "Master Minds of Grid Will Match Wits Saturday: Rockne and Jones Have Fine Records," *CDT*, Nov. 23, 1927; Walter Eckersall, "See Notre Dame Battle Today: Trojans, Irish Are Geared for Terrific Fight," *CDT*, Nov. 26, 1927; Walter Eckersall, "Watch Drury Is N. Dame Slogan for U.S.C. Game: Niemiec, Flanagan Also Should Be Observed," *CDT*, Nov. 24, 1927.

29. At the time, it was common to call the parts of a football game "periods," but I have gone with the more modern "quarters." Warren Brown, "Notre Dame Downs U.S.C., 7 to 6: 110,000 See Bitter Fight for Victory," *CHE*, Nov. 27, 1927; George Strickler, "Passes Bring Touchdowns as Irish Beat Trojans," *CHE*, Nov. 27, 1927; Sperber, *Shake Down the Thunder*, 267–68; Edward Burns, "Police, Ushers Make Traffic Job Look Easy," *CDT*, Nov. 27, 1927; Walter Eckersall, "117,000 See Notre Dame Win: Trojans Fal, 7 to 6; Drury, Flanagan Star," *CDT*, Nov. 27, 1927; University of Notre Dame Athletic Department, Notre Dame record sheet, in *Notre Dame Football Supplement* (South Bend: University of Notre Dame, 2006), 49 (through what is most likely a typo, this team background book gives the date of the 1927 USC game as Nov. 1, 1927). On the game's record attendance, see, for example: http://www.chicagobears.com/tradition/sf_timeline.asp (accessed June 2, 2006); *Official NCAA 2005 Football Records Book, Divisions I-A and I-AA* (Indianapolis: National Col-

legiate Athletic Association, 2005), 425, at http://www.ncaa.org/library/records/football/
football_records_book/2005/2005_d1_football_records.pdf (accessed June 2, 2006).

30. Walter Eckersall, "120,000 See Notre Dame Whip Navy," *CDT*, Oct. 14, 1928; Alan
J. Gould (AP), "Notre Dame Downs Navy for Its Third Successive Loss of the Season," in
Kingsport (TN) *Times*, Oct. 14, 1928; Gems, "Prep Bowl," 279–80; "Mayor Jimmie Does a
Gridiron Victory Prance," *CDT*, Oct. 14, 1928.

31. "90,000 See Notre Dame Beat Badgers, 19–0," *CDT*, Oct. 20, 1929; Sperber, *Shake
Down the Thunder*, 315.

32. "The General Rejoins His Troops" (photo), *CDT*, Nov. 13, 1929; "Rockne Directs
N. Dame Drill for Trojans," *CDT*, Nov. 13, 1929; "N. Dame Confident; U. S. C. Arrives
Today," *CDT*, Nov. 15, 1929.

33. Arch Ward, "120,000 View Notre Dame Victory," *CDT*, Nov. 17, 1929; Sperber,
Shake Down the Thunder, 316–18; Don Maxwell, "Rockne Gives 1 Order; Boys Obey—and
Win," *CDT*, Nov. 17, 1929.

34. Sperber, *Shake Down the Thunder*, 339–40; "N. U. Presents $100,000 to Unem-
ployment Fund," *CDT*, Dec. 9, 1930; Grantland Rice, "Notre Dame Triumphs over Army,
7 to 6," *LAT*, Nov. 30, 1930; "Stagg Says Bad Weather Spoiled Army-Irish Game," *CDT*,
Nov. 30, 1930; Paul Mickelson (AP), "Notre Dame Downs Soldiers by Single Point Margin:
Irish Outplay Fine Cadet Team; Soggy Field Hampers Play," in *Ogden Standard-Examiner*,
Nov. 30, 1930.

35. "Tuskegee, Wilberforce Elevens Ready," *CD*, Oct. 26, 1929; "Chicago Buildings,
'Big and Copious,' Thrill Dixie Team," *CDT*, Oct. 25, 1929; "'Wilberforce' and 'Tuskegee'"
(photo), *CD*, Oct. 26, 1929.

36. "Tuskegee Wins 6–0 Game from Wilberforce," *CDT*, Oct. 27, 1929.

37. Mills Stadium, built in 1911 at Kilpatrick Avenue and Lake Street and known for years
as Garden Field, was torn down in 1941 to make way for a factory.

38. "Battle Four Quarters to a Draw," *CDT*, Oct. 26, 1930; "Wilberforce and Tuskegee
Game Here," *CD*, July 9, 1932; "Wilberforce and Tuskegee Game Here Canceled," *CDT*,
Oct. 14, 1937; "Wilberforce's Air Attack Defeats Tuskegee," *CD*, Oct. 22, 1938; "Tuskegee
Vs. Wilberforce Football Classic Sets New Spectator Record as Soldier Field Evening
Event," *CD*, Oct. 22, 1938.

39. Frank "Fay" Young, "'Force Attack Downs 'Skegee Tigers, 22–7," *CD*, Oct. 15,
1949; Frank Young, "Athletics Serves Purpose: Fay SAYS" (column), *CD*, June 24, 1950;
Joel Sternberg, "Frank A. 'Fay' Young," in *Dictionary of Literary Biography: American
Sportswriters and Writers on Sport*, ed. Richard Orodenker (Detroit: Gale Group, 1996),
332; "A Year of Honors for Lou Rawls," *American Profile Magazine*, Nov. 28, 2004, http://
www.americanprofile.com/article/4456.html (accessed July 2, 2006).

CHAPTER 4

1. "Olympic Games Transferred from Chicago to St. Louis," *CDT*, Feb. 12, 1903; John
E. Findling, "Chicago Loses the 1904 Olympics," *Journal of Olympic History* 12, no. 3
(Oct. 2004): 26–27; John A. Lucus, "Caspar Whitney," *Journal of Olympic History* 8, no.
2 (May 2000): 33.

2. "Ogden Entries Win Honors in Horseshoe Meet: Dan Cooper Brings State Title
Back to Local Park," *Southtown Economist*, Dec. 17, 1924; "Dan Cooper of Ogden Park
Wins Horseshoe Title," *CDT*, Dec. 14, 1924.

3. South Park Commissioners, "Record of Uses, Soldier Field Stadium, 1924–1931,"
ca. 1931, CPD/SF; Fayette Krum, "Brilliant Field of Girls in Track Meet," *CDN*, Sept. 26,
1924; "Women Champions to Enter Finnish Games," *CDT*, May 18, 1925.

4. Allen Guffman, The Olympics: A History of the Modern Games (Champaign: University of Illinois Press, 2002), 39–42, 47–51; "Paavo, Rivals Race Today at Loyola Relays,"
CDT, April 19, 1925; "Nurmi Beats Ritola in 3,000-Meter Run," NYT, April 20, 1925; "Willie

Ritola, 86, Track Star; Won 5 Olympic Gold Medals," NYT, April 28, 1982; "Finns Refuse to Discuss Charges on Visit Here," CDT, May 8, 1925; Walter Eckersall, "Myyra Smashes Javelin Record at Finn Games," CDT, June 1, 1925; "Weather," CDT, June 1, 1925.

5. Jimmy Corcoran, "World's Marks Fall in Girl's Track Meet," CA, June 2, 1928; William Shirer, "Chicago Girl Breaks World's 100 Meter Record," CDT, Aug. 1, 1928; Andrew Bagnato, "She Blazed a Trail of Gold," CT, June 5, 1988; Karen Craven, "Olympic Gold Medalist Betty Robinson Schwartz," CT, May 20, 1999; " 'Welcome Home,' Riverdale Tells Betty Robinson," CDT, Aug. 29, 1928; "Chicago Girls Break World Records in A.A.U. Meet," CDT, July 28, 1929.

6. Charles Nevada, "14 Marks Fall in prep Relays at Marquette," CDT, May 4, 1930; "Chicago Boy Ties U. S. Interscholastic Record," CD, June 8, 1929; "Carrying the Stars and Stripes to Victory" (photos), CDT, Aug. 28, 1930; Wilfrid Smith, "United States Beats British Athletes, 9–5," CDT, Aug. 28, 1930; Wilfrid Smith, "Post Olympic Meet Produces 2 World Marks," CDT, Aug. 19, 1932; "A.A.U. Meet Is Great Show, but Flops at Gate," CDT, July 2, 1933; "Negro Track Stars in National Meet at Soldier Field," CDN, Aug. 2, 1933; "Ajax Club, Gary, Captures Title in Negro Meet," CDT, Aug. 13, 1933.

7. Delia O'Hara, "Gymnastics," CT, March 28, 1979; "25,000 Attend Czecho-Slovak Festival Here," CDT, June 17, 1929; Earl Mullin, "50,000 Witness Sokol Festival at World's Fair," CDT, June 26, 1933; "Soldiers' Field Sokol Festival Thrills 50,000," CDT, June 30, 1947; Howard Barry, "Illinois Star Takes Sokol Gym Crown," CDT, June 28, 1954.

8. John E. Findling, "Chicago Loses the 1904 Olympics," Journal of Olympic History 12, no. 3 (Oct. 2004): 27–29; "Presents Chicago's Claims for 1924 Olympic Games," NYT, Aug. 7, 1920; "Want College Games Held Here as Olympic Lead," CDT, Dec. 12, 1922; " Ski Team Will Take Chicago Olympic Bid," CDT, Jan. 16, 1924; "Approve Chicago Site for Final Olympic Trials," CDT, Feb. 24, 1931; William Fay, "Olympic Chief Calls Chicago Facilities Best," CDT, Jan. 24, 1947; Edward Prell, "Chicago Steps Up Tempo of '52 Olympic Bid," CDT, Feb. 6, 1947; Edward Prell, "Tribune Man Carries City's Olympic Bid," CDT, June 19, 1947; "Chicago Gets '60 Olympics Bids Meeting," CDT, Nov. 10, 1954.

9. V. K. Brown, letter to George Hjelte, Feb. 15, 1945, 2, CPD/SF; Walter Eckersall, "Coast Track Stars Arrive for Meet Here," CDT, June 9, 1927; Wilfrid Smith, "Nation's Track Stars Vie for Titles Today," CDT, June 16, 1933.

10. "Chicago's Day Recalls 53 Yrs. of City Growth," CDT, Oct. 9, 1924; "Polo Series Is Planned as Part of Rodeo Show," CDT, July 22, 1928; "Climax Holiday Today; Bright Skies Promised," CDT, July 4, 1938; "Lary Kelley to Fly to Chicago for Rugby Game," CDT, Nov. 7, 1939; Judith Cass, "Rugby Team to Meet New York Club Tomorrow," CDT, Nov. 11, 1939; Edward Prell, "Chicago Beats New York at Rugby, 24 to 9," CDT, Nov. 13, 1939; "East-West Polo for Legion Show," Southtown Economist, June 19, 1940.

11. "Youngster of 50 Is South Parks Marbles Champ," CDT, May 24, 1929; AP, "Sports Tourney at Chicago Fair," in Reno Evening Gazette, April 15, 1933.

12. "Sparta Eleven Defeated 1–0 by Uruguay," CDT, May 16, 1927; "Bricklayers Defeat Uruguay, Olympic Soccer Champs, 3–2," CDT, May 23, 1927.

13. "Most of Europe Represented on Hapoel Eleven," CDT, May 8, 1947; William Fay, "Heading for a Deadlock," CDT, May 12, 1947; "Austrians, All-Stars Win Soccer Games," CDT, July 29, 1961; "Soccer Attendance Marks Set in '62 in Collegiate, International Play," CDT, Dec. 16, 1962; "Top Foreign Soccer Clubs to Play Here," CDT, March 11, 1962.

14. Photograph of softball teams (with "Becker Weiner" and "Edison" jerseys) in Soldier Field, photo # 1-25-167A, Chicago Park District Special Collections, Burnham Park photographs box; "Softball Meet Opens Today at Soldiers' Field," CDT, Sept. 12, 1936; "U. S. Softball Finals to Be Held Tonight," CDT, Sept. 16, 1936; "Softball Brief," CDT, Sept. 17, 1936; Amateur Softball Association, "National Softball Hall of Fame Member Harold (Shifty) Gears," http://www.softball.org/hall_of_fame/memberDetail.asp?mbrid=177 (accessed April 24, 2006).

15. Although some accounts of the Golden Gloves tournaments say Ward had the idea to begin them in 1923, that is not the case. Ward did not start at the Tribune until

1925; someone else at the *Tribune* had originated the Golden Gloves tournament in 1923, though Ward appears to have popularized the idea after boxing became legal again.

16. Jon Enriquez, "Coverage of Sports," in *American Journalism: History, Principles, Practices*, ed. W. David Sloan and Lisa Mullikin Parceil (Jefferson, NC: McFarland & Co., 2002), 201; Arch Ward, editorial, *CDT*, July 10, 1955; Wilfrid Smith, "Loop Crowds Cheer French Ring Champions," *CDT*, May 8, 1931.

17. Arch Ward, "Seats for 125,000 at Golden Gloves Battles," *CDT*, April 19, 1931; "Early Birds Take No Chances; Begin Roosting at 4 O'clock," *CDT*, May 13, 1931; Wilfrid Smith, "American, French Boxers Ready for Battle," *CDT*, May 12, 1931; Wilfrid Smith, "Rodak First Foreign Bout Glove Victor," *CDT*, April 12, 1949; "U.S. Amateur Boxers Defeat French, 5 Bouts to 3, before 40,000 in Chicago" (Wide World Photo), *NYT*, May 13, 1931.

18. Arch Ward, "Champions of Germany to Fight in Chicago," *CDT*, March 7, 1932; "Phagan's Right Travels 12 Inches; Campe Sails 12 Feet," *CDT*, July 28, 1932; Olympic medal winner results, http://www.olympic.org/uk/athletes/results/search_r_uk.asp (accessed July 12, 2006).

19. Arch Ward, "Golden Gloves Team to Fight Irish in July," *CDT*, March 31, 1933; Howard Barry, "200,000 Hail Irish Fighters on West Side," *CDT*, July 22, 1933; Wilfrid Smith, "Hail Irish Fighters; Hold Reception Tonight," *CDT*, July 21, 1933; Arch Ward, "48,000 See Chicago Boxers Beat Irish," *CDT*, Aug. 4, 1933; Warren Brown, "Chicagoans Whip Irish Fighters, 6 Bouts to 2," *CHE*, Aug. 4, 1933.

20. "C.Y.O., New York Fight July 22 at Soldiers' Field," *CDT*, June 17, 1936; Wilfrid Smith, "New York C.Y.A. Boxers Hope to Break Tradition," *CDT*, July 19, 1936; Wilfrid Smith, "C.Y.O. Defeat New York Boxers, 11–5, before 38,000," *CDT*, July 23, 1936.

21. "C.Y.O. Boxers to Fight South American Champions," *CDT*, June 28, 1937; Howard Barry, "30,000 Extend a Welcome to South American Boxers," *CDT*, Aug. 21, 1937; Howard Barry, "C.Y.O. Conquers South American Fighters, 11 to 5," *CDT*, Aug. 26, 1937; Wilfrid Smith, "Irish Boxers Tie C.Y.O., 5–5, before 35,372," *CDT*, July 20, 1939; Wilfrid Smith, "C.Y.O. Boxing Team Beats Hawaiians, 8–3," *CDT*, July 11, 1940; Frank Mastro, "Chicago CYO Boxers Defeat Hawaiians, 6 to 4," *CDT*, Sept. 18, 1941.

CHAPTER 5

1. "Hearst Is Expelled on Visit to France for 'Hostile' Action," *NYT*, Sept. 3, 1930.

2. "Hearst Back, Takes a Fling at France," *NYT*, Sept. 16, 1930; Douglas Bukowski, *Big Bill Thompson, Chicago, and the Politics of Image* (Urbana: University of Illinois Press, 1998), 111; "Parade to Mark Chicago Day on October 9th," *CDT*, Sept. 28, 1930; "Hearst to Speak over Radio Network," *NYT*, Sept. 28, 1930. An AP story that ran in the *New York Times* just below "Hearst Welcome Planned" (*NYT*, Sept. 14, 1930) noted that Curley had invited Hearst to speak at a celebration of Boston's tercentenary.

3. Philip Kinsley, "Mayor Greets W. R. Hearst in Soldiers' Field," *CDT*, Oct. 10, 1930.

4. Ibid.

5. Institute of Public Opinion, "Majority of Americans Favor Change in Neutrality Act," *Lincoln Sunday Journal and Star*, Sept. 24, 1939.

6. "Father Coughlin Is Denied Field," *Olean* (NY) *Times-Herald*, May 29, 1935; UP, "Coughlin Is Barred at Chicago Stadium," in *Oakland Tribune*, May 29, 1935.

7. "Reverend Coughlin's Agent Seeking Hall for Rally," *CDT*, May 30, 1935.

8. "Deny Coughlin Soldiers' Field a Second Time," *CDT*, June 2, 1935.

9. "Coughlin Plans Lawsuit to Get Soldiers' Field," *CDT*, June 8, 1935.

10. See, for example, Contract No. 156, between Grand Commandery Knight(s) of Templars of Illinois and the Chicago Park District, signed April 30, 1934, for Review of Parade on Sept. 15, 1934, and Contract No. 153, between Polish Interorganizational Sports Committee of Chicago and the Chicago Park District, signed April 20, 1934, for Central A.A.U. Track Meet, May 27, 1934; both in CPD/SF.

11. "Coughlin Enlists Aid of Ettelson in Fight for Meeting Permit," *CDT*, June 4, 1935.

12. "Don't Be Uncouth, Please," *Chicago Heights Star*, June 4, 1935.

13. "Coughlin Loses His Battle for Soldiers' Field," *CDT*, June 11, 1936.

14. Parke Brown, "U.S. Rallies to Constitution," *CDT*, Sept. 18, 1935.

15. "Lindy Takes Ford Riding," *CDT*, Aug. 12, 1927.

16. "City Will Greet Lindbergh as He Circles Loop," *CDT*, Aug. 12, 1927.

17. "Boys to Escort Lindbergh at Soldiers' Field," *CDT*, Aug. 10, 1927.

18. "Chicago Sees Lindy Today," *CDT*, Aug. 13, 1927.

19. "Lindy Beckons City to Air," *CDT*, Aug. 14, 1927.

20. "Girl Tries 3 Times to Get Lindbergh's Autograph," *CDT*, Aug. 14, 1927. For an illustration of Lindbergh and Thompson's dress on the day of Lindbergh's visit, see photographs in the Chicago History Museum's Chicago Daily News collection, including "William Hale Thompson holding a bullhorn to his mouth, standing with Charles Lindbergh in a sports stadium," 1928 [*sic*], DN-0086095C (the car and clothing match other photographs dated 1927; it appears the photograph has been incorrectly dated by museum staff). Other photographs confirm reports describing Lindbergh's stance as he rode in the car in Comiskey Park and Soldier Field; see, for example, "Crowd sitting in the bleachers at Soldier Field, watching aviator Charles A. Lindbergh riding in an automobile on the field," 1927, DN-0083868.

21. "Lindy Beckons City to Air," *CDT*, Aug. 14, 1927.

22. "Anti-War Rally to Hear Clark and Lindbergh," *CDT*, July 24, 1940.

23. Ralph Ingersoll, "Denouncing Charles Lindbergh," *PM*, Aug. 6, 1940; FBI file of Charles A. Lindbergh, 117–18, http://foia.fbi.gov/lindberg/lindberg1a.pdf (accessed Sept. 27, 2005).

24. "Highlights of Huge Welcome for MacArthur," *CDT*, April 27, 1951.

25. "MacArthur—I'll Fight On," *CDT*, April 27, 1951; William R. Conklin, "MacArthur Demands Policy to Replace Korea 'Vacuum,'" *NYT*, April 27, 1951.

CHAPTER 6

1. "Bouquet," *Time*, May 31, 1926.

2. Kathleen McLaughlin, "'We Are Ready,' Says Chicago as Pilgrims Pour into City," *CDT*, June 19, 1926.

3. "Pope Is Told Million May See Chicago Rite," *WP*, Feb. 25, 1925; George Seldes, "Pope Beams When Told Chicago's Eucharist Plan," *CDT*, Feb. 25, 1925; "Pilgrims to Rome Will Return Today," *NYT*, March 20, 1925.

4. "Pope Is Told Million May See Chicago Rite," *WP*, Feb. 25, 1925.

5. "3,000 in Hymn Competition," *NYT*, Jan. 7, 1926; PSPC, Jan. 20, 1926; "Eucharistic Congress Prize Awarded," *NYT* Jan. 22, 1926.

6. W. B. Norton, "Catholics to Open Congress Here June 17," *CDT*, Feb. 15, 1926.

7. "Pick Eucharistic Delegates," *NYT*, March 16, 1926.

8. John Cornyn, "2,000 Mexicans Sign to Attend Eucharist Meet," *CDT*, May 23, 1926; AP, "Belgian Pilgrimage Cut," in *CDT*, May 23, 1926.

9. "Catholics Plan Meetings Here in 16 Tongues," *CDT*, April 27, 1926.

10. Claude J. Pernin, "The Eucharistic Congress," *CDT*, April 11, 1926.

11. Kathleen McLaughlin, "Meaning of Eucharistic Congress Here," *CDT*, May 23, 1926.

12. Kathleen McLaughlin, "Plan Religious Building Show for Catholics," *CDT*, April 26, 1926.

13. "Chicago Prepares to Entertain 1,000,000 Catholics at Eucharistic Congress," *Bridgeport* (CT) *Telegram*, May 22, 1926.

14. "Catholics to Tell World of City's Wonders," *CDT*, May 14, 1926.

15. "$15,000,000 to Be Spent Here by Catholics," *CDT*, May 21, 1926.

16. Kathleen McLaughlin, "Plan Religious Building Show for Catholics," *CDT*, April 26, 1926.

17. Earl J. Johnson, "Chicago Leaders Prepare for Eucharistic Congress of Roman Catholic Church," *Atlanta Constitution*, May 22, 1926; "Count D'Yanville Arrives to Direct Eucharistic Work," *CDT*, May 22, 1926.

18. Earl J. Johnson, "Chicago Leaders Prepare for Eucharistic Congress of Roman Catholic Church," *Atlanta Constitution*, May 22, 1926. For evidence of the state of construction, see the photographs taken by Chicago Architectural Photographing Co., June 12 and July 9, 1926, in Soldier Field construction photograph album no. 2.

19. "Six Cardinals Sail for Chicago Visit; Headed by Bonzano," *WP*, June 6, 1926.

20. See "50 More Delegates Here for Conclave," *NYT*, June 16, 1926.

21. AP, "Prelates Leave New York," in *LAT*, June 17, 1926.

22. "Pilgrims Flock to Chicago," *NYT*, June 18, 1926.

23. "Crowds Stimulate Cardinals on Trip," *NYT*, June 18, 1926; Earl J. Johnson, "Cardinals' Train Reaches Chicago for Big Congress," *Atlanta Constitution*, June 18, 1926. The subhead of the latter article states that 200,000 people greeted the cardinals, but the body of the article says that "fully half a million persons" were in the crowds that day. See also AP, "Cardinals' Party Is Wildly Greeted by Chicago Throng," in *WP*, June 18, 1926, and John Clayton, "Chicago Growth since Last Visit Amazes Bonzano," *CDT*, June 18, 1926, which estimates the crowd at 150,000.

24. John Clayton, "Chicago Growth since Last Visit Amazes Bonzano," *CDT*, June 18, 1926.

25. Cornelius Francis Donovan, *The Story of the XXVIII Eucharistic Congress* (Chicago: Eucharistic Committee, 1927), 104.

26. Ibid., 102.

27. Ibid., 138–39.

28. "Place Visitors Now in City at Some 600,000," *CDT*, June 22, 1926; "Notes of the Eucharistic Congress," *CDT*, June 22, 1926.

29. Donovan, *Story*, 138–39; AP, "Rush of Throngs," in *LAT*, June 22, 1926.

30. Donovan, *Story*, 105, 140. Donovan writes that the organ began playing at 10 a.m., after which bishops were seen ascending the steps "immediately." Other accounts indicate that the procession was not completed, as had been planned, by 10 a.m.; I tend to believe them over Donovan but have left the timeframe ambiguous because of these conflicting accounts.

31. Ibid., 140–41.

32. Ibid., 141; Glenn Dillard Gunn, in *Herald-Examiner*, June 22, 1926, excerpted in Donovan, *Story*, 163.

33. "Notes of the Eucharistic Congress," *CDT*, June 22, 1926.

34. "250,000 Hear Mass outside Stadium," *NYT*, June 22, 1926.

35. Steve Kloehn, "Catholic Rally Holds Echoes of the Past," *CT*, June 22, 2000.

36. Donovan, *Story*, 141–47.

37. AP, "Epoch-Marking Worship at the Great Chicago Congress of Catholic Church," *Helena Independent*, June 22, 1926; AP, "Rush of Throngs," in *LAT*, June 22, 1926.

38. AP, "Rush of Throngs," in *LAT*, June 22, 1926.

39. "New Crowd Mark Made by Pilgrims, Overflowing Field," *WP*, June 23, 1926. For the remark on the June 22 events' possibly having been more heavily attended than even the Monday events, see "325,000 Attend Open-Air Services in Chicago Stadium," *NYT*, June 23, 1926.

40. "325,000 Attend Open-Air Services in Chicago Stadium," *NYT*, June 23, 1926.

41. Earl J. Johnson, "Catholic World Joins in Tribute to Sacred Host," *Atlanta Constitution*, June 23, 1926; "325,000 Attend Open-Air Services in Chicago Stadium," *NYT*, June 23, 1926.

42. "Quebec Premier Lauds Chicago for Hospitality," *CDT*, June 24, 1926.

43. W. B. Norton, "Dawn of Greater Day for Christianity Seen by Dr. James S. Stone," *CDT*, June 23, 1926.

44. *Herald of Christ's Kingdom* 9, no. 14, July 15, 1926.

45. See discussion below; there are some reasons to doubt that the 1954 Marian event actually surpassed the Eucharistic Congress events in size, and the 1954 event was not held over multiple days.

46. "Homage Paid to American Flag in Big Service," *Times of Northwest Indiana*, June 28, 1926.

47. "Youth of Chicago Unite for Easter Sunrise Services," *CDT*, April 17, 1933.

48. John Evans, "1,500 Churches Have Record Easter Crowds,"*CDT*, April 22, 1935.

49. John Evans, "Sunrise Service to Hail Easter at Soldier Field," *CDT*, March 22, 1936.

50. The conflict over which anniversary to celebrate cropped up again at Chicago's sesquicentennial, marked by Mayor Jane Byrne in 1983 and by Mayor Harold Washington in 1987. Mayor Richard M. Daley has always favored 1837, as the date of incorporation, March 4, coincides with his mother's birthday.

51. "Southeast Churches to Join Easter Celebration," *Chicago Southeast Economist*, March 25, 1937; "Weather," *CDT*, March 29, 1937.

52. "Weather," *CDT*, April 18, 1938.

53. John Evans, "Prepare Rites to Hail Sun on Easter Morning," *CDT*, March 27, 1938; John Evans, "40,000 Attend Soldiers' Field Dawn Service," *CDT*, April 18, 1938.

54. John Evans, "Expect 100,000 to Motor for Easter Service," *CDT*, March 26, 1939, SW1; AP, "Easter Celebrated in World Torn by Strife, War Fears," in *Galveston Daily Star*, April 10, 1939, 1.

55. "City Bundles Up for Its Coldest Easter Parade," *CDT*, March 24, 1940; Marcia Winn, "City's Churches Crowded with Easter Throngs," *CDT*, March 25, 1940; India Moffett, "Frigid Faithful Keep an Easter Date on Avenue," *CDT*, March 25, 1940; "Weather," *CDT*, March 25, 1940.

56. John Evans, "Decorate Soldiers' Field for 50,000 Worshipers," *CDT*, April 13, 1941.

57. Gladys Priddy, "Thousands Hail Easter's Dawn and Take Hope," *CDT*, April 26, 1943; John Evans, "Devout Throngs Pay Homage to Risen Savior," *CDT*, April 18, 1949; Jim Bowman, "Sun, Snow, and a Parade of Spectacular Easter Hats," *CT*, April 11, 1982.

58. "Plan Elaborate Easter Rites in City's Churches," *CDT*, April 8, 1950.

59. John Evans, "Expect 200,000 at Holy Name Field Service," *CDT*, Sept. 14, 1941.

60. "150,000 Attend Catholic Peace Prayer Service," *CDT*, Sept. 15, 1941.

61. John Evans, "120,000 Pray for U. S. Fighting Men," *CDT*, Sept. 14, 1942.

CHAPTER 7

1. Edward J. Kelly, speech at dedication of Soldier Field, Nov. 11, 1925, CPD/SF, speeches folder.

2. "Postmen Sell 100,000 Tickets for War Show," *CDT*, Aug. 27, 1918; "Exposition Great Living Picture of Modern Warfare," *CDT*, Sept. 1, 1918; E. M. Newman, "The Battle of Grant Park," *CDT*, Sept. 3, 1918; "Chicago Swarms War Exposition despite Rains," *CDT*, Sept. 3, 1918.

3. "What Defense Day Means," *LAT*, Sept. 10, 1924.

4. "Millions Rally to Colors," *CDT*, Sept. 13, 1924.

5. "Defense Day," *Time*, May 17, 1926, http://www.time.com/time/magazine/article/0,9171,769322,00.html (accessed April 14, 2006).

6. "Big War Show in Chicago Opens Next Friday," *Cook County Herald*, May 15, 1925; "You Won't See the Sham in This Sham Battle," *CDT*, May 3, 1925; "Cavalry Charge to Give Thrill at Army Show," *CDT*, May 11, 1925; "Mayor Orders Chicago Day of Military Show," *CDT*, April 5, 1925.

7. "Cold to Relax Its Hold on Chicago Today," *CDT*, May 25, 1925; "Dawes among 25,000 Who See Big Army Show," *CDT*, May 23, 1925.

8. "Planes High Up Obey Orders of Radio on Earth," *CDT*, May 24, 1925; "Military Show Closes; Backers Call It Success," *CDT*, May 25, 1925.

9. "Outdoor Fans Hear Square Dance Is Back," *CDT*, May 12, 1932.

10. "1,500 Soldiers Will Move into Loop Wednesday," *CDT*, June 13, 1932; Kathleen McLaughlin, "City Welcomes Miss Earhart Home," *CDT*, July 20, 1928.

11. Kathleen McLaughlin, "Amelia Flies to City; Given Noisy Ovation," *CDT*, June 25, 1932.

12. "Planes Thrill Crowd at Military Show," *CDT*, June 25, 1932.

13. "Troops Finish Their Drilling for War Show," *CDT*, May 29, 1933; William O'Neil, "50,000 Witness War Spectacle at Guard Show, *CDT*, Aug. 15, 1937; "Draw Up Battle Lines for Show of Army Might," *CDT*, June 18, 1938, 7.

14. Illinois National Guard, "Chicago's 1940 Military Show: Soldier Field, June 29–30, 1940" (program), Chicago History Museum; Jack Thompson, "Progress of 33d Division Draws Praise, Blame," *CDT*, Nov. 17, 1941.

15. Roger Biles, "Edward J. Kelly: New Deal Machine Builder," in *The Mayors: the Chicago Political Tradition*, ed. Paul Michael Green and Melvin G. Holli, 3rd. ed (Normal: Southern Illinois University Press, 1995), 118–19.

16. "Battle Troops Start Here for Army War Show," *CDT*, Aug. 28, 1942; "City Gets Taste of War in Army Show's Preview," *CDT*, Sept. 2, 1942; "War Show Arms Are on Display in Battle Depot," *CDT*, Sept. 3, 1942.

17. Charles Leavelle, "51,000 Thrill to Battle Din at Army Show," *CDT*, Sept. 4, 1942.

18. Paul Healy, "Gay and Lively War Bond Show Warms Throng," *CDT*, Sept. 17, 1943; "Americanism Rally Pledges to Crush Japs," *CDT*, May 21, 1945.

19. "Chicagoans See Two Jet Planes—but Not Long," *CDT*, April 7, 1946.

20. "Militia Holds Motor Drill in Soldiers' Field," *CDT*, April 23, 1945; George Schreiber, "Militia to Hold Disaster Relief Maneuver Here," *CDT*, Sept. 16, 1945; "Trophies Awarded Reserve Militia," *CDT*, Sept. 24, 1945.

21. "10,000 Watch Park District Water Show," *CDT*, Aug. 8, 1960; "Crowds Watch Park District Water Show," *CDT*, Aug. 6, 1962.

22. "Men and Missile" (photo), *CDD*, Sept. 15, 1960.

23. "1,200 March to Dedicate Stadium," *CA*, Sept. 6, 1924; Walter Eckersall, "Police Games to Open New Chicago Stadium," *CDT*, Sept. 5, 1924.

24. "60,000 Voice City's Spirit at Stadium Fete," *CDT*, Oct. 10, 1924; "60,000 Invited to See Chicago Fire Pageant," *CDT*, Oct. 8, 1924.

25. "New Chief May Abolish Annual Police Games," *CDT*, April 22, 1927. See, for example, Walter Eckersall, "30,000 Attend Police Games; Finals Today," *CDT*, Aug. 19, 1928.

26. "Recalls Steam Pumper at Fire Show of 1877," *CDT*, June 30, 1940. For a description of the first test of Chicago's first horseless fire engine on January 27, 1877, see "The City-Hall," *CDT*, Jan. 28, 1877.

27. "Bud's Junior Firemen Win Honors at Show," *CD*, June 7, 1930.

28. Charles Leavelle, "Police and Fire Teams Perfect Thrilling Acts," *CDT*, July 12, 1938.

29. Charles Leavelle, "70,000 Thrilled by Police and Fire Spectacle," *CDT*, July 18, 1938; William Moore, "American Flag Biggest Thrill at Thrill Show," *CDT*, July 15, 1940.

30. James P. Allman, Michael J. Corrigan, and Roger F. Shanahan, "Thrill Show Receipts," *CDT*, Nov. 10, 1943. See also Biles, "Edward J. Kelly," 119–20.

31. Chicago Park District, annual reports (1936–1965). Annual reports prior to 1952 detail attendance at individual events held at Soldier Field; in subsequent years, the reports became more aesthetically pleasing, adding photographs and other graphics, but provided less information about specific activities. Revenue for the 1960s appears to have peaked in 1960, at about $113,000 (about $810,000 in 2008 dollars).

32. James O'Donnell Bennett, "Chicagoland Joins in Great Music Festival," *CDT*, June 15, 1930; Philip Maxwell, "Minneapolis to Enter Chorus in Music Festival," *CDT*, June 7, 1936; "Death of Patrick S. Gilmore," *CDT*, Sept. 27, 1892; "The Great Chicago Jubilee," *CDT*, May 18, 1873, 16; "The Jubillee," *CDT*, June 6, 1873.

33. James O'Donnell Bennett, "150,000 Hear Feast of Song," *CDT*, Aug. 24, 1930.

34. Judy Roberts, "James A. Mundy Just Keeps Right on Singing," *CT*, Feb. 22, 1970.

35. "You'll Enjoy Yourself," *CDT*, Aug. 3, 1930; Judy Roberts, "James A. Mundy Just Keeps Right on Singing," *CT*, Feb. 22, 1970; Seymour Korman, "Negroes to Sing Songs of Race at Music Fest," *CDT*, Aug. 10, 1934.

36. Nahum Daniel Brascher, "Random Thoughts," *CD*, Aug. 17, 1935.

37. "An Elevator Boy Sings to Victory in Festival Test," *CDT*, Aug. 13, 1930.

38. Marian Anderson, "James A. Mundy" (letter to the editor), *CD*, Feb. 10, 1940.

39. Philip Maxwell, "2,000 to Play in Festival's Accordion Unit," *CDT*, April 26, 1959. Also see, for example: "The Woman's World: Bands Will Compete in Music Festival," *Oshkosh* (WI) *Northwestern*, Aug. 23, 1957; Philip Maxwell, "Accordion Band of 1,000 to Play at Music Fete," *CDT*, April 26, 1953; Philip Maxwell, "Open Accordion Tests Monday for Festival," *CDT*, July 31, 1952.

40. "1,000 South Side Girls to Dance at Tribune Fete," *CDT*, June 12, 1932; Charles Leavelle, "Fats Waller to Swing It at Music Festival," *CDT*, Aug. 17, 1939; "Fats Waller Sets Precedent and 'Sends' 90,000 with Swing at Chicago Festival," *CD*, Aug. 26, 1939; Irene Powers, "Final Music Festival Luncheon Will Bring Back Memories," *CT*, Aug. 11, 1966.

41. See, for example, "Fats Waller Sets Precedent," *CD*, Aug. 26, 1939; "Local Singers Go to Chicago," *Waukesha Daily Freeman*, Aug. 24, 1954; Kermit Holt, "90,000 Cheers Reward Man Who Fought for Folk Music," *CDT*, Aug. 12, 1951; "28th Annual Chicagoland Music Festival Program," 6–7, CPD/SF, 1957; Robert Wiedrich, "Music Festival Fans await Match Thrill," *CDT*, Aug. 19, 1960; "Miss Hawaii Arrives for Music Fest" (photograph), *CDT*, Aug. 19, 1960, C10.

42. See, for example, Edward Moore, "Chorus Contest Launches Great Music Festival," *CDT*, Aug. 20, 1931, and 28th Annual Chicagoland Music Festival (script), 1957 Chicagoland Music Festival folder, 11, CPD/SF.

43. See, for example, the Southern Illinois University Web site, http://www.siu.edu/~music/faculty/Best.html (accessed May 12 and Dec. 8, 2006).

44. "Contest Winners Appear at Festival—Sousa Applauded," *CDT*, Aug. 23, 1931; "Edward Moore, Al Jolson Will Sing Tonight at Music Festival," *CDT*, Aug. 18, 1934; Edward Moore, "Festival Thrills 100,000," *CDT*, Aug. 19, 1934; "Jolson Arrives for Music Festival," *CDT*, Aug. 20, 1949; "Liberace, Colorful Pageantry for Music Festival," *CDT*, Aug. 15, 1954; Clay Gowran, "The Big Names Begin Arriving for Festival," *CDT*, Aug. 23, 1957; "Here's the Program for Music Festival," *CT*, Aug. 17, 1963; Larry Wolters, "Folk Music, Waltzes, Jazz Set 35th Festival Aglow," *CT*, Aug. 9, 1964.

45. "Huge Audience Thrills Stars of Music Fete," *CT*, Aug. 17, 1964.

46. Philip Maxwell, "Music Festival Match Lighting Copied Widely," *CDT*, June 7, 1953; Thomas Carvlin, "Match Lights to Glow Again at Music Fete," *CDT*, Aug. 15, 1961.

47. 28th Annual Chicagoland Music Festival (script), 1957 Chicagoland Music Festival folder, 14, CPD/SF.

48. South Park Commissioners, "Record of Uses of Soldier Field"(unpublished manuscript), Soldier Field general events folder, 1 CPD/SF; display advertisement, *CDT*, July 3, 1925.

49. "40,000 See 'Birth of Chicago' in Old Indian Days," *CDT*, July 5, 1926.

50. Henry Bolles, *Industrial History of the United States: From the Earliest Settlements to the Present Time* (Boston: Henry Bill Publishing, 1878), 476–77; "It's July 4th!" *CT*, July 4, 1973.

51. William Shinnick, "50,000 Cheer Legion Show in Soldiers' Field," *CDT*, July 5, 1935; "Legion in County Plans 2d Annual July 4 Program," *CDT*, June 5, 1936; "Legionnaire's [*sic*] Huge Fireworks Show July 4," *Garfieldian*, June 23, 1938.

52. "Fireworks Ban to Be Enforced," *Garfieldian*, June 23, 1938; "Fireworks Ban to Mean First Really Sane 4th," *CDT*, June 14, 1942.

53. "For a Safe and Sane Fourth," *CDT*, June 26, 1938; "Expect 75,000 Lie Tests Considered at Legion Fete for Evanston Police," *CDT*, July 4, 1961; "Police Get Orders to Enforce Ban on Sale of Fireworks," *CDT*, June 27, 1935. Some later reports, such as the 1961 article, incorrectly state that the Legion show began after a municipal ban passed in 1935, but reports in 1934 also mention the ban. Kelly does, however, appear to have spurred police and fire officials to enforce the ban more vigorously around this time, and the Chicago Park District—still under Kelly's heavy influence—worked with the American Legion and other groups to provide alternatives to private fireworks.

54. "City's Millions Fete Freedom's Birth in Nation," *CDT*, July 5, 1940; "Legionnaire's [*sic*] Huge Fireworks Show July 4," *Garfieldian*, June 23, 1938.

55. Mimeographed program, 22nd Annual 4th of July Show—Cook County Council of the American Legion, 1–2, July 4th, 1956, folder, CPD/SF; "American Top Entertainers Booked by Alameda County Fair," *Oakland* (CA) *Tribune*, June 9, 1954; "Fair Will Open at Kingsville on Tuesday," *Valley Morning Star* (Harlingen, TX), Nov. 8, 1949; photo, *Ada* (OK) *Evening News*, Aug. 26, 1956.

CHAPTER 8

1. "Norse, Germans Celebrate Deeds of Their Races," *CDT*, Sept. 21, 1925; "70,000 Expected to Attend Second Annual German Day Festival," *CDT*, June 3, 1926; "Austrians Here to Get Pointers on Industries," *CDT*, June 13, 1926; "50,000 to Fete German Day at Soldiers' Field," *CDT*, June 19, 1927; "30,000 Sing in Praise of U.S. on German Day," *CDT*, June 4, 1928; "City's Germans Honor Schurz at Annual Festival," *CDT*, May 27, 1929.

2. Annette R. Hofmann, "150 Years of Turnerism in the United States," speech given at the Athenaeum in Indianapolis, Aug. 3, 1998, http://www.iupui.edu/~hoyt/Hofmann.htm (accessed Oct. 13, 2006).

3. AP, "Reviews Contributions of Germans to Culture of the United States," in *Daily Northwestern* (Oshkosh, WI), Aug. 14, 1933.

4. "Jewish Group Protests Use of Nazi Flag," *CDT*, June 10, 1936; "Norse, Germans Celebrate Deeds of Their Races," *CDT*, Sept. 21, 1925; "45,000 Attend Annual German Day Pageantry," *CDT*, June 15, 1936.

5. Betty Browning, "Two-Day Fete to Honor First Swedes in U. S.," *CDT*, July 7, 1938.

6. Lisa Boehm and Beth Krissof, *Popular Culture and the Enduring Myth of Chicago, 1871–1968* (New York: Routledge, 2004), 109–10.

7. Roger Biles, "Edward J. Kelly: New Deal Machine Builder," in *The Mayors: the Chicago Political Tradition*, ed. Paul Michael Green and Melvin G. Holli, 3rd. ed (Normal: Southern Illinois University Press, 1995), 112–13; Special to *NYT*, "Chicago Fair Opened by Farley; Rays of Arcturus Start Lights," *NYT*, May 28, 1933; James O'Donnell Bennett, "Exposition Starts with Pageant in Soldiers' Field," *CDT*, May 28, 1933.

8. Arthur A. Goren, *The Politics and Public Culture of American Jews* (Bloomington: University of Indiana Press, 1999), 30–47.

9. Meyer W. Weisgal, *Meyer Weisgal . . . So Far* (New York: Random House, 1971), 103–7.

10. Ibid., 110.

11. Ibid., 103–8; Walter Roth, *Looking Backward: True stories from Chicago's Jewish History* (Chicago: Academy Chicago Publishers, 2002), 27–28.

12. Weisgal, *Meyer Weisgal* , 106–9; David Garfield, "The Romance of a People," *Educational Theatre Journal* 24, no. 4 (Dec. 1972): 436–42.

13. Weisgal, *Meyer Weisgal*, 110; Michael Smith, "Israel Science Chief Tells of Debt to City," *CT*, Dec. 21, 1967.

14. Weisgal, *Meyer Weisgal*, 110; Edward Moore, "Jewish Musical Event Revives

Ancient Forms," *CDT*, July 2, 1933; Edward Moore, "Stage Effects at Jewish Fete to Make History," *CDT*, June 17, 1933.

15. John Evans, "Jewish Pageant to Depict 40 Centuries of Religion," *CDT*, June 9, 1933. See also "Pageant to Depict Rise of Religion," *NYT*, June 11, 1933.

16. Michael Smith, "Israel Science Chief Tells of Debt to City," *CT*, Dec. 21, 1967.

17. Weisgal, *Meyer Weisgal*, 59, 110–12.

18. Ibid.; Garfield, "Romance of a People," 437. For more on Weizmann, see, for example, Elinor Slater and Robert Slater, *Great Jewish Men* (Middle Village, NY: Jonathan David Publishers, 2003), 319–23.

19. Weisgal, *Meyer Weisgal*, 112–13; John Evans, "3,600 Jews Hold Full Rehearsal of Fete Tonight," *CDT*, June 25, 1933; AP, "125,000 to See Big Spectacle: Jews to Present 'Romance of a People' at Chicago World's Fair," in *Lowell* (MA) *Sun*, July 3, 1933.

20. "800 Policemen Clear Jam at Jewish Play," *CDT*, July 4, 1933; Weisgal, *Meyer Weisgal*, 112; Edward Moore, "Stage Effects at Jewish Fete to Make History," *CDT*, June 17, 1933; James O'Donnell Bennett, "125,000 Witness Jewish Spectacle," *CDT*, July 4, 1933; S. J. Duncan-Clark, "Jewish 'Romance of a People' Kindles Thrill of Faith in 150,000 Spectators," *CDN*, July 5, 1933; John Evans, "Pageant Tells 4,000 Year Epic of a Great Race," *CDT*, July 2, 1933; Garfield, "Romance of a People," 441.

21. Weisgal, *Meyer Weisgal*, 112–14; James O'Donnell Bennett, "Great Jewish Play Repeated before 55,000," *CDT*, July 6, 1933.

22. "Jewish Pageant Grosses $450,000," *NYT*, Oct. 20, 1933; Weisgal, *Meyer Weisgal*, 114–40; Roth, *Looking Backward*, 27–28.

23. Marian M. Ohman, "Major N. Clark Smith in Chicago," *Journal of the Illinois State Historical Society* 96, no. 1 (2003): 49–79; Christopher Robert Reed, "A Reinterpretation of Black Strategies for Change at the Chicago World's Fair, 1933–1934," *Illinois Historical Journal* 81 (Spring 1988): 2–12; Christopher R. Reed, "In the Shadow of Fort Dearborn: Honoring De Saible at the Chicago World's Fair of 1933–1934," *Journal of Black Studies* 21, no. 4. (June 1991): esp. 400–405.

24. Oscar DePriest, "DePriest Not to Take Part in 'Negro Day' Program," *CD*, Aug. 5, 1933; Ohman, "Major N. Clark Smith," 62–66; "'Negro Day' at Fair Flops," *CDD*, Aug, 19, 1933; "Rise of Negro Dramatized in Pageant at Fair," *CDT*, Aug. 13, 1933; Dewey R. Jones, "The Last Day at the Fair," *CD*, Nov. 18, 1933.

25. Percy Wood, "Test in House Faces World's Fair Measures," *CDT*, Feb. 21, 1934.

26. Ohman, "Major N. Clark Smith," 66–68.

27. Ibid., 66–70; Kirk, Elise, *American Opera* (Champaign: University of Illinois Press, 2001), 186–88; Giles Oakley, *The Devil's Music: A History of the Blues* (New York: De Capo Press, 1997), 40–48; Reginal T. Buckner, "Rediscovering Major N. Clark Smith," *Music Educators Journal* 71, no. 6 (Feb. 1985): 41.

28. T. C. Jones, "Rites Set for Dr. J. Wesley Jones," *CDD*, Feb. 13, 1961; "Well Done, Faithful Servant," *CDD*, Feb. 15, 1961.

29. Nahum Daniel Brascher, "Hail National Auditions throughout Country," *CD*, March 17, 1934.

30. Display ad for *O, Sing a New Song*, *CD*, April 7, 1934.

31. "Big Indiana Choir to Sing at Auditions Music Fest," *CD*, June 30, 1934; "Rosenwald Fund in O.K. of Auditions," *CD*, July 7, 1934.

32. "National Auditions Wins Support of Music Masters," *CD*, May 5, 1934.

33. Nahum Daniel Brascher, "National Auditions Wins Support throughout East," *CD*, June 30, 1934.

34. "Chorus of 5,000 to Be Heard in Negro Pageant," *CDT*, Aug. 5, 1934; Judy Roberts, "James A. Mundy Just Keeps Right on Singing," *CT*, Feb. 22, 1970.

35. "Africans to Aid Pageant," *CD*, Aug. 11, 1934.

36. "Expect 75,000 to See Negro Pageant Tonight," *CDT*, Aug. 25, 1934; "Negro Pageant Makes Jobs for Multitude Here," *CDT*, Aug. 22, 1934.

37. "Expect 75,000 to See Negro Pageant Tonight," *CDT*, Aug. 25, 1934; Seymour Kor-

man, "Mighty Pageant of Negro People Seen by Throng," *CDT*, Aug. 26, 1934; AP, "Negroes in a Pageant," Aug. 25, 1934.

38. "Name Winners in $3,000 Auditions Contests," *CD*, Sept. 15, 1934; "First Pianist of Race with Detroit Symphony," *CD*, March 19, 1938.

39. Albert G. Barnett, "O, Sing a New Song," *CDD*, Sept. 1, 1934.

40. "Chicago Will View 'Pageant of Celt,'" *NYT*, Aug. 3, 1934; Larry Kelly, "Old Irish Glory Thrills Throng at Celt Pageant," *CDT*, Aug. 29, 1934; "Irish Pageant Is Rehearsed; 1,000 in Chorus," *CDT*, Aug. 27, 1934; "'Pageant of Celt' Given Second Time at Soldiers' Field," *CDT*, Aug. 30, 1934.

CHAPTER 9

1. See Bill Gleason, *Daley of Chicago* (New York: Simon and Schuster, 1970), 112, on Richard J. Daley not wanting to be called a "Stock Yards cowboy" by opponents. But see Len O'Connor, *Clout: Mayor Daley and His City* (New York: Avon Books, 1975), 23–24, on how, late in life, Daley seems to have embraced his past at the Stock Yards.

2. Michael Allen, *Rodeo Cowboys in the North American Imagination* (Reno: University of Nevada Press, 1998), 22–23; Beverly J. Stoeltje, "Rodeo: From Custom to Ritual," *Western Folklore* 48, no. 3. (July 1989): 244–55.

3. AP, "Facing Blindness, Tex Austin Takes His Own Life," in *Albuquerque Journal*, Oct. 27, 1938; "'Tex' Austin Killed by Gas in His Garage," *NYT*, Oct. 27, 1938; "Tex Austin Expected to Reach City Soon," *Indianapolis Star*, May 18, 1919; "Riders Are Thronging to Fort Bayard Rodeo," *Deming* (NM) *Headlight*, Dec. 16, 1921.

4. The Pendleton Roundup celebrates its hundredth anniversary in 2010.

5. "World Title Rodeo to Limn Frontier Here," *CDT*, May 3, 1925; "Rodeo Fans to See Country's Wildest Horses," *CDT*, July 5, 1925.

6. H. J. Streibert, "Against the Rodeo" (Voice of the People letter), *CDT*, May 12, 1925; "Protests Aimed at Rodeo Fall on Deaf Ears," *CDT*, May 13, 1925; "Gents of Range Offer Refined but Real Rodeo," *CDT*, Aug. 7, 1925.

7. Richard W. Slatta, *The Cowboy Encyclopedia* (New York: W. W. Norton, 1996), 319–20; "Champ Woman Steer Roper to Compete Here," *CDT*, July 12, 1925; "Chicago Is Lassoed by Cowgirl Champs," *CDN*, Aug. 14, 1925; "Patter of Cowboys Pithy and Expressive; A 'Salty' Horse Is No Dead One," *CDN*, Aug. 15, 1925; "Riders Parade Loop, Opening 9-Day Rodeo," *CDN*, Aug. 15, 1925; Frank Ridgway, "Farm & Garden," *CDT*, Aug. 20, 1925.

8. Genevieve Forbes Herrick, "15,000 Women Shout Approval as Rodeo Opens," *CDT*, Aug. 16, 1925; "Record Crowds Come by Train for Rodeo," *CDN*, Aug. 18, 1925; "Chicago Rodeo Is to Be Made Annual Event," *CDT*, Aug. 24, 1925; "Rodeo Here," *Riverdale* (IL) *Pointer*, Aug. 21, 1925; "Southern Boosters Will Witness Rodeo," *CDN*, Aug, 19, 1925; "Soldiers' Field Becomes Ranch Today for Rodeo," *CDT*, Aug. 14, 1927.

9. "Gored Cowboy's Nerve Thrills 70,000 at Rodeo," *CDT*, Aug. 17, 1925; Clifford Peter Westermeier, *Man, Beast, Dust: The Story of the Rodeo* (Omaha: University of Nebraska Press, 2005), 325.

10. "Only $5.50 Round Trip—Chicago, Sunday, Aug. 22" (advertisement), *Cedar Rapids* (IA) *Republican*, Aug. 20, 1926; "35,000 Brave Rain to Watch Cowboy Stunts," *CDT*, Aug. 16, 1926; "Wild West Feats Thrill 80,000 in a Day at Rodeo," *CDT*, Aug. 22, 1926; "35,000 Cheer Broncho Riders as Rodeo Opens," *CDT*, Aug. 21, 1927; "Rodeo's Close Puts Laurels on New Riders," *CDT*, Aug. 30, 1927; "Mayor's Advisory Group to Take Charge of Rodeo," *CDT*, Sept. 5, 1927; "Rodeo Contests for $33,000 in Prizes Opened," *CDT*, July 29, 1928; AP, "Facing Blindness, Tex Austin Takes His Own Life," in *Albuquerque Journal*, Oct. 27, 1938.

11. "Duties of WAAC Get Top Billing over Gene Autry," *CDT*, July 26, 1942; "Local Brevities," *Valparaiso Vidette-Messenger*, July 22, 1942; John McBride, *Searching for John Ford* (New York: St. Martin's Press, 2001), 57–58; "Big Crowds See Rodeo Acts in Soldiers' Field," *CDT*, Sept. 6, 1943; "Rodeo and Thrill Show at Soldiers' Field for 2 Days," *CDT*, Sept.

5, 1943; "Our Town," *CDT*, July 27, 1947; "N. Siders Have Part in Rodeo Set for Today," *CDT*, July 20, 1947; "Chicago Model Ropes in Title of Rodeo Queen," *CDT*, July 15, 1947; Larry Wolters, "New Antenna for Television Improves View," *CDT*, July 22, 1947.

12. "Rodeo and Thrill Show to Be Held at Soldiers' Field," *CT*, June 29, 1966; Herb Lyon, "Tower Ticker," *CT*, July 10, 1966; David Condon, "In the Wake of the News," *CT*, July 15, 1966; "Gala Shows Set for Soldier Field," *CDD*, March 25, 1975.

13. "35,000 Brave Rain to Watch Cowboy Stunts," *CDT*, Aug. 16, 1926; "Rodeo Broncho Kills Girl," *CDT*, Aug. 21, 1926; "Award $35,000 Cowboy Prizes as Rodeo Ends," *CDT*, Aug. 23, 1926.

14. For Dempsey and Tunney background, sources include Nathan Miller, *New World Coming: The 1920s and the Making of Modern America* (New York: Scribner, 2003), 336–39; Randy Roberts, *Jack Dempsey: The Manassa Mauler* (Champaign: University of Illinois Press, 2003), 3–66, 212–35; and Gavin Evans, *Kings of the Ring: The History of Heavyweight Boxing* (London: Weidenfeld & Nicolson, 2005), 74–87.

15. "N.Y. Turns Tex's Dempsey-Tunney Ring Bout Down," *CDT*, June 23, 1926; "Rickard Talks of Bouts Here," *CDT*, June 24, 1926; AP, "Rickard Hopeful of Chicago Bout," in *NYT*, July 19, 1926; Walter Eckersall, "Dempsey Fights Tunney Here Sept. 11," *CDT*, July 22, 1926; "Tex Grows Cool to Title Fight Here," *CDT*, July 23, 1926; "Title Bout Here, Chicagoans Claim," *CDT*, July 23, 1927; Teddy Hayes, *With the Gloves Off: My Life in the Boxing and Political Arenas* (Houston: Lancha Books, 1977), chap. 10, http://www.genetunney.org/gloves1.html (accessed Oct. 10, 2005); "In the Wake of the News," *CDT*, July 1, 1927.

16. Charles J. McGuirk, "The Inside Story of the Fight Racket," *New McClure's* 61, no. 5 (Nov. 1928): 18ff; Roberts, *Jack Dempsey*, 230–32; James Dawson, "Tunney Title Bout Set about Sept. 10," *NYT*, June 20, 1927; "The Dempsey Tunney Fight" (memorandum on South Park Board's role in the fight), Dempsey-Tunney folder, CPD/SF.

17. "Jack Dempsey a Happy Man," *LAT*, June 16, 1920; "Jury Loses Little Time in Acquitting Champion," *WP*, June 16, 1920; "Dempsey on Stand Replies to Charges," *NYT*, June 15, 1920; "Legionnaires Plan to Halt Dempsey Bout," *Atlanta Constitution*, July 26, 1927; AP, "Chicago Councilmen Dislike Dempsey," in *Atlanta Constitution*, July 26, 1927; "$100,000 Rental to Help Pay Expenses for Soldier Field," *NYT*, Aug. 28, 1927; "Petition to Prevent Fight Filed by Chicago Lawyer," *WP*, July 28, 1927; "Dempsey Balks at Rickard's Date for Fight," *LAT*, Aug. 2, 1927; Walter Eckersall, "Stadium Terms for Title Bout Are Outlined," *CDT*, July 28, 1927.

18. McGuirk, "Inside Story," 18; "Dempsey's Training Camp at Lincoln Fields Track," *WP*, Aug. 12, 1927; "Mates Cringe at Blows of Dempsey," *WP*, Aug. 28, 1927; James Dawson, "5,000 See Dempsey Go through Drill," *NYT*, Sept. 1, 1927; Walter Eckersall, "Tunney to Groom Self for Battle in Sylvan Camp," *CDT*, Aug. 19, 1927; Walter Eckersall, "Gene Says He Is Fit to Defend Title Now," *CDT*, Sept. 4, 1927; "Bout Applications Opened in Chicago," *NYT*, Aug. 9, 1927; "100,000 Railroad Stations to Sell Chicago Bout Tickets," *NYT*, Aug. 12, 1927; "Days Ticket Sale for Bout $200,000," *NYT*, Aug. 16, 1927; James Dawson, "To Issue Seat Plat 4 Days before Bout," *NYT*, Sept. 8, 1927; Don Maxwell, "Rickard Reveals Allotment of Front Row Seats," *CDT*, Sept. 14, 1927.

19. Robert J. Schoenberg, *Mr. Capone: The Real—and Complete—Story of Al Capone* (New York: HarperCollins, 1993), 179; McGuirk, "Inside Story," 131.

20. James R. Harrison, "Tunney Will Defend His Crown Tonight; Betting Now Even," *NYT*, Sept. 22, 1927; Paul Lowry, "Jack Picked by Lowry: Fight Viewed as Epic or Farce," *LAT*, Sept. 22, 1927; Gene Fowler, "Forecasts on Outcome of Bout Widely Different," *Bridgeport Telegram*, Sept. 22, 1927; Tom Mix, "Who Wins in Chicago?" *Life*, Sept. 15, 1927; Damon Runyon, "Tunney Clashes with Dempsey Tonight," *Bridgeport Telegram*, Sept. 22, 1927.

21. South Park District, agreement in re Tunney-Dempsey boxing match, paragraph 10, 2, Dempsey-Tunney Agreements folder, CPD/SF; "Trib Announcers to Put Dempsey Battle on Air," *CDT*, Sept. 11, 1927; AP, "Huge Radio Chain to Describe Big Battle," in *Bridgeport Telegram*, Sept. 22, 1927; Miller, *New World Coming*, 337; Ed Frayne, "Boxing

Board to Have Final Say as to Winner of Battle Tonight by Setting Precedent," *Bridgeport Telegram*, Sept. 22, 1927.

22. AP, "Final Statements from Fighters and Managers," in *LAT*, Sept. 22, 1927; Louella O. Parsons, "Estelle Taylor Confident Jack Will Win Battle," *Bridgeport Telegram*, Sept. 22, 1927.

23. Miller, *New World Coming*, 337; AP, "Chicago Is a Fistic Mecca," in *LAT*, Sept. 22, 1927; AP, "Over 150,000 Seek Lakefront Arena," in *Decatur Daily Herald*, Sept. 22, 1927.

24. "Army of Police Smooths Fight Traffic Lanes," *CDT*, Sept. 23, 1927; Don Maxwell, "150,000 at Fight Tonight," *CDT*, Sept. 22, 1927; AP, "Dry Agents Busy," in *Decatur Daily Herald*, Sept. 22, 1927; James Dawson, "Fight Fast and Furious," *NYT*, Sept. 23, 1927.

25. "Armored Auto Carries Tunney from Camp Here," *CDT*, Sept. 23, 1927; "Story of Tunney-Dempsey Bout as Broadcast from Ringside," *NYT*, Sept. 23, 1927; "Yale Okun Beaten by George Manley," *NYT*, Sept. 23, 1927; UP, "Dry Agents Wink at Hip-pocket 'Heating Units,'" in *Charleston Gazette*, Sept. 23, 1927; Walter Eckersall, "Tunney's Ring Craft Is Credited for His Victory; Given 8 of 10 Rounds," *CDT*, Sept. 23, 1927; James O'Donnell Bennett, "Crowd Screams at Tense Drama as Gene Rises," *CDT*, Sept. 23, 1927; "Blow by Blow Story of Dempsey-Tunney Battle," *LAT*, Sept. 23, 1927; William Nack, "The Long Count," *Sports Illustrated*, Sept. 22, 1997; Damon Runyon (Universal Service), "Ex-Marine Rallies to Get Victory after His First Taste of Canvas," in *Charleston Gazette*, Sept. 23, 1927; AP, "Gene Admits Fear of Fighting Jack," in *Charleston Gazette*, Sept. 23, 1927; "Three Seconds Saved Gene, Says Lytton," *CDT*, Sept. 23, 1927.

26. "Champion Placid after the Fight," *NYT*, Sept. 23, 1927; AP, "Jack Balks Short Count Alibi Claim," in *Charleston Gazette*, Sept. 23, 1927; AP, "Radio Fight Returns Kill Twelve Fans in Six States," *CDT*, Sept. 24, 1927.

27. South Park Commissioners, statement of Soldier Field maintenance and operation for the fiscal year ending Feb. 28, 1929, financial statements folder, CPD/SF; Wilfrid Smith, "Close Soldiers' Field to N.Y. Charity Bout," *CDT*, Feb. 1, 1931; Westbrook Pegler, "Walker Fights 15 Round Draw with Sharkey," *CDT*, July 23, 1931.

28. PSPC, May to Dec. 17, 1924.

29. Linn White, "Soldier Field in Chicago," unpublished bound manuscript (1936), 12, CPD/SF; Bert M. Thorud, "Architectural Engineering: Stadia Sight Lines," *American Architect* 124, no. 2435 (Dec. 19, 1923): 563.

30. "Cards and Bears in Clash Today at Soldier Field," *CA*, Nov. 11, 1926; "Dunn Hurt as Bears Batter Cards, 10 to 0," *CDT*, Nov. 12, 1926.

31. "Packers Drill on Icy Grid for Tilt with Bears," *CDT*, Dec. 16, 1926; "Bears Fight Green Bay to Tie, 3–3," *CDT*, Dec. 20, 1926; "Gibbons Is Dead; J. Carr Slated for Treasurer," *CDT*, April 20, 1921; Chicago Park District, eleventh annual report (1945), 66; David Condon, "A Nun's Idea in 1926 Piles Up Touchdowns for Charity," *CDT*, Oct. 24, 1946; David Condon, "In the Wake of the News," *CDT*, Sept. 8, 1959; Edward Prell, "Hornets Seek Franchise Sale," *CDT*, Jan. 15, 1950.

32. Cooper Rollow, "Cards' Top Draft Pick: Soldiers' Field," *CDT*, Feb. 27, 1959; Cooper Rollow, "Cards' Hopes for Soldiers' Field Rise: Park Board Votes for Improvements," *CDT*, March 11, 1959; "Soldier Field Ready to Give Cardinals a Home," *CA*, March 10, 1959; Cooper Rollow, "Bears Rout Cards, 31–7; Fifth in Row!" *CDT*, Nov. 30, 1959; George Strickler, "It's Official, Final, Permanent; Cards Go," *CDT*, March 30, 1960; "Grid Cards Pay City $110,000," *CA*, Aug. 23, 1960.

33. Bob Verdi, "Fans Grin, Bare Fire Pyromania," *CT*, July 11, 1974; Cooper Rollow, *Cooper Rollow's Bears Football Book* (Ottawa, IL: Jameson Books, 1985), 62; Leo Zainea, "Origer Seeks to Put Out Fire," *CT*, Oct. 29, 1974.

34. George Halas, with Gwen Morgan and Arthur Vesey, *Halas by Halas: The Autobiography of George Halas* (New York: McGraw-Hill, 1979), 217–20; "Bears, Cards Ready for Benefit Duel," *CDD*, Sept. 1, 1966.

35. "Tribune Gives $21,000 to Charity Funds," CDT, Oct. 25, 1934.

36. Arch Ward, "College All-Star Voting Opens thruout Nation: Contributions to Army

Relief Rise to $81,800," *CDT*, July 12, 1942; "Donations to All-Star Fund Reach $70,500: 'Tribune Booster' Gives $1,500," *CDT*, July 5, 1942; Arch Ward, "All-Star Drive Nears Goal," *CDT*, July 19, 1942.

37. Howard Roberts, "It's Foot-Baugh Tilt as All-Stars Win 6–0," *CDN*, Sept. 2, 1937; John C. Hibner, "The Death of an All-Star Game," *Professional Football Researchers Association Annual, 1986* (Huntingdon, PA: Professional Football Researchers Association, 1986), http://www.footballresearch.com/articles/frpage.cfm?topic=y-allstargame (accessed April 12, 2006).

CHAPTER 10

1. Billy Graham, *Just As I Am: The Autobiography of Billy Graham* (New York: HarperCollins, 1999), 92–93; Martin Emil Marty, *Modern American Religion: Under God, Indivisible, 1941–1960* (Chicago: University of Chicago Press, 1996), 150–53; Torrey Johnson and Robert Cook, *Reaching Youth for Christ* (Chicago: Moody Bible Institute, 1944), 12; interview with Torrey Maynard Johnson by Robert Shuster, Oct. 23, 1984, transcript of tape T1, collection 285, BGC/PTMJ, http://www.wheaton.edu/bgc/archives/trans/285t01.htm (accessed Sept. 14, 2005). Some sources have May 20 or May 26 as the date of the first Saturday night rally of twenty weeks over the summer of 1944. Johnson and Cook put it on May 27—the Saturday that immediately preceded Memorial Day, at the time always observed on May 30.

2. Interview with Torrey Maynard Johnson, Dec. 13, 1984, transcript of tape T3, collection 285, BGC/PTMJ, http://www.wheaton.edu/bgc/archives/trans/285t03.htm (accessed Sept. 14, 2005).

3. Ibid.

4. "25,000 Are Expected at 'Youth for Christ' Rally Tomorrow Night," *CDT*, Oct. 20, 1944, 19. On evangelicals, including Graham, using sports stars such as Dodds to attract young people, especially men, see Marjorie Garber, "Two Point Conversion," in *Religion and American Culture*, ed. Marjorie Garber and Rebecca Walkowitz (New York: Routledge, 1999), 284–85. See also Bayard B. Browne, assistant regional administrator, War Production Board, Nutrition in Industry Program, letter to the Rev. Torrey M. Johnson, Oct. 28, 1944, folder 2, box 45, collection 285, BGC/PTMJ.

5. Tom E. Nash, secretary, Chicago Park District Board, letter to the Rev. Torrey M. Johnson, Jan. 15, 1945, folder 27, box 14; "Itinerary of Gospel Teams for Week of May 7, 1945," folder 27, box 14; Torrey Maynard Johnson, letter to pastors, May 10, 1945, folder 27, box 14; interview of Torrey Maynard Johnson by Robert Shuster, Aug. 14, 1985, tape 6. All in collection 285, BGC/PTMJ.

6. Torrey Maynard Johnson, general letter to eight thousand Christian leaders, April 26, 1945, folder 27, box 14; Dwight H. Green, letter to Torrey M. Johnson, March 13, 1945, folder 45, box 3; C. J. Ulrich, Radio Program Sponsors Letter, undated (spring 1945), folder 27, box 14; Charles Palmquist, Poster Committee Letter, undated (spring 1945), folder 27, box 14. All in collection 285, BGC/PTMJ.

7. Proposed program for May 30, 1945, Youth for Christ Rally at Soldier Field (unpublished typed manuscript), folder 45, box 2; program for May 30, 1945, Youth for Christ Rally at Soldier Field, folder 27, box 14; microphone cue sheet for May 30, 1945, Youth for Christ Rally at Soldier Field, folder 27, box 14. All in collection 285, BGC/PTMJ. See also AP, "Evangelistic Meet in Soldier Field," *The Era* (Bradford, PA), May 31, 1945. For information on Graham's short speech, see Joel Carpenter, "Youth for Christ and the New Evangelicals' Place in the Life of the Nation," in *Religion and the Life of the Nation: American Recoveries*, ed. Rowland A. Sherrill (Champaign: University of Illinois Press, 1990), 128–52; Robert Wuthnow, *The Restructuring of American Religion: Society and Faith since World War II* (Princeton: Princeton University Press, 1990), 175–76; and Robert Bruns, *Billy Graham: A Biography* (Westport, CT: Greenwood Press, 2004), 23–26.

8. Edward J. Kelly, letter to Torrey Maynard Johnson, May 22, 1945, folder 45 box 3, collection 285, BGC/PTMJ.

9. *The Protestant Voice*, June 22, 1945, 1, folder 27, box 14, collection 285, BGC/PTMJ.

10. AP, "'Youth for Christ' Plans Own Invasion," in *Austin* (TX) *American*, Aug. 24, 1945.

11. John Evans, "City Churches to Mark Start of Family Week," *CDT*, May 4, 1946; John Evans, "Memorial Week Services Will Open Tomorrow," *CDT*, May 25, 1946.

12. For further discussion of Youth for Christ's role in the early postwar evangelical awakening, see Carpenter, "Youth for Christ."

13. Mark A. Noll, *A History of Christianity in the United States and Canada* (Grand Rapids: Wm. B. Eerdsmans Publishing, 1992), 390–94.

14. Marty, *Modern American Religion*, 151; Chesly Manly, "Faith Rally Draws 125,000," *CDT*, Aug. 16, 1954; John Evans, "World Church Meetings Set for Midwest," *CDT*, May 3, 1954; John Evans, "Religious News Notes," *CDT*, July 17, 1954; E. V. Toy Jr., "The National Lay Committee and the National Council of Churches: A Case Study of Protestants in Conflict," *American Quarterly* 21, no. 2, pt. 1 (Summer 1969): 198–201; John Evans, "Religious News Notes," *CDT*, July 17, 1954; Richard Philbrick, "Thousands to Join in Prayer Sunday at Festival of Faith," *CDT*, Aug. 12, 1954; Chesly Manly, "Begin Church Parley Today," *CDT*, Aug. 15, 1954; Ruth Moss, "Besiege Church Dignitaries for Autografs after Service," *CDT*, Aug. 16, 1954; John Evans "Devout Service Opens World Church Rally," *CDT*, Aug. 16, 1954.

15. John Evans, "100,000 in Holy Ritual Pray to Chicago Saint," *CDT*, Sept. 23, 1946; "250,000 Jam Church Rites," *LAT*, Sept. 9, 1954; Joseph Egelhof, "Catholic Rally of 200,000!" *CDT*, Sept. 9, 1954; "260,000 Attend Church Festival," *NYT*, Sept. 9, 1954; Michael D. Wamble, "Public Offerings of Faith Part of Our Tradition," *Catholic New World*, June 25, 2000; Linn White, "Soldier Field in Chicago," unpublished bound manuscript (1936), 27–28, CPD/SF; Pat Kelly, (Chicago Civil Defense Corps) Staff Study of Mass Assembly and Dispersal Conducted with the Religious Assembly at Soldier Field on Wednesday, Sept. 8, 1954, esp. 4–10, 12, 16–17, Chicago Public Library Special Collections.

16. Richard Philbrick, "Begin Planning for '62 Graham Revival Here," *CDT*, Oct. 6, 1959; "Another Evangelist Named Billy," *CDT*, Sept. 2, 1961; "Billy Graham Asks Help for Revival Here," *CDT*, Dec. 24, 1961.

17. Herbert J. Taylor, letter to George T. Donoghue, superintendent, Chicago Park District, Oct. 13, 1959, and various other letters; W. G. Haymaker, Crusade Director, Suggested Plan of Organization for a Billy Graham Crusade (pamphlet—undated). All in folder 10, box 37, collection 20, Papers of Herbert J. Taylor, Billy Graham Center (Wheaton, Ill.). See also Bruns, *Billy Graham*, 103–4; "Billy Graham's Crusade Costs Half a Million," *CDT*, June 1, 1962; Richard Philbrick, "'Regain the Frontiers of Morality': Graham," *CDT*, May 31, 1962; Richard Philbrick, "Graham Heard by 116,000," *CDT*, June 18, 1962; Howard James, "Heat Overcomes 400 in Soldiers' Field," *CDT*, June 18, 1962; J. Edward Bing, "Crowd Finds Inspiration in Graham Talk," *CDT*, June 18, 1962; UPI, "Billy Graham Likens U.S. to Roman Empire," in *Washington Post and Times-Herald*, June 18, 1962.

18. Richard Philbrick, "Graham Heard by 116,000," *CDT*, June 18, 1962; "1965 Billy Graham Revival Slated Here," *CDT*, Jan. 27, 1963; "Graham Aids Expect 30,000 to Hear Talk," *CT*, June 6, 1964; Richard Philbrick, "Graham Rally Opens Today," *CT*, June 3, 1971; Richard Philbrick, "Graham Ends His Chicago Revival, Has Praise for City," *CT*, June 14, 1971; David Meade, "Graham's Crusade Here: An $818,355.77 Success," *CDN*, Nov. 1962 (undated clipping); "Graham Took in $818,335—Crusade in Chicago Found a Success," *Fortune Magazine*, Nov. 1962 (undated clipping).

19. Christopher Robert Reed, *The Chicago NAACP and the Rise of Black Professional Leadership, 1910–1966* (Bloomington: Indiana University Press, 1997), 161–73, esp. 166.

20. "Open Church Classes for Pupils Boycotting 'Willis Warehouse,'" *CDD*, Jan. 31, 1963.

21. "Willis Favors Bogan Parents over Negroes," *CDD*, Sept. 16, 1963; "Willis, Board Cited for Better Schools," *CT*, Sept. 7, 1963; "Plan to Urge Support for Willis in City," *CT*, Sept. 22, 1963.

22. "Race Equality Group Pickets School Board," *CDT*, Dec. 7, 1963.

23. "Soldiers' Field Ok'd as Site of Rights Rally," *CDT*, May 13, 1964.

24. "Rights Law Tests Mapped in 6 Cities," *NYT*, June 22, 1964.

25. The *Tribune* quoted estimates that put the crowd at fifty-seven thousand ("Rally Told: Push Rights," *CT*, June 22, 1964); the *Defender* and the *Daily News* estimated between seventy and seventy-five thousand people ("They Were at the Illinois Rally for Civil Rights Sunday," *CD*, June 20–26, 1964; Dean Gysel, "Rights Test Coming, King Tells Rally," *CDN*, June 22, 1964).

26. "Rights Rally Set Today in Soldier Field," *CT*, June 21, 1964.

27. Dean Gysel, "Rights Test Coming, King Tells Rally," *CDN*, June 22, 1964.

28. Ibid.

29. Archbishop Arthur Brazier, interview with author, Sept. 16, 2003; portions published in Liam Ford, "A Stadium for the Times," *CT*, Sept. 29, 2003, Soldier Field special section.

30. "Dr. King to Open Drive in Chicago," *NYT*, July 8, 1965.

31. "27 Seized in Rights March," *CT*, July 11, 1965.

32. Austin C. Wehrwein, "Dr. King Attends Winnetka Rally," *NYT*, July 26, 1965; Thomas Fitzpatrick, "King Leads Loop March," *CT*, July 27, 1965.

33. Coretta Scott King, "King Meets Conflict Here" (excerpt from *My Life with Martin Luther King, Jr.* [New York: Holt, Rinehart and Winston, 1970]), *CT*, April 11, 1970.

34. Betty Washington, "Dr. King Travels in Secret to Chicago," *CDD*, Jan. 6, 1966; "King Launches Rights Fight at Secret Session," *CT*, Jan. 6, 1966; David Halvorsen, "King Tells Chicago Strategy," *CT*, Jan. 8, 1966.

35. "Dr. King's Campaign in Chicago," *CT*, Jan. 13, 1966.

36. Coretta Scott King, "King Meets Conflict Here," *CT*, April 11, 1970.

37. "Clergy, King Map Chicago Boycotts," *CD*, Feb. 5, 1966; Betty Washington, "Dr. King Meets with Top Cops; Map Plan to Prevent Violence," *CD*, Jan. 29, 1966; Arnold Rosenzweig, "Big Freedom Festival? It Was a Smash!" *CDD*, March 14, 1966.

38. "King Discloses Plan for Rally, March on City Hall on June 26," *CT*, May 27, 1966.

39. "Momentum Building for Two Marches," *CDD*, June 9, 1966; "King to Seek City Income Tax, $2 Wage," *CT*, June 9, 1966.

40. Coretta Scott King, "King Meets Conflict Here," *CT*, April 11, 1970.

41. Alan D. Wade, letter to members of the National Association of Social Workers, June 23, 1966; John A. McDermott, letter to members of the Catholic Interracial Council, July 1, 1966; the Rev. Canon Paul S. Kyger Jr., letter to Edwin C. Barry, Chicago Urban League, July 8, 1966; Freedom Rally Committee, memorandum to executive director and deputy director, July 2, 1966. All in accession 76-116, box 168, folder 27, CUL.

42. Martin Luther King, statement to the press, July 8, 1966, accession 76-116, box 168, folder 27, CUL.

43. "Hits 'Black Power,'" *CT*, July 2, 1966; "Jackson, SCLC Rights Concept Split Is Widening," *CD*, July 9, 1966; William Kling, "Peace among Teen Gangs Still in Doubt," *CDT*, Aug. 1, 1966.

44. "Dr. King to Stage Big Rally Today," *NYT*, July 10, 1966; Austin C. Wehrwein, "Dr. King and CORE Chief Act to Heal Rights Breach," *NYT*, July 11, 1966.

45. Basil Talbott Jr., "Dr. King Declares War on Inequality," *CST*, July 11, 1966; Stephen A. Rothman, "Why They Braved Heat: To See Dr. King," *CST*, July 11, 1966; "Thousands Go to Soldiers' Field Rights Rally," *CT*, July 11, 1966.

46. "30,000 Hear Dr. King at Soldier Field Rally," *CDD*, July 11, 1966; Basil Talbott Jr., "Dr. King Declares War on Inequality," *CST*, July 11, 1966; Austin C. Wehrwein, "Dr. King and CORE Chief Act to Heal Rights Breach," *NYT*, July 11, 1966.

47. Martin Luther King Jr., "Address Delivered at Rally at Soldier Field," July 10, 1966, box 55, folder 1259, accession 80-102, CUL.

48. Ibid.

49. Basil Talbott Jr., "Dr. King Declares War on Inequality," *CST*, July 11, 1966; "Thousands Go to Soldiers' Field Rights Rally," *CT*, July 11, 1966.

50. Martin Luther King Jr., "Address Delivered at Rally at Soldier Field," July 10, 1966, box 55, folder 1259, accession 80-102, CUL.

51. Austin C. Wehrwein, "Dr. King and CORE Chief Act to Heal Rights Breach," *NYT*, July 11, 1966; Basil Talbott Jr., "Dr. King Declares War on Inequality," *CST*, July 11, 1966; "Thousands Go to Soldiers' Field Rights Rally," *CT*, July 11, 1966.

52. "Daley, King, Aids Meet on Rights," *CT*, July 12, 1966.

53. "Dr. Jackson Joins Archbishop in Peace Plea," *CT*, July 16, 1966; "Rather, Berry 'Explain' Riots on Westside,"*CD*, July 23, 1966.

54. "Common Sense Prevails," *CT*, July 12, 1966.

55. "Next: Civil Rights Action," *CDN*, July 12, 1966.

56. Partial transcript from videorecording of press conference by Martin Luther King Jr., Aug. 5, 1966; David Halvorsen, "Cancel Rights Marches," *CT*, Aug. 27, 1966.

57. "K.K.K. Barred from Rally in Soldiers' Field," *CT*, Aug. 11, 1966.

58. Nancy McArdle, Theresa Osypuk, and Dolores Acevedo-Garcia, "Disparities in Neighborhood Poverty of Poor Black Children and White Children," *Diversity Data Briefs*, 1, May 2007, http://diversitydata.sph.harvard.edu/brief7.pdf (accessed June 24, 2008).

59. Steve Kloehn and Byron White, "One Bridge Left to Cross; Promise Keepers Is Thriving, but Attracting Minorities Remains Its Biggest Struggle," *CT*, June 30, 1996; Steve Kloehn, "Catholic Rally Holds Echoes of the Past," *CT*, June 22, 2000.

60. Lori Lessner, "Daley, Cops Meet about Weedfest; City Permit in Doubt Unless Pot Use Stops," *CT*, May 17, 1996; Jan Crawford Greenburg, "Top Court OKs Chicago Park Permits," *CT*, Jan. 16, 2002.

CHAPTER 11

1. Bert M. Thorud, "Architectural Engineering: Stadia Sight Lines," *American Architect* 124, no. 2435 (Dec. 19, 1923): 566–67; Holabird & Roche, "Description Submitted with Design for a Stadium on the Lake Front, Chicago," *American Architect* 117, no. 2304 (Feb. 18, 1920): 208.

2. "80,000 Enjoy Thrill Show of City's Firemen," *CDT*, Aug. 4, 1958; "Police Widows, Orphans to Benefit from Circus," *CDD*, May 19, 1959.

3. Stanley R. Sarbarneck, "Voice of the People," *CDT*, March 30, 1959.

4. James L. Merriner, *Grafters and Goo Goos: Corruption and Reform in Chicago, 1833–2003* (Carbondale: Southern Illinois University Press, 2004), 174–75.

5. "Wilson Orders Reform," *CDT*, March 13, 1960. Also see "50 Clowns in Police Circus," *CDD*, April 21, 1960; "Gas Stations to Sell Police Show Tickets," *CDT*, May 23, 1960; Robert Wiedrich, "Thrill Show Crowds Reach Record 93,000," *CDT*, June 20, 1960; "Police Benefit Show Thrills 93,000 Here," *CDD*, June 21, 1960.

6. "Police Benefit Fund Mail Plea Approved," *CDT*, May 12, 1962.

7. Robert Nolte, "Lakefront Show Thrills 38,000," *CT*, Aug. 15, 1971.

8. Philip Maxwell, "Hail Rodgers, Hammerstein at Chicagoland Festival," *CDT*, April 15, 1956.

9. Charles Leavelle, "85,000 in Mass Music Fete," *CDT*, Aug. 21, 1938.

10. Philip Maxwell, "Bozo's Circus Billed as Festival Highlight," *CT*, April 7, 1963.

11. "Local Singers Go to Chicago," *Waukesha Daily Freeman*, Aug. 24, 1954.

12. "Here Is Tonight's Festival Program; Clip It and Take It," *CDT*, Aug. 19, 1939; "Former Sousa Musician Dies," *Gettysburg Times*, Sept. 26, 1960.

13. Clay Gowran, "Hear Lincoln vs. Douglas—at Music Fete," *CDT*, Aug. 16, 1958; "South Siders Boost Big Music Fete," *CDT*, Aug. 9, 1942; "Night of Music to Unfold as 90,000 Listen," *CDT*, Aug. 11, 1946; "Music Festival to Give Fantasy, 'Dutch Wedding,'" *CDT*, June 30, 1946; John McCutcheon Jr., "70,000 Cheer Music Festival Pageantry," *CDT*, Aug. 20, 1950; Shirley Lowry, "Night of Song for 80,000!"*CDT*, Aug. 21, 1955.

14. Chicago Park District Board, letter regarding March 19, 1957, authorization for 1957 Chicagoland Music Festival; Erwin Weiner, letter to Phil Maxwell regarding complimentary tickets (undated 1957 carbon copy). Both in 1957 *Tribune* Music Festival folder, CPD/SF.

15. Thomas Fitzpatrick, "56,000 Cheer Music Fete," *CT*, Aug. 16, 1964; Philip Maxwell, "Festival to Honor Song Writers," *CT*, May 2, 1965; Thomas Fitzpatrick, "Music King for Tonight at Festival," *CT*, Aug. 7, 1965; "Luncheon to Honor Woman, 90, for Song," *CT*, July 29, 1965; "Music Festival Fans Laud New Setting," *CT*, Aug. 9, 1965; Philip Maxwell, "Music Fete Luncheon to Relive Past," *CT*, March 6, 1966; Donna Gill, "Past Glories of Music Festival Relived," *CT*, Aug. 12, 1966; "Serve on Paper a Total of 191 Years," *CT*, Jan. 14, 1967.

16. "Fireworks Displays Periled by Mishaps," *CT*, July 6, 1972; "Fireworks Cap Holiday Events; Children Frolic," *CT*, July 5, 1972.

17. "Fireworks Show on Lakefront," *Suburbanite Economist*, July 2, 1975; "Lakefront Fireworks," *CT*, July 3, 1975 "Legion Bows Out on Fourth," *CT*, June 30, 1976.

18. "It's July 4th!" *CT*, July 4, 1973; Robert Enstad, "Legion Hears Mayor," *CT*, July 21, 1973; "July 4th Music, Fireworks Planned," *CT*, July 2, 1976; William Griffin "Vets Seek 2,500 New Cab Licenses," *CT*, Jan. 6, 1978; "Soldier Field Fireworks Cap July 4 Festivities," *CT*, July 4, 1978; Ralph Frammolino, "Fireworks Make July 4 Skies Glisten," *CT*, July 4, 1978; Douglas Frantz and Andy Knott, "Gas Aplenty on 4th, but Most Here Stay Close to Home," *CT*, July 5, 1979.

19. Anthony Cotton, "Where to Get Thoroughly (and Legally) Dazzled on 4th," *CT*, July 2, 1978; John Von Rhein, "350,000 Music Lovers Usher in Early 4th," *CT*, July 4, 1979; Robert Benjamin, "200,000 Crowd Park on Gut Feeling," *CT*, July 5, 1982; Howard Reich, "Happenings," *CT*, July 3, 1981; Rich Lorenz, "Fire Tops Shreveport with Interceptions," *CT*, July 5, 1981.

20. Robert Benjamin, "200,000 Crowd Park on Gut Feeling," *CT*, July 5, 1982.

21. "50,000 Watch Polish Pageant of City's Rise," *CDT*, Aug. 9, 1937; "Toward the Millennium," *Time*, April 22, 1966, http://www.time.com/time/magazine/article/0,9171,899144-1,00.html (accessed Aug. 14, 2006); "Poland Bars Cody Visa for Celebration," *CT*, April 5, 1966; UPI, "Explains Why Poland Bars Visit by Pope," in *CT*, April 18, 1966; "Polish Ban on Churchmen Hit," *CT*, April 17, 1966.

22. Richard Philbrick, "Soldiers' Field to Be Filled for Mass," *CT*, Aug. 28, 1966; UPI, "Polish-Americans Gather to Hail Christian Millennium," in *Pacific Stars & Stripes*, Aug. 30, 1966; Richard Philbrick, "75,000 See Poles Mark Millennium," *CT*, Aug. 29, 1966.

23. "His Morning Tub," *CDT*, Aug. 10, 1919; "Circus to Exhibit under Canvas at Soldiers' Field," *CDT*, July 23, 1935; "Old Fashioned Circus Opener Thrills Throng," *CDT*, July 26, 1936; "Girl Rider Rehearses Her Stunts for Circus Opening," *CDT*, July 23, 1937.

24. Marcia Winn, "Streamlined Big Top Pays Rich Circus Dividends," *CDT*, July 30, 1939.

25. Gladys Priddy, "It's Same Old Circus—under the Blue Skies," *CDT*, Aug. 23, 1944.

26. Copy of letter from Robert J. Dunham, Chicago Park Board president, to James A. Haley, first vice president, Ringling Bros. and Barnum and Bailey, Combined Shows, Inc. (Chicago office), Sept. 13, 1943, CPD/SF; "Circus Cancels Soldiers' Field Date in Dispute," *CDT*, July 17, 1945.

27. List of events at Soldier Field, 1954, CPD/SF; Arch Ward, "In the Wake of the News," *CDT*, Nov. 16, 1954; Chicago Park District, handwritten list of circus safety and health violations, undated, CPD/SF; "Ringling Circus Coming June 12," *CDT*, May 10, 1959; Lucy Key Miller, "Front Views & Profiles," *CDT*, May 29, 1959.

28. "Gala Shows Set for Soldier Field," *CDD*, March 25, 1975; "Daley Boosts Summer Activities," *CT*, June 7, 1975; Lisa Daniels, "Just Call Him Emmett Kelly Jr.," *Frederick* (MD) *News-Post*, Nov. 16, 1988; "Something Special," *Arlington Heights Daily Herald*, Nov. 15, 1985.

29. Chicago Park District, annual reports (1941, 265; 1942, 257; 1943, 255–56; 1944,

65–66); "Opera Trustees Plan Pons Concert in Soldiers' Field," *CDT*, June 19, 1941; "Lily Pons Concert and Opera Slated for Soldiers' Field," *CDT*, June 30, 1942; Cecil Smith, "Storm Skirts 30,000 Hearing Outdoor Opera," Aug. 9, 1942; "Service Men Get Boxes for Opera Company Presentations," *CDT*, July 22, 1942; Claudia Cassidy, "Two Outdoor Operas Scheduled for Soldiers' Field," *CDT*, July 11, 1943; Claudia Cassidy, "'Aida' Is Sung Adequately in Soldiers' Field," *CDT*, July 22, 1944; Claudia Cassidy, "Soldier's Field 'Il Trovatore' Outraces Rain," *CDT*, July 24, 1944.

30. "Amateur Bands to Seek Swing Prizes Tonight," *CDT*, Aug. 23, 1938; Wayne Thomis, "City's Swing Fete Runs Riot," *CDT*, Aug. 24, 1938; "Tonight's Program in Grant Park," *CDT*, Aug. 23, 1938; "200,000 Jitterbugs," *Time*, Sept. 5, 1938, www.time.com/time/magazine/article/0,9171,760137,00.html (accessed Oct. 17, 2006).

CHAPTER 12

1. John Leusch, "83,750 See Weber Win Prep Bowl, 14–12," *CDT*, Dec. 3, 1961; John Leusch, "91,328 See Fenwick Rout Schurz, 40–0," *CDT*, Dec. 2, 1962; John Leusch, "St. Rita All-Chicago Champion," *CT*, Dec. 1, 1963; John Leusch, "City Prep Football Title to Weber," *CT*, Dec. 6, 1964; John Leusch, "75,400 Watch Loyola Take Title," *CT*, Dec. 5, 1965; John Leusch, "Loyola Defeats Vocational, 20 to 14," *CT*, Dec. 4, 1966; John Leusch, "Mount Carmel Crushes Dunbar, 37-0," *CT*, Dec. 3, 1967.

2. Taylor Bell, "Prep Bowl Must Find New Home," *CST*, Nov. 7, 1988; John Montgomery, "Site Shift Surfaces for 1988 Prep Bowl," *CST*, Nov. 8, 1988; Ray Hanania, "Prep Bowl OKd for Soldier Field," *CST*, Nov. 19, 1988; "Rescheduled Prep Bowl Stays at Soldier Field," *CT*, Nov. 19, 1988; Kathy O'Malley and Hanke Gratteau, "O'Malley & Gratteau INC.," *CT*, Nov. 16, 1988; Reid Hanley, "Loyola Runs Off with Prep Bowl," *CT*, Nov. 29, 1988; Bill Jauss, "Triple-Threat's Treat Greyhounds' Hayden Puts On Prep Bowl Show," *CT*, Nov. 27, 1999.

3. Steve Tucker, "Thrill of a Lifetime at Soldier Field," *CST*, Aug. 25, 2006.

4. "Air Force and Army to Play Here in 1963," *CDT*, Jan. 11, 1962; Robert Wiedrich "City to Welcome 5,000 Cadets," *CT*, Nov. 1, 1963; "Military Ball Lures Girls," *CT*, Oct. 5, 1963; "Kennedy Plans Visit Here for Grid Game," *CT*, Oct. 9, 1963; "Democrats Seek Crowds for Kennedy," *CT*, Oct. 30, 1963.

5. Chicago Park District, annual report (1963), 8; Charles Bartlet, "3 Illinoisans Help Air Force Fly High," *CT*, Oct. 30, 1963; Charles Bartlet, "Army, Air Force Squads Arrive Today," *CT*, Nov. 1, 1963.

6. AP, "Army and Air Force Sign to Meet in Chicago Nov. 6," in *NYT*, Jan. 14, 1965; "Dedicate Game Nov. 6 to Men in Viet Nam," *CT*, Oct. 19, 1965; "Service Game to Honor Viet Fighting Men," *CT*, Oct. 21, 1965; "2,000 Cadets Parade Today," *CT*, Nov. 6, 1965; Allen Gray, "Men in Blue and Gray Hold the Colors High," *CT*, Nov. 7, 1965; David Condon, "Air Force Pins Down Army, 14–3," *CT*, Nov. 7, 1965; James Fitzgerald, "Big Mistake Hurt at Start, Says Dietzel," *CT*, Nov. 7, 1965.

7. Andrew Beyer, "Underdog Navy Rated Possible Victor Today," *Washington Post and Times-Herald*, Oct. 12, 1968; Edward Prell, "Navy Shot Up by Air Force, 26–20," *CT*, Oct. 13, 1968.

8. "Chicago Circle Triumphs, 20–17, on Late Tally," *CT*, Oct. 30, 1966; "Circle Beats Ind. Central in Inaugural," *CT*, Sept. 22, 1968; "Playin' the Game with Lloyd Hogan," *CDD*, Sept. 18, 1969; Mike Conklin, "Area Football: No Big Thing," *CT*, Sept. 6, 1971; "Circle Shut Out by Wayne State 34–0," *CT*, Oct. 29, 1972.

9. Vernon Jarrett, "This Football Game Is Something Else," *CT*, Sept. 15, 1971; Mike Conklin, "Grambling Rips Alcorn 21–6," *CT*, Sept. 18, 1971; Mike Conklin, "Tenn. State Passes Take Toll of Alcorn," *CT*, Sept. 24, 1972; "Joe Louis: 'Athlete of Century!'" *CDD*, Sept. 12, 1972; Mike Conklin, "No Urban League Football Contest This Season," *CT*, May 10, 1974; Ralph Stewart, "Football and Sickle Cell: Things to Know," *CDD*, Sept. 12, 1974; Mike Conklin, "Tigers Squash Central State, Stewart Stars," *CT*, Sept. 14, 1974.

10. Jack McCarthy, "40,000 Watch Delta Devils Dominate on 'D,' " *CT*, Sept. 3, 2006; "Northern Illinois–Iowa Football Game at Soldier Field in 2007: Hawkeyes to Play Football in Chicago," press release, University of Iowa, June 5, 2006, http://hawkeyesports.CSTv. com/sports/m-footbl/spec-rel/060506aab.html (accessed Oct. 21, 2006); "Stadium in a Park: The Lakefront Redevelopment Project," press release (information sheet), Chicago Park District, http://www.chicagoparkdistrict.com (accessed about Dec. 1, 2003).

11. V. K. Brown, letter to George Hjelte, Feb. 15, 1945, 2, CPD/SF; Walter Eckersall, "Coast Track Stars Arrive for Meet Here," *CDT*, June 9, 1927; Wilfrid Smith, "Nation's Track Stars Vie for Titles Today," *CDT*, June 16, 1933.

12. Erwin Weiner, Chicago Park District Board of Commissioners, letter in re amendment to existing agreement with Mayor's All-Chicago Citizens' Committee, Aug. 3, 1956, International Folk Festival 1956 folder, CPD/SF; Mayor Daley's All Chicago Citizens Committee, information circular on 1956 International Folk Festival, International Folk Festival 1956 folder, CPD/SF; Erwin Weiner, Soldier Field Special Events 1956, Inter-Office Bulletin no. 10, Sept. 6, 1956, International Folk Festival 1956 folder, CPD/SF; "Folk Festival Raises $10,338 for Olympics," *CDT*, Oct. 12, 1956; Howard Barry, "Foreign Born Give Fete to Aid U. S. Team," *CDT*, Sept. 16, 1956; "Chicagoans Out to Land Olympics," *CDT*, March 27, 1957; David Condon, "In the Wake of the News," *CT*, Aug. 2, 1977.

13. "Pan-Am Site Search Turns to Guatemala," *CDT*, April 18, 1957; "Daley Bid for Pan-American Gains Support," *CDT*, April 12, 1957; "Council Urges Fund Group for Pan-Am Games," *CDT*, June 8, 1957; "Says Chicago Is Likely '59 Pan-Am Games Site," *CDT*, June 21, 1957; AP, "Award Pan-American Games to Chicago," in *CDT*, Aug. 4, 1957.

14. Charles Bartlett, "The Order of the Day in Sports Was Business," *CDT*, Oct. 23, 1958; "Pan-Am Track Will Get New Speed Surface," *CDT*, Oct. 17, 1958; "Pan-Am Track Budget O.K.'d by Park Board," *CDT*, Oct. 24, 1958; "$56,059 Contract Awarded for Pan-American Track," *CDT*, Oct. 29, 1958 (although the contract with the English company was for $56,000, the total appropriation for the track was about $100,000); "Let Contract for 3 Canopies to Aid Parkers," *CDT*, Nov. 26, 1958; "Chicago to Get Olympia Soil," *NYT*, Nov. 19, 1958. The traditional opening date of the Olympics, 776 BC, is based on one source from about 400 BC and is thought to be inaccurate; for a discussion, see Mark Golden, *Sport and Society in Ancient Greece* (Cambridge: Cambridge University Press, 1998), 53–65.

15. Robert Cromie, "Open Fund Drive for Pan-Am Games," *CDT*, Jan. 20, 1959; "Announce Ticket Sale for Pan-Am," *CDD*, May 6, 1959; "Scouts Carry Pan-Am Torch," *CDD*, April 13, 1959; "Pan-Am Track to Have Students' Day," *CDT*, May 24, 1959; "Chicago Scout to End 1,400 Mile Torch Run," *CDD*, July 9, 1959; Irene Powers, "Plan Varied Events for Festival," *CDT*, Aug. 5, 1959; "Seek 600 Girls for '59 Pan-Am Games Event," *CDT*, Jan. 29, 1959; "Testing" (AP wirephoto), *NYT*, June 5, 1959.

16. Robert Cromie, "25,000 See Pan-American Games Open," *CDT*, Aug. 28, 1959; Paul Zimmerman "Chicago Greets More Than 2,000 Athletes to Pan-American Games," *LAT*, Aug. 28, 1959; Joseph M. Sheehan, "Third Pan-American Games Open with Ceremony before 40,000 at Chicago," *NYT*, Aug. 28, 1959; Permanent and Temporary Seat Layout, Soldier Field (schematic and chart), Oct. 24, 1949, revised 1955, Armed Forces Benefit Game (1955) folder, CPD/SF; Howard Barry, "Pan-Am Sports to Open Today," *CDT*, Aug. 28, 1959; "Pan-American Games Champions" (chart), *CDT*, Sept. 8, 1959; Louise Mead Tricard, *American Women's Track and Field: A History, 1895 through 1980* (Jefferson, NC: McFarland & Co., 1996), 387, 407–8; Thomas Picou, "Jones Wins Hurdle Thriller," *CDD*, Sept. 2, 1959.

17. Gerry A. Carr, *Fundamentals of Track and Field*, 2nd ed. (Champaign: Human Kinetics, 1999), 87; Howard Barry, "Pan-Am Judges Trim Connolly's Mark," *CDT*, Aug. 29, 1959; Paul Zimmerman, "Five More Pan-Am Titles Won by U.S.," *LAT*, Sept. 3, 1959; "Officials Catch Fish at Pan-Am Games," *Washington Post and Times-Herald*, Sept. 2, 1959; AP, "U. S. Riders Earn Games' Last Title," in *NYT*, Sept. 8, 1959.

18. "Ski Stars Meet Tomorrow at Soldiers' Field," *CDT*, Feb. 15, 1936; "Ski Riders

Will Meet Today at Soldiers' Field," *CDT*, Feb. 16, 1936; "Wilson Takes Class A Title in Ski Tourney," *CDT*, Feb. 17, 1936; "Novelty Acts to Support Skiing Events Sunday," *CDT*, Feb. 3, 1937; "Summer Time Ski Jumping," *CDT*, Aug. 28, 1954; Howard Barry, "Open Ski Meet Tonight; Snow at Lake Front," *CDT*, Sept. 17, 1954; "Swedish Ski Star to Jump at Lake Front," *CDT*, Sept. 12, 1954; Howard Barry, "Olson Takes First in Lake Front Ski Meet," *CDT*, Sept. 18, 1954; "Hauge Takes Summer Ski Meet Crown," *CDT*, Sept. 20, 1954; Herb Lyon, "Tower Ticker," *CDT*, Dec. 2, 1957; Alfred Borcover, "New Trends Encourage Wary Novice to Reconsider His Aversion to Skiing," *CT*, Nov. 18, 1984; Herb Lyon, "Tower Ticker," *CDT*, April 20, 1958.

19. "Fun Is Hard for Some," *CT*, Jan. 9, 1966; Eunice Kennedy Shriver, letter to Miss Anne McGlone, Jan. 29, 1968, Judge Anne Burke papers about the Special Olympics, Chicago History Museum.

20. William H. Freeberg, letter to Miss Anne McGlone, Feb. 2, 1968, Judge Anne Burke papers about the Special Olympics, Chicago History Museum; David Condon, "In the Wake of the News," *CT*, July 12, 1968; Steve Neal, "35 Years Later, Special Olympics Still Owes Big Debt to Burke," *CST*, March 17, 2003; "4 Youths Enter Chicago Games," *Charleston Gazette*, July 17, 1968; "Drive to Help D.C. Retarded," *Washington Post and Times-Herald*, July 16, 1968; Canadian Press, "Mikita, Armstrong to Coach 'Olympics,'" in *Winnipeg Free Press*, July 17, 1968, 45.

21. David Condon, "In the Wake of the News," *CT*, July 12, 1968; "Special Olympics" (photograph) *CT*, July 19, 1968; "Area Duo to Spark Olympics," *Woodlawn* (Chicago) *Booster and Bulletin*, July 16, 1968.

22. Bill Jauss, "Now Special Olympics Really Are Special," *CT*, Aug. 2, 1987; quote from Shriver's address, http://www.specialolympics.org (accessed July 19, 2006); Sara Jane Goodyear, "1,000 Retarded Kids Compete in Chicago Special Olympics," *CT*, July 21, 1968.

23. Eunice Kennedy Shriver, letter to Anne Burke, July 23, 1968, Judge Anne Burke papers about the Special Olympics, Chicago History Museum.

24. David Condon, "Everybody Is a Big Star in Our Special Olympics," *CT*, Aug. 15, 1970; "Another Olympics Set," *Washington Post and Times-Herald*, Feb. 11, 1972. Two representative studies, both by Jonathan A. Weiss and Terry Diamond, are "Involvement in Special Olympics and Its Relations to Self-concept and Actual Competency in Participants with Developmental Disabilities," *Research in Developmental Disabilities* 24, no. 4 (July–Aug. 2003): 281–305, and "Stress in Parents of Adults with Intellectual Disabilities Attending Special Olympics Competitions," *Journal of Applied Research in Intellectual Disabilities* 18 (2005): 263–70. See also Malcolm Moran, "30 Years Later, Chicago Veteran Stays in the Game," *CT* , May 10, 1998; Mike Houlihan, "Birthday Boy Kevin Won't Let Any Syndrome Keep Him Down," *CST*, Sept. 5, 2004; Raymond R. Coffey, "How Caring People Made Kevin Special," *CST*, July 11, 1993. On the running track, see, for example, Mike Prizy, "The Soldier Field Track Is Gone, but the Memories Are Still Here," *Chicago Athlete*, May 2005, http://www.chicagoaa.com/features/speedplaysoldierfieldMay05.html (accessed Aug. 4, 2006).

CHAPTER 13

1. "Sparta, Ulster Soccer Teams Play 4–4 Tie," *CDT*, Oct. 11, 1926; "Chicago to See 2 Title Soccer Battles Today," *CDT*, June 11, 1933; "Toronto and Swedes Take Soccer Games," *CDT*, June 12, 1933; "Scots Win Soccer Title," *NYT*, June 12, 1933; Robert Cromie, "German Soccer Team Defeats Plymouth, 4–0," *CDT*, May 8, 1954.

2. "Austrians, All-Stars Win Soccer Games," *CDT*, July 29, 1961; "Top Foreign Soccer Clubs to Play Here," *CDT*, March 11, 1962; "Mexicans Bow, 2–1, to Yugoslavs," *CDT*, June 16, 1962; "Soccer Attendance Marks Set in '62 in Collegiate, International Play," *CDT*, Dec. 16, 1962.

3. "Poles Beat Swedes, 5–2, in Soccer," *CT*, July 18, 1963; "Dukla Beats Britain, 1–0,

in Soccer," *CT*, Aug. 8, 1963; "1964 Soccer Proves Year of Schwaben," *CT*, Dec. 20, 1964; James Fitzgerald, "Spurs and Roy Beat St. Louis in Mud, 2 to 1," *CT*, April 17, 1967; "Spurs Agree to Move Out of Chicago," *CT*, Dec. 14, 1967; Abe Korsower, "Pro Soccer in Chicago Proves Financial Flop," *CT*, Dec. 24, 1967.

4. Mike Conklin, "Sting Announces '76 Home Schedule," *CT*, Feb. 12, 1976; Neil Milbert, "Wrigley Field to Be Sting's Second Home," *CT*, Nov. 23, 1977; "Sting History Filled with Playoff Misery," *CT*, Aug. 15, 1979; "Sting to Split Home Dates between Cubs, Sox Parks," *CT*, Nov. 27, 1979; "Sports Notes," *CT*, Dec. 14, 1982; Mike Conklin, "Sting Considers Escape to Wisconsin," *CT*, June 17, 1983.

5. "Chidome Could Doom City's Shot at World Cup," *CT*, Jan. 29, 1990; Phil Hersh, "Soldier Field Impresses Organizers as World Cup Site in '94," *CT*, April 5, 1990; Joe Knowles, "World Cup Games Set in Chicago," *CT*, Oct. 21, 1992; John Schmeltzer, "Judge Declines to Redistribute Soldier Field Tickets," *CT*, June 11, 1994; Paul Sullivan, "World Cup to Chicago: Now What?" *CT*, March 24, 1992; "Strip Soldier Field for Safety," *CST*, Oct. 21, 1971; John Kass, "Daley's Goal during World Cup Will Be Polishing City's Image," *CT*, June 1, 1994; Steve Johnson, George Papajohn, and Ellen Warren, "Producers of Extravaganza Send Striker the Mascot to the Doghouse," *CT*, June 17, 1994.

6. Tom McNamee, "Chicago, Goodwill Triumph at Opening," *CST*, June 18, 1994; Fred Lief, "World Cup Starting to Fill Defending Champion, Germany Slips Ahead; U.S. Starts Play Today," *Peoria Journal Star*, June 18, 1994; Tim Franklin, "Fans Heat Up at Cup Opener," *CT*, June 18, 1994; Colin McMahon and Sue Ellen Christian, "Chicago Says Welcome to the World," *CT*, June 18, 1994.

7. Johnette Howard, "Soccer's Grand Welcome; World Cup Opens amid Chicago Swelter," *WP*, June 18, 1994; "World Cup Kicks Off with a Flurry of Red and Yellow Cards," *Manchester Guardian*, June 18, 1994; Andrew Bagnato, "New Turf Shows a Slippery Side," *CT*, June 18, 1994; Julie Deardorff, "Even in Defeat, Proud Bolivians Come Up Winners," *CT*, June 18, 1994.

8. Steve Johnson and George Papajohn, "Cup Passes, Scoring More Than Just a Few Points," *CT*, July 3, 1994; Robert Markus and John von Rhein, "Spain Reigns, but Defender's Sweet Day Has Bitter End," *CT*, June 28, 1994; "A Champion Crowd-Pleaser," *CT*, June 28, 1994.

9. "Chicago Scores Big in World Cup" (editorial), *CT*, July 10, 1994; Ted Gregory, "End of the World, Part II: Germans Leave," *CT*, July 9, 1994.

10. Bonnie DeSimone, "Name Game Ends: It's Fire; New MLS Franchise Balks at Nike Suggestion," *CT*, Oct. 9, 1997; Len Ziehm, "Fire Won't Practice at Soldier Field: Saturday's Home Debut Will Be Team's First Time on Its Turf," *CST*, April 3, 1998; Len Ziehm, "Fire Lights Up First Night before 36,444," *CST*, April 5, 1998.

11. "Lewis Takes Auto Race for Midwest Title," *CDT*, May 20, 1935; Alan E. Brown, *The History of America's Speedways, Past and Present*, 3rd ed. (Comstock Park, MI: self-published, 2003), 268; Gordon Eliot White, *Lost Race Tracks: Treasures of Automobile Racing* (Hudson, WI: Iconographix, 2006), 33; Chicago Park District, annual report (1939), 169; "Leading Midget Auto Drivers to Fight for Title," *CDT*, May 7, 1940; Chicago Park District, annual report (1940), 249; Chicago Park District, annual report (1941), 265; Robert Cromie, "Midget Autos Will Roar for Cops' Benefit," *CDT*, Sept. 12, 1950; "Hot-Rod Cars Race Tonight in Soldiers' Field," *CDT*, June 9, 1948; Hal Foust, "Auto Racing Sets Records in 3 Phases," *CDT*, Dec. 19, 1954; Chicago Park District, annual report (1947), 59–61; "17 Week Midget Auto Race Card to Open Tonight," *CDT*, June 1, 1947; Pete Lyons, "Track Roadsters Roar Again; Special Exhibit at NHRA Museum Recalls Midcentury Stepping-stone to the 500," *Auto Week*, Dec. 19, 2005, 50.

12. Records of the Chicago Park District regarding 1954 stock car racing season, Stock Car Racing 1954 folder, CPD/SF; Mary Cameron Frey, "Fearless Racing Circuit Drivers Start Season in . . . Rosemont?" *CST*, Jan. 24, 1990.

13. "Roberts Wins Nascar Race by Car Length," *CDT*, July 22, 1956; "Brown Takes 50 Lap Race on Lake Front," *CDT*, June 16, 1957; ". . . And Then Today," *CDT*, June 29, 1957;

"Lake Front 100 Lap Race to Virginian," *CDT*, June 30, 1957; Mike Brudenell, "A Real Mom and Pop Operation; Old-Fashioned Wood Brothers Racing Keeps Plugging Along," *WP*, Feb. 13, 2005; "60,000 See Marmor Win Stock Race, *CDT*, May 29, 1955.

14. "Stock Cars Rolling Fast at Soldier's Special," *CDD*, May 22, 1962; Henry Martin, "Auto Racing Hits Record Heights in 1963," *CT*, Dec. 22, 1963; "Top Stock Car Races Slated," *CDD*, May 3, 1967; David Condon, "In the Wake of the News," *CT*, May 1, 1968.

CHAPTER 14

1. "Find Stadium Walls Veneer," *CA*, July 8, 1935.

2. "Two Million Park Building Hit as Needless Expense," *CA*, Dec. 16, 1936.

3. "Parks to Seek U.S. Funds," *CHE*, Dec. 16, 1936.

4. Stadium revenues in 2005 were significantly higher in equivalent dollars—about $20 million—although that figure included money from taxes on hotel rooms funneled through the Illinois Sports Facilities Authority and paid to the park district for upkeep of the stadium.

5. "Soldier Field Money Maker," *CHE*, undated 1927 clipping; South Park Commissioners, statement of Soldier Field maintenance and operation for the year ending Feb. 28, 1930, Operations folder, CPD/SF; Chicago Park District, statement showing income and expenses for Soldier Field stadium, Jan. 1, 1937, to Dec. 31, 1944, Operations folder, CPD/SF; Paul M. Dolak, Soldier Field marketing study (Chicago Park District, Feb. 26, 1990), 1, Marketing Study folder, CPD/SF. The 1934 attendance figures seem low; they appear not to include all the Century of Progress events held that year.

6. Harry Sheer, "Soldier Field Costly Item on C.P.D. Budget," *CDN*, Jan. 28, 1944 (the figures released to the *Daily News*, showing 1943 as a profitable year, contradict the 1945 memo summarizing Park District accounts from 1937 through 1944, which show it is as a deficit year; given the more complete figures in the memo [preserved in Park District files], I am inclined to believe it rather than the *Daily News* account, although both end up making the same point); Arch Ward, "All-Star Game Moved to Dyche Stadium," *CDT*, May 27, 1943.

7. "New Management Policy Pays Off" (advertisement), *Billboard*, Feb. 5, 1955, 50; "Chatter—Chicago," *Variety*, April 16, 1958 (in clippings folder, CPD/SF); Chicago Park District, annual report (1970), 10. After 1970, the Park District often failed to include statistics about Soldier Field attendance in its annual report, although the 1990 marketing study by Paul M. Dolak makes clear that in the first twenty years of the Bears era, attendance never went above one million, even in the 1985 Super Bowl season. See also "Soldiers' Field Pistol Range to Be Opened Today," *CDT*, Dec. 28, 1936; "Parks' Chief for Soldiers Field Courts," *CDT*, Dec. 11, 1947.

8. Edgar Munzel, "Chicago's Sports White Elephant: Soldier Field Maps Ball Diamond," *CST*, Feb. 1, 1958.

9. "Soldier Field Conversion Snags Heard," *CA*, Feb. 11, 1958; "Pan Am Games Stall New Arena," *CST*, Feb. 12, 1958; "Mayor Tells Plan for Pro Sport Field," *CDT*, Jan. 3, 1959; "Plan $300,000 Expenditure at Soldier Field," *CDT*, April 22, 1956; "Chicago's White Elephant of Sports Is Ready to Change Colors," *CDN*, April 11, 1959.

10. "Limit Preps on Lakefront Grid Games," *CA*, Sept. 28, 1959.

11. Nails Florio, "Nailing 'em Down," *Community Publications* (Chicago), March 20, 1963; Dolak, *marketing study*, 1.

12. "Mayor Reveals Plan to Convert Soldier Field," *CT*, Nov. 19, 1963; "Soldiers' Field Repair Costs Are Estimated," *CT*, Nov. 27, 1964; "Daley Hits All Foes of Arena," *CT*, Dec. 12, 1964.

13. "No. 1 Civic Project for 1964," *CT*, Jan. 3, 1964.

14. "Philadelphia Voters Back Sports Arena," *CT*, Nov. 6, 1964; "Hope Glows Faintly for Field's Use," *CDT*, Nov. 8, 1964; "New Stadium Is Inevitable; Let's Start Now—Halas," *CT*, Dec. 22, 1964.

15. "Raze McCormick Place, Soldier's Field: Unit Asks," *CA*, Dec. 1, 1965; "Will Chicago Be Left Behind?" *CT*, July 15, 1967.

16. Campbell Gibson, *Population of the the 100 Largest Cities and Other Urban Places in the United States, 1790 to 1990* (Washington, DC: Population Division, U.S. Census Bureau, June 1998), tables 14–21; "Soldiers' Field Seats Fall in Safety Test," *CT*, June 24, 1970; Chris Agrella, "Parks Chief Calls for New Stadium," *CO*, June 24, 1970; AP, "Bears Schedule Exhibition Games," in *Post-Herald* (Beckley, WV), April 4, 1968; Bob DiPietro (UPI), "Halas' Bet Nixed by Rozelle," in *Elyria* (OH) *Chronicle-Telegram*, Sept. 11, 1970.

17. Roy Damer, "Big Ten Closes Dyche to Bears: Allows N.I.T.," *CT*, March 9, 1971.

18. Cooper Rollow, "Wrigley Blasts Halas' Tenant Tactics," *CT*, March 23, 1971; "Bears to Play on Lakefront? Decision Due," *CO*, April 7, 1971; Bill Jauss, "Bears Headed for Soldier Field?" *CO*, April 14, 1971; Jack Griffin, "Soldier Field Is Bear Home for 3 Years," *CST*, May 14, 1971; Ed Stone, "Halas Goal New Stadium in '74," *CO*, May 14, 1971; "Soldier Field O.K.—Halas," *CO*, July 29. 1971; Roy Damer, "Bears' Move Draws Mixed Fan Reaction," *CT*, May 14, 1971.

19. Michael Sneed, "Mini'pinions," *CDT*, July 5, 1970; Jerry Shnay, "Plan Lake Stadium," *CT*, *July* 2, 1971; Tom Watts, "Revolt in Fun City, West: Daley, Chicagoans Don't See Eye to Eye on Stadium," *CO*, July 11, 1971; "Letters to the Editor: No, No, No to Lakefront Stadium,' " *CDN*, July 8, 1971; Lois Wille, *Forever Open, Clear, and Free: The Struggle for Chicago's Lakefront* (Chicago: University of Chicago Press, 1991), 141–44; Peter Negronida, "Tax May Be Needed for New Stadium," *CT*, July 3, 1971; "Indians Occupy Missile Base," *CT*, June 15, 1971; "Indians Ousted from Park; Reject Apartment Offer," *CT*, July 2, 1971; Mike Royko, "The Ugh-lie American," *CDN*, July 2, 1971; Adam Cohen and Elizabeth Taylor, *American Pharaoh: Mayor Richard J. Daley: His Battle for Chicago and the Nation* (Boston: Back Bay Books, 2001), 513; Edward Schreiber, "Daley Names 5 Men to Restudy Stadium," *CT*, July 9, 1971.

20. Wille, *Forever Open*, 142–43; Edmund Kelly, telephone interview with author, Jan. 17, 2002.

21. "Astro Turf Picked for Soldier Field," *CT*, May 19, 1971; Ronald Koziol, "City Asphalt Costs under Two Probes," *CT*, April 15, 1966; Ronald Koziol, "Tell Asphalt Trucking Loss," *CT*, April 18, 1966; Ronald Koziol and Thomas Powers, "Tell Road Contract Scandal," *CT*, Jan. 23, 1972; "Road Contracts Probed for Fraud," *CT*, Oct. 7, 1971.

22. "Bare 3-Year Deal for Soldier Field," *CO*, Sept. 15, 1971; Jerry Shnay, "Arena Revamp Possible: Report," *CT*, *July* 29, 1971; "Tests Say Stadium Repairs Possible," *CT*, Oct. 12, 1971; Special Architectural Committee on Soldier Field, *Soldier Field Report*, Nov. 10, 1971, esp. 2–3, 16–22, Municipal Reference Collection, Harold Washington Library Center.

23. Erlin, Hime Associates, *Boroscope Studies of Core Holes and Petrographic Studies of Holes from Columns at Soldier Field* (1971) , C-1 to C-4 ff, Municipal Reference Collection, Harold Washington Library Center.

24. Rick Talley, "Could Bear Victory Be Good Omen?" *CO*, Sept. 20, 1971; Ed Stone, "O'B, Burp Save Face, Bears," *CO*, Sept. 20, 1971; Cooper Rollow, "Bears Explode to Nix Steelers, 17–15," *CT*, Sept. 20, 1971; Cooper Rollow, *Cooper Rollow's Bears Football Book* (Ottawa, IL: Jameson Books, 1985), 59–60; Jack Schnedler, "Butkus Blitz Keys Victory," *CDN*, Sept. 20, 1971; Cooper Rollow, "Bears Rally, Stun Redskins 16–15," *CT*, Nov. 15, 1971.

25. Rollow, *Bears Football Book*, 59–63; Cooper Rollow, "Bears Err, Pack Back on Top Alone," *CT*, Nov. 13, 1972.

26. Stanley Ziemba, "$15 Million Facelifting Planned at Soldier Field," *CT*, Oct. 10, 1973; Leo Zainer, "Origen Seeks to Put Out Fire," *CT*, Oct. 29, 1974; "New Plans for Soldier Field North Sector," *CT*, Oct. 21, 1973; Dan Moulton, "Soldier Field Host to Tennis Festival," *CO*, May 23, 1974; Jack Mabley, "Chicagoland Tennis Is Ripe for Davis Cup," *CO*, June 26, 1974; Robert Markus, "Soldier Field Great Place for Tennis," *CT*, July 24, 1974; Steve Nidetz, "Tanner Wins 6–3, 6–4 in Festival Quarters," *CT*, *July* 19, 1975; Steve Nidetz, "Tanner—a Winner in ITC Final," *CT*, July 21, 1975; David Condon, "Wake of the News," *CT*, Sept. 13, 1975.

27. Earl Calloway, "Waiting for Marvin Gaye Was Too Long," *CDD*, Aug. 12, 1975.

28. Richard Philips, "80,000 Hear Emerson, Lake, and Palmer," *CT*, June 5, 1977; Chicago Park District, annual report (1976), 22; Pamela Zekman, "Contract for Rock Concerts at Soldier Field Questioned," *CST*, June 12, 1977; Pamela Zekman, "Park Dist. Board Not Told of Kelly Rock-Concert Ties," *CST*, June 13, 1977; Pamela Zekman, "BGA Demands Bidding for Soldier Field," *CST*, June 14, 1977; Pamela Zekman, "Park District Sets 4th Rock Concert, Lauds Supt. Kelly," *CST*, June 29, 1977; Pamela Zekman, "Data on Rock Concerts Subpoenaed," *CST*, July 12, 1977; Gary Deeb, "FCC Fines WDAI $7,000 for Concert Payola Fraud," *CT*, May 21, 1978; Jay Branegan, "Soldier Field Rock Promoters Indicted," *CT*, Sept. 19, 1980; "2 Rock Promoters Sentenced," *CT*, June 25, 1981; "Rock Concert Aide Pleads Guilty in Ticket Fraud," *CT*, May 15, 1981; AP, "Three Rock Music Promoters Plead Guilty," April 10, 1981.

29. Lynn Van Matre, "Stones Prove They're the Best," *CT*, July 9, 1978; Lynn Van Matre, "Funk Festival Is Infectious, Uptempo Fun," *CT*, Aug. 28, 1978; Chicago Park District, annual report (1969), 21.

30. Rollow, *Bears Football Book*, 63; Leo Zainea, "WFL Tosses Out Winds for Shortage of Money," *CT*, Sept. 3, 1975.

31. Don Pierson, "Bears Draft Back Payton in First Round," *CT*, Jan. 29, 1975; "Broncos Ruin Finale for Bears, Payton," Don Pierson *CT*, Dec. 13, 1976; Rollow, *Bears Football Book*, 66–81; Don Pierson, "Super Walter's 275 Sets Rushing Mark," *CT*, Nov. 21, 1977.

32. Eleanor Randolph, "Mayoral Opponents Blast Daley's Soldier Field Plan," *CT*, Jan. 6, 1975; Edward Schreiber, "No New Stadium Planned for Soldier Field, Daley Says," *CT*, Jan. 7, 1975; Edmund Kelly, telephone interview with author, Jan. 17, 2002; "The Stadium Flap," *CT*, Jan. 13, 1975; David Condon, "Bears Accelerate Stadium Search in Suburbs," *CT*, Feb. 8, 1975.

33. David Condon, "Bears Accelerate Stadium Search in Suburbs," *CT*, Feb. 8, 1975; Scott Simon, *Home and Away: Memoir of a Fan* (New York: Hyperion Books, 2000), 145–46; Kurt Baer, "'We Want In': Bears, Stadium 'Could Earn Arlington Million a Year,'" *Arlington Heights Daily Herald*, May 29, 1975; Charles Mount, "Upper Deck, 100 'VIP Rooms' Recommended for Soldier Field," *CT*, Nov. 6, 1976.

34. Robert Davis, "New Construction Projects in City Told by Bilandic," *CT*, April 12, 1977; Robert Davis, "Bilandic Calls for a City Racetrack, Stadium Complex," *CT*, Feb. 8, 1978; Robert Davis, "Soldier Field Out: Ogilvie," *CT*, Feb. 23, 1978; Robert Davis, "Ogilvie Hits Kelly Plan to Renew Soldier Field," *CT*, March 3, 1978; Robert Davis, "Soldier Field Frame for Arena?" *CT*, May 27, 1978; George Halas, with Gwen Morgan and Arthur Vesey, *Halas by Halas: The Autobiography of George Halas* (New York: McGraw-Hill, 1979), 328; Mitchell Locin, "Repair Cost Put at $3.5 Million," *CT*, Jan. 9, 1979.

35. David Israel, "Byrne's Victory Puts Stadium on Back Burner," *CT*, March 2, 1979; Rudolph Unger, "3-Phase Soldier Field Plan Revived," *CT*, May 23, 1979; Patrick G. Ryan, "Let's Build New Stadium" (letter), *CT*, July 6, 1979.

36. Rudolph Unger, "Park District to Seek 21 Food Concession Bids," *CT*, March 12, 1980.

37. John Husar, "More Than Just 10-Cent Beer Caused Baseball Riot," *CT*, June 30, 1974; Rich Rzyski, "Beer with the Bears?" *CT*, Nov. 20, 1975; Rudolph Unger, "Park District to Seek 21 Food Concession Bids," *CT*, March 12, 1980; Daniel Egler, "Liquor Sale in Parks OKd," *CT*, June 20, 1980; "Beer Down," *CT*, June 21, 1980; Stephanie Zimmerman, "New Stadium, Packer Clash Pump Up Interest in Bears," *CST*, July 20, 2003; "Bears Tickets on Sale July 19," *CT*, June 24, 2003.

38. Bob Logan, "Bears, Park District Agree to New 20-Year Lease," *CT*, July 18, 1980; Kurt Baer, "Stadium Panel's Report Not the Final Word: Kelly," *Arlington Heights Daily Herald*, March 3, 1978.

39. Bob Logan, "Park District May Veto Bear Beer Sale Plan," *CT*, July 23, 1980; Monroe Anderson, "Concession Study May Lead to Beer at Bear Games," *CT*, July 23, 1981; "Week Ahead," *CT*, July 27, 1981; David Schneidman, "Parks OK Bears' No. 1 Draught Choice," *CT*, July 29, 1981; Mike Kiley, "Bear Rookies Learned Some Hard Lessons," *CT*, Aug. 9, 1981.

40. G. J. Klein, "New Life for an Old Soldier: Rehabilitation of Chicago's Soldier Field," in *Evaluation and Rehabilitation of Concrete Structures and Innovation in Design: Proceedings of ACI International Conference Hong Kong, 1991* (ACI SP-128, vol. 1), ed. V. M. Malhotra (Detroit: American Concrete Institute, 1991), 473–83.

41. Bob Logan, "Soldier Field Gets a Facelift: What $32 Million Will Buy," *CT*, July 27, 1980; Klein, "New Life for an Old Soldier"; Edmund Kelly, telephone interview with author, Jan. 17, 2002.

42. Mike Ditka, with Don Pierson, *Ditka: An Autobiography* (Chicago: Bonus Books, 1986), 156–59; Paul Sullivan, "The Ditka Years: A Look Back over Mike Ditka's Successful and Stormy 11 Seasons as Head Coach of the Bears," *CT*, Jan. 6, 1993; Don Pierson, "Bears Await Victory's Price," *CT*, Nov. 5, 1984.

43. Ditka, *Ditka*, 184–85; Fred Mitchell, "Sweetness a Quiet Leader: Payton's Achievements Made Noise," *CT*, Aug. 13, 1995, 13; Rob Karwath and Barbara Mahany, "A Blessed Event for Fans," *CT*, Jan. 6, 1986; Don Pierson, "Superb Bears in Super Bowl," *CT*, Jan. 13, 1986; Fred Mitchell, "Those 1985 Bears Posters Are Starting to Yellow; Few Remain Who Know Steps to the Super Bowl Shuffle," *CT*, Aug. 13, 1989; "Da Shuffle," *CT*, Aug. 14, 1995. The hype surrounding the Bears also ushered in a new era in sports betting: some Las Vegas bookies credit the hype surrounding the team with giving the Super Bowl a central place in each years' sports book. See Chad Millman, *The Odds: One Season, Three Gamblers and the Death of Their Las Vegas* (Cambridge, MA: De Capo Press, 2002), 176.

CHAPTER 15

1. Robert A. Baade and Allen R. Sanderson, "Bearing Down in Chicago," in *Sports, Jobs and Taxes*, ed. Roger G. Noll and Andrew Zimbalist (Washington, DC: Brookings Institution, 1997), 330–31; William Rechtenwald and James Strong, "NFL Chief in Push for Bears Stadium," *CT*, Dec. 14, 1989.

2. John Schmidt, telephone interview with author, around April 17, 2002 (portions unpublished).

3. John Schmidt, telephone interview with author; author's personal recollections; Richard M. Daley, "Announcing the Plan for the New Soldier Field House" (speech), Sept. 13, 1996, author's personal collection; Jacquelyn Heard and Sue Ellen Christian, "Daley Plan Raises Roof," *CT*, Sept. 14, 1996; John Kass and Rick Pearson, "Bears Offer Deal to Keep Stadium Alive; Dome Scuttled," *CT*, Nov. 16, 1996; John Kass and Rick Pearson, "Daley Fighting to Keep His Turf," *CT*, Nov. 17, 1996.

4. Robert Becker, "Long Way to Go on Stadium Issue, Daley Says," *CT*, Nov. 19, 1996; Benjamin Wood, interview with author, Chicago, April 2002; Andrew Martin, Liam Ford, and Laurie Cohen, "Bears Play, Public Pays," *CT*, April 21, 2002.

5. Gary Washburn, "Bears Plan Would Save Soldier Field's Columns," *CT*, May 19, 1999; Fran Spielman, "Plans for Soldier Field Leave Daley Impressed," *CST*, July 7, 1999; Patrick G. Ryan, "Let's build new stadium," (letter) *CT*, July 6, 1979; Andrew Martin, Liam Ford, and Laurie Cohen, "Bears Play, Public Pays," *CT*, April 21, 2002; author's interview with confidential source.

6. Stacy St. Clair, "Soldier Field Renovation Hinged on Old Blueprints," *Arlington Heights Daily Herald*, Sept. 28, 2003.

7. Mayor's office, City of Chicago, "Lakefront Revitalization Plan to Protect and Enhance Vital Asset for All the People of Chicago," press release, Nov. 15, 2000; Gary Washburn and Ray Long, "Bears, City Say They Have a Winner," *CT*, Nov. 16, 2000; Matt Walberg (City News Service), "Daley Comments," CNS-22, Dec. 4, 2000; Richard M. Daley, "Stadium Plan Protects Taxpayers," *CST*, Dec. 4, 2000, 31; Andrew Martin, Liam Ford, and Laurie Cohen, "Bears Play, Public Pays," *CT*, April 21, 2002; Liam Ford, "Soldier Field Busts Budget," *CT*, Oct. 15, 2003.

8. Liam Ford, "Soldier Field Control at Issue," *CT*, June 17, 2001; governor's press office, "Ryan Approves Lakefront Improvement Plan" (press release), Jan. 5, 2001; "Report

Finds New Stadium 'Feasible,'" *CT*, Dec. 10, 1964; Daniel Egler, "Lawmakers Seek Funds for Stadium," *CT*, July 2, 1986; Mark Eissman and John McCarron, "City, Sox Agree to Stadium Proposal," *CT*, Dec. 2, 1986; Andrew H. Malcolm, "Chicago, Playing Hardball Politics, to Replace Aging Stadium," *NYT*, Dec. 18, 1986; John McCarron and Daniel Egler, "Hotels Aim to Strike Out Sox Park Tax," *CT*, Feb. 9, 1987; "Another Plan for Soldier Field" (editorial), *CT*, Dec. 14, 1975; Liam Ford, "Soldier Field Revamp Leaps onto Fast Track," *CT*, July 12, 2001; Liam Ford and Andrew Martin, "Bears Win Stadium Ruling," *CT*, April 26, 2002.

9. Liam Ford and Jon Yates, "Era Ends at Soldier Field," *CT*, Jan. 20, 2002.

10. Liam Ford, "Solis Brother's Firm Wins Stadium Pact," *CT*, Sept. 13, 2003; "The New Soldier Field: Melding Tradition with Modern Convenience," *Consulting-Specifying Engineer Magazine*, Nov. 1, 2004, http://www.csemag.com/article/CA494990.html (accessed Aug. 14, 2006); National Restoration Systems, "Soldier Field Renovation," http://www.nrsys.com/soldier_field.html (accessed Feb. 19, 2007).

11. Liam Ford, "Clock Ticking at Soldier Field; Work Crews Aim to Complete Shell before It's Winter," *CT*, Oct. 23, 2002; Liam Ford and Rick Jervis, "Soldier Field Getting 1st Reviews: Critics Still Harp, but It Has Backers," *CT*, June 15, 2003; Kent McDill, "Legends Like Look of New Soldier Field," *Arlington Heights Daily Herald*, Aug. 14, 2003.

12. Barry Rozner, "The New Soldier Field: Looks Great, Less Filling," *Arlington Heights Daily Herald*, Sept. 18, 2003; Fred Mitchell, "Ted Phillips: The Bears President Talks about His Expectations," *CT*, May 1, 2003.

13. Tony Proscio and Basil J. Whiting, *After-School Grows Up: How Four Large American Cities Approach Scale and Quality in After-School Programs* (New York: Robert Wood Johnson Foundation, 2004), 58; Yvette Shields, "Firms Working with Chicago Gave to Daley-Linked Fundraiser," *Bond Buyer*, Sept. 29, 2003; Mary Cameron Frey, "Mayor Carries the Ball at Soldier Field Kick-Off," *CST*, Sept. 24, 2003; Julian Green, "Soldier Field Rededication Ceremony & Public Opening" (Chicago Park District Media Advisory), Sept. 24, 2003; Liam Ford and Gayle Worland, "Bears Fans Get a Taste of New Digs," *CT*, Sept. 28, 2003; David Haugh, "Stadium Fixed: Can the Bears Be?" *CT*, Sept. 30, 2003.

14. Liam Ford, "Not All Events at Soldier Field Are Bear-Sized: Park District Has Variety of Uses," *CT*, Nov. 24, 2003.

15. Liam Ford, "Bears Draft Potty Plan: Team Is Seeking to Shorten Line for Men's Toilets," *CT*, April 25, 2004.

16. Liam Ford, "Soldier Field Busts Budget: Bears Will Pay $49 million in Cost Overruns," *CT*, Oct. 15, 2003.

17. Christopher Steiner, Liam Ford, and Angela Rozas, "Time to Honor and to Remember; Veterans Day Observances throughout the City and Suburbs Call Attention to the Sacrifices of Those Who Served Our Nation in Many Wars," *CT*, Nov. 12, 2003.

18. Blair Kamin, "Bowled Under: Still a Work-in-Progress, Soldier Field Is Disfigured and No Longer Worthy of Its Landmark Status," *CT*, Oct. 30, 2002; Hal Dardick and David Mendell, "Stadium Has Lost Landmark Look, U.S. Says," *CT*, July 21, 2004; AP, "Federal Committee Might Not Withdraw Landmark Status for Soldier Field," Dec. 3, 2004; Tom Hardy, "Soldier Field Debate Heats Up: We Can Keep Chicago Mainstay on Lake, Where It Belongs, and Stay Out of Local Taxpayers' Pockets," *CST*, Aug. 8, 2001; Blair Kamin, "Soldier Field Gets What It Deserves," *CT*, April 24, 2006; Noreen S. Ahmed-Ullah "Soldier Field Loses Landmark Status," *CT*, April 22, 2006; Barnaby Dinges, "*Tribune*'s Kamin Fumbles in Latest Soldier Field Rant," April 24, 2006, http://dingesgang.com/blog/?p=133 (accessed May 1, 2006). The portions of Kamin's "Bowled Under" article regarding the connection between place and history were suggested by an e-mail I wrote to him a few days before the article was published.

.

INDEX

Page numbers in italics refer to illustrations.

SOLDIER FIELD: A STADIUM AND ITS CITY

Designed and typeset by Michael Brehm
Printed and bound by Sheridan Books

Composed in Warnock Pro, a typeface designed by Robert Slimbach in 2007.
The display type used is Berthold Akzidenz Grotesk which was released by
the H. Berthold AG type foundry in 1896 and later modernized by
Günter Gerhard Lange in the 1950s.
Printed on 60# Glatfelter natural offset
Bound in Arrestox linen